AF600695

VALUE CHANGE IN THE SUPREME COURT OF CANADA

Value Change in the Supreme Court of Canada

MATTHEW E. WETSTEIN AND C.L. OSTBERG

UNIVERSITY OF TORONTO PRESS
Toronto Buffalo London

Toronto Buffalo London
www.utppublishing.com

ISBN 978-1-4875-0139-6

Library and Archives Canada Cataloguing in Publication

Wetstein, Matthew E., 1963–, author
Value change in the Supreme Court of Canada / Matthew E. Wetstein, C.L. Ostberg.

Includes bibliographical references and index.
ISBN 978-1-4875-0139-6 (cloth)

1. Canada. Supreme Court – Decision making. 2. Social values – Canada. I. Ostberg, C.L. (Cynthia L.), 1963–, author II. Title.

KE8244.W48 2017 347.71'035 C2017-901029-8
KF8764.ZA2W48 2017

This book has been published with the help of a grant from the Federation for the Humanities and Social Sciences, through the Awards to Scholarly Publications Program, using funds provided by the Social Sciences and Humanities Research Council of Canada.

University of Toronto Press acknowledges the financial assistance to its publishing program of the Canada Council for the Arts and the Ontario Arts Council, an agency of the Government of Ontario.

Canada Council for the Arts
Conseil des Arts du Canada

Funded by the Government of Canada
Financé par le gouvernement du Canada

This book is dedicated to our respective families.

Contents

Tables and Figures

Tables

Figures

Acknowledgments

No book is possible without outside advice, support, and guidance, and this book is no exception to that rule. We have benefited from the assistance of many individuals during the course of writing this book, and we owe a debt of gratitude to many individuals for their assistance. First, we would like to acknowledge the generous support of the Canadian Federation for the Humanities and Social Sciences for providing a grant to help underwrite production costs for this manuscript. Second, we would like to acknowledge the University of the Pacific for providing a sabbatical leave to help this project come to fruition. We are also grateful for permission from *Social Science Quarterly* for allowing us to reprint portions of our previously published material. Chapter 2 presents some updates from our prior work on environmental cases (Matthew E. Wetstein and C.L. Ostberg, "The Environmental Revolution and the Supreme Court of Canada: Empirical Analysis of Post-materialist Value Change across Four Decades," *Social Science Quarterly* 2016, doi:10.1111/ssqu.12272).

We are grateful to the many colleagues who provided commentary and advice on our research throughout the development of this project when segments of it were presented at conferences throughout the years. We are particularly grateful to Christopher Manfredi of McGill University for his constant willingness to read our work, provide helpful commentary, and extend continued support on the rough drafts that we presented. Likewise, we would like to thank Ian Greene and Carl Baar for their in-depth, insightful commentary on our work. Some arguments advanced are the product of exchanges with Donald Songer, a mentor and friend who was always willing to help us along on our Canadian intellectual travels, given that he was a fellow Canadian judicial traveller himself. Donald passed away recently, and the judicial field will not be the same kind and cordial atmosphere without his presence. We will miss him greatly. We are also grateful to several Canadian scholars who have also provided valuable advice and supported our efforts, including Laurie Hausegger of Boise State, Troy Riddell of Guelph, Matt Hennigar of Brock University, James Kelly of Concordia University, and countless others who have anonymously read and reviewed our work over the years. Their commentary has always been helpful and has inspired us to think differently and hone our work.

We are grateful to several individuals who helped us improve this work through the editing process at the University of Toronto Press. The anonymous reviewers provided insightful tips to strengthen our analysis. A big assist in the revision process came from editor Daniel Quinlan, who was generous with his comments and supportive nudges to help us refine our thinking in the environmental chapters. His helpful guidance strengthened the book's overall impact. Finally, we benefited from the remarkable copy editing work of Stephanie Stone. We are grateful to all the individuals at the Press who devoted time and energy to improving our manuscript.

At our home universities, we have had the benefit of supportive colleagues and students who have listened to our various commentaries on Canadian judicial politics. Our research has benefited from many college colloquiums, which have allowed us to present some of this research for the first time and receive valuable commentary on it.

We would also like to acknowledge the support of some of the former faculty in the political science department at Northern Illinois University, who played a critical role in our development as scholars in the field. First, we would like to acknowledge Lettie McSpadden, who worked with us on our first research project, ensured that we received financial support for it over the summer, and, as promised, made sure that it became a publication. We cannot thank her enough for her kindness and willingness to mentor us during this critical period. Second, we would like to thank Mike Wyckoff for his tutelage in empirical research. His valuable advice was drilled into us so well that, to this day, we hear his voice telling us always to make sure we have sound hypotheses that are worth exploring. We would also like to extend special thanks to Craig Ducat, who helped us begin to develop the initial database that has served as a springboard for our research over the past 25 years. Craig was instrumental in sparking our interest in Canadian judicial politics in the first place, and his enthusiasm, willingness to collaborate, and constant words of wisdom have been invaluable to us over the years. His gastronomical knowledge is invaluable since he always knows the best restaurants to dine at in both Canada and the United States.

Last, we would like to thank our family and friends for their patience and support during this long writing process. Specifically, we would like to thank our mothers, brothers, and sisters, who were sometimes left in the lurch when we were working on the manuscript, and Scout, who sat by our side throughout the process of writing, providing constant companionship. We miss you greatly.

VALUE CHANGE IN THE SUPREME COURT OF CANADA

Chapter One

Value Change in the Supreme Court of Canada

Introduction

In 2004, the Supreme Court of Canada gave its constitutional stamp of approval to the legal equality of gays to marry in *Reference re Same-Sex Marriage*, [2004] 3 S.C.R. 698. It was a historic decision that had its roots in a constellation of forces: a series of earlier rulings by the court itself that had leaned towards the principle of gay equality, a long run of legal-mobilization strategies by equality-focused groups in Canadian society, and changing opinions on gay marriage within the Canadian mass public. The concordance of the value shift taking place in the mass public and in the judicial opinions of the Canadian Supreme Court is the subject of this book. We explore the Supreme Court's changing attitudes towards gay rights and other key issues across four decades (1973–2010) and across the leadership of four chief justices (Laskin, Dickson, Lamer, and McLachlin). Our theoretical touchstone throughout the enquiry is the theory of postmaterialist value change in advanced post-industrial societies documented by Ronald Inglehart (1971, 1977, 1990, 1997), Inglehart, Nevitte, and Basanez (1996), Inglehart and Abramson (1999), and Inglehart and Welzel (2005). Put simply, this book is an examination of postmaterialist value change in the Supreme Court of Canada and an analysis of whether, and the extent to which, the opinions of Supreme Court justices reflect a long-term societal shift in attitudes that have reshaped overall priorities away from notions of economic self-interest and order to concerns like protecting the environment and promoting equality and free expression rights. Such an enquiry has far-reaching political implications as the Canadian Supreme Court and other high courts move to centre stage in high-profile policy disputes within their respective democracies.

The examination of the relationship between the public's views on key political and legal issues and those held by high court justices represents an enduring area of interest for modern democratic theorists. Before examining this relationship, however, it is first necessary to survey competing paradigms of judicial behaviour that have emerged in the literature over the past 75 years because they provide an important theoretical backdrop to the research questions we are examining in this book. These paradigms have gained greater prominence in Canada in recent years, since the Charter of Rights and Freedoms was added to the Canadian Constitution in 1982. The Charter has placed the court at centre stage in some of the most dramatic policy debates in Canada; this in turn has transformed the high court into a more politicized institution. This dramatic shift has sparked greater interest among Canadian judicial scholars, and comparative law scholars alike, in examining the veracity of these theories in the decision-making process of Canadian Supreme Court justices.

Literature Review: Models of Judicial Behaviour

Judicial scholars in the United States and elsewhere have sought to unravel the complex process of judicial decision making on high courts for over 75 years. Scholarship providing a more complete understanding of this process has garnered increasing attention as high courts in advanced industrial democracies, and elsewhere, become a dominant force in the larger body politic (see Tate and Vallinder 1995). Of course, there are numerous competing theories of judicial decision making at the Supreme Court level that have led scholars, like Lawrence Baum (1997), to suggest that judicial behaviour remains a "puzzle" despite decades of empirical analysis of this institution.

One approach or model for explaining judicial behaviour is the legal model, or interpretivism, which dominated in law schools throughout the United States and Canada in the later nineteenth and twentieth centuries. This theory of judicial decision making is based on the assumption that justices act as unbiased arbiters of the law when they seek to enforce it. The task of deciding cases becomes a mechanical one, whereby a judge applies the law, statutes, and precedents to the facts of an existing controversy. Put another way, advocates of this approach believe that high court justices simply apply rules in the written law to facts in the cases when resolving disputes, and they do not let their own attitudes and values influence them when they hand down rulings (see

Rohde and Spaeth 1976; Segal and Spaeth 1993, 2002; Ducat 2013). The legal model, then, views justices as simple norm enforcers of rules and not judicial policymakers.

The second approach to judicial decision making, the attitudinal model, had its origins in the mid-twentieth century, when political scientists began questioning the viability of the proposition that justices were "unbiased" in the decision-making process. Relying on the seminal work of rule sceptics such as Justice Oliver Wendell Holmes (1881, 1897) and Jerome Frank (1930), Pritchett (1941) began systematically examining the voting behaviour of US Supreme Court justices. These scholars asked a rather straightforward question: If justices were truly unbiased and only enforced legal rules, why did they not reach the same conclusion in the application of the law? This scepticism led to the publication of the now-classic work by Pritchett (1941, 1948) on the Roosevelt Court, which subsequently sparked the rise of more systematic attitudinal research on appellate courts in the United States.

Over the last 75 years, the attitudinal model has become one of the most prominent theoretical explanations for how justices resolve disputes. In short, this model posits that high court justices rely on their own attitudes and values when resolving a given dispute and that their written opinions, which seem to follow the norms of precedent and legal texts, simply act as mere covers for advancing the justices' own beliefs and values in the cases they decide (Spaeth 1963; Schubert 1965, 1974; Rohde and Spaeth 1976; Segal and Spaeth 1993, 2002). This makes sense when one realizes that high court justices come to the bench as independent decision makers who do not seek higher office and have the freedom to decide controversies without fear of retribution or removal from office. As a result, the justices are free to invoke their own ideology and attitudes when they decide cases (Segal and Spaeth 1993, 2002). The most sophisticated presentations of the attitudinal model in the contemporary literature have featured a more comprehensive argument, one that extends the model to include specific case facts that can provide shorthand cues to guide the justices in the resolution of cases (see Segal 1984, 1986; Segal and Cover 1989; Segal and Spaeth 1993, 2002; Ostberg and Wetstein 1998, 2007; Wetstein and Ostberg 1999). These models demonstrate the importance that case facts, such as an unreasonable search or right-to-counsel violation, have in "triggering" attitudinal responses by the justices.

In the literature on Canadian Supreme Court justices, the attitudinal model has gained prominence among a host of scholars who have applied empirical techniques to the decisions of the Supreme Court. The findings of these scholars have suggested that attitudinal decision making is prevalent in many issue areas of the Canadian Supreme Court, although the impact of attitudes and ideology are less prominent and more nuanced than in the more polarized US Supreme Court setting (see Tate and Sittiwong 1989; Ostberg and Wetstein 1998, 2007; Wetstein and Ostberg 1999; Ostberg, Wetstein, and Ducat 2002; Alarie and Green 2008, 2009a, 2009b; Songer 2008; Wetstein et al. 2009; Songer et al. 2012). In some cases, the attitudinal differences have been motivated by remarkable gender splits within the Canadian Supreme Court, such as in free expression and equality cases. In other areas of law, such as search and seizure, right to counsel, and tax disputes, the ideological rifts are more clearly along liberal-conservative or libertarian-communitarian lines (Ostberg, Wetstein, and Ducat 2002; Ostberg and Wetstein 2007; Wetstein et al. 2009; Songer et al. 2012). Recent work by Alarie and Green has focused on the ways that judicial cooperation operates as a pervasive norm that helps explain why the Canadian justices are less ideologically strident than their US counterparts (see also Songer et al. 2012). For example, their findings reveal weak to moderate ideological voting records in Charter cases decided by the McLachlin Court, with the strongest attitudinal voting appearing in equality disputes (Alarie and Green 2009a, 501–2). Yet the balance of decisions led them to conclude that the period between 2000 and 2009 reflected a court that was "weakly ideological and cooperative" in its orientation towards Charter cases (Alarie and Green 2009a, 501).

The attitudinal model does have its critics, especially in Canada. Some argue that an empirical focus on case outcomes misses the nuance in the written opinions and the importance of the give and take that occurs among a small group of appellate justices in the decision-making process. In addition, the attitudinal model does not take into consideration how justices perceive their role: what it means to be a justice (Macfarlane 2013). However, even some prominent attitudinalists recognize the limitation of missing the important interplay that occurs among justices and the resulting rationale that is published in their opinions. We address this criticism in this book by examining the language and rationale used by justices in salient cases in the environment, discrimination, and free expression areas of law.

One of the reasons we focus on the written reasons for judgment is that researchers have noted that justices seek to meet several broad goals when crafting their opinions in cases (see Songer et al. 2012; see also Greene et al. 1998; Songer 2008). First, they want to get the law right and write a sound legal decision. Second, they want to maintain a collegial dialogue within their own institution and stay on good terms with their colleagues. This results in the occasional bargaining over language and rationale in their opinions. Third, they recognize that there are bound to be ideological and attitudinal disagreements in critical cases and there is no way around those attitudinal schisms (Songer et al. 2012, 87–93). As Songer et al. (2012, 6) put it, justices are often addressing competing tensions when they write opinions. "They must have a firm legal grounding, comport with the norms of their colleagues, and reflect their ideological vision of the law." As a result, dissenting opinions and the occasional concurrence reflect honest ideological differences that are bound to emerge within a court. Seen in this light, judicial opinions are the by-product of a social group that includes individuals who have differing views on the law – in short, opinions flow from the socio-attitudinal interaction of the court and its actors.

A second criticism of the attitudinal model is that its supporters tend to treat each case as an equal unit of analysis in their empirical results, missing the point that some cases are more important than others. We address this criticism throughout this book by providing two methodological approaches to the study of judicial behaviour. While we engage in a sophisticated analysis of case outcomes that comports with earlier attitudinal studies, our recognition of the dynamic social forces that shape judicial opinions leads us to include an extensive analysis of the legal rationale and writings of justices in landmark rulings that have garnered significant legal commentary. In short, we blend the quantitative approach that is so prominent in attitudinal studies with the qualitative approach that is the hallmark of legal studies. In doing so, we honour the comments of the justices themselves, who say that the law and precedent clearly shape their thinking and their desire to write good, sound opinions.

A third model of judicial behaviour – namely, the strategic model – derives from the seminal work of Murphy (1964) and later scholarship by Epstein and Knight (1998) and Maltzman, Spriggs II, and Wahlbeck (2000). The strategic approach is rooted in the notion that justices are strategic, or "rational," actors that respond to other actors, both within the Supreme Court and in other institutions. This model acknowledges that while justices are driven by their own policy preferences, they are often forced to modify or mute their "ideal" policy position in favour of a less ideal one to work with their colleagues to build more unified opinions, whenever possible. Another mode of strategic action occurs when justices stake out a less optimal position to safeguard against the court reaching a "least desired outcome" (Epstein and Knight 1998). Other scholars have documented this strategic interplay in their interviews with court justices (see Greene et al. 1998; Songer 2008; Songer et al. 2012). This model also recognizes that the court may act strategically as a unified institution in a manner that fosters its legitimacy in the eyes of other government institutions and the mass public. As noted by these scholars, justices "need to be attentive to the informal norms that reflect dominant societal beliefs about the rule of law in general and the role of the Supreme Court in particular" (Epstein and Knight 1998, 138). As such, one can see Supreme Court decisions as reflecting the strategic calculations that justices make in response to intra-court norms, the mass public, and larger political forces in society.

These three main models of judicial behaviour – namely, the legal, attitudinal, and strategic models – have come to dominate judicial scholarship in recent years and have been presented in the literature as competing paradigms for explaining judicial decision making on high courts. Yet in recent years, some scholars, such as Ostberg and Wetstein (2007) and Songer et al. (2012), have begun to suggest that all three models act together and play complementary roles, like the different layers of an onion, in explaining the judicial decision-making process. While none alone provides a complete explanation of the complex puzzle of judicial behaviour on high courts, taken together they provide a clearer and more robust and nuanced understanding of this activity. More important for this book, we believe that current attitudinal scholarship has failed to acknowledge that there is still another, more nebulous, but intriguing onion layer that can help explain the decision-making process and direction that high courts are taking in advanced industrial societies. Unlike the attitudinal model discussed earlier, which tends to focus on the immediate decision-making process, this new approach, which we call the socio-attitudinal model, provides a longer and broader framework of analysis to augment our understanding of how justices decide cases.

The theoretical origins of this approach are found in the sociological background-behavioural studies that appeared in the scholarly literature from the 1970s to the 1990s. Several scholars during this period sought to make connections among certain personal and sociological background characteristics of justices, such as religion, region of origin, gender, race, party affiliation, education, and prior law practice and judicial decision making (see Ulmer 1973, 1986; Tate and Sittiwong 1989; Tate and Handberg 1991; Songer and Johnson 2007). However, most of these studies yielded mixed results, leading one scholar to postulate that these types of studies were problematic because they were time bound (see Ulmer 1986). The critical problem of such enquiry, as noted by Ulmer (1986), stems from the fact that social-background conditions change over time, making it difficult to pinpoint how various background factors actually impact judicial behaviour beyond a short time frame of analysis. If such studies are "time bound," they provide limited help in understanding judicial behaviour over time. This underlying problem, along with the mixed results from some of these studies, appeared to dissuade many scholars from further exploring whether background behavioural characteristics make an important contribution to understanding judicial behaviour.

We believe that a new, socio-attitudinal model can be built from the foundation of these studies, one that helps shed considerable light on the direction that judicial decision making is taking in the foreseeable future in advanced industrial societies like Canada. However, we do not dispute that many of the background-behavioural studies in the past were time bound and that the key characteristics analysed were likely to change across a small time frame of a decade or so. Yet what if scholars expanded the attitudinal framework of analysis across space and time to examine the impact that the gradual shift in attitudes across the mass public have on the behaviour of judicial elites? Under this expanded rubric, the time-bound problem noted by Ulmer loses most of its punch because, on this expanded societal level, at least, the most important changes in mass attitudes and opinions are bound to resonate in a culture for an extensive period of time. Our book seeks to explore this thesis, looking at the attitudes that judicial elites develop, which are shaped by social forces in their formative years, and whether they are reflected in later rulings in key issue areas. We believe that this approach builds on the attitudinal model because it explores the impact that changing world views among citizens in a society have on current judicial decision making, and it provides a broader framework for understanding where high courts in advanced democracies are heading in critical issue areas in the foreseeable future.

The societal value changes that Ronald Inglehart (1997; Inglehart and Welzel 2005) has documented among the mass public are discussed at length throughout this book, and the role they play in the socio-attitudinal model of judicial decision making cannot be ignored. Yet one cannot forget the critical role that key social groups have played over a series of decades in transmitting changing value positions to justices by advocating for a cleaner environment, more liberal free expression laws, and equality concerns using various political and legal strategies. One of the most prominent strategies has been to use the court system to advocate for legal change when other political institutions have not been responsive enough. This legal mobilization, catalogued by a host of scholars (see Epp 1998; Morton and Knopff 2000; Hein 2001; Brodie 2002; Manfredi 2004; Langer 2005; Hausegger, Hennigar, and Riddell 2009, chap. 7; Alarie and Green 2010), represents a set of social forces that help shape the attitudinal positions taken by the justices. In short, the attitudes of the justices are the by-product of their own views, the views brought forward by litigants and interveners, and the views that are evident in the larger body politic. Thus, the decisions of the court reflect the interplay between individual-level factors (their own views and how they acquired them) and the views and perspectives advanced by key actors in the legal arena.

In the end, our book examines whether gradual intergenerational shifts in public opinion also transform the value priorities of judicial elites over time and, if so, whether these changing values are embodied in the rulings of the Canadian court in predictable ways. We examine these shifts through the lens of postmaterialist value change theory, and we assess whether the votes of individual justices and the arc of their legal writing over time act as empirical barometers of a prior, predictable value change taking place in Canadian society. If so, our findings could have important implications for the future direction of the court in critical policy areas in Canadian society. Throughout our analysis, readers should keep in mind that our vision of judicial behaviour is one that is grounded in a socio-attitudinal perspective. We recognize justices as individual decision makers with unique attitudinal make-ups, but we also recognize that they operate in a group setting that influences their relationships with each other and that their attitudes are often the product of their individual upbringing and the broader social and economic factors that were in play during their formative years. To fully understand this relationship, we turn our attention to a detailed discussion of the postmaterialist value change thesis, postulated by Inglehart (1971, 1977, 1990, 1997; Inglehart and Welzel 2005), that is occurring in advanced industrial societies around the world.

Inglehart's Theory of Postmaterialist Value Change in Democratic Societies

The theoretical foundation for our study is drawn from Ronald Inglehart's theory of postmaterialist value change. Inglehart's extensive research on public opinion over the past 35 years has led him to advance a new theory of global modernization. He argues that systematic changes in mass belief systems have had a profound impact on the larger political, economic, and social structures of societies (1971, 1977, 1997; Inglehart, Nevitte, and Basanez 1996; Inglehart and Welzel 2005). At the heart of his thesis is the contention that the attitudes and values of the mass public across a host of countries are changing in predictable ways over time. He suggests that as societies become more economically developed throughout the world, they move along two successive trajectories – first from an agrarian to an industrial stage and then, with subsequent economic advancement, to a post-industrial stage (Inglehart 1997, chap. 1; Inglehart and Welzel 2005). Inglehart's analysis of advanced democracies reveals that, over the past six or seven decades, a new postmodern world view is emerging that is gradually replacing the materialistic one that existed in these societies throughout the bulk of the twentieth century. Inglehart suggests that prolonged periods of economic prosperity after the Second World War in countries like Canada have triggered a gradual intergenerational shift away from materialistic value priorities, which emphasize economic security and physical survival concerns, to postmaterialist ones, which place greater emphasis on freedom, individual well-being, and quality-of-life concerns (Inglehart and Abramson 1994, 336; Inglehart, Nevitte, and Basanez 1996; Inglehart 1997, chap. 1; Inglehart and Welzel 2005, 23–5).

Inglehart and others have collected a vast amount of public opinion data across scores of countries to support this postmaterialist transformation thesis. His findings from a battery of value questions outlined in the World Values Surveys, which have been administered regularly since 1970 (Inglehart and Welzel 2005, 97), demonstrate that a value shift is indeed taking place among the pre- and post-Second-World-War-generation birth cohorts in advanced democracies because of the changing nature of their economic conditions. Inglehart argues that as the citizens of advanced industrial societies have become more economically secure and less concerned about their survival needs, they have begun to turn their attention to striving for more esoteric goals of individual well-being and self-fulfilment and concerns like protecting the environment (1990, 1995, 1997).

Inglehart claims that data from the pre-Second-World-War-generation cohort indicate that they placed a higher priority on materialist values pertaining to economic accumulation and physical security (1997, chap. 1). This emphasis on physical and economic scarcity is not surprising since this birth cohort lived through two world wars and experienced the Great Depression, which left many penniless and without shelter. However, the data for the post–Second World War generation paint a much different picture. Inglehart contends that this birth cohort, and successive ones, are gradually developing a much different world view because they grew up in a time of relative economic abundance and political security (ibid.). As a result, this cohort has begun to develop a new value structure, one that places a greater priority on the development of individual freedom, well-being, and quality of life. Inglehart suggests that this new, postmodern world view, which is sweeping across a multitude of advanced, post-industrial societies, can also be attributed to the vast technological and scientific achievements that have occurred in the last half-century, along with the rise of the modern welfare state, which has provided individuals with higher levels of social security (Inglehart, Nevitte, and Basanez 1996; Inglehart 1997, 32). He argues that the rise in this new world view, in turn, has begun to have a profound impact on the sociopolitical landscape that is emerging in these societies as the mass public becomes gradually more sensitive to issues pertaining to environmental protection, the status of women, protection of minorities, homosexual rights, and freedom of speech (Inglehart, Nevitte, and Basanez 1996; Inglehart 1997, chap. 1).

Even though Inglehart identifies the post–Second World War economic boom period as a starting point for the development of postmaterialist values in societies such as Canada, he points out that his intergenerational value change thesis is founded on two underlying, interrelated hypotheses, which he labels the scarcity and socialization hypotheses (Inglehart 1997, 33; Inglehart and Welzel 2005, 97). The scarcity hypothesis predicts that individuals will place the highest subjective value on what constitute the most pressing needs they face in society. For example, if people live in poor economic conditions, they will give the highest priority to materialist, economic-survival concerns. In contrast, if they live in conditions of economic abundance, they will be able to place a greater emphasis on postmaterialist goals. His socialization hypothesis, in turn, forecasts that since people develop their attitudes and values during their formative years, cultural change in society will principally occur through intergenerational population replacement. Thus, Inglehart predicts that there will be a time lag before public opinion data demonstrate changes in the value priorities at a societal level (Inglehart 1997, 33; Inglehart and Welzel 2005, 97).

Scholarship in the developmental psychology and political socialization literature reinforces Inglehart's contention that people's overarching world view is formed during their teenaged years to their early twenties as they begin to grapple with their political beliefs, concepts of inequality, and issues pertaining to international relations, poverty, war, and environmental concerns (see Greenstein 1965; Merelman 1971; Jennings and Niemi 1974; Niemi and Hepburn 1995; Griffin 2004). Research in this area has shown that while adults change their views in response to specific experiences that they may have as adults, the overall world view they developed in their teens and early adulthood can have a strong influence on their attitudes and values throughout their life (see Niemi and Hepburn 1995). Ultimately, Inglehart claims that the postmaterialist value change that is taking place in post-industrial societies is gradual and part of a larger modernization process occurring throughout the world as societies move along the two successive sociopolitical trajectories as a result of economic advancements (1997, chap. 1). Before turning our attention to the application of Inglehart's thesis to the Supreme Court of Canada, it is important to describe the data and measures that Inglehart has marshalled to support his theory of postmaterialist value change in advanced industrial societies.

Inglehart's Measures of Postmaterialist Values

To test the intergenerational value shift thesis, Inglehart developed a four-item question index, and later a more sophisticated, 12-item question index, from cross-national public opinion surveys, which have been conducted at regular intervals since 1970 (1997, 108). Inglehart created the latter index after he factor-analysed a series of questions that had respondents rate 12 goals, in order of importance, that their country should achieve over the next 10 years. While six of the question goals clustered neatly at the materialist end of the factor, including the desire to maintain order and develop a strong defence force, fight rising prices and crime, and ensure economic stability and growth, five other goals clustered at the postmaterialist end of the factor, including ensuring freedom of speech and a less impersonal society, having more say in government and on the job, and having a belief that one's ideas count more than money in society (Inglehart 1997, 108).[1]

Although these two indices of values are not without their critics, Inglehart and others have tested their micro-level validity extensively over a series of decades in relation to other theoretically relevant variables, using factor analysis, and across numerous countries (Inglehart and Abramson 1999, 665). The data that they have accumulated systematically show that these indices do a remarkable job of accurately identifying the shifting movement of values away from materialistic economic and physical survival needs towards postmaterialist values of individual well-being and quality-of-life concerns. Moreover, Inglehart's index of postmaterialism correlates strongly with question responses describing attitudes about discrimination, women's rights, gay rights, support for the environment, pollution regulations, and free speech rights (Inglehart 1997, 82, 89–90; Inglehart and Welzel 2005, 115, 272, 299).

The data results from the Canadian samples in the World Values Survey help illustrate Inglehart's intergenerational theory. Surveys conducted in 1982, 1990, and 2000 asked Canadians to identify first- and second-priority rankings across the 12 societal goals mentioned earlier; this resulted in a 0–5 index of postmaterialist values (0 = materialist, 5 = postmaterialist). Based on survey responses across the three data points, Inglehart found that Canadian society had moved in a postmaterialist direction across the 18-year period. Indeed, the percentages of people with postmaterialist values (constituting a score of 5 on the index) increased 10 percentage points in Canada between 1982 and 1990, from 16 to 26 per cent, and then to 35 per cent in 2000. In contrast, priority for materialist values in Canada dropped from a high of 22 per cent in 1982 to just 9 per cent in 2000 (World Values Survey 2000). Although most people surveyed could be found in the mixed category, these findings clearly support Inglehart's contention that a generalized, gradual shift towards postmaterialist values is occurring in Canada over time. If one simply focused on the youngest cohort of Canadians across these three periods, those between the ages of 15 and 29, one would also find evidence of a rise in postmaterialist values and a decline in materialist ones. This cohort's postmaterialist index increased from 15 per cent in

---

1 Inglehart dropped one question from his initial 12-item index – namely, the desire for more beautiful cities – because it did not seem to cluster at either end of the materialist-postmaterialist spectrum.

1982 to 35 per cent in 2000, while its materialist value score fell from 23 per cent in 1982 to 6 per cent in 2000 (ibid.).

A similar pattern holds for even the oldest cohort in the Canadian survey sample across these three periods. Collectively, these data provide compelling evidence that Inglehart's gradual shifting values thesis is indeed taking place in modern Canadian society and that the Canadian public is moving in an increasingly predictable direction towards postmaterialist values. Moreover, there is a high correlation between the value scores found in Inglehart's 12-item index and other critical questions, showing a shift from materialist to postmaterialist values in Canadian society. These attitudes, drawn from questions dealing with issues like support for equality-seeking groups, support for protecting the environment, and endorsing the right to free expression, are part and parcel of a postmaterialist mindset that is increasingly evident among the general public in societies like Canada. Having said this, it is still an open question whether Canadian political elites – namely, Supreme Court justices – have taken a similar postmaterialist turn in their written opinions.

Criticisms of Inglehart's Modernization Theory

Before we turn to an explanation of Inglehart's thesis in the setting of the Supreme Court of Canada, we should note that his modernization theory is not without its detractors. Scholars have taken issue with his theory on both a practical and a theoretical level. First, some have criticized Inglehart's measurement techniques. They have questioned whether the cross-national surveys administered since 1970 actually measure the values that Inglehart claims they do and what types of questions most accurately identify materialist and postmaterialist values. Inglehart's early work was based on factor analysis and the creation of indexes based on a series of survey questions. Arguing for greater attention to value complexity, some scholars have questioned whether his initial one-dimensional explanation for the postmaterialist value shift sufficiently captures the degree of cultural changes that were taking place in advanced industrial societies around the world (see Clarke et al. 1999; Davis and Davenport 1999). Inglehart has attempted to answer these criticisms by refining and expanding his theory and providing further data and complex dimensions to support his thesis (Inglehart and Welzel 2005, 22–47). He also contends that the postmaterialist shift is only one type of change in a larger societal transformation taking place throughout these societies (ibid.).

On a theoretical level, other scholars have questioned Inglehart's contention that a shift towards postmaterialist values is actually occurring across multiple societies. For example, van Deth (1983) and Boltken and Jagodzinski (1985) assert that the intergenerational shift Inglehart found between the older and younger cohorts in various countries might simply be explained by life cycle events, suggesting that as a cohort of the mass public grows older, its members become less interested in quality-of-life concerns and more interested in monetary concerns, security, and survival. Inglehart has subsequently demonstrated that this life cycle criticism does not hold up because "the data strongly suggest that generational replacement has been a major long-term force pushing postmaterialism upward" (Inglehart and Abramson 1994, 350). Other scholars have pointed out that values can fluctuate over time and that this implies that postmaterialist value trends are hampered by period effects, or short-term forces, which can change value orientations in a society (see Thomassen and van Deth 1989, 64).

In more contemporary work, Inglehart and his colleagues acknowledge that period effects can dampen or accelerate the postmaterialist trend, but they argue that these factors influence all cohorts simultaneously and thus do not undermine the overall transformation thesis (Inglehart and Abramson 1994, 339–44; Inglehart and Welzel 2005, 38). More important, Inglehart recognizes that the postmaterialist value shift is not simply linear and that societies can regress to materialistic concerns if economic survival becomes salient once again (Inglehart and Welzel 2005, 46). This implies that, in economic hard times, the public and possibly even elites will become more concerned with putting food on the table and conditions of economic security rather than quality-of-life issues such as environmental protection and free expression rights. It can be argued that citizens' concerns about terrorism, pensions, health care, levels of household debt, retirement savings, and homelessness reflect a resurgence of materialist values in recent years. Despite these current economic concerns, it is clear that Canadian citizens living in the 1970–2010 period, as a whole, were living in some of the most affluent decades in history. Inglehart would argue that, despite possible dips in a materialist direction, there was a steady movement in a postmaterialist direction in the period of our study, and we seek to test his theory among Canadian judicial elites.

Although we are testing Inglehart's intergenerational value shift thesis among judicial elites in the post-industrial setting of Canada, other scholars take issue with his overarching claims that societies throughout the world are experiencing predictably uniform patterns of economic, cultural, and political change in values and that this change necessarily leads to more flourishing democratic institutions, characterized by liberal democracies (Inglehart and Welzel 2005, 173). Jackman and Miller (2005, 129) claim that Inglehart fails to provide systematic evidence that changing cultural values are necessarily linked to the establishment of long-term, viable democratic institutions. They argue that his modernization thesis is grounded in numerous questionable empirical decisions and ad hoc assumptions, which cast doubt on his overall modernization thesis. Ultimately, they contend that it is more plausible that mass values are a result of, and not the driving force behind, changes in the political, social, and economic structures of society. In other words, Jackman and Miller believe that changes in public values, such as trust, tolerance, and equality, occur because individuals live in wealthy democratic societies that value individual freedom and mass participation in politics, not the other way around (2005). Once one turns Inglehart's modernization theory on its head, it casts doubt on his contention that a change in cultural values necessarily fosters a rise in democratic institutions in societies.

Inglehart's global modernization theory might strike a raw note with some critics because it harks back to classical modernization theories articulated in the 1950s and 1960s. Indeed, one scholar suggested a generation ago that many saw modernization as a "dead" theory that had been largely rejected (Roxborough 1988, 753). Classical modernization theory has experienced a barrage of criticism over time from advocates of dependency, world systems, and neo-Marxist theories (for this kind of critique, see Roxborough [1988]; Armer and Katsillis [2000]). These theorists place greater emphasis on the exploitative patterns of capitalism that emanate from industrial power brokers in the "centre" of the developed world, patterns that shape the continuing underdevelopment on the "periphery." The implication of this line of thought is that any evidence of value change that scholars find simply reflects the values imposed by the dominant capital interests of the colonial powers that have exploited the resources of peripheral countries.

The idea that modernization leads inevitably to democratization, or that human development is necessarily tied to liberal democracies (Inglehart and Welzel 2005, 272), is bound to draw criticism from scholars in other disciplines. Sociologists and others have tended to cast a sceptical eye towards Eurocentric notions of development and modernization, and Inglehart's early work tends to emanate from such a

Western, democratic viewpoint. Yet his later application of the World Values Survey to a host of non-Western states suggests that there is a strong kernel of truth to the postmaterialist and modernization theory. For instance, as countries move from an industrial-focused economy to one featuring a greater share of the workforce in the service sectors, there tend to be greater levels of support for postmaterialist values (Inglehart and Welzel 2005, 61). It is certainly the case that some societies are more porous and open to value change in their political, economic, and social structures, while other societies are less open to such forces. Even so, increasing globalizing forces are eroding differences across many international boundaries, especially in Europe, and Inglehart (1997) suggests that a postmaterialist drift is evident wherever economic development and prosperity take root. His recent findings seemingly undermine earlier dependency theory critics and provide support for the proposition that economic development does seem to lead to advances in democratization – a position advanced by an earlier cadre of scholars such as Lipset, Trow, and Coleman (1956), Dahl (1971), and Rostow (1971); and see also Inglehart (1997, 160). He goes so far as to suggest that satisfaction with life and overall happiness are also evident in societies where economic development has increased standards of living and where the freedom to make choices is flourishing in the political sphere (Inglehart et al. 2008). Yet he acknowledges that two countries have not documented significant postmaterialist changes: India and Nigeria (Inglehart 1997, 148).

Despite the various criticisms that have been levelled at his theory on both a practical and a theoretical level and the fact that a few countries have weak records of postmaterialist change, the volume of cross-national studies that Inglehart continues to generate cannot be ignored, and they invite scholars to test the theory's veracity in various contexts, including its application to legal elites. The particular context of judicial elites is the focus of this book, which presents an assessment of postmaterialist value change in the Canadian Supreme Court between 1973 and 2010.

Rights Revolution in Advanced Democracies and Judicial Behaviour in Canada

Notwithstanding the criticisms of Inglehart's theory, there are a couple of important reasons why evidence of value change should appear in the decisions of Canadian Supreme Court justices. First, we contend that the justices themselves are the product of the society and socializing forces that shape them as they emerge from young adulthood to careers in law. Some justices of the late twentieth century grew up during the Depression and two world wars, and therefore faced the generational forces of scarcity and insecurity that reflect Inglehart's findings of a more materialistic generation of people. Later justices who came of age after the important "break point" of the Second World War experienced gradually improving conditions of economic security, at least compared to the earlier cohort of justices, and these more contemporary justices came of age in a generation possessing an increasingly postmaterialist mindset. As this cohort of newer justices replaces the retiring ones, Inglehart's theory implies that the gradual intergenerational replacement that occurs will result in more justices who are receptive to postmaterialist arguments and claims advanced by litigants.

A second reason for expecting more postmaterialist Supreme Court rulings over time is tied to the legal-mobilization strategies employed by key groups in post-industrial society. As we noted earlier, throughout the twentieth century and into the twenty-first century, interest groups in advanced democracies have turned to the judiciary to instigate policy changes in society after being shut out of the traditional forums of the political process (Epp 1998). The failure of minority and specialized interest groups to secure desired policies and protective rights in the legislative and executive branches, at both the state and the federal levels, has led these groups to pursue a concerted and methodical strategy to secure policy change through the court docket. For example, in the United States, groups such as the National Association for the Advancement of Colored People were able to win major victories to desegregate public schools with the *Brown v. Board of Education*, 347 U.S. 483 (1954) and the *Brown v. Board of Education II*, 349 U.S. 294 (1955) rulings of the 1950s. Their successes were noticed and followed by other groups in the United States, such as environmental protection and equality rights groups, starting in the 1970s. Collectively, these efforts signified a widespread rise of legal-mobilization strategies by groups across the political spectrum. Today, interest group litigation and intervention is a commonplace strategy used by groups of all stripes seeking to defend victories they have won in the legislature and to reverse losses they have suffered in other political arenas.

In the Canadian context, there was much speculation about whether interest group activity would accelerate with the adoption of the Charter of Rights and Freedoms in 1982. Since that document recognized numerous constitutional rights and protections for Canadians for the first time, it seemed likely that groups would take to the courts in an effort to breathe strong life into the protections in these clauses. Subsequent scholarship by Brodie (2002, 39) indicated that in the five years after the Charter was adopted, citizen groups representing various sections of the political arena filed 340 applications to intervene in judicial disputes at the Supreme Court level. This trend is even more obvious in cases raising Charter claims. Indeed, in the 1984–9 time period, appeals to intervene in Charter cases skyrocketed, and various interest groups and individuals participated as interveners more than 370 times (Brodie 2002, 45).

One of the most prominent groups to use legal-mobilization strategies in Canada is the Women's Legal Education and Action Fund (LEAF), which, according to Manfredi (2004, 15), participated in 36 Supreme Court cases between 1988 and 2000. More important, Manfredi documented that the court ruled in favour of the LEAF position in 84 per cent of the cases it participated in during that period (Manfredi 2004, 18–20). According to Hein (2001) and Brodie (2002), other prominent interveners at the Supreme Court level since the Charter's enactment have been the Canadian Civil Liberties Association, the Sierra Legal Defence Fund (now called Ecojustice Canada), and First Nations and other indigenous peoples. Surprisingly, Hein (2001, 223) noted that activity by these groups has been surpassed by corporate interests, with business groups making 468 appearances in the 1988–98 period alone.

These findings suggest that the Charter has not only accelerated legal mobilization by groups advocating postmaterialist positions and the "have-nots" but also fuelled extensive interest group activity by the groups advancing materialistic interests in Canadian society. More recently, Alarie and Green (2010, 395–6) have documented that, between 2000 and 2008, nearly half of all appeals featured an intervention of some form, and 91 per cent of all parties seeking leave to intervene were successful. Moreover, their analysis suggests that, all other things being equal, justices of the Supreme Court vote more conservatively when conservative-oriented interveners appear in a case and that the impact is slightly higher than when liberal interveners file arguments with the court (Alarie and Green 2010, 408). Surprisingly, they find that neutral interveners can boost liberal voting by the justices by 4 to 6 percentage points (ibid.). Collectively, these findings document the importance of intervener activity as a social force because it has the power to promote value change within the Supreme Court of Canada, regardless of the perceived ideology of the justices.

The accelerated pace of interest group activity in the Canadian Supreme Court makes intuitive sense given the extensive use of such activity south of the border. Moreover, it fits with the broader rights revolution discussed by Charles Epp (1998, 171, 175–6), who claimed that interest groups were engaging in efforts to enact policy changes through the Canadian courts well before the Charter was enacted. Epp (1998) also contended that rising support for rights protections within constitutions was evident across a number of democracies, including the United Kingdom, India, and Canada, and that legal elites were largely supportive of this movement. As a result, post-Charter legal mobilization was not surprising and was foreseeable given the favourable groundwork and various efforts instituted during the pre-Charter period. In addition, scholars such as Tate and Vallinder (1995) and Ran Hirschl (2004) have argued that the broader rights revolution instigated by the entrenchment of rights in constitutional documents, like the Charter, has helped trigger an increase in the "judicialization of politics" around the world. They have contended that this is one of the most significant governmental trends of the late twentieth and early twenty-first centuries and that this larger global transformation has placed high courts at the centre of resolving critical policy disputes. Tate and Vallinder (1995) claimed that the heightened profile of high courts in judicial policymaking around the world came at the expense of democratically elected legislative institutions that had traditionally been given oversight in this area.

In the Canadian context, some scholars have been critical of "the Court Party" coalition of postmaterialist interest groups that has emerged since the Charter was enacted and the highly effective partisan political pressure it has placed on the courts (see Morton and Knopff 2000, 27–8). They argue that a loose, sometimes antagonistic, coalition of groups has instigated a Charter revolution that is both undemocratic and anti-majoritarian and that their collective efforts could seriously undermine the democratic process (2000, 149). Morton and Knopff also argue that liberal democracies can remain strong only if majorities rule, rather than a loose coalition of minorities, and they contend that the prevalence of representative institutions facilitates the democratic process, while judicial ones do not (ibid.). While Morton and Knopff (2000) lament the anti-majoritarian nature of judicial policymaking that seems to be on the rise in the post-Charter era, the fact that high court justices decide cases ideologically cannot be overlooked. US scholars, such as Segal and Spaeth (1993, 2002), have empirically documented the politicized nature of Supreme Court rulings for decades, and they have provided compelling evidence that the justices routinely hand down rulings that reflect their own attitudes and values. Since these justices secure long-term appointments, sit at the pinnacle of their careers, and aspire to no other office, they are unconstrained decision makers who are able to let their own attitudes and values influence their opinions. Moreover, since their rulings set a precedent for lower federal and state courts throughout the United States, they necessarily leave a far-reaching policy imprint on society.

Although numerous scholars have documented the politicized nature of high court rulings in both Canada and the United States (see Segal and Spaeth 1993, 2002; Ostberg and Wetstein 2007; Songer et al. 2012), Rosenberg (1991) points out that it is a "hollow hope" for groups to secure enduring policy advantages without the support of the legislative and executive branches. His argument rings true for contentious issues in the US context, such as affirmative action, in which officials are still struggling to desegregate schools some 60 years after the Supreme Court handed down the two *Brown v. Board of Education* rulings. Although interest groups of all stripes regularly use the judiciary to try to secure policy advantages they have failed to win in other institutions, those victories may be short lived if executive- and lower-level officials drag their feet or fail to effectively implement those rulings. This is especially true if they do not support the rulings in the first place. Moreover, lasting policy change is guaranteed only if the views of the mass public are ultimately supportive of that change.

For all these reasons, it is important to understand how value change in society is reflected in the decisions of Supreme Court justices. Our book addresses this fundamental question. Regardless of the desirability or prudence of having high courts involved in policymaking in democratic societies, the question remains: Are the current legal-mobilization efforts and the postmaterialist value change that is taking place in the general public in these societies readily documented in the written opinions and voting behaviour of their judicial elites?

Goals and Issue Areas Examined in the Book

The overarching goal of this book is to test the veracity of Inglehart's intergenerational value shift thesis in the Canadian Supreme Court context. More specifically, this book seeks to assess whether the postmaterialist value changes that Inglehart has documented in public opinion polls are reflected in the voting and writing behaviour of the judicial elites over the four decades studied. Such an analysis is important because it can provide insights into how the Canadian Supreme Court will resolve controversies in these critical policy areas in the future. The two general research questions we seek to address are as follows: Do Canadian Supreme Court justices hand down rulings that reflect the value changes taking place in Canadian society over time? Can we document, in the written opinions of the Supreme Court justices in salient issue areas, a movement away from materialistic towards post-materialist concerns that present a classic tension between materialist and postmaterialist values? Since Inglehart's research indicates that Canada, along with other advanced democracies, is at the forefront of adopting postmaterialist values, it makes intuitive sense to believe that these value changes would occur in the judicial rulings of the Canadian Supreme Court.

To answer these questions, we employ both quantitative and qualitative approaches and assess judicial rulings on both an individual (micro) and an aggregate (macro) level in environmental, free expression, and discrimination cases. This type of dual analysis is important because it provides a more robust and complete understanding of how the court is approaching and resolving these critical disputes. The time frame chosen for this study dovetails with the period when justices who had come of age during the global, postmaterialist generational shift were replacing those who had come of age during the Depression and two world wars.

After the Canadian Supreme Court became the court of last resort in 1949, it favoured the individual in a series of Quebec civil liberties cases in the early 1950s (Baar 1976, 370–1; Russell 1987, 342; Ostberg 1995, 3). Key cases during this period related to the rights of Jehovah's Witnesses, with the court promoting freedom of speech on narrow grounds within the limited constitutional means available to it (Baar 1976, 370–1; Berger 1981; Hogg 2011, s. 34-2). The leading proponent of civil liberties at this time was Justice Ivan Rand, followed in the 1960s by Justice Emmett Hall and in the 1970s by Justice Bora Laskin, but there were no consistent majorities supportive of an expansion of civil liberties and civil rights until the 1980s (Baar 1976, 371; Epp 1998, 168). Other data indicate that, between 1960 and 1982, the Supreme Court heard only 34 claims referring to the Canadian Bill of Rights and favoured the individual litigant in only 5 of those cases (see Russell 1987, 343; Morton, Russell, and Withey 1991, 61–2).

In light of the inconsistent and relatively weak civil liberties record up until the 1970s, we think the critical postmaterialist breaking point occurs when older, more materialist justices occupy the court along with their younger, post–Second World War cohorts throughout the 1970s and 1980s. As a result, our study begins in 1973, the era marked by the beginning of the Laskin Court, followed by the Dickson Court (1984–89), the Lamer Court (1990–99), and the early McLachlin Court (2000–10). If Inglehart's theory of intergenerational value change applies to Supreme Court justices, we should see increasingly postmaterialist rulings and legal language as we move forward in time.

We test Inglehart's postmaterialist value shift thesis in three broad areas of law: the environment, free expression, and equality/discrimination. We selected these legal areas for analysis because they generate disputes that raise obvious materialist and postmaterialist fulcrums of conflict. Moreover, Inglehart's index, which measures the prevalence of public support for postmaterialist values, is highly correlated with a host of other postmodern values, including endorsement of self-expression values, protection of the environment, tolerance of homosexuals and human diversity, and support for gender equality (Inglehart 1997, 82; Inglehart and Welzel 2005, 115, 272, 299). The strong correlation with support for self-expression values is not surprising since support for free speech is one of the core questions in the 12-item postmaterialism index. Thus, it makes intuitive sense to evaluate changes in the patterns of judicial rulings over time in these three broad areas of law because they lie at the foundation of a postmodern society and can provide evidence of whether elite justices have moved in a postmaterialist direction, in line with Inglehart's finding for the Canadian public at large. If Inglehart's theory cannot be documented in these three areas of law, which represent some of the most obvious testing grounds, then the theory's overall applicability to judicial elites can be called into question.

It is important to understand how cases in these three issue areas reflect the materialist and postmaterialist tension articulated by Inglehart. These tensions are readily exemplified in the environmental area, where many disputes feature one side advancing an argument to develop or exploit resources for material or economic gain, while the other side typically seeks to limit the development or taking of resources to protect the environment from lasting harm. Lawyers on each side of these cases represent the opposing value priorities reflected in the questions in the World Values Survey and embodied along Inglehart's survival–well-being values continuum. Even so, some disputes in the environmental area, especially those pertaining to First Nation individuals' rights to hunt and fish, present an element of complexity in the coding of cases because the justices may be endorsing the postmaterialist value of protecting the environment or the postmaterialist goal of enhancing the political and economic equality of a historically marginalized group in Canada that seeks the right of self-government (Macklem 1995). Some scholars might argue that First Nations peoples are not exploiters of the environment because they engage in sustainable practices drawn from a long history of wise resource management and that they have rights to do so granted by treaty (see Collins and Murtha 2010). As a result, there is an equality element and a degree of postmaterialist ambiguity in the First Nation environmental cases that must be discussed in more detail; this is done in chapters 2 and 3.

Disputes in the area of free speech and equality/discrimination raise a social tension that pits an individual's rights to free expression and equality against a governmental, corporate, or societal interest in maintaining order and security or promoting economic liberty in the marketplace. Disputes in the equality area typically feature a conflict between an equality-seeking individual or group and a government or private entity, which seeks the freedom to provide services or benefits as it sees fit and in a manner that others in society may consider discriminatory. For example, when the government excludes gay couples from receiving federal benefits that are given to heterosexual couples, this reflects an equality-versus-order conflict, with gays seeking equal treatment and government representatives arguing for the freedom to create distinctions in the law that promote traditional values in society.[2]

Disputes in the free expression area, in turn, characteristically feature a conflict between an individual's or entity's right to engage in free expression and government's interest in protecting the order, safety, and well-being of society at large. Yet free speech claims sometimes

---

2 Our discussion of the tensions articulated by Inglehart are also discussed in US government texts, in which scholars such as Janda, Berry, and Goldman (2004, 26) explain political ideology in terms of value conflicts along two attitudinal dimensions. According to Janda, while the first dimension pits the values of equality versus freedom along the y-axis, the other dimension pits freedom versus order along the x-axis. Collectively, these two dimensions provide a framework for describing the value difference among four ideological archetypes: liberals, libertarians, populists (or communitarians), and conservatives.

contain a tension between two postmaterialist values, which Inglehart has acknowledged – namely, freedom of speech versus the value of protecting the equality of individuals and groups in society. Examples of this tension can be found in cases involving restrictions on campaign contributions, which pit the freedom to use money to back political candidates against the societal interest in ensuring equal participation in the political arena. We address this tension in more detail in chapters 4 and 5 of the book, recognizing that postmaterialist value change takes on different guises over four decades.

Although discrimination and free speech disputes are typically social in nature, they still track well along Inglehart's materialist-postmaterialist value dimension because government's interest in law, order, and traditional values reflects materialist tendencies, while the desire of individuals or others to engage in free expression or advance equality interests reflects postmodern values that foster well-being and individual self-fulfilment. In subsequent chapters, we highlight a hierarchical vision of postmaterialist-materialist values, which suggests that despite the complexity of the value conflicts found in certain cases, one can evaluate Inglehart's theory of postmaterialist value change across these three distinct areas of law.

Since we are interested in examining whether value changes are taking place among judicial elites in Canadian society, it is important to look briefly at the political culture of Canada. Like other advanced democracies, Canada has a core set of political values that endorse equality before the law and the right to hold private property, along with freedom of speech and the right to assemble and vote (Nevitte 1991, 3–4). Aside from these common liberal, Western traits, there are several factors that argue against the development of a singular national identity for Canada, including its geographic size, harsh climate, a small and widely dispersed population, cultural and linguistic diversity, and proximity to the more hegemonic US culture (Nevitte 1991, 3–6).

Seen in this light, Canadian political culture does not project a single clear, unifying, powerful image like the United States, but rather reflects a mosaic of diverse cultures. Several scholars studying the early political development of Canada highlight different cultural elements of the two countries: different settlement patterns; different responses to founding events (such as the American Revolution); the influence of powerful, tight-knit elites; and the economic forces that shaped the development of the two countries (see Innis 1956; Hartz 1964; Porter 1965; Kornberg 1988; Lipset 1990). They, along with others such as Nevitte (1991) and

Jackson, Jackson, and Baxter-Moore (1986), argue that Canadian political culture is characterized by higher levels of trust, greater deference to the authority of leaders, a more positive view of government action, and a greater interest in seeing the state do more to promote the well-being of society, at least when compared to US citizens. Canadians also have a higher distaste for disorder and a greater preference for actions that promote the collective good, being good citizens of the world, and placing less emphasis on individual rights and greater emphasis on group rights (Lipset 1990; Nevitte 1991, 18–19; Ostberg 1995; Berger 2005). These collective value differences suggest that postmaterialist value change in Canada might lead Canadian justices to value the promotion of equality interests and the rights of collective groups, such as First Nations, over the unfettered right to freedom and individual liberty that is so prominent in US political culture.

Main Research Questions and Structure of the Book

In light of Inglehart's research documenting intergenerational changes in values in the Canadian public in the post–Second World War era, we seek to explore whether that same value shift has occurred among judicial elites in Canadian society by examining five specific research questions across the six main chapters of the book (2 to 7). The first research question, explored in the three quantitative chapters (2, 4, and 6), is whether a gradual intergenerational shift occurred across the Canadian Supreme Court between 1973 and 2010. Inglehart's intergenerational value change thesis leads us to expect the levels of support for postmaterialist positions to increase in these areas of law as we move through the Laskin (1973–84), Dickson (1984–90), Lamer (1990–99), and McLachlin (2000–10) Courts. Obviously, the court's movement in the postmaterialist direction does not occur in a vacuum. Rather, courts are reactive institutions that depend on dissatisfied individual and group litigants to bring forward postmaterialist arguments that reflect this shifting values landscape.

In keeping with this theme, the second research question we explore in the three quantitative chapters is whether there is an increase in postmaterialist interest group activity in the court over time that provides the legal rationale and insight that prompts it to move in a postmaterialist direction. It is expected that, across the four decade period analysed, there will be an increase in intervener activity in the Supreme Court that reflects the changing values and norms in the Canadian public. Our specific tracking of this second research question is based on counts of postmaterialist interveners over the 1973–2010 period and the proportion they represent of all interveners in the disputes.

The third main research question testing Inglehart's theory in the quantitative chapters tracks each justice's support for postmaterialist claims over time by examining the bivariate relationship between a justice's year of birth and his or her career support for postmaterialist values in the three issue areas. If the intergenerational values thesis is correct and applies to judicial elites, we expect the scatterplot to feature a line of best fit with a positive slope that moves from low to high in the three areas of law as we move forward to the current McLachlin Court.

To examine the fourth main research question, we use logistic regression analysis to examine the voting patterns of the four most recent courts in relation to each other. If Inglehart's intergenerational theory is valid for the study of judicial elites in Canada, we postulate that justices serving on the two most recent courts (Lamer and McLachlin) will vote more consistently for postmaterialist values in the three issue areas than their earlier counterparts on the Laskin and Dickson Courts. We chose to analyse this relationship using logistic regression methodology because it allows us to control for rival factors that might explain individual voting behaviour in the cases we study. It also enables us to assess the impact that judge-level variables have on voting behaviour as well as the impact of a combined model, which has both judge-level and case-level variables in the equation. The beauty of logistic regression is that it allows us to not only examine the overall impact of serving on a court at a particular time but also, simultaneously, study the impact of a multitude of case and individual justice-level variables in a single equation. In the face of multiple control variables, we expect to find increasingly positive coefficients for the Dickson, Lamer, and McLachlin Court indicators in the three areas of law, and we believe that such a finding is emblematic of the latent intergenerational forces that shaped the justices during their formative years. This test moves beyond the simple bivariate relationships examined in the third hypothesis and provides the most robust, two-stage quantitative test of Inglehart's intergenerational values thesis.

The last main research question in this book turns to a qualitative analysis of the language and rationale used by the justices in their written opinions in landmark cases in the three issue areas over the time period studied (chapters 3, 5, and 7). We employ content analysis techniques to highlight key language that either reflects, or does not reflect, a postmaterialist mindset. In line with Inglehart, we expect to see stronger postmaterialist language reflected in the rationale and wording of the written opinions in various sub-fields in environmental, free expression, and equality areas of law. In this area of the book, we focus our attention on reviewing one or two landmark cases from each court period, which we distil into the Laskin/Dickson, Lamer, and early McLachlin Courts. Moreover, given the sheer volume of cases across these areas, our analysis of landmark rulings homes in on the environmental sub-areas of pollution, energy, and First Nation fishing rights cases; the free expression sub-areas of commercial advertising and political speech; and the equality areas of gay rights and sex discrimination. Although the cases reviewed represent just a sample of those in each of these areas of law, our findings are compelling because the cases embody some of the most salient, high-profile political controversies in Canada over the four decades studied.

We explore Inglehart's intergenerational values thesis both quantitatively and qualitatively in this book because these two methodological techniques complement each other and provide us with a more complete, robust understanding of the degree to which individual justices and the four most recent, modern Canadian courts have embraced postmaterialist values over time. The importance and benefits of conducting statistical analysis are numerous. First, it gives readers a comprehensive overview of the types and percentage of cases that the courts have heard in the three areas of law over the past four decades. Second, it helps us understand the actual voting behaviour of individual justices across a wide array of cases in each of these areas and identify the percentage of postmaterialist rulings that individual justices and courts have handed down. Third, quantitative logistic analysis allows us to systematically determine the degree to which the four most recent courts have moved in a postmaterialist direction, while controlling for other possible rival variables, such as the adoption of the Charter, which may alternatively explain such behaviour. As a result, the empirical analysis focuses on individual justices and their patterns of support for postmaterialist outcomes across different court periods under the leadership of Chief Justices Laskin, Lamer, Dickson, and McLachlin. These findings help shed light on the degree to which various factors in the socio-attitudinal model explain judicial voting behaviour, especially the impact that latent attitudes and values acquired by the justices during their formative years have on postmaterialist voting behaviour.

It is equally important to conduct qualitative analysis of critical rulings in the three areas of law because it allows us to examine whether the justices use legal language or principles that embrace postmaterialist values over time. Second, a qualitative approach allows us to understand the doctrinal direction the court is taking in the sub-fields of the three areas of law. The emphasis on doctrinal development is critical because the language of opinions can shape the course of the law for decades. Moreover, this attention to detail in the language reflects what the justices say is a vital component of their work: writing good decisions that align opinions with law and precedents (Songer et al. 2012, 6, 62). In addition, detailed analysis of the written opinions in certain subfields may unmask critical postmaterialist movement that an overarching statistical analysis of a given area of law might miss. Using these two methodological techniques in a single book is a unique addition to the judicial discipline, and it provides readers with the most comprehensive way to assess whether Inglehart's intergenerational values thesis is occurring among judicial elites in modern Canadian society.

One of the overarching findings emerging from the book is that a relatively clear pattern of postmaterialist value transformation has taken place in the Supreme Court of Canada. Readers will note, however, that the movement in a postmaterialist direction is stronger in some areas of law than in others. One of the strongest pieces of evidence of an intergenerational value shift within the Supreme Court can be found in the environmental area of law, which is highlighted by the increasingly postmaterialist outcomes across the Dickson, Lamer, and McLachlin Court tenures. While the qualitative analysis of landmark pollution cases demonstrates a clear postmaterialist ethic in the Supreme Court opinions, the same pattern does not hold in the energy cases. Yet even in these cases, most of the justices have come to recognize the "fundamental value" of environmental protection in Canadian society. Across the complex mosaic of issues in the fishing rights cases, readers will not be surprised to find a good deal of constitutional and historical nuance and mixed results in relation to Inglehart's thesis. Yet overall, these cases do provide some evidence of strong postmaterialist language in the opinions as the court struggles to balance a First Nation individual's right to fish using traditional, sustainable methods against the need to protect fisheries from further encroachment. Overall, the language and rationale in the arc of landmark cases examined in the environmental area seem to provide strong, although occasionally mixed, evidence supporting the Inglehart thesis that a gradual postmaterialist movement is playing out in the Supreme Court in many environmental disputes.

Evidence of a postmaterialist value transformation also predominates across most of the quantitative tests in the free expression area. However, there is an apparent retrograde movement during the first 10 years of the McLachlin Court towards materialist stances when controlling for all other variables in the equation. The qualitative analysis of landmark commercial advertising and political speech cases reinforces the empirical results, with the Lamer Court taking a much more postmaterialist stance in the language of its opinions than the Laskin and Dickson Courts. However, these postmaterialist gains in these subfields of law were seemingly undercut in the first 10 years of the McLachlin Court. Even so, we present evidence in the book to suggest that a kind of postmaterialist sentiment is evident in the McLachlin Court rulings pertaining to the importance of equal participation in the political process. This transformation has reflected a shift from the postmaterialist value of unfettered freedom of expression towards the postmaterialist norm of equality. Turning to a quantitative analysis of equality cases, Inglehart's proposed shift seems least apparent among the justices' voting records. However, we believe that there is a dominant factor in the equation – namely, the gender of the justices – that is confounding the empirical findings. In other words, the bloc of female justices and the distinctive positions they have taken in equality disputes in recent decades has overpowered any postmaterialist movement made by the male justices.

This conclusion becomes even more evident when reading the language used in the opinions of the justices. Indeed, some of the most ardent postmaterialist language in favour of securing equality rights appears in the gay rights and sex discrimination cases. These equality cases indicate that the female justices have played a leading role in elevating the postmaterialist value of defending equality rights over those professing the freedom to treat individuals as they see fit; this fits with the cultural emphasis on equality rights more readily apparent in Canadian society than in the United States. Overall, the results demonstrate that a slow, gradual shift towards postmaterialist values, identified by Inglehart in the mass public, is taking root in the environmental, free speech, and equality decisions of Canada's high court.

In the closing chapter, we summarize the major findings of the qualitative and quantitative chapters of the book and provide a table that catalogues the evidence of a postmaterialist shift in the Supreme Court of Canada. We discuss what the overarching findings of the qualitative and quantitative approaches have to say about the applicability of Inglehart's intergenerational value shift theory to Canadian judicial elites. We highlight some of the important tensions that emerge in cases that pit two postmaterialist values against each other – namely, equality and freedom. We also discuss the implications that the sweeping postmaterialist value shift seen in some areas will have on various actors in the Canadian political system, including interest groups, members of Parliament, and the justices themselves. The chapter explores some normative questions that emerge from our findings, focusing on issues like the political interplay between the Supreme Court and Parliament, the role of the court in a constitutional democracy, the continuing pace of interest group mobilization, and the court's place in an era of increasing judicialization of politics. We close the book by speculating about the prospects of a materialistic resurgence in postmodern society as Western states, including Canada, grapple with the lingering effects of the Al Qaeda terrorist strikes, the economic meltdown in the late 2000s, continuing globalizing forces in the world economy, and rising economic disparity between the haves and have-nots in the last decade.

Chapter Two

Postmaterialist Outcomes in Environmental Disputes

Introduction

Environmental issues provide an obvious place to begin to test the veracity of Inglehart's intergenerational values thesis in the rulings of the Canadian Supreme Court. If one remembers, at the heart of his thesis is the contention that the prolonged period of prosperity after the Second World War fostered a slow and gradual shift in the public away from materialistic economic growth and security concerns to postmaterialist quality-of-life concerns (Inglehart 1997, chap. 1; Inglehart and Welzel 2005, 23–5). Since justices necessarily develop overarching world views in their formative years that reflect the values of their society, the postmaterialist value change reflected in Canadian public opinion should eventually become evident in the voting behaviour of the judicial elites. Moreover, justices appointed more recently to the high court should exhibit voting behaviour that supports quality-of-life concerns, such as protection of the environment, to a greater extent than their older, more materialistic cohorts.

With justices on the Canadian Supreme Court seen in this light, this chapter assesses whether they exhibit a gradual shift towards embracing postmaterialist values in environmental cases heard between 1973 and 2010. We begin with environmental disputes because they highlight a tension between postmaterialist and materialist concerns that frequently juxtaposes environmental protection against economic development and resource exploitation. Moreover, these disputes represent salient political disputes that burst on the political stage in the early 1970s, at the same time that Inglehart (1971, 1990, 1997) began documenting a postmaterialist awakening in public opinion polls.

Last, we begin here because Inglehart's (1995) research indicates that the Canadian public has been near the forefront of postmaterialist value change in the area of environmental protection.

Postmaterialist Values and the Environment

In a 1996 book exploring the cultural and economic ties among Canada, the United States, and Mexico, Inglehart, Nevitte, and Basanez (1996, 151) stated that "postmaterialism has a very significant impact on environmental attitudes in the American and Canadian publics." Over the years, Inglehart has collected a wealth of public opinion data documenting this intergenerational value change in environmental issues over successive generations in Canada (World Values Survey 2011). For example, in a 2000 survey, 64 per cent of Canadians indicated that they preferred "protecting the environment" as a priority "even if it causes slower economic growth and some loss of jobs" (ibid.). In surveys conducted in 1990 and 2000, more than 50 per cent of Canadians were willing to accept increased taxes if they were used to protect the environment. In addition, between 1982 and 2000, the percentage of Canadians saying that they belonged to a conservation, environmental, or animal rights group doubled (ibid.).

Despite this high level of support, however, it is interesting to note that Inglehart found that Canada ranked only in the middle of the pack among advanced, post-industrial countries in supporting environmental protection across a multi-item index of survey questions he conducted in 1990–91 (Inglehart 1995, 60–1). The countries exhibiting the highest levels of support for the environment and willingness to make economic sacrifices were Sweden, Denmark, the Netherlands, and Norway. Inglehart noted that this is not surprising since they have relatively high proportions of postmaterialists among their citizenry (Inglehart 1995, 57, 61). Even so, the polling data clearly demonstrate that the Canadian public has increasingly embraced postmaterialist values that endorse environmental protection, and this is particularly true for younger Canadian cohorts (Inglehart 1995, 62).

According to Inglehart (1995), it is not surprising that the mass public in many countries supports protecting the environment in the abstract; however, the question remains: Are people willing to make financial sacrifices or give up other societal needs to protect the environment? As he stated, "The crunch comes when a difficult choice is needed between roads or trees, dams or endangered species, to burn fossil fuels that may lead to global warming or to remain non-industrialized" (Inglehart 1995, 59). In other words, attitudes are one thing, but actual pro-environmental behaviour among members of the public more clearly cements the belief that a pro-environmental shift is occurring.

There is evidence of this behavioural shift in Canada. A 2006 study by Babooram (2008, 7) found that nearly half (45 per cent) of all Canadians had taken four to six actions to engage in household behaviour that reduced energy consumption and water use, and/or promoted recycling. Among those steps, fully 30 per cent of households reported composting waste on their property, while another 37 per cent reported installing reduced-volume toilets (Babooram 2008, 8–9). He also found that more active environmental households were associated with higher income and education levels (Babooram 2008, 11), a fact that aligns well with Inglehart's postmaterialist values thesis in highly developed regions. These data suggest that there is no doubting that Canadian citizens place a high value on protecting the environment. David Boyd goes so far as to suggest that, with public opinion so strongly pro-environment, countries like Canada should consider giving environmental protections constitutional status to ensure the future preservation of the country's natural heritage (Boyd 2012a, 92; 2012b, 197–9).

Although Canadians have embraced environmental values, there are critics who claim that the notion of Canadian environmental exceptionalism is a myth. For instance, Boyd noted that, across a wide range of ecological rankings for advanced Western democracies, Canada actually placed near the bottom. Only the United States ranked lower among developed states on the release of sulphur oxides per capita and water consumption, while Canada was among the three worst countries for greenhouse gas emissions, energy efficiency, the volume of timber harvested, and nuclear waste (Boyd 2003, 6–7). In a recent survey of constitutional documents, Boyd found that Canada was among 15 nations that had yet to enshrine a constitutional right to live in a healthy environment (Boyd 2012a, 97). This suggests that Canada's policymaking institutions have not matched the expectations of Canadian citizens on environmental issues. For example, 99 per cent of Canadians surveyed in 2000 believed that reducing air pollution was important, but Canada was one of the worst air-polluting countries at that time (Prescott-Allen 2001; Boyd 2003, 10). Similarly, while the Canadian public wants clean, secure water supplies, governmental policies are shaped, in part, by the mistaken belief that the country possesses an endless supply of water (Boyd 2003, 15). This contradiction reflects a populace with high expectations of environmental protection, but environmentalists point to a poor track record on key regulatory fronts.[1]

The apparent gap between pro-environmental public opinion and public policy points to the importance of testing Inglehart's postmaterialist value change thesis among political elites. If decisions by elite policymakers do not jibe with the expectations of the public, then government institutions are open to the criticism that they do not reflect the values of the majority of the body politic. The expectation is that in a democratic system, legislatures and courts should not be radically out of step with the mass public and the gradual attitudinal shifts that come with intergenerational change in values over time. In fact, elites are often more accepting of postmaterialist value change because they are more likely to come from high-income socio-economic backgrounds (Inglehart and Welzel 2005, 219–20). However, we would contend that since high-level policy officials tend to come from earlier birth cohorts, they are more likely to hold value positions that reflect a more materialist value structure. Rosenberg (1991) suggests that it may be a hollow hope in any case to expect courts and judges to be in lockstep with changing public opinion, but representative democratic theory postulates that if courts are too out of step with public opinion, they are bound to face a backlash from other governmental institutions and have their legitimacy questioned by the larger public (Epstein and Knight 1998).

Our test of postmaterialist value change in the Supreme Court of Canada analyses whether a gradual shift in values has occurred over time in one of the most salient postmaterialist issue areas. In doing so, our study also evaluates the degree to which the justices are relatively in or out of step with these gradual changes in Canadian society. Given the decisive shift in the postmaterialist direction of citizen values in Canada over the last 40 years, a study that looks at the voting record of Canadian justices can provide a valuable link in the chain of postmaterialist theory, especially in cases involving environmental protection issues.

---

1 Not all is grim in terms of governmental protection of the environment. For example, federal and provincial agencies have taken steps to protect more and more open space and marine areas. Between 1990 and 2011, land and water protected from development grew by 95 per cent, to a total of roughly 10 per cent of Canada's total land area (Environment Canada 2012).

Data and Methods for Descriptive Statistics and Judicial Voting Patterns

The data for this part of the study are drawn from published opinions in the *Canadian Supreme Court Reports* from 1973 to 2010. Cases were included in the analysis if an environmental issue was a central component of the case ($N = 74$).[2] The 1973–2010 time period was selected because it allowed us to analyse the environmental rulings handed down by the court under the tenures of the last four chief justices – namely, Justices Laskin (1973–84), Dickson (1984–90), and Lamer (1990–99) and the first 10 years under Justice McLachlin (2000–10). Moreover, this time frame enabled us to test the applicability of Inglehart's shifting values priority thesis among judicial elites over time in the Canadian setting.

The chapter uses three separate stages of analysis to provide a robust explanation of the patterns of judicial behaviour in the environmental area and to examine these cases according to Inglehart's postmaterialist theory. We begin by providing general statistics on the 74 environmental rulings handed down during the period, including the types of environmental issues heard by the court, the percentage of pro-environmental rulings in each issue area, and an analysis of the various litigants and interveners in the cases. In the second stage, we assess the pro-environmental voting patterns of the justices over time and in terms of authorship, majority voting behaviour, and dissent activity. We also provide a scatterplot of judicial pro-environmental rulings by year of birth across the four courts to examine whether the patterns of voting agree with Inglehart's intergenerational value change theory. In the third stage, we conduct logistic regression analysis to evaluate the

2 A list of cases included in the study is provided in the appendix. Nine potential environmental cases were excluded from the analysis because some of them did not feature written reasons for judgment and others were more appropriately identified as property, contract, insurance, or jurisdiction disputes: *McKinney v. The Queen*, [1980] 1 S.C.R. 401; *Oregon Jack Creek Indian Band v. Canadian National Railway Co.*, [1989] 2 S.C.R. 1069; *Delgamuukw v. British Columbia*, [1997] 3 S.C.R. 1010; *Opetchesaht Indian Band v. Canada*, [1997] 2 S.C.R. 119; *Reference re Upper Churchill Water Rights Reversion Act*, [1984] 1 S.C.R. 297; *Mastermet Cobalt Mines v. Canada*, [1980] 2 S.C.R. 119; *Lac d'Amiante du Québec Ltée v. 2858-0702 Québec Inc.*, [2001] 2 S.C.R. 743; *British Columbia Hydro and Power Authority v. British Columbia (Environmental Appeal Board)*, [2005] 1 S.C.R. 3; *Teck Cominco Metals, Ltd. v. Lloyd's Underwriters*, [2009] 1 S.C.R. 321.

Table 2.1. Canadian Environmental Cases by Issue Area, 1973–2010

Issue area	Cases (N = 74)	
	No.	%
Pollution	**15**	**20.3**
Air pollution	2	2.7
Land pollution	6	8.1
Water pollution	9	12.2
Wildlife protection	**44**	**59.5**
Fisheries regulations	30	40.5
Hunting regulations	17	23.0
First Nation issues	**24**	**32.4**
Treaty claims/issues	23	31.1
Customs/religion	2	2.7
Land and sea preservation	**30**	**40.5**
Forests and public land	20	27.0
Maritime protection	2	2.7
Laws preventing extraction	11	14.9
Open space	7	9.5
Energy	**6**	**8.1**
Oil and gas	2	2.7
Hydro	3	4.1
Nuclear	1	1.4
Government takings and land use	**12**	**16.2**
Takings	4	5.4
Land use/zoning	10	13.5

Note: Readers should be careful when interpreting the table. The subgroup counts across five of the six broad issue areas are larger than the overall category counts because many environmental cases feature multiple issues and facts. For example, in the pollution area, two cases feature two different forms of pollution, one with both air and land and a second with both land and water. Thus, across the 74 cases, multiple issues may arise, resulting in a larger count within the subcategories than in the total number.

relative explanatory power that various judge-level and case-specific variables have on judicial voting patterns in environmental cases.

Descriptive Statistics and Judicial Voting Patterns

The first set of data results, found in Table 2.1, show that the court heard a range of environmental issues, which were classified into six distinct categories relating to pollution control, wildlife protection, First Nation issues, land and sea preservation, energy issues, and government takings/land use. Although the court heard a total of 74 cases during this period, the data in Table 2.1 indicate that the bulk of these legal disputes actually fell into two or more of the environmental

Table 2.2. Pro-environmental Rulings in Canadian Environmental Cases by Broad Issue Area, 1973–2010

Issue area	Cases (*N* = 74)	
	No.	%
Pollution	15	80.0
Takings/land use	12	75.0
Wildlife protection	44	56.8
Land/sea preservation	30	56.7
First Nation issues	24	45.8
Energy	6	33.3

categories. The largest percentage of cases was heard in the areas of wildlife protection and land and sea preservation, and collectively, they represent over half of the disputes heard by the court (60 per cent and 41 per cent, respectively). Those two categories were followed by cases dealing with First Nation issues (32 per cent) and pollution issues (20 per cent). One should note that 23 of the 24 cases in the First Nation category involved treaty issues and that many of these also fell into the wildlife protection category because they typically involved First Nation individuals that sought to fish or hunt either without a licence or in direct violation of a specific regulation that conflicted with some kind of treaty right. The fewest environmental cases appeared in the areas of government takings/land use and energy (16 and 8 per cent, respectively). Collectively, the data suggest that two areas of paramount importance in the environmental area relate to wildlife protection and land and sea preservation, particularly in relation to First Nation individuals and their attempt to exercise historically protected rights to use natural resources.

Table 2.2 provides a breakdown of the percentage of pro-environmental rulings that the court handed down in the cases that dealt with six of the categories discussed above. Readers should note that we coded the following outcomes as pro-environmental decisions: cases supporting pollution regulations or supporting hunting, fishing, or wildlife regulations; cases that upheld land or resource preservation, or upheld restrictions on the extraction of resources, or imposed regulations on energy producers; and government takings in favour of open space, parks, or the preservation of natural resources. The data reveal that the court ruled in favour of the environmental claim over 56 per cent of the time in four of the six issue areas, a result that mirrors the average support of environmental claims among all the justices in the cases. The greatest percentage of pro-environmental rulings occurred in the pollution and takings/land use cases (80 and 75 per cent, respectively). These findings suggest that the Canadian justices were particularly interested in protecting the environment from pollution and supporting government efforts to expropriate property in the interest of environmental protection and preservation.

However, since the court heard only a moderate number of cases in these two issue categories (15 and 12, respectively), one should not read too much into these findings. The smallest number of cases appeared in the energy area, where it heard only six cases. Energy was one of the two issue areas in which the court handed down the lowest percentage of pro-environmental rulings (33 per cent), while First Nation disputes featured only a 46 per cent pro-environmental rate. These results indicate that the Supreme Court was most willing to promote economic and materialist interests in cases involving oil and power generation and in disputes that featured First Nation claimants seeking the right to exploit wildlife resources in conflict with government regulations. We have much more to say about the unique features of First Nation cases in chapter 3, but overall, the data in Table 2.2 suggest that the modern Canadian court has a greater proclivity than not to rule in favour of litigants that bring forward pro-environmental claims in a bulk of the issue areas, and the fact that there is an overall support score of almost 60 per cent provides some limited support at first blush for the proposition that Inglehart's postmaterialist values are prominent in the minds of some of the modern Canadian justices.

Inglehart's thesis obtains more qualified support in Table 2.3, which lists the number and percentage of pro-environmental rulings by decade and by tenure of the four most recent chief justices of the Canadian Supreme Court. The data reveal that there was an increase in the number and percentage of rulings handed down in favour of the environment throughout the 1970s, 1980s, and 1990s and under Chief Justices Dickson and Lamer compared to Chief Justice Laskin. Indeed, the percentage of pro-environmental rulings rose from 53 per cent under the Laskin Court to 71 and 67 per cent, respectively, during the Dickson and Lamer Courts of the 1980s and 1990s. However, the table also indicates that the percentage of pro-environmental rulings fell below the rate of Chief Justice Laskin's Court during the first 10 years of Chief Justice McLachlin's leadership, from 53 to 50 per cent. The question remains whether that drop in pro-environmental rulings reflects a situation in which the McLachlin Court was less willing to

Table 2.3. Pro-environmental Rulings by Decade and Court in the Supreme Court of Canada, 1973–2010

Court	Cases	
	No.	%
Decade		
1970s (1973–79)	9	55.5
1980s	20	65.0
1990s	21	66.7
2000s (2000–10)	24	50.0
Period		
Laskin Court (1974–84)[a]	15	53.3
Dickson Court (1984–90)	14	71.4
Lamer Court (1990–99)	21	66.7
McLachlin Court (2000–10)	20	50.0

[a]The Laskin Court rulings start in 1974 instead of 1973 because the first Laskin Court decisions were handed down that year.

Table 2.4. Number of Environmental Issues Decided by the Supreme Court of Canada by Decade, 1973–2010

Issue area	1970s	1980s	1990s	2000s	Total
Pollution	4	1	5	5	15
Wildlife protection	8	12	15	9	44
First Nation issues	2	8	6	8	24
Land/sea preservation	1	10	3	16	30
Energy	0	1	2	3	6
Takings/land use	1	5	2	3	12

support the environment, which would undermine Inglehart's thesis, or one in which it was facing more complex environmental issues. One can answer this question by controlling for competing variables in a regression model, which we turn to in the third stage of our analysis. However, given the data presented, it seems that Inglehart's thesis of postmaterialist value change was alive and well under three of the four modern Canadian courts, but under the current chief justice's tenure, it appears to have fallen into disfavour.

Table 2.4 documents the trend of cases across the six broad issue areas over time. What stands out in this table is that wildlife protection was a prominent issue on the court throughout the last four decades, but its proportion of the docket has declined from a high in the 1970s (8 of 9 cases) to a second-tier status in the 2000–10 time period (9 of 24).

Table 2.5. Appellants and Respondents in Canadian Environmental Cases, 1973–2010

Appellant	Respondent						
	Individual (non-native)	Individual (native)	First Nation	Government	Corporation	Environmental interest group	Total
Individual (non-native)	0	0	0	9	1	0	10
Individual (native)	0	0	0	**23**	0	0	**23**
First Nation	0	0	0	3	0	0	3
Government	2	8	6	3	4	2	**25**
Corporation	0	0	0	**12**	0	0	**12**
Environmental interest group	0	0	0	1	0	0	1
Total	2	8	6	**51**	5	2	74

The court's contemporary docket now seems more focused on land and sea preservation cases, although this issue was prominent in the 1980s as well. Aside from these two issue areas, environmental disputes involving First Nation groups or individuals have constituted a fairly steady proportion of the court docket since the 1980s.

Table 2.5 highlights the pattern of litigants that appeared in environmental cases decided by the Supreme Court in the last four decades. The data reveal that the most frequent litigants in the 74 cases featured in disputes between First Nation individuals and government (31 of 74 cases, 42 per cent). In three-fourths of those cases (23 of 31), an individual appealed a lower court ruling upholding the government's effort to enforce environmental or wildlife protection regulations. Overall, cases involving First Nation issues, whether presented by individuals or groups, constituted fully 54 per cent of the environmental docket heard by the Supreme Court over the last four decades (40 of 74 cases). The next most frequent set of litigants involved corporate interests pitted against the government, comprising 16 of the 74 cases (22 per cent), with corporations seeking to overturn pro-environmental rulings in three-fourths of the cases. It is interesting to note that, in the Canadian context, environmental groups played almost no role as lead litigants in environmental disputes, appearing as respondents in only two cases and as an appellant in only one case across the 1973–2010 period. This is in marked contrast to the litigation patterns of environmental groups found in the United States (Wenner 1982).

Table 2.6. Litigant Pro-environmental Stances and Environmental Victories, 1973–2010

Party	Appellant	Respondent	Total	Pro-environment as either appellant or respondent, no.	Anti-environment as either appellant or respondent, no.	Environmental wins	
						No.	%
Government[a]	25	51	76/73	**58**	15	41	70.7
Individual (native)	23	8	31	0	**31**	0	0.0
First Nation	3	6	9	**8**	1	3	37.5
Individual (non-native)[b]	10	2	12	2	10	1	50.0
Corporation	12	5	17	0	17	0	0.0
Environmental interest group	1	2	3	3	0	2	66.7

[a]Three cases pit government against government, resulting in 76 appearances for government across 73 cases.
[b]One of the 74 cases does not involve a government party (individual versus corporation).

Table 2.6 provides a description of the appearances and pro-environmental victories of litigants across the time frame of our study. It appears that government, far more than any other litigant, acted as the champion of environmental interests and garnered the highest percentage of pro-environmental victories (58 appearances as a pro-environmental litigant, 71 per cent win rate). This high win rate aligns with party capability theory: the notion that well-financed and experienced litigants have an advantage in the legal system (Galanter 1974, 2003; McCormick 1993; Kritzer 2003). In contrast to government, First Nation individuals represented the largest group of anti-environmental litigants (in 31 of the 74 cases), and since they were always contesting the application of hunting, fishing, and wildlife regulations, they were obviously unable to achieve any pro-environmental victories in those cases. The position of First Nation individuals stands in stark contrast to the success of First Nation groups, which litigated on behalf of the environment in eight of the nine cases they appeared in before the Supreme Court. Yet they won only three of the eight cases, a 38 per cent win rate. The sharp divide in the stance taken by First Nation individuals and groups in environmental cases is important, and it explains why the 24 cases raising First Nation issues resulted in only 46 per cent pro-environmental rulings.

Another point of interest in Table 2.6 is that, aside from corporations, individual non-natives principally brought claims against the environment in most of their appearances (10 of 12, or 83 per cent of the time). Overall, the most significant finding in the table is the overwhelming prominence of government defence of environmental interests and the sustained rate of victories that governments obtained in those cases. These data align well with Inglehart's overarching thesis that the value of protecting the environment is important to the mass public in post-industrial societies. There are clear indications that environmental issues have become more salient in recent years, with Canadian governments playing an increasing role in the protection of the environment and touting an impressive winning record in the Supreme Court of Canada.

Some might take issue with the fact that we coded judicial votes against First Nation individuals as being anti-environment. Our counterargument would point to the fact that these individuals have engaged in sustainable practices of resource use for centuries, and, in reality, they are often seen as better environmental stewards than the government. Moreover, they are seeking to enforce various treaty rights that have been enacted throughout Canadian history and have been subsequently entrenched in the Canadian Constitution (see, e.g., Collins and Murtha 2010). Indeed, these cases are imbued with an equality element that adds complexity to the coding of them along Inglehart's materialist-postmaterialist spectrum. Although Inglehart's thesis recognizes equality as a value on the postmaterialist side of the spectrum, as do we, it is our contention that the equality position is a less purely postmaterialist value in these cases than the pure protection of the environment, and thus we have coded these particular cases as anti-environment.

We recognize that this makes it more difficult to prove our hypothesis. Our coding scheme puts the balance in favour of government, which in these cases is defending an environmental protection rule or law to advance the cause of ensuring resource management for the collective good. In some ways, we see these First Nation cases presenting a tension between, on the one hand, the traditional and historical argument for a privileged status to use and manage resources and, on the other, government's modern efforts to balance the demands of multiple actors who seek to hunt and fish in the same resource domain (individuals who hunt and fish, First Nation individuals, and commercial interests). Although we acknowledge that seeking equality rights is postmaterialist in nature, in the environmental context we look at each case to determine which party is taking the purest pro-environmental stance. In all the cases involving government enforcement of hunting and fishing restrictions, we ultimately coded the cases as pro-environment if the justices voted to support those regulations.

Having said this, we do recognize that First Nation individuals engage in sustainable practices, and we expect that some of the justices will sympathize with the equality claims advanced by First Nation individuals, given their historical marginalization as a group in Canadian society and the constitutionally protected rights they retain. Ultimately, these specific environmental cases pit two postmaterialist values against each other – namely, the pure protection of wildlife resources in the face of increasing environmental encroachment versus the equality-seeking claims of First Nation individuals. Although First Nation individuals can make a legitimate argument that they engage in sustainable practices, government agencies have an equally valid concern in limiting the increasing encroachment on pristine habitats and the need for sound limits. As such, support for modern hunting and fishing regulations should be seen as trumping First Nation concerns under most circumstances, and this guided our coding scheme. We delve into these issues in more depth in chapter 3, but for the moment, we highlight the notion that pro-environmental rulings in this quantitative chapter reflect the consistent application of our coding rules: that pro-environmental decisions are (1) those favouring governmental enforcement of hunting and fishing limits and (2) those opposing development projects on First Nation lands.

Table 2.7 provides more evidence to support Inglehart's postmaterialist argument by identifying the trends of intervention in environmental cases. The table is broken into two parts, with the top portion cataloguing the *total* number of interveners over the last four decades, while the bottom portion highlights the number of *pro-environmental* interveners. The totals found at the bottom of each portion illustrate a clear upward trend in the overall number of interveners, as well as those favouring the environment, across the four decades studied. Total intervening activity climbs from a low of 2 and 41 in the 1970s and 1980s to 105 and 244 in the 1990s and 2000s. A similar trajectory of growth for pro-environmental intervention is found at the bottom of Table 2.7. Remarkably, government interveners have dominated this landscape: a total of 144 instances reflect participation in environmental disputes, with 105 of those interventions featuring a pro-environmental stance. First Nations follow a close second, intervening in 139 cases, with the bulk of that activity occurring in the 1990s and 2000s. Yet unlike their activity as lead litigants, as interveners, First Nation groups struck a

Table 2.7. Intervener and Pro-environmental Intervener Activity in Environmental Cases, 1973–2010

Intervener	1970s	1980s	1990s	2000s	Total
Government agency	2	22	33	87	144
Corporation/trade association	0	12	6	33	51
First Nation	0	5	39	95	139
Environmental group	0	2	25	23	50
Other group	0	0	2	6	8
Total	2	41	105	244	392
Pro-environmental intervener tallies in environmental cases, 1973–2010[a]					
Intervener	1970s	1980s	1990s	2000s	Total
Government agency	**2**	**22**	**26**	**55**	**105**
Corporation/trade association	0	12	3	0	15
First Nation	0	0	4	38	42
Environmental group	0	2	25	23	50
Other group	0	0	2	5	7
Total	2	36	60	121	219
Proportion pro-environment	100.0	87.9	57.1	49.6	55.9
Proportion anti-environment	0.0	12.1	42.9	50.4	44.1

[a]We coded the direction of the interveners in reference to whether they supported a pro-environmental stance based on a reading of the Supreme Court cases.

pro-environmental stance in only 30 per cent of the cases (42 of 139). It seems that First Nation representatives were primarily using intervener activity as a means to provide supportive arguments and resources for individuals seeking to advocate for their historical treaty rights to hunt and fish. For their part, environmental groups appeared as interveners in 50 cases over the 1973–2010 time frame, and 48 of those appearances occurred in the last two decades.

Overall, a very prominent flurry of postmaterialist environmental activity occurred in the 1980s, with pro-environmental interveners making up 88 per cent of all interveners in that decade. This lopsided distribution gave way to a more equalized distribution between pro- and anti-environmental intervener activity in the 1990s and 2000s (see the bottom of Table 2.7). This transformation suggests that the rise of pro-environmental groups in the 1980s prompted a counter-mobilization by materialist anti-environmental groups in the subsequent two decades. These findings coincide with the overall rise of interest group mobilization in Canadian courts documented by Epp (1996) and Brodie (2002). Recent work by Alarie and Green (2010, 398–400) indicates that during the first nine years of the McLachlin Court (2000–9), it granted environmental groups leave to intervene in Supreme Court cases 98 per cent

Table 2.8. Canadian Supreme Court Justices' Environmental Voting Records, 1973–2010

Justice	Cases, no.	Pro-environment	
		No.	%
Laskin	*9*	*7*	*77.8*
Bastarache	22	15	68.2
La Forest	25	17	68.0
Gonthier	32	21	65.6
Beetz	25	16	64.0
Cory	22	14	63.6
McIntyre	16	10	62.5
Estey	13	8	61.5
Fish	13	8	61.5
Wilson	13	8	61.5
Major	30	18	60.0
Martland	12	7	58.3
Iacobucci	31	18	58.1
L'Heureux-Dubé	27	15	55.6
Sopinka	18	10	55.6
Lamer	*31*	*17*	*54.8*
Dickson	*22*	*12*	*54.5*
LeBel	22	12	54.5
Arbour	13	7	53.8
McLachlin	*41*	*22*	*53.7*
Ritchie	15	7	46.7
Binnie	26	12	46.2
Chouinard	11	5	45.5
Deschamps	16	6	37.5

Note: The table includes voting records for all justices participating in 10 or more environmental cases. Chief Justice Laskin is included in the table to draw comparisons with other chief justices. Justices omitted from the table are Justices Abbott, Abella, Charron, Cromwell, de Grandpré, Fauteux, Hall, Judson, Pigeon, Pratte, Rothstein, Spence, and Stevenson.

of the time, while 70 per cent of the time, it sided with their position on the disposition of the case. The pace and success of environmental interventions lends further credence to Inglehart's arguments about the rise of postmaterialist value transformation over time; however, this transformation in the environmental area has also fuelled competing interest group activity on the side of materialist interests.

Judicial Voting and Authorship Patterns

In the second stage of analysis, we look at the patterns of voting by Canadian Supreme Court justices in the environmental area. Table 2.8 sorts 24 of the justices from high to low in terms of their career support for environmental stances during the period studied. The justices who stand out as staunch supporters of environmental causes include Chief Justice Laskin and Justices Bastarache and La Forest, all of whom sided with the environmental argument in over two-thirds of the cases they heard. The true standout is Chief Justice Laskin, who supported the pro-environmental position in seven of the nine cases he heard, for a career support record of 78 per cent, but the career records of 68 per cent for Justices Bastarache and La Forest are more reliable since they heard 22 and 25 cases, respectively. On the other end of the spectrum stand two of the newer members of the Canadian court – namely, Justices Binnie and Deschamps – who, along with Justices Chouinard and Ritchie, supported environmental causes less than 47 per cent of the time.

When comparing the chief justices, only Justice Laskin stands out as a leading environmental advocate, while Justices Lamer, Dickson, and McLachlin fall below the median level of environmental support, with scores of 55, 55, and 54 per cent, respectively. Each of these three chiefs cast votes below the two median justices on the court: Martland and Iacobucci, who both favoured the environment 58 per cent of the time. It seems that, collectively, the three most recent chief justices are not demonstratively pro-environmental leaders.

Figure 2.1 provides a scatterplot of career voting support for pro-environmental positions by the ideology of the justices. The ideology measure is derived from our earlier work (Ostberg and Wetstein 2007) that catalogued the ideological leanings of Supreme Court nominees based on newspaper reports at the time of their nomination. As expected, the figure demonstrates that justices who are perceived to be liberal tend to have higher support scores for pro-environmental positions. Indeed, the slope of the relationship suggests that the most liberal justice is 10 percentage points more likely to support an environmental claim than the most conservative justice. Overall, the data confirm that liberal justices are more predisposed to support environmental claims than their conservative colleagues.

Another way to test the Inglehart thesis is to place the justices into a scatterplot that juxtaposes the year of their birth with their career support for environmental rulings. When all the justices were put into a single scatterplot assessing pro-environmental voting by year of birth, the data were not supportive of Inglehart's thesis (see Figure 2.2). Indeed, the slope was in the unexpected direction, with more contemporary justices exhibiting lower support for the environment than their

Figure 2.1. Pro-environmental Voting by Ideology Score

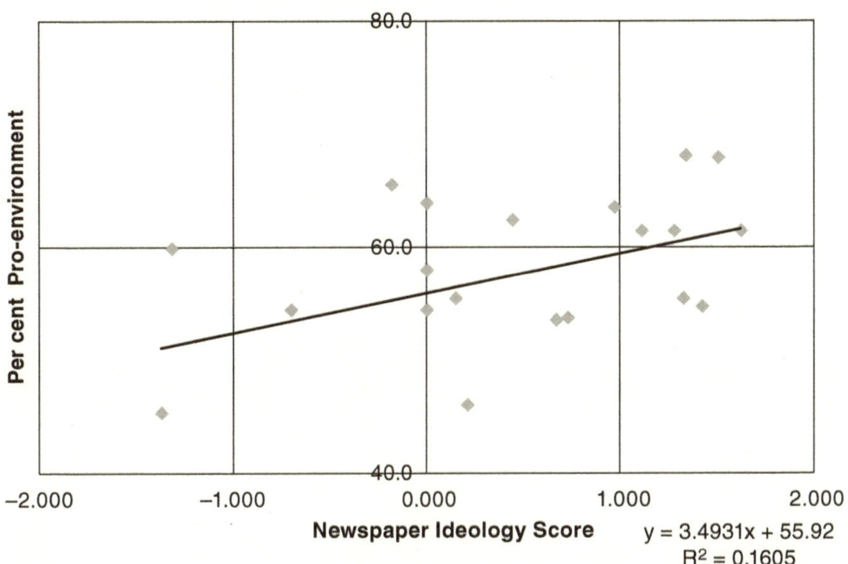

Note: Figure 2.1 excludes 15 justices because they either participated in fewer than 10 cases in the environmental area during the 1973–2010 period or did not have ideology scores: Justices Abbott, Abella, Charron, Cromwell, de Grandpré, Fauteux, Hall, Judson, Laskin, Martland, Pigeon, Pratte, Ritchie, Rothstein, Spence, and Stevenson.

earlier colleagues (*b*, or slope, = −.244, R-square = .117). In the interest of teasing out Inglehart's thesis, we decided to split the justices into two distinct groups: Figure 2.3a documents the justices elevated to the bench between 1958 and 1985, and Figure 2.3b covers justices appointed between 1987 and 2003.[3] The justices appointed between 1958 and 1985 have birth years that range between 1907 and 1928; this roughly coincides with Inglehart's pre–Second World War cohort, which prioritized materialist values and economic safety concerns.

The data from these justices provide nice confirmation of the postmodern transformation among early judicial elites in environmental cases. Indeed, there is an upward slope in the pro-environmental

3 Justices Abella, Charron, Cromwell, and Rothstein were omitted from the analysis in Figure 2.3b because they cast too few votes to record a meaningful career-vote score in environmental cases.

Figure 2.2. Pro-environmental Voting by Year of Birth

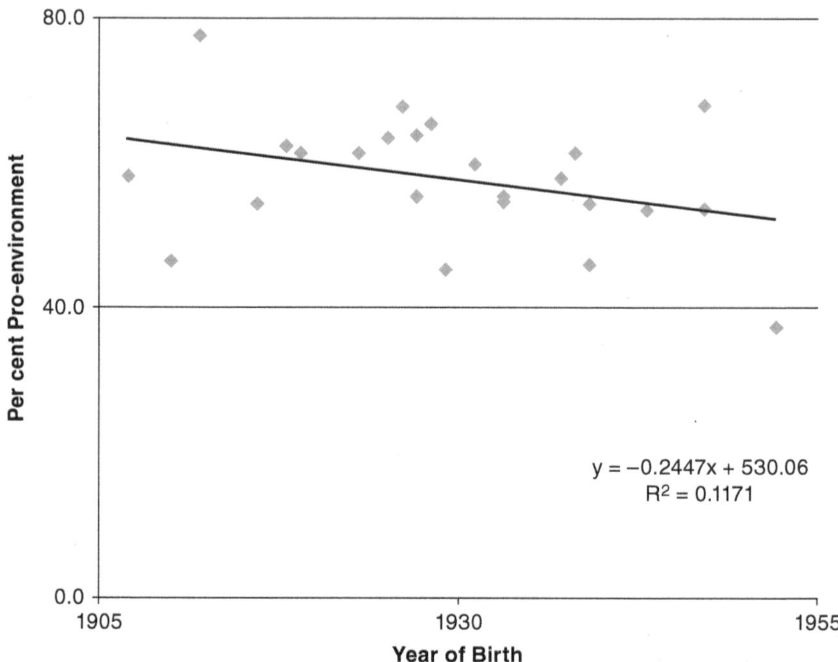

direction, indicating that for every 10 years added to a typical justice's year of birth, support for environmental claims increased by 2.5 per cent up to 1985 (slope of .245 × 10 = 2.45). Figure 2.3b documents later appointments made to the Canadian court, starting with Justice L'Heureux-Dubé, who came of age as a teenager in the wake of the Second World War. The data from this cohort of justices suggest that support for environmental rulings declined as more recent, younger justices were added to the court between 1987 and 2003. These latter data suggest that, over a 10-year period, there was roughly a 2-percentage-point drop in support for environmental claims (slope of −.173 × 10 = −1.73). This downward shift, which coincided with more recent justices appointed to the court, seems to present contrary evidence to Inglehart's thesis in the environmental area, but the problem with analysing a simple bivariate scatterplot is that it does not control for the issues and parties involved in the cases.

We next assess the patterns of majority voting, majority authorship, and dissenting activity in environmental cases (see Table 2.9). One should note that there has been a high degree of consensus among

Figure 2.3a. Pro-environmental Voting by Year of Birth, 1907–1928

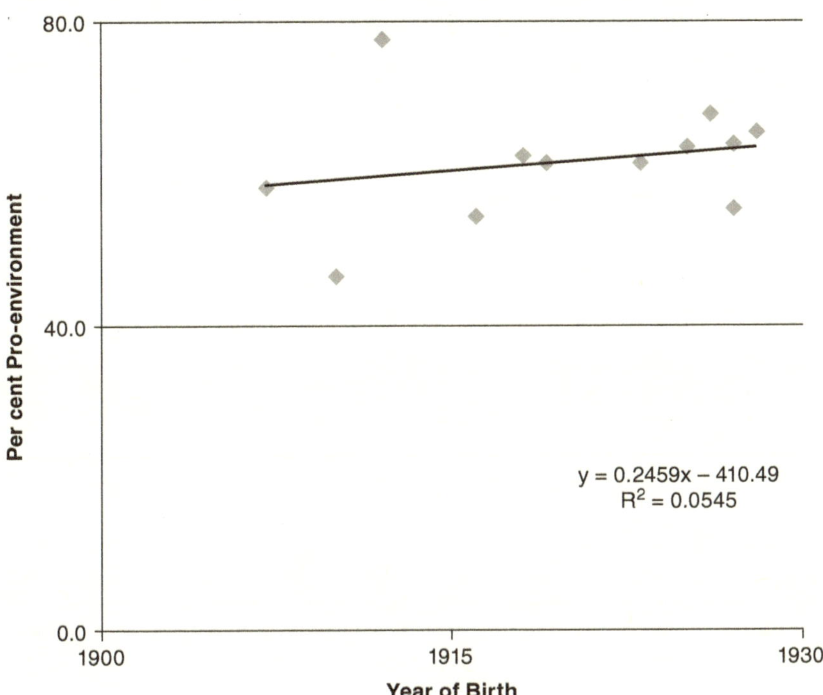

the justices in the environmental area: 78 per cent of the cases handed down over this period were unanimous decisions (58 of the 74 cases). This track record is even higher than usual for the Canadian Supreme Court, which typically hands down unanimous rulings in 70 per cent of its cases.[4] The table indicates that Chief Justice Dickson stands out as the decisive opinion, or task, leader in the environmental area, authoring majority opinions in 41 per cent of the cases that he heard (9 of 22 cases). Task leaders are individuals who typically dominate a court because they possess a towering intellect, are skilled debaters, and are seen as being adept at handling the difficult cases. Thus, other members of the court tend to defer to their intellectual prowess (Danelski 1989; Ostberg, Wetstein, and Ducat 2004).

4 The 70 per cent figure for unanimous rulings by the court was calculated across all cases featuring written reasons for judgment between 1973 and 2008.

Figure 2.3b. Pro-environmental Voting by Year of Birth, 1929–1955

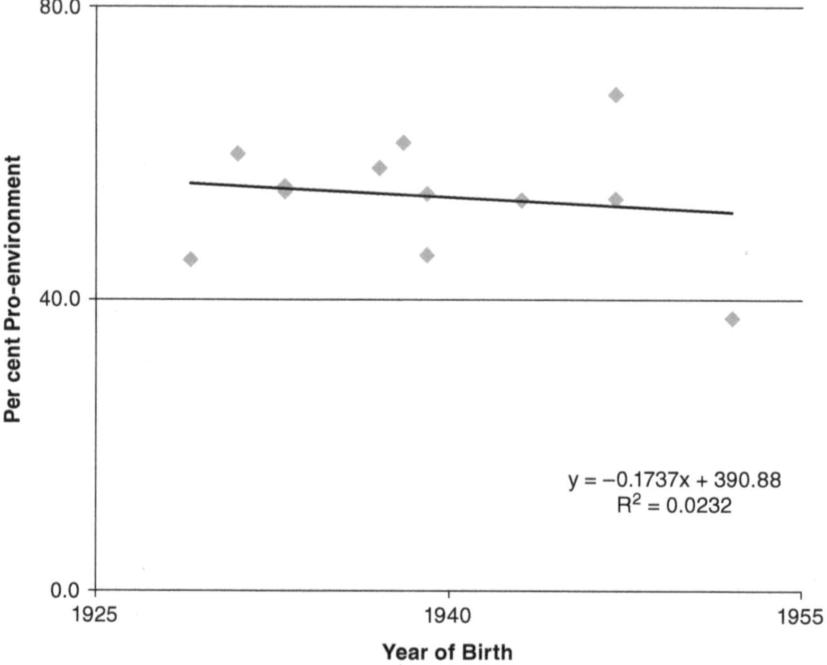

Chief Justice Dickson's pre-eminent leadership status is followed at a lower level by Justices Martland and Beetz and Chief Justice Laskin, who were majority-opinion authors in 25, 24, and 22 per cent of the cases they heard, respectively, in the environmental area. Relatively speaking, all four of the chief justices have high majority-opinion authorship rates relative to the court average of 13 per cent; this is noteworthy since scholars who have interviewed the chiefs indicate that they all tended to say that they made a conscious effort to distribute the workload evenly among the justices based on seniority, specialized expertise, and existing workloads (see Greene et al. 1998, 123–4; Songer et al. 2012, 88). Our findings show, at least in the environmental area, that the chief justices liked to assign themselves a disproportionate number of majority opinions. At the other end of the authorship spectrum are Justices McIntyre, Arbour, and Chouinard, who always voted with the majority but never authored an opinion. Moreover, Justices Sopinka and Fish also cast a large percentage of majority votes without

Table 2.9. Canadian Supreme Court Justices' Opinion Authorship Patterns in Environmental Cases, 1973–2010

Justice	Cases, no.	Voting in majority, %	Majority author, %[a]	Voting in dissent, %	Dissenting author, %[b]
Dickson	*22*	*95.5*	*40.9*	4.5	0.0
Martland	12	100.0	25.0	0.0	0.0
Beetz	25	96.0	24.0	4.0	0.0
Laskin	*9*	*88.9*	*22.2*	11.1	11.1
Lamer	*31*	*90.3*	*19.4*	9.7	3.2
Binnie	26	100.0	19.2	0.0	0.0
Cory	22	100.0	18.2	0.0	0.0
McLachlin	*41*	*87.8*	*17.1*	13.2	12.2
LeBel	22	90.9	13.6	9.1	9.1
Iacobucci	31	93.5	12.9	6.5	0.0
Deschamps	16	93.8	12.5	6.2	0.0
La Forest	25	88.0	12.0	12.0	8.0
Major	30	93.3	10.0	6.7	3.3
Gonthier	32	96.9	9.4	3.1	0.0
Bastarache	22	86.4	9.1	13.6	0.0
Wilson	13	92.3	7.7	7.7	7.7
Estey	13	100.0	7.7	0.0	0.0
L'Heureux-Dubé	27	81.5	7.4	18.5	11.1
Ritchie	15	93.3	6.7	6.7	6.7
Sopinka	18	94.4	0.0	5.6	0.0
McIntyre	16	100.0	0.0	0.0	0.0
Fish	13	84.6	0.0	15.4	0.0
Arbour	13	100.0	0.0	0.0	0.0
Chouinard	11	100.0	0.0	0.0	0.0

Note: The table includes voting records for all justices participating in 10 or more cases. Chief Justice Laskin is included to draw comparisons with other chief justices.

[a]Majority authorship is calculated by dividing the number of majority opinions authored by the total number of cases heard by a justice.

[b]Dissenting authorship is calculated by dividing the number of dissenting opinions authored by the total number of cases heard by a justice.

authoring a majority opinion. Collectively, these justices acted as the quintessential followers among the 24 justices in the environmental area, and the data make sense when thinking about the legal expertise they brought to the court in other issue areas.

Since Justice L'Heureux-Dubé is known as the great dissenter, it is not surprising that she voted most often in dissent in the environmental area (18.5 per cent) and ranked second in authoring dissents (11 per cent, 5 of 27 cases). Other high rates of dissent in environmental cases were registered by Justices Fish, Bastarache, and McLachlin (15, 14, and 13 per cent, respectively). It is noteworthy that Justice McLachlin penned the highest rate of dissenting opinions in the environmental area, even surpassing Justice L'Heureux-Dubé and Chief Justice Laskin. Overall, the opinion leadership, dissenting behaviour, and joining activity identified in environmental cases parallel findings from the literature on authorship and dissent activity in other issue areas (see McCormick 1993, 1994; Ostberg and Wetstein 2007).

Data and Methods for the Logistic Regression Analysis

All the data presented to this point rely on bivariate or univariate distributions of data and, as such, take our analysis only so far. Our most stringent test of the Inglehart thesis required taking a multivariate logistic regression approach. When conducting logistic regression analysis, each justice's vote was used as the unit of analysis, and, depending on the variables in the model, we examined patterns based on as many as 562 voting outcomes. The dependent variable is a dichotomous variable highlighting whether a justice handed down a pro-environmental ruling in the case or not (1 = pro-environmental/postmaterialist ruling, 0 = anti-environmental/materialist ruling). As we noted earlier, our scoring of postmaterialist votes encompassed the following types of outcome: votes to uphold pollution regulations, votes to uphold fishing and hunting restrictions, votes to require environmental assessments by government agencies, votes to prevent land development or protect open spaces, votes to preserve First Nation lands from development, and votes to protect fish and wildlife from further endangerment and possible extinction.[5] Ultimately, the dependent variable reflects each justice's willingness to hand down a ruling protecting the environment from encroachment by individuals, corporations, First Nations, and, occasionally, the government. The cases in this portion of the analysis span environmental issues pertaining to pollution, First Nation issues, and governmental takings and zoning cases, to name a few. If Inglehart's thesis holds true, that a postmodern value shift is indeed taking place in the mass public across advanced industrial societies, we expect more pro-environmental rulings to be handed down by Canadian justices over time.

The independent variables include a host of judge-level and factual variables that allow us to address the following overarching

---

5 In the next chapter, we provide more extensive commentary on the types of First Nation claims that personify materialistic interests.

question: Are judicial rulings in environmental cases driven by judge-level variables, such as the ideology or gender of the justice, or by parties and interveners, such as the number of pro-environmental interveners; or are case facts (case-level variables), such as cases featuring pollution or claims raised by indigenous peoples, paramount in influencing judicial votes? This collection of variables reflects our attempt to apply a socio-attitudinal model to the voting behaviour of justices in environmental cases. More important in regard to Inglehart's thesis, if control variables denoting the tenures of the different chief justices over time prove statistically significant in the equation, it will provide further evidence that a postmodern, intergenerational value shift is taking place among elite justices in the Canadian court.

There are seven judge- and court-level variables that reflect the individual justices' attitudes and the forces that shaped their overall world views. The first judge-level variable identifies whether or not a female justice participated in the case (1 = yes, 0 = no). This variable was included in this study to examine whether prior patterns of gender differences, which have been uncovered in the literature, also appear in environmental disputes (Ostberg and Wetstein 2007; Songer et al. 2012). One hypothesis might be that female justices are more prone to support environmental causes than men because of their greater tendency to display an "ethic of care" towards others and the community at large (Ostberg, Wetstein, and Ducat 2002). As such, they may be willing to hand down rulings supporting the environment because they tend to foster a higher quality of life for society writ large. A competing hypothesis might be that women will be more supportive of promoting the equality of vulnerable groups in society, and since many of the cases in this area feature economically vulnerable First Nation individuals contesting governmental wildlife regulations, female justices may actually exhibit more equality-focused, postmaterialist voting patterns than their male counterparts in this narrow set of cases. In other words, the female justices' votes might appear to be rooted in promoting greater equal treatment of historically disadvantaged First Nations. Ultimately, we included the gender variable to test these two competing propositions, and the subsequent textual analysis of some of the opinions sheds some interesting light on these complex differences (see chapter 3).

The second judge-level variable is a sophisticated and nuanced measure of ideology drawn from our earlier work (Ostberg and Wetstein 2007). We used newspaper accounts of the attitudes of a justice at the time of his or her appointment, garnered from content analysis of news stories obtained from nine newspapers across Canada.[6] The scoring for this newspaper ideology measure is based on an assessment of journalists' comments and runs along a continuum ranging from +2 for very liberal comments to −2 for very conservative comments, while neutral or moderate comments received a 0 score (for further commentary, see Ostberg and Wetstein [2007, 49–58]).[7] For this book, we used the cumulative ideology scores for 26 of the 35 justices, with scores ranging from the most conservative score tabulated for Justice Chouinard (−1.375) to the most liberal score for Justice Wilson (1.618); see Ostberg and Wetstein (2007, 55).[8] It is hypothesized that justices who obtained positive, more liberal newspaper ideology scores are more likely to rule in favour of environmental interests than their more conservative colleagues. This is a hypothesis in line with the expectation that justices emerging from a liberal background are more likely to endorse progressive policies aimed at protecting the environment as opposed to individual, corporate, and governmental interests in pursuit of economic and resource development.

The third judge-level variable is a dichotomous indicator that identifies whether or not a justice spent any time teaching in academia or as a law professor (1 = spent time teaching, 0 = no time teaching in the academy). Our use of this variable follows earlier studies by Tate and Sittiwong (1989) and Songer at al. (2012) that have shown a link between academia and liberal voting patterns. Since individuals working in the academic environment tend to be more liberal than those in the corporate setting, we hypothesized that the Canadian justices

---

6 The papers that we analysed were the *Globe and Mail, Ottawa Citizen, Halifax Chronicle-Herald, Gazette* (Montreal), *Toronto Star, Winnipeg Free Press, Calgary Herald, Edmonton Journal,* and *Vancouver Sun*.

7 Some might have concerns that coding from newspapers is tautological because the newspaper commentary is based on patterns of voting in the lower courts. Although there is truth to this, we contend that it is not tautological because the voting record and the commentary about it constitute an a priori measure that precedes a justice's appointment to the high court and thus precedes his or her voting record as a Supreme Court justice.

8 We were unable to use newspaper ideology scores for nine of the justices included in the study because the early newspaper commentators did not provide any ideological references or commentary in their coverage of new appointments to the Canadian Supreme Court and because Justice Rothstein had too few votes to include in the analysis.

who had engaged in full- or part-time teaching are more likely to hand down a pro-environmental ruling than their colleagues who had never worked in academia.

A fourth judge-level variable tests for the impact of Quebec justices in a socio-attitudinal model of voting behaviour. The hypothesis here is that distinctive social forces that flow from being raised in Quebec result in more conservative stances on many civil liberties issues (Lipset 1990; Songer et al. 2012, 140–2). In keeping with this earlier scholarship, we hypothesize that Quebec justices are likewise to be less protective of the environment than their counterparts, all other things being equal. If true, a negative coefficient will appear for justices from Quebec (1 = yes, 0 = no).

The last three judge-level variables are dichotomous indicators that identify whether or not a vote occurred under one of the three most recent chief justices (1 = vote under the Dickson or Lamer or McLachlin Court, 0 = otherwise). As mentioned earlier, if Inglehart's thesis holds up, we expect that the three most recent courts will hand down successively more pro-environmental rulings than the Laskin Court, which was left out of the equations for comparison purposes. In short, positive coefficients for these indicators will show a positive postmaterialist shift by the court over time.

If the judge-level variables noted above reflect individual attitudinal factors and the latent forces that shaped the justices' overall world view, the 10 case-level variables, in turn, seek to examine whether and to what extent various case facts impact judicial voting in environmental cases. These case-level variables are included in the model to test for unique legal and social forces that shape judicial votes on a case-by-case basis. Since cases often instigate interveners on both sides of a legal issue, we included four types of interveners that might influence judicial behaviour. First, we tabulated the number of pro-environmental interveners that were featured in each case (for a similar approach, see Alarie and Green [2010]). This variable ranged from 0 to 20 across the 74 cases, and it was hypothesized that the more pro-environmental interveners that joined the suit, the greater the likelihood that the justices would hand down a ruling in favour of the environment. Our hypothesis is rooted in litigant resource theory, which suggests that justices can draw important cues from interveners who bring forward specialized legal arguments regarding the specific dispute or interveners who are "repeat players" in the judicial system (Galanter 1974, 2003; Brodie 2002; Manfredi 2004; Alarie and Green 2010).

We next included a variable identifying whether or not the Canadian Environmental Law Association (CELA) had intervened in a case or not (1 = yes, 0 = no). Obviously, we expected that the justices would be more likely to hand down a ruling in favour of the environment in such instances because the presence of CELA would provide a cue to the justices of the salience of the environmental cause in the case. We also included two variables identifying the number of other groups or First Nation groups that intervened in the cases. Since these two types of interveners could support either side of the environmental issues, we simply tallied the number of groups that favoured an environmental outcome and gave them a positive count, and we gave those that supported an anti-environmental outcome a negative count. In the end, the range of scores for the other intervener variables ranged from −1 to +4, while the First Nation group interveners ranged from −13 to +7. Similar to the previous intervener variables, it was expected that the more pro-environmental groups or pro-environmental First Nation groups that joined the suit, the greater the likelihood that the justices would favour the environmental interest in the case.

We included three important issue characteristics as dichotomous variables in the equation – namely, whether or not a case dealt with pollution (1 = yes, 0 = no) or government takings and land use (1 = yes, 0 = no) or whether a case involved a First Nation issue (1 = yes, 0 = no). All other things being equal, we expected justices to be more likely to rule in favour of the environmental interest in a case if pollution was at issue – at least in relation to other cases not featuring pollution. The rationale for this hypothesis was that pollution could trigger the most protective sentiment in the environmental area, given the shock to the conscience that incidents of pollution can foster in the minds of the Canadian public.[9] Likewise, we hypothesized that justices would be more favourable to the government in cases where land was being taken away or preserved for environmental purposes or to ensure the protection of natural wilderness. In short, under Inglehart's postmaterialist thesis, we expected justices to show positive deference to governmental efforts to protect the environment in takings and land use cases.

9 Although our logistic models initially analysed various types of pollution, such as air, land, and water pollution, these indicators were kept out of the final logistic regression because the *N*s for each sub-area were too small and the indicators were highly correlated with the broader pollution measure.

Last, since the bulk of the First Nation cases involved individuals attempting to trump governmental hunting, fishing, and resource regulations on the basis of treaty or constitutionally protected rights, we were interested to see whether the justices would side more often than not with the government in such cases because it was trying to protect natural resources and species from excessive taking by First Nation individuals. Again, this hypothesis is derived from Inglehart's notion of value change towards environmental/postmaterialist sentiments and away from strictly material concerns, but we recognize that, in this area of law, the justices' votes might have been motivated by a desire to promote the postmaterialist equality interests of a historically marginalized group and side with its pursuit of recognized cultural practices.

The logistic equation also included a variable identifying whether or not the government favoured an environmental outcome in the case (1 = yes, −1 = no, 0 = no government participation in the case). Since justices tend to take government's interest into serious consideration when handing down rulings, and governments are the most frequent repeat players in court, it was expected that when government supported an environmental interest, the justices would have a greater likelihood of handing down a pro-environmental ruling. The last two case-level variables in the equation pertained to whether or not a case involved a federal or provincial environmental regulation (1 = yes, 0 = no), and both were juxtaposed to the existence of a municipal law, which was kept out of the equation for comparative reasons. In line with party capability theory, it was expected that the justices would be more likely to favour the environment in cases where federal and provincial environmental restrictions were at issue rather than a municipal ordinance because federal and provincial governments have more resources, litigate more environmental cases, and tend to have better win records than municipalities (Galanter 1974, 2003; McCormick 1993; Kritzer 2003).

Overall, the logistic regression models provide insight into the kinds of variables that play a critical role in influencing judicial decision making in environmental disputes in the modern Canadian court. Our model is designed to present a socio-attitudinal collection of variables to explain judicial voting behaviour. Moreover, it provides us with a deeper understanding of the veracity of Inglehart's postmodern transformation thesis because we can control for various rival variables that may influence judicial voting as well as take into consideration the evolution of the complexity in case facts as increasingly more difficult environmental disputes reach the court over time.

Explaining Pro-environmental Outcomes Using Logistic Regression

In the third stage of analysis, three distinct logistic regression models were developed, with the final model culminating in a regression equation that combined all 17 variables (see Table 2.10). Our goal was to identify the factors that help explain why justices cast pro-environmental/ postmaterialist votes. Moreover, the combined model helps identify whether, and the degree to which, a more robust socio-attitudinal model explains judicial behaviour. The model takes into consideration the role that current and past attitudinal forces, social background traits, types of legal issues, case facts, intervener activity, and litigants play in shaping judicial outcomes.[10] Logistic regression analysis was required for this part of the study because the dependent variable is dichotomous (Aldrich and Nelson 1984). Table 2.10 provides logistic regression maximum-likelihood estimates for the judge-level, case-level, and combined models, along with goodness-of-fit statistics at the bottom. A quick perusal of the summary statistics indicates that the judge-level model does not produce statistically significant results, but both the case-level and combined equations do. The case-level model, with 10 factual variables, was able to accurately predict 74 per cent of the judicial votes, which provided a 41 per cent reduction in error over the modal guessing model.[11] The combined model, featuring 17 variables taken from the two previous equations, accurately predicted 71 per cent of the case votes and provided a 36 per cent reduction in error. Although the overall explanatory power of the combined model dropped slightly, this last model is theoretically important because it tests the relative impact of various factors evident in a socio-attitudinal model of judicial behaviour. Clearly, the latter two equations explain a

10 While there were 562 judicial votes for the logistic regression equation pertaining to the case-level model found in Table 2.10, there were only 496 judicial votes in the equations involving the judge-level and combined model because we were unable to code ideology scores for several of the early justices in the analysis, including Justices de Grandpré, Judson, Laskin, Martland, Pigeon, Pratt, Ritchie, Spence, and Rothstein. As a result, there were 66 fewer case votes in the latter two equations.

11 A modal guessing strategy is often used as a yardstick to measure logistic regression models. It assumes that if one tried to "guess" each justice's vote in each case, you could be right if you always guessed "pro-environment" 55.7 per cent of the time. Any decent regression model should improve considerably over that guessing strategy, and in this case, the 73.8 per cent accuracy rate represents a 40.9 per cent improvement over that modal approach.

Table 2.10. Estimating the Odds of a Pro-environmental Vote in Canadian Supreme Court Environmental Cases, 1973–2010

Variable (min., max.)	Judge-level model			Case-level model			Combined prediction model		
	Coefficient	Standard error	Change in probability	Coefficient	Standard error	Change in probability	Coefficient	Standard error	Change in probability
Female justice (0, 1)	–.442*	.230	–.110				–.530*	.260	–.131
Ideology score (–1.375, 1.618)	.101	.126	+.075				.141	.140	+.103
Academic (0, 1)	–.175	.212	–.043				–.170	.234	–.041
Quebec justice (0, 1)	–.022	.196	–.005				–.086	.218	–.021
Dickson Court (0, 1)	.648*	.363	+.154				.724*	.409	+.167
Lamer Court (0, 1)	.768*	.324	+.185				1.061**	.376	+.246
McLachlin Court (0, 1)	.496	.318	+.121				1.797***	.445	+.399
Pollution case (0, 1)				.484*	.284	+.115	.516	.337	+.122
First Nation issue (0, 1)				–1.045***	.230	–.255	–.925***	.246	–.226
Takings and land use case (0, 1)				.725*	.368	+.166	.956*	.416	+.213
Number of pro-environmental interveners (0, 20)				–.091***	.030	–.416	–.141***	.039	–.571
CELA intervenes in case (0, 1)				1.521***	.460	+.304	1.840***	.560	+.347
Other pro-environmental interveners (–1, 4)				.546	.353	+.493	.359	.361	+.369
First Nation pro-environmental interveners (–13, 12)				.129***	.032	+.657	.172***	.035	+.781
Government favours environment (–1, 1)				.690***	.161	+.330	1.105***	.215	+.490
Federal law (0, 1)				.491	.425	+.117	.747	.519	+.174
Provincial law (0, 1)				1.303**	.439	+.314	1.361**	.528	+.327
Constant	–.149	.337		–.795	.433		–1.903	.649	
Number of cases	496			562			496		
Chi-square –2 log likelihood	11.523			97.552***			113.36***		
Pseudo R-square	.031			.213			.273		
Per cent correct predictions	59.3%			73.8%			71.2%		
Reduction in error	9.2%			40.9%			35.7%		

*Significant at 95% confidence level; **significant at 99% confidence level; ***significant at 99.9% confidence level.

significant proportion of variance in the dependent variable and generate robust model-fit statistics.

Only three variables prove statistically significant in the judge-level model – namely, gender and two of the three court variables (Dickson and Lamer Courts). The positive coefficients for the Dickson and Lamer Courts (b = .648 and .768) are in the hypothesized direction, and the change in probabilities reflected in the third column are in line with Inglehart's expected thesis. Indeed, while the justices on the Dickson Court were 15 per cent more likely to hand down a pro-environmental ruling than those on the Laskin Court, those on the Lamer Court were fully 19 per cent more likely to do so. In this initial model, the McLachlin Court indicator did not attain statistical significance, although we have yet to control for case facts and interveners, which prove to be a critical consideration for explaining pro-environmental voting patterns on the current court. Interestingly, the gender variable is significant: it indicates that the female justices appear to be more materialistic than their male colleagues: the odds of them casting a pro-environmental vote are 11 per cent below those of the male justices.[12] In light of the duelling hypotheses discussed earlier, this finding suggests that the female justices seem more inclined to protect the postmaterialist equality claims of First Nation groups and individuals than environmental claims, at least when compared to their male counterparts. We believe this voting pattern is reflective of their greater endorsement of the value of equality, recognizing the historical practices and rights of First Nation individuals. Although these three variables proved statistically significant, the model as a whole does not perform well and is able to correctly predict only 59 per cent of the judicial votes. This is not a significant improvement over the modal guessing strategy (56 per cent).

In contrast to the first set of results, fully 8 of the 10 case-fact variables in the second equation are statistically significant and 5 of them at the 99.9 per cent confidence level. Looking more closely at the second model in Table 2.10, three of the four intervener variables were statistically significant, but only two of those three were in the expected direction. As expected, the positive parameter estimates listed for CELA (b = 1.521) and

12 We did introduce interaction effects into the regression models that looked at the relationship between gender and ideology and gender and court period, but the results did not add any substantive findings beyond what is already highlighted in Table 2.10.

the First Nation groups ($b = .129$) suggest that when these two groups took pro-environmental stances when intervening in cases, the justices were more likely to hand down a ruling in favour of the environment than in cases where either they did not intervene or they intervened on the opposite side of the environmental issue. For example, since the First Nation group variable ranged between –13 and +12, the odds-ratio analysis at the end of the row indicates that the presence of 12 First Nation groups in favour of the environment led the justices to be 66 per cent more likely to cast a pro-environmental vote in cases than in those in which 13 groups intervened against the environmental claim (change in $p = +.657$).

Similarly, if CELA intervened in a case, the justices were 30 per cent more likely to rule in favour of the environment than when it did not. Clearly, the presence of First Nation groups and CELA as advocates for pro-environmental stances sent a significant signal and influenced the Canadian justices' vote in these types of cases. These results align well with recent findings documenting the impact of liberal and conservative interveners in McLachlin Court decisions (see Alarie and Green 2010). However, the presence of too many pro-environmental interveners may be problematic. For instance, our results show that if a case featured 20 pro-environmental interveners, the justices would be 42 per cent *less* likely to hand down a ruling in favour of the environment than if a case featured no interveners at all. This suggests that intervening activity that becomes too extreme may have a counter-intuitive effect on the justices in environmental cases. In short, the quantity of all interveners may be less important than the presence of particular environmental interveners such as CELA and First Nation representatives.

The parameter estimates for two of the three types of environmental issues included in the equation – namely, whether a case involved pollution ($b = .484$) or a government takings or land use case ($b = .725$) – were statistically significant and in the expected direction. The odds ratios indicate that if a case involved pollution, there was a 12 per cent greater likelihood that the justices would vote in favour of the environment than if the case did not feature pollution. Similarly, the odds of a pro-environmental vote go up 17 per cent if the case involved government takings or land use. Given the concern for environmental pollution and the need for government to take land to preserve open spaces and natural resources, these findings are not surprising, and they square well with Inglehart's postmaterialist thesis. However, the parameter estimate for a First Nation issue ($b = -1.045$) was statistically significant, but in the anti-environmental direction. The odds ratio for this variable suggests that when First Nation issues are in play in a case, principally aimed at securing historical hunting and fishing rights, the odds of a pro-environmental ruling go down 26 per cent. This suggests that when controlling for all other factors, First Nation issues tended to produce more anti-environmental rulings than pro-environmental ones. We attribute this statistical outcome to the heavy weight the justices accorded to the treaty and constitutional claims that First Nation representatives brought to these cases and the postmaterialist equality value embedded in those claims – namely, that siding with the First Nation argument reflected an endorsement of the equal but distinctive standing of these groups in Canadian society.

The parameter estimates for federal law ($b = .491$) and provincial law ($b = 1.303$) were in the expected direction, but only the provincial indicator was statistically significant. The results suggest that when a provincial law was at issue, the justices would be 31 per cent more likely to favour the environment than when it featured a municipal ordinance, which was kept out of the equation for comparative purposes. This finding squares with prior work by Morton (1995) indicating that the Canadian Charter of Rights and Freedoms would provoke more activist rulings by the Supreme Court in provincial government cases. However, it is surprising that the federal indicator is not significant when stacked up against a municipal ordinance. This is contrary to expectation because scholarship suggests that since the federal government is a "bigger gorilla" in the litigation realm in terms of resources, staff, and expertise, it is likely to be more effective at persuading justices to embrace its side of the environmental argument in a given case than attorneys from lower levels of government. Meanwhile, the results for the last variable in the equation suggest that if government supported an environmental ruling, the justices were 33 per cent more likely to cast a pro-environmental vote than in cases in which government was lined up against environmental interests ($b = .690$). Taken together, the data results from the second equation suggest that the justices overwhelmingly relied on case-level variables when resolving environmental disputes, and there are strong indications that interest groups advancing postmaterialistic claims have had a powerful impact on case outcomes in the Canadian court over the past four decades.

The third equation in Table 2.10 reflects the fullest test of a socio-attitudinal model in environmental cases, and it combines the variables in the first two equations. This equation yields virtually identical results as the other two, but with two small exceptions. As mentioned earlier, this model correctly predicted 71 per cent of the case votes and produced a 36 per cent reduction in error in predicting voting outcomes correctly. Although there were small shifts in the coefficients and slight changes in the probabilities, all the variables that proved statistically significant in the first two equations were significant in the combined equation, save one (the pollution variable). Moreover, in the combined model, the McLachlin Court variable, like the other two, obtained statistical significance in relation to the Laskin Court.

While only two of the three court-level variables were statistically significant in the first equation, which featured only judge-level characteristics, all three obtained statistical significance in the correct hierarchical order when both case- and judge-level variables were thrown together in the combined model (Dickson Court $b = .724$, Lamer Court $b = 1.061$, and McLachlin Court $b = 1.797$). It is important to remember that these variables were included in the equation to test whether Inglehart's post-materialist transformation thesis is taking place among judicial elites over time, and the last equation demonstrates that when important rival explanatory variables are included in the model, Inglehart's thesis pans out nicely in the environmental area of law. The data indicate that the Dickson Court justices were 17 per cent more likely to hand down a pro-environmental ruling than the Laskin Court, and the odds increased to 25 per cent for the Lamer Court and 40 per cent for the McLachlin Court. What this means is that if two identical environmental cases presenting the same case facts, types of litigants, and interveners appeared before the Laskin and McLachlin Courts, and everything was identical except for the justices hearing the dispute, our logistic model suggests that the later-serving justices were actually 40 per cent more likely to cast a pro-environmental vote than the Laskin Court.

This is a critical finding, and it points to the importance of conducting logistic regression analysis. If we simply relied on the descriptive statistics found in the first stage of our analysis, we would conclude that while there was an upward swing in pro-environmental rulings over time during the Dickson and Lamer Courts, this pattern did not seem to hold during the first 10 years of the McLachlin Court (see figures 2.3a and 2.3b). Yet when all other things are held equal in a case, the McLachlin Court indicator in the regression analysis documents that this court did hand down significantly more pro-environmental rulings than the Laskin Court. Moreover, the McLachlin coefficient produces a greater swing in pro-environmental judicial voting than did the Dickson and Lamer Courts when controlling for case characteristics and interveners. In short, by placing the court variables into the large socio-attitudinal equation, we are able to control for the potential impact that increasingly difficult case facts and increasing numbers of interveners can have on Supreme Court justices over time. When holding such variables constant, the McLachlin Court justices look considerably more postmaterialist than at first blush.

There are two other variables worth mentioning in the full model: namely, that the pollution variable (b = .516) is no longer statistically significant and that gender remains a statistically significant predictor of environmental votes (b = –.530). Although the pollution indicator is just below statistical significance at the 94 per cent confidence level, its b and odds ratio measures are very similar to the results in the prior model, and there is an indication that pollution cases are 12 per cent more likely to foster pro-environmental votes than all other cases. The gender variable, in turn, indicates that female justices, all other things being equal, are 13 per cent more likely to cast an anti-environmental vote than male justices in these cases. The pattern appears to be driven by disputes in which female justices have sided with the historical and cultural arguments advanced by First Nation individuals in support of traditional fishing, hunting, and logging rights, which are juxtaposed against environmental regulations. Thus, as mentioned earlier, female justices view the postmaterialist, equality-seeking values of the societal underdog as being more important than government's effort to protect environmental resources through generalized laws.

One important, overarching conclusion to be drawn from the logistic analysis is that the ideology of the justices, measured by newspaper ideology scores, does not appear to have an impact on judicial voting in environmental cases. This is a critical attitudinal finding because past research has indicated that, in some prominent areas of economic and criminal law, judicial ideology does indeed influence voting behaviour on the Canadian Supreme Court in the post-Charter era (see Ostberg and Wetstein 2007; Songer et al. 2012). The question remains: What distinguishes environmental rulings in the modern Canadian context from rulings handed down in some economic and criminal areas? One explanation for why ideology might not matter in environmental cases may be derived from earlier findings in another specialized area of law – namely, tax cases (Ostberg and Wetstein 2007). It seems that, in particular areas of law, where justices may not possess subject matter expertise and ideology is less salient to the issue, they tend to rely on other critical cues to help them resolve a case, such as case facts, a lower regulatory agency ruling, or expert litigants and interveners. As such, they are less likely to be influenced by their personal ideological views when handing down such rulings. In a way, this suggests that social cues are more important to the justices than individual attitudinal forces. The judge-level model in Table 2.10 seems to confirm this conclusion since only a few of the judge-level variables proved statistically significant in the equation, while the bulk of the case-level variables in the second and third equations were statistically significant. Thus, it seems that, in select fields of law, like the tax and environmental areas, modern Canadian justices will rely on case facts and litigant/intervener cues, rather than judge-level variables, to resolve disputes. This finding demonstrates that ideology, which dominates the judicial decision-making process in the US setting, plays a more nuanced and muted role in Canada, particularly in the context of environmental disputes.

The findings also point to the relevance of the socio-attitudinal model for explaining judicial votes in environmental cases. If judicial outcomes are seen to be the potential product of multiple forces, including current ideology, intergenerational changes in values, gender effects, pressure group strategies, various case facts, the significance of repeat players, and the prominence of government players in the field of law, then our understanding of the decisions becomes more layered, nuanced, and accurate. For the purposes of the postmaterialist theory of value change, we believe that an empirical analysis of nearly 40 years of decisions identifies intergenerational value change as one of the important factors in explaining the greater odds of a pro-environmental outcome as cases progress through time. When seen through the lens of a socio-attitudinal model of judicial behaviour, gradual postmaterialist value change helps provide one key explanatory variable for pro-environmental outcomes in the modern Supreme Court of Canada.

Chapter Three

Qualitative Analysis of Pollution, Energy, and Fishing Rights Disputes

Introduction

In the previous chapter, we documented a decisive, quantitative shift in Canadian Supreme Court outcomes across all environmental disputes, indicating a movement away from materialistic concerns towards facilitating environmental protection. This evidence of who wins and loses in environmental cases supports the shifting postmaterialist values landscape that Inglehart has documented among the mass public over the last 40 years. In this chapter, we provide a detailed qualitative assessment of a number of landmark environmental rulings to tease out the degree to which justices use postmaterialist language and rationales to justify the outcomes they reach. We believe this type of analysis is important because it identifies the legal direction the Canadian court is taking in an area of law that features postmaterialist concerns. Moreover, looking at case outcomes in terms of wins and losses gets you only so far in a postmaterialist analysis. To understand the judicial mindset more fully, an assessment of the language and rationale developed in these opinions is critical because it helps legal practitioners understand the principles and values that shape these legal claims. For example, if the Supreme Court determines that individuals who infringe a government pollution regulation must bring forth *compelling evidence* showing that the violation does not cause demonstrable harm to Canadian society, this stringent standard will have important implications for who wins the current and future similar disputes. The focus on language is also important because it fits with what the justices say is an important part of their work: that they strive to write sound legal opinions that are acceptable to the key audiences they are addressing (Baum 2006, chap. 3; Songer et al. 2012).

Clearly, the language that justices use is important because attorneys, lower court judges, scholars, and other political actors rely on that language to guide their own work.

Since it is unrealistic to review all 74 environmental cases decided by the Supreme Court of Canada between 1973 and 2010, we focus on analysing one or two landmark cases decided by the Laskin, Dickson, and Lamer Courts, and during the first 10 years of the McLachlin Court, in three of the six issue areas discussed in the previous chapter. We decided to examine the written reasons for judgment in landmark pollution and energy cases because they garnered the highest and lowest levels of pro-environmental support by the justices across the 40-year period, and we included the First Nation fishing rights cases because of the volume and political importance of these disputes. Moreover, these disputes reflect a classic tension between two postmaterialist values: the pursuit of greater equality and protection of treaty rights by First Nation individuals against the government's interest in protecting fisheries as a vital natural resource for the benefit of all. We used the published work of renowned constitutional law scholar Peter Hogg (2011) and environmental scholar David Boyd (2003, 2012a, 2012b) to help identify which landmark cases to examine across the tenures of the four chief justices.

Readers should keep in mind that we envision the written opinions of the justices as a social construct that is the result of the individual justices and the values and attitudes they bring to cases, along with a variety of social pressures and interactions that influence them. Ultimately, we believe that numerous factors influence judicial rulings, including the world views the individual justices acquired during their formative years, their current attitudes and values, their relations with other high court justices, their strategic view of the larger political and societal landscape, and litigant group arguments. Amid all these influences, we believe it is important to seek out evidence of whether justices are embracing postmaterialist values. If one recalls, environmental disputes typically involve an economic tension between protecting scarce resources and exploiting these resources for economic development purposes. This is a tension that fits nicely into Inglehart's postmaterialist-materialist dichotomy. For example, pollution and energy cases necessarily involve disputes that pit government interests in protecting the environment from harm resulting from contamination of pristine resources against the commercial development of natural resources for economic gain.

Yet cases involving First Nation fishing regulations necessarily have an additional equality element that adds complexity to these types of cases. These cases feature constitutional and treaty arguments that confound any effort to classify them simply as representing materialist or postmaterialist conflicts. Instead, the issues raised in these cases represent components of both value perspectives. First, they turn on important historical, social, and cultural values that First Nation representatives advance. First Nation representatives contend that their customs and traditions reflect a long pattern of wise resource use based on traditional ecological knowledge, should remain undisturbed by governmental regulation (Haggan and Brown 2002, 18). In their view, they have a right to continue following the handed-down cultural and social norms of hunting and fishing that align with their connection to place, seasonal cycles of fishing, patterns of cultural exchanges of goods, and traditional group customs (ibid.; see also Collins and Murtha 2010). The ability to continue these traditions is essential to maintaining the strong cultural heritage of First Nations and the ability to pass on these norms to future generations. These traditional cultural values are especially important in the face of historically recognized treaty rights and constitutional rights to fish and hunt, which have been enshrined in agreements with Canadian governments over the last three centuries. Critics argue that environmental fishing regulations should take into consideration indigenous constitutional interests.

Closely connected to this historical argument for special recognition is a second value perspective – namely, the claim that indigenous communities deserve differentiated treatment to ensure that they are able to maintain their distinctive minority culture from encroachment from larger economic, cultural, and social forces. Proponents of this argument claim that to ensure genuine equality in Canada's multicultural society, Canada must correct its past mistreatment and accommodate the historically disadvantaged First Nation peoples, who have struggled to sustain their community identity through local autonomy, guaranteed representation, land claims, language rights, and hunting and fishing rights (see Kymlicka 1994, 1995; Greene 2006, 143–6; Collins and Murtha 2010). When viewed from this standpoint, First Nation arguments advance three overlapping value perspectives: (1) upholding traditional social customs and practices reflected in the materialist value of order; (2) promoting postmaterialist equality rights, a perspective that is reflected in ensuring more equal status for a group of Canadians that has been traditionally marginalized; and (3) advancing their view of environmental protection, which emanates from a belief that indigenous practices built up over centuries actually result in better resource management than the government can enact and enforce.

This multifaceted set of First Nation materialist-postmaterialist arguments is pitted against government's heightened interest in protecting the environment through generalized restrictions on hunting and fishing established in recent decades in the face of a dramatic depletion of the Canadian fisheries stock. These regulatory efforts were intensified after the northeastern cod fishing crisis of the early 1990s. Given this complexity of value perspectives, it is important to examine what the justices say in their written reasons for judgment in these disputes. Cases that feature outcomes in favour of First Nation groups may embody multiple, layered value priorities. Justices might side with First Nation individuals on the basis of historical agreements and traditions, making the opinions reflect a desire to protect traditional economic and materialist patterns over governmental efforts to enforce environmental protection. This approach stems from a desire to recognize rights that have been granted to First Nations throughout governments' historical interaction with them (Kymlicka 1994, 24–5; 1995, 116–20). Note how this perspective maintains a traditional order of how things have been and should continue to be.

A second value perspective that justices might advance to counteract the environmental ones advanced by government are statements that focus on the marginalization of First Nations throughout history and the negative treatment they have faced from governments. Such arguments reflect a desire to promote their equitable status as Canadians in a multicultural democracy and to recognize historical arguments that give them preferred status (Kymlicka 1994, 24–5; 1995, 108–9). Depending on the language used by the justices, these arguments can embody the postmaterialist value of equality more so than advancing the economic interests or historical traditions of First Nations people.

In the end, the First Nation cases involving fishing rights present an interesting and distinctive set of value conflicts when examined through the lens of postmaterialist value change theory. Our view is that the purest endorsement of postmaterialist thinking reflects language in support of generalized environmental regulations that are aimed at protecting the depletion of and extinction of scarce resources and species. Scientific studies show that less than 50 per cent of Canadian fisheries are healthy and sustainable, and the collapse of the northern cod fishery in the early 1990s highlighted the need for governmental intervention

Table 3.1. Postmaterialist-Materialist Values: Examples of Value Conflicts in Cases

Type of dispute	Postmaterialist value priority		Materialist value
	Environmental protection	Equality	Economic freedom and order
Water and air pollution control	Restrict water and air pollution to protect the environment and endangered species		Allow commercial development of natural resources
Energy development	Restrict energy development to protect land, water, and species		Allow commercial development of natural resources
Fishing and hunting regulation	Restrict fishing and hunting by all groups to protect the environment from harm	Uphold First Nation treaty and constitutional rights to promote the equality of a traditionally marginalized group	Endorse traditional customs and historical practices of First Nation individuals

to change the structure of fishing-management practices to rebuild fish stocks (see Thomson 2013; Sharpless and Laughren 2016). Having said that, it is clear that the pro-equality arguments advanced by First Nation representatives reflect postmaterialist values. However, our value conception envisions a hierarchy in these cases, placing protection of the environment in the top spot on the postmaterialist hierarchy, followed by equality concerns and, finally, by the economic interests and protection of tradition as embodiments of materialist thought. Our depiction of this hierarchy in First Nation and other types of environmental cases is presented in Table 3.1.

The methodology we use to characterize the postmaterialist or materialist language patterns of the justices is qualitative content analysis. This methodology was introduced as a scientific method by political scientist Harold Lasswell in the middle of the twentieth century, and it later became popular in many fields of social science, medicine, public health, and other disciplines (Lasswell and Leites 1965; Woodrum 1984; Hsieh and Shannon 2005; Prasad 2008). The approach draws inferences about the meaning of a text and the sender of a message based on reading and coding its content. In some ways, the technique is similar to textual analysis, which has been a hallmark of a distinct mode of constitutional interpretation for generations, sometimes called interpretivism (Ducat 1978).

Like interpretivists, who believe that the meaning of a country's constitution and statutes is derived from the text used by the framers and legislative body, we believe that content analysis of the keywords in judicial opinions divulges the belief system that a justice brings to the interpretive process. We assume that the language and tone used in an opinion *matter* and reflect the value structure a justice brings to the writing of an opinion. For example, if justices take a postmaterialist, pro-environmental stance, we expect them to use language identifying environmental protection as a "core fundamental value" or expressing the need to "protect the environment from economic development" or "overuse" or for "future generations to enjoy." In addition, they might use language citing the need to "protect species from extinction" as an "overriding value of societal importance" or pollution events as "shocking the conscience" of society. Such phrases reflect our view of Inglehart's postmaterialist mindset in its purest form.

Similarly, justices may develop tests that place the burden of proof on those interested in exploiting the environment to provide "compelling evidence" or meet a high standard before infringing on Canadian natural resources. Collectively, these phrases and examples can provide key markers of a postmaterialist mindset or belief system. However, if the justices are embracing equality values in the First Nations cases, we expect to see language referencing "disparate treatment" in the past and the need to ensure "the protection of a traditionally marginalized group" or the need to uphold their "protected status in treaties and the Constitution." Such statements reflect an interest in upholding the postmaterialist value of equality over unfettered protection of the environment.

Alternatively, justices might use language depicting the need to "uphold traditional cultural patterns" of fishing and "ensure that customs and traditional norms" are protected and remain intact. Inglehart's theory would characterize this language as being rooted in the values of tradition and order, and thus more reflective of a materialist world view. Meanwhile, in the pollution and energy cases, materialist language is more evident in its reliance on words like "commercial benefit" or the "economic good that flows from development of natural resources" and its "greater benefit to society." If our test of Inglehart's theory is valid, we expect pro-environmental and equality language to be more evident in the language of the justices' written reasons for judgment as we move forward in time.

Although we focus on the materialist or postmaterialist language used by the majority author in landmark pollution, energy, and fishing cases over time, we also analyse important concurring and dissenting opinions. The logic behind this tactic is the common understanding that the language and rationale used by justices in concurrences and dissents often become the controlling language and rationale used by the future court (Baum 1998, 139). These opinions also highlight the fulcrum of conflict among the justices. Similarly, we also describe, in some cases, obiter dicta, or what legal scholars call non-binding language in the opinions. We do so because such language provides a critical window for examining the gradual shifting values that are taking place in the milieu of the Canadian Supreme Court over time.

Obviously, Canadian Supreme Court cases can raise multiple issues in a given dispute. It is not uncommon for an environmental issue to be embedded in a larger federal, constitutional, or jurisdictional context. For example, a case might involve a dispute between a provincial and a federal government over which level of government has power and control over scarce environmental resources. Alternatively, a dispute could address whether a federal agency has the right to stop or deny a permit or has overstepped its jurisdictional authority in some way. In cases where the environmental issue is superimposed on a larger federal, jurisdictional, or constitutional framework, the environmental concern may be a secondary component of the case. In these multifaceted disputes, it is important to recognize the salient issues that are fundamental to the resolution of the case, but also to assess whether the federal, judicial, or constitutional principles announced by the justices are imbued with value statements that either promote or diminish environmental protection and stewardship. In light of these concerns, we devote the rest of the chapter to an analysis of the language used by the justices to reach their decisions in key cases touching on pollution regulation, energy, and First Nation fishing rights.

Our reading of the cases is designed to look for nuance and directional value positions lying at the core of the justices' rationale for their rulings. The strength of this approach is that it values what the justices write instead of just looking at the votes cast for one party or another. This type of analysis captures the nuanced patterns of value transformation taking place in a high court that quantitative analysis cannot provide. A weakness in this methodology, however, is that Supreme Court justices work in dynamic groups of usually five, seven, and nine justices. Thus, opinions are sometimes the product of compromises, which may have the effect of not necessarily reflecting a justice's values, but rather a mediated amalgamation of value positions. Even so, these written reasons for judgment result in narrative choices that reflect the justices' authoritative expression of what the law means, and they are likely to reflect a movement in societal values over time.

A second concern is that sometimes justices will discuss value positions at the beginning of their opinions that they do not support or that serve as counterpoints to the true value positions reflected in their opinions. However, this language is easily understood as obiter dicta because it does not comprise the core language that is central to the rationale for the ruling in the case. Overall, we suggest that the balance of word choices at the crux of a ruling reflects the legal value priorities in the minds of the justices. All things considered, we are concerned with the content of the language and values at the heart of the rationale, which dictates the future direction of the law. If Inglehart's theory of value change is correct, more modern justices should be using a postmaterialist narrative more regularly than justices of earlier courts.

Pollution Cases – Landmark Decisions of the Laskin and Dickson Courts

The Supreme Court of Canada heard 15 cases dealing with pollution between 1973 and 2010, and in 12 of the disputes, it handed down a pro-environmental ruling. Yet the question remains whether the justices used decisive postmaterialist language to resolve the disputes. The three landmark pollution cases that we chose to analyse under the Laskin and Dickson tenures (1974–90) collectively showed a willingness of the Canadian court to recognize the importance of pollution as a societal problem that needed to be addressed by government in a cogent and aggressive way. The court recognized the saliency of this issue in *Fowler v. The Queen*, [1980] 2 S.C.R. 213 and *Northwest Falling Contractors Ltd. v. The Queen*, [1980] 2 S.C.R. 292 (hereafter *Fowler* and *Northwest Falling*). Although the Laskin Court appeared to hand down a pro-environmental ruling in only one of these cases, the language it used in both of these water pollution disputes set the tone for the early modern Canadian court in the environmental area. The overarching legal question in this pair of cases was whether Parliament had the constitutional authority to enact two sections of the National Fisheries Act or whether such enactments fell within provincial legislative powers. This was a critical early test of the viability of the act, passed by Parliament in 1970. The central question in *Fowler* was whether a blanket prohibition on any logging or land clearing that put any amount of wood debris into any water in Canada containing fish was outside the scope of power of the federal government (*Fowler*, [1980] 2 S.C.R. 213, at 213–4).

Justice Martland, writing for a unanimous court, determined that Parliament had overstepped its authority because the scope of the legislation was far too sweeping and broad, failed to require a clear link between the prohibited activity and actual harm to fisheries, and prohibited certain kinds of activity that are typically under provincial, and not federal, jurisdiction (*Fowler*, [1980] 2 S.C.R. 213, at 226). In reaching his conclusion, Justice Martland highlighted a point made by the lower provincial judge at trial, who stated,

> This [section] would affect every log, piece of lumber or tree that is so placed or dumped into any river, lake, stream or ocean in Canada. ... I cannot conceive that the ... log drives and similar type of logging enterprises could be carried out without depositing some debris into the waters. ... If section 33(3) does not require the additional proof that the deposit of the debris affects the preservation of fish then every such booming operation and log drive would be committing an offence. ... (*Fowler*, [1980] 2 S.C.R. 213, at 225–6)

Although Justice Martland used this rationale to strike down parts of the law, the language used in his opinion suggested that the National Fisheries Act was clearly aimed at ensuring the preservation of the Canadian fishery, and it documented that fishery stocks were a precious natural resource that needed to be protected from exploitation.

If *Fowler* represented an easy call in favour of provincial power, the factual circumstances were very different in *Northwest Falling*. In this case, an individual had dumped 3,000 gallons of diesel fuel into an inlet. Like *Fowler*, the legal question in this case was whether s. 33(2) of the National Fisheries Act, which prohibited individuals from depositing "deleterious substance" into water frequented by fish, was outside the scope of the legislative powers of the federal government. Unlike *Fowler*, Justice Martland upheld the statutory provision as being constitutionally valid because it was narrowly tailored and the deposit of deleterious substance into water frequented by fish would directly harm and deplete the fish population in the area. He concluded that since the law was aimed at the protection and preservation of fish, not regulating water pollution generally, it was indeed within the purview of federal government power. What distinguished this provision was that it was limited in scope and strictly aimed at "the prohibition of deposits that threaten fish, fish habitat or the use of fish by man" (*Northwest Falling*, [1980] 2 S.C.R. 292, at 301).

The language, rationale, and case precedent that Justice Martland used in both cases reinforce the notion that subsequent parliamentary regulations in the water pollution area would be upheld as long as they were narrowly tailored and aimed at regulating, protecting, and preserving fish as a natural resource for all Canadians to enjoy. Moreover, the *Northwest Falling* case foreshadowed a rising environmental ethic within the court.

One of the most salient and critical cases handed down in the water pollution area under the Dickson tenure was *R. v. Crown Zellerbach Canada Ltd.*, [1988] 1 S.C.R. 401 (hereafter *Crown Zellerbach*), which also addressed the scope of federal power in relation to the provinces in regard to dumping by a logging company, but this time it was *in provincial marine waters*. The question was whether the federal government had jurisdiction to regulate dumping in provincial waters for substances not shown to have any effect on marine life or navigation at sea (*Crown Zellerbach*, [1988] 1 S.C.R. 401, at 417). Although both lower courts had determined that the provision was outside the scope of federal power, the Supreme Court, in a 4–3 ruling, disagreed. Justice Le Dain relied on the rationale put forth by Justice Pigeon in *Interprovincial Cooperatives Ltd. v. The Queen*, [1976] 1 S.C.R. 477 to conclude that the provision of the Ocean Dumping Control Act was constitutionally valid under the national concern doctrine, which emanated from the peace, order, and good government power of the federal government. He went on to suggest that prior cases firmly established that the doctrine applied to new subject matter that had acquired singleness, distinctiveness, and indivisibility of purpose. In determining whether a subject matter met the conditions above and qualified for national concern and federal jurisdiction, one had to assess the effect on interests outside the province if the provincial government did not control the problem within its own boundaries (*Crown Zellerbach*, [1988] 1 S.C.R. 401, at 432). Justice Le Dain indicated that this last factor, identified as the "provincial inability" test, constituted the most satisfactory rationale for determining whether federal jurisdiction was justified under the national concern doctrine.

When Justice Le Dain subsequently applied the test to the case at hand, he argued that the pollution of provincial marine waters had predominantly extra-provincial and international characteristics that necessarily made it a matter of national concern. He argued that marine-water pollution necessarily differed in composition and action, which made it distinct from freshwater pollution. Moreover, since the Ocean Dumping Control Act recognized this distinction and limited the power of the federal government to regulating only marine-water dumping, it necessarily met the requirements of the national concern doctrine (*Crown Zellerbach*, [1988] 1 S.C.R. 401, at 437–8). In taking a stance in favour of federal power, Justice Le Dain's opinion had the impact of importing postmaterialist concerns about the environment into the jurisprudence of federalism.

Justice La Forest, in dissent, had a different view. He argued that the law dealt with subject matter that fell entirely within the confines of the province and that there was no evidence to link the conduct by the logging company to any actual or potential harm outside the province. Since the act was a blanket prohibition against depositing any substance in marine waters, he concluded that it mirrored the facts in the *Fowler* case and thus the law was outside the scope of federal power (*Crown Zellerbach*, [1988] 1 S.C.R. 401, at 448–51). However, even if one were to assess the provision under the new approach, Justice La Forest claimed that the subject failed to meet the singleness, distinctiveness, and indivisibility requirement necessary to qualify as a matter of national concern, most notably because there were no clearly demarcated boundaries between salt and fresh water. Moreover, since a wide range of activities along the coasts involved dumping some substances into the ocean, Justice La Forest argued that this provision would have an irreconcilable impact on the division of power articulated in the Constitution (*Crown Zellerbach*, [1988] 1 S.C.R. 401, at 458). Last, since there was no evidence that the dumping harmed any ocean marine life, he thought there was no need to consider any impacts beyond the province's boundary (*Crown Zellerbach*, [1988] 1 S.C.R. 401, at 458–9).

The *Crown Zellerbach* ruling exposed clear tensions in the Supreme Court over federalist principles in water pollution regulations. Even though Justice Le Dain appeared to confine the scope of federal power by requiring a singleness, distinctiveness, and indivisibility of purpose that distinguished it from provincial concerns, and by requiring that courts assess such issues in light of the constitutional division of powers, it seems that, in *Crown Zellerbach*, the Dickson Court opened an avenue for expansion of the federal government's power to control and regulate water pollution issues at the expense of the provinces. As long as the water pollution issue could be labelled "a national concern," the federal government was justified in regulating water pollution that was completely confined within a given province, irrespective of whether it harmed the ocean. Ultimately, the majority in *Crown Zellerbach* gave the federal government a new basis of constitutional authority over water pollution and environmental matters, and it greatly expanded federal authority over the provinces pertaining to dumping waste exclusively within provincial waters. Only time would determine whether the court and other actors would use this provision to control other types of environmental pollution that took place exclusively within the confines of a Canadian province and whether it would confine its interpretation of this statute exclusively to water pollution.

Pollution Cases – Landmark Decisions of the Lamer Court

The effort to recognize environmental pollution as a salient issue that government must combat gained even greater traction under the Lamer Court (1990–99). In the two landmark cases reviewed below, *Ontario v. Canadian Pacific Ltd.*, [1995] 2 S.C.R. 1031 (hereafter *Canadian Pacific*) and *R. v. Hydro-Québec*, [1997] 3 S.C.R. 213 (hereafter *Hydro-Québec*), the Lamer Court gave an increasing level of ammunition to government entities to combat the complex issue of environmental pollution. *Canadian Pacific* shifted the federalist discussion to air pollution, with the court addressing a provision of the Ontario Environmental Protection Act (EPA) that prohibited anyone from releasing contaminants into the air that "cause impairment of the quality of the natural environment for any use that can be made of it." The legal question was whether the law was vague and overbroad, and thus violated principles of fundamental justice in s. 7 of the Charter of Rights and Freedoms, because it failed to provide an intelligible standard for people to follow (*Canadian Pacific*, [1995] 2 S.C.R. 1031, at 1066). Although all nine justices agreed that Ontario's EPA was neither vague nor overbroad, three members of the court provided a different rationale for finding Canadian Pacific Railway criminally liable for causing injuries to the health and property of nearby residents from dense smoke emanating from two controlled burns conducted along the railway line.

Justice Gonthier, writing for the majority, determined that the Ontario EPA was written in broad and general terms to provide Ontario with the necessary flexibility to deal with numerous types of pollution issues. He stated, "Such an approach is hardly surprising in the field of environmental protection, given that the nature of the environment (its complexity, and the wide range of activities which might cause harm to it) is not conducive to precise codification" (*Canadian Pacific*, [1995] 2 S.C.R. 1031, at 1068). Justice Gonthier argued that the Ontario statute clearly applied to the smoke pollution that was at issue and passed the vagueness test established by the court in *R. v. Nova Scotia Pharmaceutical Society*, [1992] 2 S.C.R. 606. He also maintained that the judiciary must take a deferential approach when assessing legislation that promoted important policy goals (*Canadian Pacific*, [1995] 2 S.C.R. 1031, at 1071–2).

Although Canadian Pacific objected to the "open-ended" nature and "standardless sweep" of the provision, Justice Gonthier concluded that the scope of the statute was reasonable and that a fact-sensitive interpretation of the law was needed to ensure that it did not criminalize minor activities that caused minimum impairment to the environment in Ontario (*Canadian Pacific*, [1995] 2 S.C.R. 1031, at 1069–71, 1079–83). He also concluded that the dense smoke clearly contaminated the natural environment and significantly impaired its use by the surrounding residents in the community (*Canadian Pacific*, [1995] 2 S.C.R. 1031, at 1087). He determined that s. 14(1)(a) of Ontario's EPA was not overbroad. Since the Crown needed to prove that the polluting substance had been released, and significantly impaired the use or likely use of the air in the environment, this prevented the provision from being used in trivial situations that failed to meet the overall objective of environmental protection (*Canadian Pacific*, [1995] 2 S.C.R. 1031, at 1092).

Chief Justice Lamer, writing for a three-member concurrence, agreed that the statute was not overbroad or vague, but he thought a more narrow interpretation was needed so that it would not fail the overbreadth analysis established by the court in *R. v. Haywood* (*Canadian Pacific*, [1995] 2 S.C.R. 1031, at 1048). When he compared the overall objectives of the statute with the means chosen to achieve those objectives, as required under *R. v. Haywood*, he claimed that the court needed to focus on the specific examples of pollution activity that would significantly impair the quality of the natural environment (*Canadian Pacific*, [1995] 2 S.C.R. 1031, at 1054–9). Thus, Chief Justice Lamer's interpretation of s. 13(1)(a) would restrict the confines of the Ontario provision to specific types of harm identified in the statute, while Justice Gonthier gave a much broader interpretation of the Ontario law. Regardless of which interpretation the Canadian court adopted in the future, the Lamer Court, under either interpretation, greatly expanded the protection of the environment to numerous types of air pollution and, in doing so, breathed more postmaterialist life into its ruling.

The language used by Justice Gonthier to justify the court's ruling reinforces the expansive approach taken by the Lamer Court in this case and coincides well with a postmaterialist vision of environmental decision making. At one point, he discussed the need for broad-based legislation in the area of environmental protection, claiming, "Environmental protection legislation has, as a result, been framed in a manner capable of responding to a wide variety of environmentally harmful scenarios, including ones which might not have been foreseen by the drafters of the legislation" (*Canadian Pacific*, [1995] 2 S.C.R. 1031, at 1068). Moreover, he claimed, "Not only has environmental protection emerged as a fundamental value in Canadian society, but this has also been recognized in legislative provisions such as s. 13(1)(a) EPA" (*Canadian Pacific*, [1995] 2 S.C.R. 1031, at 1076). These statements and others like them illustrate the expansive interpretation that the Lamer Court seemed willing to give to air pollution laws in the mid-1990s through its interpretation of the Ontario EPA in *Canadian Pacific*.

Two years later, the Lamer Court recognized the federal government's right to punish environmental polluters through criminal law power in a water pollution case whose federalist features were reminiscent of *Crown Zellerbach*. In *Hydro-Québec*, [1997] 3 S.C.R. 213, the Lamer Court addressed the extent to which the federal government could control, regulate, and prohibit Hydro-Québec from dumping toxic substances into a river exclusively within the confines of Quebec.

Hydro-Québec had filed a motion to have several provisions of the Canadian EPA struck down, and all three lower courts had ruled that these sections of the federal provision were outside the scope of federal power because they could not be justified under any federal head of power under s. 91 of the Constitution Act, 1867 (*Hydro-Québec*, [1997] 3 S.C.R. 213, at 284). The Supreme Court, unlike the lower courts, ruled that Part II of the act was constitutionally valid because it was not aimed at protecting the environment generally, but rather focused on controlling specific toxic substances using a series of criminal sanctions. Justice La Forest reasoned that since the purpose and effect of the provision provided federal ministers only with guidelines for assessing, and subjecting a limited number of toxins to, regulation and penalty, it was a valid limited objective under Parliament's criminal law power (*Hydro-Québec*, [1997] 3 S.C.R. 213, at 266; see also 304). He buttressed his conclusion by stressing the critical role that environmental protection had come to play in Canadian society. In the opening passage of his opinion, he stated, "This Court has in recent years been increasingly called upon to consider the interplay between federal and provincial legislative powers as they relate to environmental protection. … There can be no doubt that these measures relate to a public purpose of superordinate importance" (*Hydro-Québec*, [1997] 3 S.C.R. 213, at 266). A few sentences later, he wrote, "The Constitution must be interpreted in a manner that is fully responsive to emerging realities and the nature of the subject matter sought to be regulated. Given the pervasive and diffuse nature of the environment, this reality poses particular difficulties in this context" (*Hydro-Québec*, [1997] 3 S.C.R. 213, at 267).

With these postmaterialist sentiments at the forefront, Justice La Forest concluded that the Constitution gave the federal government broad power in the criminal law area and that Parliament had a wholly legitimate public objective to protect the health of Canadian citizens and ensure a clean and safe environment through its criminal law power. Indeed, in his assessment of the scope of federal criminal law power, he cited Justice Gonthier's approval of a government report in *Canadian Pacific*, writing, "I agree … that the stewardship of the environment is a fundamental value of our society and that Parliament may use its criminal law power to underline that value. The criminal law must be able to keep pace with and protect our emerging values" (*Hydro-Québec*, [1997] 3 S.C.R. 213, at 297).

It is important to keep in mind that Justice La Forest had written for the minority in *Crown Zellerbach*, where he raised concerns about granting the federal government exclusive control over environmental pollution found *exclusively within a province* because it would disturb the balance of power enshrined in the Constitution. But the *Hydro-Québec* case gave Justice La Forest the opportunity to clarify his position in the *Oldman River* case: that both levels of government would have to work together strategically to combat the evils of environmental pollution (*Hydro-Québec*, [1997] 3 S.C.R. 213, at 288). As Justice La Forest wrote,

> The two levels of government frequently work together to meet common concerns. … Here again [in the water pollution area] there is a wide measure of cooperation between the federal and provincial authorities to effect common or complimentary ends. … The fear that the legislation impugned here would distort the federal-provincial balance seems to me to be overstated. (*Hydro-Québec*, [1997] 3 S.C.R. 213, at 299)

Overall, the Lamer Court in these two cases readily recognized the overarching importance of regulating environmental pollution in Canadian society, and in *Hydro-Québec,* it was even willing to support Parliament's efforts to criminalize the actions of certain polluters. In that sense, the Lamer Court's pollution rulings featured narrative themes that squarely adopted a postmaterialist viewpoint of protecting the environment as a fundamental value.

Pollution Cases – Landmark Decisions of the McLachlin Court

If the earlier cases stood for the proposition that both the federal and the provincial governments must be given leeway to legislate in the area of pollution control, the 2001 *Hudson* ruling extended the regulatory logic down to the level of local governments (*114957 Canada Ltée. v. Hudson,* [2001] 2 S.C.R. 241, hereafter *Hudson*). Acting on health concerns, Hudson's town council had adopted a by-law in 1990 that restricted the use of pesticides to specific locations and for only certain listed activities (e.g., farming, swimming in backyard pools, and indoor household use). Lawn care companies and landscapers felt unfairly targeted by the law, and they asked a municipal court judge to declare the by-law inoperative, arguing that it was incompatible with federal and provincial statutes, which allowed them to use regulated pesticides. The McLachlin Court, in a 7–0 decision, upheld the municipal by-law, essentially following the tack taken by lower court judges hearing the dispute. Justice L'Heureux-Dubé, writing for four members of the court, indicated that the town of Hudson had the authority to adopt the by-law under the Cities and Towns Act, which gave municipalities in Quebec the power to regulate for the purpose of "peace, order, good government, health and general welfare" as long as those regulations were not in conflict with federal or provincial laws. According to Justice L'Heureux-Dubé, the by-law in question clearly fell within the ambit of local government authority to regulate in the name of the health of its local residents by minimizing the use of harmful pesticides (*Hudson,* [2001] 2 S.C.R. 241, at 264).

Justice L'Heureux-Dubé's opinion used international authorities as the fountainhead of legal principles justifying local action to combat pollution. At different turns, she cited United Nations commission reports, treaties, ministerial declarations, and law-review articles drawn from the field of international law to expound on the "precautionary principle." This principle suggests that "environmental measures must anticipate, prevent and attack the causes of environmental degradation. Where there are threats of serious or irreversible damage, lack of scientific certainty should not be used as a reason for postponing measures to prevent environmental degradation" (*Hudson*, [2001] 2 S.C.R. 241, at 266–7). Justice L'Heureux-Dubé grounded her support for local environmental regulation not just in Canadian law and precedent but also in broader international communities of law and governance. As a final matter, she concluded that the local by-law did not conflict with federal or provincial powers because the companies were not put in an impossible situation when attempting to comply with all the legal regimes (*Hudson*, [2001] 2 S.C.R. 241, at 268–72). In short, a "tri-level regulatory regime" represented simply the by-product of different levels of government addressing a complex environmental problem, and for Justice L'Heureux-Dubé, the exercise of local power to promote and protect the health of its residents was not contrary to federal or provincial laws.

In concurrence, Justice LeBel reached the same fundamental conclusion, but focused on administrative law and statutory construction, stating that flowery references to non-Canadian authorities were beside the point. The case was a simple example of a town having the administrative power to legislate on normal areas of law like protecting the local environment and land and property use (*Hudson*, [2001] 2 S.C.R. 241, at 278–9).

The overall arc of law seen in the landmark pollution control cases is one that runs the gamut of governmental power. Framed within the parameters of disputes over federalism, the early decisions of the Laskin and Dickson Courts breathed life into the federal government's power to regulate water pollution, at least when the laws were not vague or overbroad. Subsequent rulings during the Lamer Court continued the progressive trend and appeared to advance the notion of cooperative federalism, indicating that protecting the environment from the harm of pollution would require concerted action from both the federal and the provincial governments. By the 2001 ruling in *Hudson*, the circle had been completed, with cities empowered to enact more stringent pesticide regulations and the majority author of the opinion citing international sources to back up the ruling. Over time, a cosmopolitan, postmaterialist language had become a regular feature of the justices' writings in pollution control cases, and the recognition that all levels of government needed to regulate complex environmental concerns had become commonplace within the modern Canadian Supreme Court.

Energy Cases – Landmark Decisions of the Laskin and Dickson Courts

The Canadian Supreme Court handed down only six cases in the energy area during the 1973–2010 period; they included disputes pertaining to hydroelectric power, nuclear energy, and oil and gas resources. The Supreme Court ruled in favour of materialist energy exploitation interests in four of the six decisions. Since two of the cases handed down in this area – namely, *Friends of Oldman River Society v. Canada (Minister of Transport)*, [1992] 1 S.C.R. 3 (hereafter *Oldman River*) and *Quebec (Attorney General) v. Canada (National Energy Board)*, [1994] 1 S.C.R. 159 (hereafter *National Energy Board*) – constitute two of the most important cases in the field of environmental law, we decided to assess the degree to which Inglehart's postmaterialist values thesis fared in this sub-field under the Laskin/Dickson, Lamer, and McLachlin tenures. Unlike the pollution area, it seems that the Canadian court has had a much more materialist record in the energy area. One possible explanation for this difference is that since advanced industrial societies are so dependent on energy resources, the modern Canadian court took a more practical and materialistic approach to these types of environmental disputes to ensure the economic well-being of society as a whole.

The only energy case heard during the Laskin/Dickson tenure was *Reference re Newfoundland's Continental Shelf*, [1984] 1 S.C.R. 86 (hereafter *Continental Shelf*). This case provided little comfort for environmentalists because neither party brought forth a pro-environmental claim. Rather, the only issue at stake was which level of government had the power to explore and exploit the natural resources of the continental shelf off the coast of Newfoundland. The court ultimately ruled that the province of Newfoundland had no legal basis, in either constitutional law or international law, to justify either the right to explore and exploit those resources or legislative jurisdiction to make laws in relation to the resources of the continental shelf (*Continental Shelf*, [1984] 1 S.C.R. 86, at 87). In the course of examining the dispute, the court determined that any continental shelf rights were "in pith and substance" an "extraterritorial manifestation of external sovereignty," and thus the assessment of such rights fell under the rubric of international law (*Continental Shelf*, [1984] 1 S.C.R. 86, at 97). Put simply, since Canada acted as a sovereign power in the international system, only Parliament possessed the authority to regulate the exploitation of resources off the country's coasts, and Newfoundland had no authority to exercise any legal power over the continental shelf.

Energy Cases – Landmark Decisions of the Lamer Court

While the Newfoundland continental shelf case turned on the exploitation of the seabed for oil, a subsequent landmark case revolved around harnessing a river for electrical power (*Oldman River*, [1992] 1 S.C.R. 3). This is one of the most important environmental cases handed down during the 1973–2010 period. In this case, the government of Alberta was in the process of building a dam on the Oldman River that impacted areas of federal responsibility, including navigable waters, fisheries, First Nations, and their lands (*Oldman River*, [1992] 1 S.C.R. 3, at 18). An environmental protection group sought to compel the Departments of Transport and Fisheries and Oceans to conduct environmental assessments on the Alberta dam to determine whether it would cause any adverse environmental effect on areas of federal responsibility. Although the province of Alberta had conducted many environmental studies, it began building the dam after obtaining approval from the minister of transport (*Oldman River*, [1992] 1 S.C.R. 3, at 5). On appeal, the Lamer Court addressed two main legal questions: (1) whether the Environmental Assessment and Review Process (EARP) Guidelines Order, authorized by the Department of the Environment Act, was outside the scope of Parliament and whether it was inconsistent with the requirements under the Navigable Waters Protection Act; and (2) whether the Court of Appeal had erred in interfering with the trial judge's determination not to grant the remedies sought by the environmental group (*Oldman River*, [1992] 1 S.C.R. 3, at 32).

Justice La Forest, writing for eight of the nine justices, used his opinion in *Oldman River* to reiterate his federalist position in *Crown Zellerbach*. In *Oldman River*, he concluded that the guidelines order was within the power of Parliament because it did not try to regulate the effects of the dam within the province of Alberta. Rather, the legislation was mandatory in nature and, in pith and substance, was aimed at matters exclusively within Parliament's jurisdiction – namely, instituting a process that required federal departments to conduct environmental impact assessments to make sound decisions regarding areas of federal responsibility such as navigable waters, fisheries, First Nations, and their lands (*Oldman River*, [1992] 1 S.C.R. 3, at 62–73). The court determined that the guidelines order was consistent with the Navigable Waters Protection Act, which did not preclude the minister of transport taking various socio-economic considerations into account in his assessment that were outside marine navigation (*Oldman River*, [1992] 1 S.C.R. 3, at 39–41).

In analysing this issue, Justice La Forest concluded that the environment was a complex phenomenon that transcended several heads of power and that collectively distributed constitutional authority to both levels of government (*Oldman River*, [1992] 1 S.C.R. 3, at 63). Since the environment involved matters pertaining to the physical, economic, and social aspects of society, both levels of government might act to effectively deal with such concerns. Yet Parliament could participate in a local or provincial environmental issue only if it could be linked to an appropriate head of power, which in this case pertained to the possible environmental damage the dam might impose on navigation, fisheries, First Nations, and their lands, all of which were under federal jurisdiction (*Oldman River*, [1992] 1 S.C.R. 3, at 63–73). In the end, the court agreed that a federal environmental assessment was necessary before the dam could be built.

After the court's pro-environmental ruling, a federal environmental assessment was completed and recommended that the dam be scuttled. Despite this assessment, the federal government went ahead and approved the dam's construction, resulting in – at least from one commentator's perspective – an "illegal" dam (see Hogg 1997, s. 29-7 [b]). However, the ruling of the Lamer Court set a strong precedent that environmental impact assessments were necessary before the development of Canadian natural resources would be allowed. In essence, *Oldman River* set in motion the court's endorsement of federal environmental reviews as being of paramount importance, even though the review in this particular case was ignored by government officials.

Two years after the *Oldman River case*, in *National Energy Board*, [1994] 1 S.C.R. 159, the Lamer Court addressed another hydroelectric energy case, this time assessing whether the National Energy Board had acted within its jurisdiction when it granted licences to Hydro-Québec to export electrical power to the United States. The licences came with strings attached, requiring the successful completion of an environmental impact assessment of future planned facilities to support the proposed exports (*National Energy Board*, [1994] 1 S.C.R. 159, at 176).

At the crux of the case, the appellants argued that the board had failed to follow the assessment requirements established in the National Energy Board Act and the EARP Guidelines Order. Justice Iacobucci concluded that the National Energy Board had been justified in requiring Hydro-Québec to assess the environmental impact of future generating facilities, for several reasons. Since the act allowed the board to "consider all factors which appear to it to be relevant" and the environmental effects were unknown at that time, Justice Iacobucci concluded that the board could give "some weight" to the environmental effects of project facilities planned in the future, especially since the electricity produced at those facilities would be critical to the export contract (*National Energy Board*, [1994] 1 S.C.R. 159, at 189–92).

Although the province expressed concern that such a broad enquiry by the board might encroach on areas of provincial concern, Justice Iacobucci argued that since the board's actions pertained to commerce and exports, its ruling clearly fell within an area of federal jurisdiction, although he acknowledged that both levels of government shared responsibilities in environmental matters. Justice Iacobucci highlighted this point by citing a passage from *Oldman River* in which the court had stated, "It must be recognized that the environment is not an independent matter of legislation under the *Constitution Act, 1867* and that it is a constitutionally abstruse matter which does not comfortably fit within the existing division of powers without considerable overlap and uncertainty" (*National Energy Board*, [1994] 1 S.C.R. 159, quoted at 193). The court concluded that the board had not exceeded its jurisdiction under the National Energy Board Act and had met its obligation when it attached the two environmental assessment conditions to the licences it granted Hydro-Québec (*National Energy Board*, [1994] 1 S.C.R. 159, at 194–8).

The court's ruling in *National Energy Board* appears to be insubstantial at first blush because it did not assess the constitutionality of either the National Energy Board Act or the EARP Guidelines Order, but rather focused exclusively on whether the National Energy Board had correctly applied the two provisions when it granted the export licences to Hydro-Québec. Yet when trying to assess the outcome in terms of Inglehart's broader postmaterialistic thesis, it is a more complex case than it first appears because it is difficult to categorize it as a pro-environmental or a materialistic economic ruling. Since the appellant Cree lost their appeal, which sought to require the board to follow more stringent procedural and substantive guidelines when conducting the licensing review process, we labelled it as a materialistic outcome because the ruling advanced the economic well-being of Hydro-Québec at the expense of the Cree. Yet one could also argue that the case established a pro-environmental standard because the Lamer Court upheld the board's stipulation that Hydro-Québec needed to successfully complete an environmental assessment for any future power generation facilities. However, as Boyd pointed out, these environmental assessments rarely have a significant impact on limiting the exploitation of water resources in Canada (Boyd 2003, 46).

Taken together, the rulings of the Lamer Court in energy cases feature an ironic component of postmaterialist thought. They clearly endorse the significance of conducting environmental assessments at the federal level, but in each case, materialistic interests ultimately won the battle to exploit water resources for electrical power.

Energy Cases – Landmark Decisions of the McLachlin Court

One of the early energy cases heard under the McLachlin tenure featured the interplay of energy exploitation and pollution in *Imperial Oil Ltd. v. Quebec (Minister of the Environment)*, [2003] 2 S.C.R. 624 (hereafter *Imperial Oil*). The court addressed the legal question of whether Quebec's minister of the environment had properly fulfilled his duty of procedural fairness and duty of impartiality when he ordered Imperial Oil to conduct site studies to assess its contamination of the land, submit a plan for rectifying the contaminated site, and, if necessary, pay for the work performed (*Imperial Oil*, [2003] 2 S.C.R. 624, at 640–1). According to Justice LeBel, the heart of the appeal turned on whether the minister had adhered to two fundamental principles of natural justice – namely, the duty of procedural fairness and duty of impartiality – when making his decision. For him, the minister had met the rules of procedural fairness set out in the law and had not followed his own personal interest, but had rather focused on what was in the best interest of the province and the public at large in protecting the environment (*Imperial Oil*, [2003] 2 S.C.R. 624, at 650). At one point, Justice LeBel indicated that the public had shifted in its views regarding the environment when he stated, "The Quebec legislation reflects the growing concern on the part of legislatures and of society about the safeguarding of the environment. … It may also be evidence of an emerging sense of intergenerational solidarity and acknowledgement of an environmental debt to humanity and to the world of tomorrow" (*Imperial Oil*, [2003] 2 S.C.R. 624, at 640). The postmaterialist language inherent in this ruling indicated that the early McLachlin Court was aware of the continuing need to protect the environment and the role that the minister of the environment had in attaining that critical goal. Justice LeBel's recognition of an intergenerational change in attitudes about the environment directly echoes Inglehart's intergenerational values thesis about postmaterialist value change.

One of the most recent energy cases handed down by the McLachlin Court was *Rio Tinto Alcan Inc. v. Carrier Sekani Tribal Council*, [2010] 2 S.C.R. 650 (hereafter *Rio Tinto*), which pitted a British Columbia provincial utilities company against a First Nation over a 2007 contract pertaining to the sale of excess hydroelectric power emanating from the Kenney Dam. The overarching legal issue raised in this case was whether the British Columbia Utilities Commission had been required to consider consultation with the Carrier Sekani Tribal Council (CSTC) First Nation in determining whether the sale of excess power under the 2007 Energy Purchase Agreement was in the public interest (*Rio Tinto*, [2010] 2 S.C.R. 650, at 657).

Justice McLachlin first discussed the three-part test established in *Haida Nation v. British Columbia (Minister of Forests)*, [2004] 3 S.C.R. 511, which required the government to consult with indigenous groups when it had "knowledge, real or constructive, of the potential existence of the Aboriginal right or title and contemplates conduct that might adversely affect it" (*Rio Tinto*, [2010] 2 S.C.R. 650, at 669). She went on to suggest that the test could be broken down into three distinct components, which included the Crown having knowledge of an indigenous claim, the Crown engaging in some conduct, and the conduct possibly adversely affecting indigenous rights. To meet the last element, the claimant had to show a causal connection between the specific, proposed Crown conduct and its adverse impact on the indigenous right. After determining that the Utilities Commission Act did give the commission the power to consider whether adequate consultation had taken place, Justice McLachlin concluded that the commission had not acted unreasonably when it approved the 2007 power agreement because the contract did not adversely affect any First Nation interests at that time.

According to Justice McLachlin, although the first two prongs of the *Haida Nation* test had been met, the third had not, even though the commission had considered the possibility of both the physical and the organizational adverse effects that might result from the contract. Justice McLachlin concluded that any changes in the water released for power generation would have no physical impact on the fisheries or the river that the CSTC First Nation was concerned about (*Rio Tinto*, [2010] 2 S.C.R. 650, at 688). In addition, the 2007 contract would not create any management or organizational policy changes that adversely impacted the CSTC First Nation's rights. Although the court concluded that there had been no adverse impact as a result of the contract in the case, it did reiterate that BC Hydro would need to consult with First Nations on any decision that might adversely impact First Nation claims or rights in the future (*Rio Tinto*, [2010] 2 S.C.R. 650, at 690).

The *Rio Tinto* case resulted in a pro-development ruling that ran against the environmental arguments of the CSTC First Nation. However, the requirement that government consult with First Nations reflected a commitment on the part of the modern court to have the traditional environmental claims of First Nations considered before development projects were initiated. This perspective reflects a growing postmaterialist, pro-environmental awareness that can serve as a check on unfettered economic development, especially if First Nation traditional land use is taken into greater consideration in the future. Yet this ruling points to the difficulty that sometimes occurs with classifying environmental disputes in relation to indigenous claims made by a First Nation group or individual because what constitutes a "pro-environmental ruling" might shift depending on who is bringing forth the claim and what stance the government takes in those claims. This issue will be discussed further in the next section of the chapter, which will explore Supreme Court rulings in environmental claims brought by indigenous peoples.

Overall, the Canadian court has had a much more mixed pro-environmental record in the energy area than in pollution cases. While it has handed down a mere six cases involving energy disputes over the four decades studied, only two of them were decisively pro-environmental outcomes, albeit *Oldman River* remains a seminal ruling in the field of environmental law because its postmaterialistic language supports the necessity of conducting environmental assessment reviews. Three other case outcomes were clearly in favour of energy development at the expense of environmental resources, yet the language used by the court recognized the continuing need for environmental impact reviews, protecting the environment against encroachment and pollution, and consulting with First Nations regarding significant environmental impacts. Although some scholars, such as Boyd (2003, 46, 113) contend that environmental assessments rarely prevent large-scale development projects from occurring, surely the existence of laws and processes that require assessments helps to reduce the degree of environmental degradation that would occur without them in place. It is clear that the qualitative analysis of energy cases provides a more robust endorsement of postmaterialist values in terms of the tests developed and the factors that justices must consider than a simple analysis of who wins and loses.

First Nation Fishing Cases – Landmark Decisions of the Laskin and Dickson Courts

The Canadian Supreme Court handed down 40 environmental rulings dealing with First Nations during the 1973–2010 period, 9 of which juxtaposed government interests against groups, while 31 pitted government interests against individuals. The cases involving First Nation groups largely addressed issues pertaining to treaty claims related to land acquisition and development, with the groups advancing a pro-environmental stance in eight of the nine cases and the court handing down a pro-environmental ruling in only three of the disputes. In contrast, virtually all the claims dealing with First Nation individuals pertained to violations of government fishing or hunting regulations restricting unlawful taking of wildlife. As suggested earlier, some might argue that subsistence fishing practices by First Nation individuals actually promote better environmental stewardship than the government. Although there is some credence to this contention, our interpretation of the value conflicts implies that government efforts to protect the environment represent the purest postmaterialist value because they are aimed at the wholesale protection of natural resources. In addition, in some of these cases, the individuals fish well beyond subsistence levels to engage in the sale and distribution of their spoils. For example, one can hardly claim that the individuals in the *Marshall* and *N.T.C. Smokehouse* cases were merely fishing for subsistence purposes when they caught 400 pounds of eel and sold more than 119,000 pounds of Chinook salmon (see *R. v. Marshall*, [1999] 3 S.C.R. 456 and *R. v. N.T.C. Smokehouse Ltd.*, [1996] 2 S.C.R. 672, hereafter *Marshall* and *N.T.C. Smokehouse*).

These examples illustrate that First Nation individuals who defy fishing regulations frequently do so to advance their own economic well-being by selling their haul in the marketplace. When the argument for historical practices is advanced, it is embedded in a value position that invokes the materialist perspective of upholding traditional practices to advance the equality claims of First Nations peoples. While acknowledging the environmental stewardship counterargument that First Nations frequently make, we think our treatment of the cases is faithful to Inglehart's theoretical proposition because the continued depletion of resources is potentially harmful to their long-term survival, especially in light of the fact that only 50 per cent of the fishery stock is deemed to be healthy. If environmental regulations and pollution restrictions are telltale signs of postmaterialist values, arguments to remain free from those restrictions must be seen as advocating for either material self-interest or special-status equality claims rather than for protecting the environmental resource. In light of our application of Inglehart's framework, we decided to focus our attention on a subset of the 14 fishing cases handed down between 1973 and 2010 because several of them constitute landmark cases that established a new framework for analysing future indigenous claims in light of the rights they secured under s. 35(1) of the Constitution Act, 1982.[1]

There were only three fishing cases handed down in the environmental area under the Laskin/Dickson tenure, although the Dickson Court's ruling in *R. v. Sparrow*, [1990] 1 S.C.R. 1075 (hereafter *Sparrow*) remains a seminal ruling in this area. *Sparrow's* impact was profound because it established a new approach, one that was more sympathetic to First Nation claims based on s. 35(1) of the Constitution Act, 1982, even though it gave top billing to conservation needs. Yet to understand the significance of the Dickson Court's approach to the claims in *Sparrow*, it is important to first review the Laskin Court's rulings in a pair of early cases in which it took a pro-environmental stance, rejecting indigenous fishing claims, and provided a historical overview of the Canadian government's approach to First Nation claims to date (*Jack et al. v. The Queen*, [1980] 1 S.C.R. 294 and *Elk v. The Queen*, [1980] 2 S.C.R. 166).

In *Jack et al. v. The Queen*, [1980] 1 S.C.R. 294, the Laskin Court addressed the overarching legal issue of whether Article 13 of the Terms of Union between British Columbia and Canada afforded protection to eight individuals who had been fishing for salmon or in possession of salmon during a prohibited fishing period. Although they had been fishing for food without a permit during a prohibited period, they argued that the Terms of Union prevented Parliament from enacting legislation that could prohibit them from fishing in the river (*Jack et al. v. The Queen*, [1980] 1 S.C.R. 294, at 300). What was unique about this case was that the First Nation individuals did not rely on a treaty or indigenous land title to back their claim, but rather based their right

1 S. 35(1) of the Constitution Act, 1982 states that "the existing aboriginal and treaty rights of the aboriginal peoples of Canada are hereby recognized and affirmed."

on Article 13 of the Terms of Union, which sanctified under the British North America Act a pre-Confederation policy in British Columbia that gave them priority in the fishery.

Chief Justice Laskin, writing for eight of the nine members of the court, ruled that regardless of what British Columbia had done in the pre-Confederation period concerning First Nation food-fishing rights in its rivers and off its coasts, there did not seem to be any statutory provision after the province joined the Union to support the First Nation claim. More important, Chief Justice Laskin concluded that even if fishing rights could be established in the law, if governmental restrictions under the Fisheries Act were aimed at conservation purposes, which the facts of the case established, they superseded any fishing rights that indigenous peoples might advance (*Jack et al. v. The Queen*, [1980] 1 S.C.R. 294, at 299–300). The majority rationale in this seminal fishing rights case provided a classic illustration of the modern court's early desire to promote postmaterialistic values in the environmental area. The Laskin Court's pro-environmental position even flew in the face of the apparently minor infringements by First Nation individuals. In short, societal interests in conservation trumped any First Nation claim to primacy over the fishery for subsistence purposes.

Although Justice Dickson agreed with Chief Justice Laskin's conservation-based conclusion, he criticized the majority's failure to recognize that Article 13 of the Terms of Union incorporated distinctive protections to indigenous peoples in the fisheries in the pre-Confederation period. According to Justice Dickson, since Article 13 required Parliament to adopt a policy "as liberal as that pursued by the British Columbia Government prior to the Union," he concluded that indigenous preference in the fishery area should remain intact. Yet Justice Dickson acknowledged that Article 13 gave Parliament the flexibility to impose restrictions on those fishing rights, which it had increasingly done between 1888 and 1917 (*Jack et al. v. The Queen*, [1980] 1 S.C.R. 294, at 311–12). More important, he argued that First Nations' fishing priority must be tempered in light of the emergence of commercial and sport fishing and the growing legislative concern to conserve scarce resources. As such, he concluded that a hierarchy should be constructed in the fishery area that gave top priority to conservation needs, followed by distinct First Nation fishing rights, while local commercial and sport fishing interests came last (*Jack et al. v. The Queen*, [1980] 1 S.C.R. 294, at 312). Even though Justice Dickson's position was *not* adopted in this case, his opinion became the foundation of the court's landmark ruling in *Sparrow*, [1990] 1 S.C.R. 1075.

One year later, in *Elk v. The Queen*, [1980] 2 S.C.R. 166, the Laskin Court handed down another brief pro-environmental ruling that contained nearly identical factual circumstances as those found in *Jack et al. v. The Queen*, [1980] 1 S.C.R. 294. In this case, a First Nation individual had been caught fishing during a prohibited period under the Fisheries Act, and the question was whether the federal statute took precedence over an agreement struck between the federal government and the province of Manitoba that allowed First Nations to trap and fish for food all year round on unoccupied Crown lands for subsistence purposes. The court summarily held that its prior ruling in *Daniels v. White and The Queen*, [1968] S.C.R. 517 dictated that the agreement under the Manitoba Natural Resources Act applied only to provincial laws and thus the appellant was not exempt from compliance with the federal law at issue (*Elk v. The Queen*, [1980] 2 S.C.R. 166, at 167–8). In the end, the *Jack* and *Elk* decisions contained pro-environmental language that upheld laws designed to conserve fisheries from overuse, even in the face of First Nation individuals fishing for subsistence purposes.

Ten years later, in *Sparrow*, [1990] 1 S.C.R. 1075, the Dickson Court for the first time took a different tactical approach to First Nation fishing rights in the course of examining the scope and parameters of rights secured under s. 35(1) of the Constitution Act, 1982. Similar to the previous two cases, the appellant had been found violating a provision of the Fisheries Act, only this time, the appellant had been catching fish with a longer drift net than allowed under the Musqueam food-fishing licence (*Sparrow*, [1990] 1 S.C.R. 1075, at 1083). The underlying constitutional question was whether the net-length licensing restrictions dictated by the federal Fisheries Act violated s. 35(1), which specifies, "The existing aboriginal and treaty rights of the aboriginal peoples of Canada are hereby recognized and affirmed" (ibid.).

Chief Justice Dickson and Justice La Forest, writing for the court, stated that they would examine the legal question by first assessing "existing aboriginal rights" and the scope of the Musqueam right to fish, followed by an analysis of how to evaluate violations under s. 35(1) of the Constitution Act, 1982. In the first part of their analysis, they concluded that "existing aboriginal rights" encompassed rights that were in place when the act was adopted in 1982, but did not revive rights that had already been extinguished (*Sparrow*, [1990] 1 S.C.R. 1075, at 1091–3). They also concluded that the trial judge had correctly determined that the appellant had a right to fish in the Fraser River, where his ancestors had fished for food since ancient times. Chief Justice Dickson and Justice La Forest went on to determine that the Crown had failed to show that this right had been extinguished by the regulations under the Fisheries Act because there was no "clear and plain" intention by Parliament to extinguish the band's right to fish (*Sparrow*, [1990] 1 S.C.R. 1075, at 1099). Rather, the permits and other regulations under the Fisheries Act were simply aimed at trying to control the fishery (*Sparrow*, [1990] 1 S.C.R. 1075, at 1101).

In the next phase of their analysis, Chief Justice Dickson and Justice La Forest examined the scope of s. 35(1) of the Constitution Act, 1982 and its impact on the power of the federal government to regulate indigenous peoples. Since the provision was the culmination of a long and difficult struggle to secure constitutional recognition for indigenous rights, and given the particular nature of s. 35(1) itself, they concluded that it should be given a broad, liberal, and purposive interpretation based on the principle that the Crown owed a fiduciary duty to indigenous peoples (*Sparrow,* [1990] 1 S.C.R. 1075, at 1097–9). They went on to conclude that the government bore the burden of meeting the "justification test" before it could legitimately infringe indigenous rights protected under s. 35(1). Chief Justice Dickson argued that this heightened level of scrutiny, or new approach, was necessary to ensure that the Crown put forth a valid legislative objective for infringement that was in keeping with the unique relationship between the Crown and indigenous peoples enshrined in the constitutional scheme (*Sparrow*, [1990] 1 S.C.R. 1075, at 1109–10).

Chief Justice Dickson and Justice La Forest went on to explain that in the first stage of s 35(1) analysis, one must determine whether the legislation in question interfered with an existing indigenous right on its face. According to Chief Justice Dickson, the onus lay on those challenging the prohibition to show that a "prima facie interference" existed or that the purpose or effect of the restriction adversely infringed an indigenous right (*Sparrow*, [1990] 1 S.C.R. 1075, at 1111). In the case at hand, the Crown had to show that Parliament was not trying to advance an unconstitutional objective, such as giving more fishing resources to non-native sporting groups than the Musqueam Band (*Sparrow*, [1990] 1 S.C.R. 1075, at 1121). If a valid legislative objective was shown, the Crown must then demonstrate a link between the justifications put forth and the allocation of priorities recognized in the fishery. Given the special trust relationship that the Crown had with indigenous peoples, the court should follow the order of priority that Chief Justice Dickson had articulated in *Jack et al. v. The Queen*, [1980] 1 S.C.R. 294, where conservation would be given top priority, followed by First Nation rights to fish, and, last, non-native commercial and sport fishing (*Sparrow*, [1990] 1 S.C.R. 1075, at 1115).

In assessing the link in the case at hand, the Crown needed to show that the net-length restriction was a necessary and reasonable conservation measure in the Fraser River. Chief Justice Dickson concluded that although the trial judge had acknowledged that some of the evidence suggested that the net-length restriction was not a necessary conservation measure and that it would impose undue hardship on the Musqueam Band's food-fishing needs, given the lack of sufficient findings of fact, the Supreme Court ordered a retrial under the new tests established in the ruling (*Sparrow*, [1990] 1 S.C.R. 1075, at 1120–1). According to Chief Justice Dickson and Justice La Forest, other questions that courts could consider at the justification stage included whether the indigenous right had been infringed as little as possible to achieve the desired results and whether indigenous groups had been consulted regarding the conservation measures being implemented or given fair compensation in warranted situations (*Sparrow*, [1990] 1 S.C.R. 1075, at 1119). Since this was the court's first articulation of the test to be used in examining the scope and parameters of First Nation rights under the Constitution, it was bound to be refined and clarified in subsequent fishing cases it handed down.

The court's ruling in *Sparrow* is a postmaterialist one that favours the protection of the environment because Chief Justice Dickson and Justice La Forest recognized that if there was a conflict of interests in the fishery, top priority should be given to reasonable conservation measures, while the rights of First Nations to fish for food were second on the list. Yet one should note that since the Supreme Court found that the government's net-length restriction on the fishing licence violated the Constitution, the case was sent back down to the trial court for further analysis. Thus, the Musqueam Band had a second opportunity to convince the trial judge that his earlier ruling should not stand. More important, the fact that the Dickson Court breathed strong life into s. 35(1) of the Constitution Act, 1982 also indicated that it was committed to protecting indigenous rights enshrined in the Constitution. Even so, scholars such as Asch and Macklem (1991, 517) justifiably note that *Sparrow* was limited in scope because it failed to embrace an "inherent theory of aboriginal right," which is necessary in ensuring First Nation forms of self-government and protection from encroachment by the state. Such an approach would foster greater political and substantive equality for First Nation peoples.

First Nation Fishing Cases – Landmark Decisions of the Lamer Court

If the *Jack, Elk,* and *Sparrow* cases spawned a trickle of individuals arguing for the right to fish, the floodgates opened during the Lamer Court period, with the Canadian court hearing nine new fishing rights cases. While four of those cases were handed down in a pro-environmental direction, five resulted in materialistic rulings that allowed indigenous peoples to fish for food for subsistence and traditional purposes. Regardless of the outcomes, our interest is in the language that members of the court used to justify their opinions. Among the cases heard was a trilogy of landmark decisions handed down in 1996 that dealt with the sale of fish. The pivotal ruling in that trilogy was *Van Der Peet v. The Queen,* [1996] 2 S.C.R. 507 (hereafter *Van Der Peet*), in which the court further clarified the prongs of the *Sparrow* test and also detailed the nature of indigenous rights protected under the Constitution. Although the Dickson Court recognized that indigenous rights had a "unique" status in *Sparrow,* it was not until the *Van Der Peet* ruling that the Lamer Court articulated the specific rights that were protected under the s. 35(1) provision.

In this case, the appellant was charged for selling 10 salmon contrary to the Fisheries Act and British Columbia Fishery (General) Regulations, and the constitutional question was whether s. 35(1) protected the Sto:lo Band's right to fish, which included the right to sell, trade, and barter fish (*Van Der Peet,* [1996] 2 S.C.R. 507, at 527). Chief Justice Lamer, writing for a seven-member majority, articulated that the *Sparrow* test had four distinct prongs determining (1) whether the appellant actions constituted an indigenous right, (2) whether that right had been extinguished, (3) whether the Crown had infringed the right, and (4) whether the infringement was justified (*Van Der Peet,* [1996] 2 S.C.R. 507, at 526).

Chief Justice Lamer began his analysis by claiming that the reason indigenous rights were given constitutional status was because indigenous peoples were living in distinctive communities that adhered to their own practices and traditions when the Europeans arrived on the continent and, thus, the purpose of the provision was to reconcile their rights with the "sovereignty of the Crown" (*Van Der Peet*, [1996] 2 S.C.R. 507, at 539). Given this foundation, Chief Justice Lamer argued that before an activity could be identified as an indigenous right under s. 35(1), it must constitute "an element of a practice, custom or tradition integral to the distinctive culture of the indigenous group claiming the right," which he labelled the "integral to a distinctive culture" test (*Van Der Peet*, [1996] 2 S.C.R. 507, at 549). For a practice to be integral to the distinctive culture, the claimant must demonstrate that the activity was of "central significance" to the indigenous society or "made the society distinctive," not that it was merely "an aspect" or simply "took place" or was "occasional" in the indigenous society (*Van Der Peet*, [1996] 2 S.C.R. 507, at 553). Although he argued that a practice could evolve over time, Chief Justice Lamer concluded that courts should consider only those practices, customs, and traditions that had roots that could be traced to the pre-contact period and could be characterized as a natural evolution of pre-contact activity (*Van Der Peet*, [1996] 2 S.C.R. 507, at 555). Three other factors that courts must consider when applying the integral-to-a-distinctive-culture test were that (1) they should focus on the "particular" indigenous group making the claimed right, instead of claims made on a "general basis"; (2) the practice, custom, or tradition at issue had independent significance; and (3) the practice, custom, or tradition constituted a distinguishing characteristic of the indigenous community in question (*Van Der Peet*, [1996] 2 S.C.R. 507, at 559–60).

When Chief Justice Lamer applied this test to the case at hand, he concluded that the precise claim made by the appellant was that she had an indigenous right to exchange fish for money because it was an integral part of the Sto:lo culture. However, the evidence indicated that her claim was unfounded because the exchange of fish in the Sto:lo culture before European contact did not constitute a central part of their culture. Since they were unable to preserve fish for long periods of time, the evidence also suggested that the exchange of salmon had been only to sell surplus food and that "no regularized trade system" had existed at the time of European contact (*Van Der Peet*, [1996] 2 S.C.R. 507, at 568–71). In light of those findings, Chief Justice Lamer concluded that the remaining three prongs of the *Sparrow* test dealing with extinguishment, infringement, or justification for violation of this right did not need to be addressed (*Van Der Peet*, [1996] 2 S.C.R. 507, at 571). Readers should note that the language and emphasis in *Van Der Peet* focuses on the analysis of evidence tied to cultural traditions. The rejection of these arguments by Chief Justice Lamer can be seen as a denial of traditional, materialistic values in favour of a postmaterialist, pro-environmental decision.

In the two companion cases to *Van Der Peet*, the court applied the same test, but reached opposite conclusions regarding whether a particular practice constituted an indigenous right under the Constitution. While the Lamer Court concluded that exchange of fish by the Sheshaht and Opetchesaht people was not sufficient to qualify as a protected indigenous right in *N.T.C. Smokehouse*, [1996] 2 S.C.R. 672, it ruled that the right had been sufficiently established in *R. v. Gladstone*, [1996] 2 S.C.R. 723 (hereafter *Gladstone*). Specifically, in *N.T.C. Smokehouse*, [1996] 2 S.C.R. 672, the court determined that the evidence supported the trial judge's findings that the exchange of fish for money or other goods by the Sheshaht and Opetchesaht before European contact had been "few and far between." Although exchange of fish had occurred at ceremonial occasions and potlatches, since this activity was only incidental to these special events, it did not constitute a sufficiently central aspect of these peoples' distinctive culture to justify protection under s. 35(1). Given this finding, the appellant's claim of an indigenous right to fish on a commercial basis must be rejected as well (*N.T.C. Smokehouse*, [1996] 2 S.C.R. 672, at 689–90). Readers should note that the *N.T.C. Smokehouse* case featured the sale of more than 119,000 pounds of salmon, so there were clear materialist interests at play in the case, and those interests lost out to a postmaterialist stance.

In *Gladstone*, [1996] 2 S.C.R. 723, the Lamer Court majority ruled that, unlike the other two cases, there was ample evidence showing that, before contact, the Heiltsuk people had engaged in extensive trading of herring spawn on kelp for money or goods with other First Nations along the coast of British Columbia. The evidence also revealed that this extensive history of commercial activity was a defining feature of this indigenous culture, one that had continued to the present day and thus deserved constitutional protection (*Gladstone*, [1996] 2 S.C.R. 723, at 745–7). Since the appellants had demonstrated that the Heiltsuk had an indigenous right to commercially trade herring spawn on kelp, the court went on to apply the remaining three prongs of the *Sparrow* test, determining whether the right had been extinguished, whether it had been infringed by government, and whether the restrictions were justified in the case at hand. The Lamer majority determined that none of the regulations showed that the Crown had extinguished the Heiltsuk Band's right, but that the regulatory scheme had the effect of impinging that right because it limited the band's ability to commercially harvest and sell herring spawn on kelp (*Gladstone*, [1996] 2 S.C.R. 723, at 750–5, 761–2). After reaching this conclusion, the court sent the case back to the trial court to assess whether the government had been justified in limiting the Heiltsuk Band's right to commercial marketing of herring spawn (*Gladstone*, [1996] 2 S.C.R. 723, at 776–9).

This trilogy of cases involving the right to sell fish fostered a good deal of disagreement within the Lamer Court. Both Justices L'Heureux-Dubé and McLachlin dissented in the first two cases because they argued that the time-period test that the Lamer majority had developed to identify existing indigenous rights was unduly restrictive and difficult for indigenous peoples to meet. Both justices thought that the Lamer Court majority had unnecessarily frozen indigenous rights to a pre-contact period, placing an undue burden on indigenous claimants and creating an inconsistent framework at odds with the liberal, interpretive approach required under the *Sparrow* test (*Van Der Peet*, [1996] 2 S.C.R. 507, at 599). Justice McLachlin indicated that the majority's deterministic approach failed to adequately consider that the modern exercise of a right may be vastly different from the traditional exercise of it (*Van Der Peet*, [1996] 2 S.C.R. 507, at 636). In light of these concerns, each of these justices argued for alternative tests that would provide a more liberal and generous interpretation of existing indigenous rights. The pointed criticisms that these two justices levelled at the majority, along with the more lenient tests that they established, highlight the fact that the Lamer Court majority took a decisively restrictive and limited approach to recognizing constitutionally protected indigenous rights. In their view, the majority did not provide the liberal and generous interpretation of indigenous rights that had been promised by the Dickson Court in *Sparrow*.

From the vantage point of postmaterialist thinking, the majority of the Lamer Court was less willing than the two female dissenters to breathe strong life into the s. 35(1) provision, indicating that the majority of the Court was more willing to uphold environmental regulations at the expense of First Nations' historical rights to fish. The trilogy of cases from 1996 exposed the materialist-postmaterialist tensions of managing a fishery in a stark manner. Most of the Lamer Court justices were willing to recognize indigenous rights only up to a point, and for them, significant historical evidence from a pre-contact period was necessary, and even then, First Nations might have their privileged materialist claims to fishing and the sale of fish restricted if the government provided reasonable justifications. Justices L'Heureux-Dubé and

McLachlin, writing in dissent in the first two cases in the trilogy, were much more willing to sacrifice conservation interests to the historical and evolving fishing and commercial practices of First Nations. As such, their writings reveal hallmark traits of materialist values in support of the traditional cultural practices that were being advocated by a historically marginalized group. But from another perspective, their position can be seen as promoting the equal standing of First Nations, so their decision reflects both a materialist and an equality-oriented value position.

Although the Lamer Court provided a seemingly narrow interpretation of the type of indigenous rights that would be recognized under s. 35(1) in *Van Der Peet*, the application of the time-period test still had the potential of securing significant fishing rights for First Nation individuals. This is a point that is driven home in *Marshall*, [1999] 3 S.C.R. 456. Here the Lamer Court addressed whether a Mi'kmaq individual, who had caught and sold over 400 pounds of eel during a prohibited period without a licence, was exempt from compliance with federal fishery regulations because of a Treaty of Peace and Friendship that had been signed by the Mi'kmaq and the British in 1760 (*Marshall*, [1999] 3 S.C.R. 456, at 467). Justice Binnie, writing for a five-member majority, ruled in favour of Donald Marshall because both the written and the oral historical evidence revealed that the Mi'kmaq had sustained themselves through hunting, fishing, and gathering activities, along with trading, since before the arrival of the Europeans in the eighteenth century.

There were several features of the case that complicated Justice Binnie's historical analysis, including the fact that the document the trial judge had relied on contained only a portion of the promises made from the oral record and that the trade clause at issue was briefly worded and framed in negative terms. Essentially, the treaty stipulated that the Mi'kmaq would engage in trade of commodities only with managers of truckhouses appointed by the Crown (*Marshall*, [1999] 3 S.C.R. 456, at 468; readers should note that truckhouses were places where First Nation individuals could bring their goods to trade with British representatives). Although the trial judge had ruled that the provision provided the Mi'kmaq with only a limited right to bring products to trade with the British at truckhouses for sustenance purposes, he had concluded that this legal trading entitlement had been subsequently extinguished when truckhouses and this licensing system were abandoned in the 1780s (*Marshall*, [1999] 3 S.C.R. 456, at 469, 479).

After close inspection of the various documents and evidence available, Justice Binnie concluded that even though the trial judge had drawn positive inferences from the restrictive trade clause, it should be read more expansively to include the right to pursue traditional hunting and fishing activities because the Mi'kmaq could not have traded products without first acquiring them and that these were the only commodities at their disposal to trade (*Marshall*, [1999] 3 S.C.R. 456, at 486). He went on to conclude that once the right to hunt, fish, and trade for sustenance had been incorporated into the 1760 treaty, it could not be removed simply because the truckhouses, or "mechanism" for that trade, had disappeared, as the trial judge had suggested (*Marshall*, [1999] 3 S.C.R. 456, at 480, 487). Since the right had not been extinguished before 1982, Justice Binnie concluded that it could be restricted only if the regulations could be justified by the Crown under a conservation rationale (*Marshall*, [1999] 3 S.C.R. 456, at 496). When the Crown expressed concerns that recognizing a right to fish and hunt for trade purposes, rather than the more narrowly restricted food purposes, could foster an *extreme exploitation of scarce resources*, Justice Binnie concluded that the treaty referenced only securing "necessaries," which translated to the modern equivalent of a moderate livelihood, and not, as the Crown suggested, the right to fish and hunt and trade for the vast accumulation of wealth (*Marshall*, [1999] 3 S.C.R. 456, at 501–2). Since the Crown failed to provide a reasonable justification for the licensing regulations or the closed-season restriction, the appellant was acquitted and had the right to continue his eel fishing and trade operation under the treaty (*Marshall*, [1999] 3 S.C.R. 456, at 505–6).

The Lamer Court's decision in *Marshall* gave an expansive and generous interpretation of the rights secured by the Mi'kmaq in the brief trading clause found in a 1760 treaty. Indeed, the ruling was so favourable to the Mi'kmaq that one eminent commentator claimed, "It seemed to confer an indigenous treaty right over the commercial exploitation of most of the natural resources of Nova Scotia and New Brunswick, where truckhouse clauses were contained in Indian treaties of peace and friendship" (Hogg 2011, s. 28-39). According to Harris (2010, 124), the *Marshall* ruling sparked intense conflict between native and non-native communities, and extensive media criticism. Concern about the potentially sweeping materialist impact of the *Marshall* decision and the threat of escalating violence prompted one of the interveners in the suit, the West Nova Fishermen's Coalition, to file a motion for a rehearing and stay in the judgment of the case. In *R. v. Marshall*, [1999] 3 S.C.R. 533

(hereafter *Marshall II*), the court denied the rehearing and concluded that the coalition had misconstrued the scope of the majority judgment in the earlier case to be more expansive than the court had intended.

Although the Lamer Court backed its earlier ruling, it tried to clarify it by stipulating that the failure of the Crown to justify the closed season and licensing restrictions in *Marshall I* did not mean that these types of restrictions could *never* be imposed to limit the commercial fishing rights of the Mi'kmaq in the future, but rather that the court would assess such regulations based on the strength of the justification, which could vary depending on factors such as the resource, species, and community at issue (*Marshall II*, [1999] 3 S.C.R. 533, at 534–5). Moreover, the court concluded that other societal objectives, such as economic and regional fairness and the historical reliance on the fishery by other constituency groups, could constitute reasonable restrictions on the Mi'kmaq treaty rights (ibid.). According to Harris (2010, 124), the Mi'kmaq felt betrayed by the *Marshall II* decision, invoking even more reasons to distrust the Canadian government and its notion of the rule of law. The implication of *Marshall II* was that the court might be more amenable to pro-environmental arguments, depending on the issue at stake.

First Nation Fishing Cases – Landmark Decisions of the McLachlin Court

Despite the Lamer Court's effort to try to clarify its earlier ruling, the tensions raised in *Marshall* would continue during the early McLachlin Court tenure. The Mi'kmaq of Nova Scotia and New Brunswick tried to stretch the fabric of the *Marshall I* ruling by subsequently engaging in commercial logging activities on Crown land without first securing provincial authorization (*R. v. Marshall*, [2005] 2 S.C.R. 221, at 222, hereafter *Marshall III*). Although the Mi'kmaq argued that the trading clauses in the various treaties of 1760 and 1761 had entitled them to engage in such activities, the McLachlin Court did not buy that argument. It concluded that these clauses were principles aimed at granting indigenous peoples the "right to trade in traditional products," which might legitimately evolve into modern eel fishing and trading, as illustrated in *Marshall I*. However, commercial logging could not be traced to any real pre-contact trading activity. Moreover, since the right to harvest resources was only ancillary to, or a by-product of, the secured right to trade in traditional products, it did not translate into granting the

Mi'kmaq unfettered permission to cut or harvest any natural resources without a licence (*Marshall III*, [2005] 2 S.C.R. 221, at 223; see also Hogg 2011, s. 28-39).

The three *Marshall* cases collectively highlight the practical difficulties that can occur when a liberal, expansive reading of treaty rights is pushed to the extremes. First Nations might take an extreme materialist position in pursuit of their economic interests, using the argument of historical treaty rights as their justification. The *Marshall* cases reflect the clear tension between the conservation of scarce resource rights on the one hand and the danger of economic exploitation on the other hand.

Moving beyond the Mi'kmaq battles over resources, the first 10 years of the McLachlin Court featured five cases relating to fishing rights. Unlike the bulk of cases heard by the Lamer Court in this area, which largely pitted First Nation individuals who sought the right to fish for food against the government's interest in protecting environmental resources, the McLachlin Court's cases largely addressed fishing rights in the context of larger First Nation claims, which sought to maintain traditional ways of life on reserve in the face of government sponsorship of development projects. In the two cases discussed below, the First Nation groups advanced the pro-environmental argument, while the government sought to confiscate reserve lands to promote economic development.

Two of the leading cases in this area are *Mikisew Cree First Nation v. Canada (Minister of Canadian Heritage)*, [2005] 3 S.C.R. 388 and *Beckman v. Little Salmon/Carmacks First Nation*, [2010] 3 S.C.R. 103 (hereafter *Mikisew Cree First Nation* and *Beckman*). The dispute in the *Mikisew* case emanated from a post-Confederation treaty that had been signed in 1899, whereby the First Nation had surrendered a tract of land (approaching the size of British Columbia, located in northern Alberta, British Columbia, and Saskatchewan, along with a southern portion of the Northwest Territories) in exchange for reserve land and various benefits, including the right to continue its traditional fishing, hunting, and trapping lifestyle on the surrendered lands (*Mikisew Cree First Nation*, [2005] 3 S.C.R. 388, at 393–4). However, the treaty had also stipulated that the government might have to "take up" portions of the land at various times for "other purposes" (*Mikisew Cree First Nation*, [2005] 3 S.C.R. 388, at 394). In 2002, the Minister of Canadian Heritage approved the construction of a winter road for transportation purposes through the middle of the Mikisew reserve without first consulting the First Nation. Although

Parks Canada, acting on behalf of the minister, altered the road to track along the border of the reserve after the Mikisew had sent a formal complaint, it failed to confer with the First Nation regarding the altered path of the road (*Mikisew Cree First Nation*, [2005] 3 S.C.R. 388, at 396–7).

The principal legal question in the case was whether the Crown had had a duty to consult the Mikisew and, if so, whether that duty had been met. Justice Binnie, writing for the court, ruled that the Crown *had* had a duty to consult the Mikisew before developing its road plans and that the Crown had so mismanaged the project that its efforts had gone a long way to further undermine relations between the Mikisew and non-natives. According to Justice Binnie, the duty to consult had been triggered because building a road along the border of the Mikisew reserve would have a clear impact on the hunting and trapping area covered by the road. However, the duty to consult under the treaty was at a lower threshold because the Crown was building only a "minor winter road" and the treaty had recognized that the Crown might "take up" surrendered land for "other purposes," which might include transportation (*Mikisew Cree First Nation*, [2005] 3 S.C.R. 388, at 406–7, 418).

In the last part of his ruling, Justice Binnie argued that a procedural duty to consult found at the lower end of the spectrum required, at a minimum, that the Crown provide notice to the Mikisew and directly consult with them. Moreover, that consultation should include providing information about the project, discussing potential adverse impacts on Mikisew interests, soliciting and listening carefully to their concerns, and trying to minimize the impact on their treaty rights (*Mikisew Cree First Nation*, [2005] 3 S.C.R. 388, at 421). In the end, Justice Binnie concluded that the Crown had failed to meet this lower duty because the government had acted unilaterally when it decided to move the road in the middle of the project. Moreover, it had not engaged in a meaningful consultation with the Mikisew Cree or tried to substantially address their concerns (*Mikisew Cree First Nation*, [2005] 3 S.C.R. 388, at 421). Seen in this light, the Mikisew case represents a postmaterialist victory for the Mikisew Cree nation and their progeny.

When the McLachlin Court addressed this same legal question five years later in *Beckman*, [2010] 3 S.C.R. 103, Justice Binnie expanded on the "duty to consult" principle but reached the opposite conclusion when applying it to the treaty negotiated between the Crown and the Little Salmon/Carmacks First Nation (LSCFN) in 1997. The dispute arose after the Yukon government approved a large agricultural land grant to a non-native individual. First Nation individuals opposed the decision, claiming that they had treaty rights to access the property for fishing, hunting, and trapping purposes. Like the *Mikisew Cree First Nation* case, the treaty stipulated that the Crown might need to confiscate land at various times for other purposes, such as agriculture (*Beckman*, [2010] 3 S.C.R. 103, at 116). The LSCFN claimed that the land grant should be overturned because the Crown had not followed proper consultation procedures and had failed to address its concerns. The Crown, in turn, argued that the treaty did not require a duty to consult in a land grant bequest.

Justice Binnie ruled that the Crown owed a duty to consult the LSCFN because the agricultural land grant would adversely affect the ability of the First Nation to fish and hunt for wildlife on a substantial tract of land that it had access to under the terms of the treaty. What distinguished this treaty from the one in the *Mikisew Cree First Nation* case is that it was far more precise and provided detailed guidelines regarding the consulting procedures that must be followed. The treaty set out a minimal consultation duty that entailed virtually the same elements that had been articulated in the *Mikisew Cree First Nation* case – namely, providing proper notice to the affected party, allowing a sufficient amount of time to prepare and present comments, and ensuring "full and fair consideration" of the affected party's views before a decision was made (*Beckman*, [2010] 3 S.C.R. 103, at 142). Ultimately, Justice Binnie concluded that the Yukon government had met its duty because the First Nation had acknowledged that it had received proper notice and information about the proposed land grant application. Moreover, it had been able to articulate its objections before the meeting of the reviewing board. Last, the objections and comments by those who had attended the meeting had been considered by the representative of the Crown before he had made the decision to approve the land grant. The upshot of the decision was that the LSCFN had been given adequate opportunities to express its environmental objections to the land grant. As a result, the case represented a materialist victory for the litigant who was seeking to farm the land in question.

Collectively, the two McLachlin Court decisions outlining a Crown duty to consult regarding development projects that might have an impact on First Nation land mimic the earlier rulings discussed by the Lamer Court in the energy area. The "duty to consult" cases feature a postmaterialist thread that is similar to the cases endorsing the practice of environmental impact reviews. Both approaches place a necessary environmental check on development projects before they take place.

In cases that encroach on First Nation interests, the government has a duty to consult with First Nation representatives about the impact that any development will have on environmental resources and minimize the impact on reserve lands and treaty rights. Such an approach would not have been thinkable in the pre–Second World War period.

The sweep of fishing rights cases across four decades reveals a classic materialist-postmaterialist tension, and early cases sketched out a largely postmaterialist position that recognized conservation interests at the top of the hierarchy, followed by First Nation claims to fishing rights, and finally by other commercial and sport fishing interests. While that hierarchy has remained consistent in the justices' opinions, the unique status of First Nation peoples has led the court to overturn some wildlife restrictions if they infringe on a distinctive activity allowed under treaty rights that existed before European contact in the 1700s. The application of these history-based tests places a tough burden on First Nation groups to advocate for their unique materialist claims, but some striking victories have been recognized under the Lamer Court, such as *Marshall* and *Gladstone*. These less frequent materialist wins make sense given the need to show that a fishing activity was integral to a distinctive culture of First Nation life. As a result, in the majority of fishing rights cases, the language and outcomes of the rulings have tended to fall on the pro-environmental, postmaterialist side of the values spectrum.

When the language in landmark environmental opinions is considered holistically, it presents a complex pattern of the development of postmaterialist thought in the Supreme Court of Canada. The pollution cases present some of the strongest evidence of consistently growing support within the court for the government's power to punish polluters. Whereas early rulings of the Laskin and Dickson Courts considered these issues through the lens of federal-provincial power disputes over the right to regulate polluters, by the 2000s, the language of the McLachlin Court justices was endorsing the need for all levels of government to regulate pollution concerns, and justices were turning to international legal doctrine to give voice to postmaterialist arguments. The handful of energy cases presents a more materialist language, although the tone of the *Oldman River* ruling carries some of the best evidence to date justifying the need for environmental assessments as part of the regimen of environmental protection measures. While several of the other energy cases favoured energy production, the language in the opinions continued to embrace the need for environmental review and the duty to consult with First Nations about significant environmental impacts. There is an underlying current of postmaterialist language throughout these cases.

The landmark First Nation fishing cases also present a complex mosaic. As a general principle, early rulings like *Jack, Elk,* and *Sparrow* helped establish a clear postmaterialist hierarchy of thought within the court. Where environmental laws seemed reasonable, the justices decided that conservation interests deserved top billing, followed by the unique interests of the First Nations (if their practices traced back to the pre-contact period), then followed by other commercial and sport fishing interests. In cases like *Marshall* and *Gladstone,* those historical arguments won the day, and indigenous peoples were given materialist victories that trumped conservation laws. Yet by 2005, the exuberance of the Mi'kmaq to use the court's constitutional principles to its advantage had resulted in a postmaterialist ruling, with the McLachlin Court endorsing governmental efforts to halt logging by the Mi'kmaq in Nova Scotia. As noted earlier, the court's jurisprudence in this area of law established a test that sets a very high standard for First Nations to document trading practices, central to their existence, that can be traced back to the pre-colonial period.

Since the time period covered by our study, the McLachlin Court has taken a major step towards repairing the country's relationship with First Nations, especially with its ruling in *Tsilhqot'in Nation v. British Columbia,* [2014] 2 S.C.R. 256. In this case, the court issued a strong, liberal decision recognizing indigenous title to a substantial tract of land in British Columbia. The ruling represents a historic movement towards reconciliation and constitutes a "landmark case in the common law doctrine of aboriginal title" (Nichols 2015, 693). It has been described as having "ground shifting" implications and setting a "new world standard" for indigenous law (Borrows 2015, 704). In short, the McLachlin Court established a broad, generous view of indigenous territorial rights. The ruling allows the Tsilhqot'in to manage their own lands and prevent environmental degradation and other misuses by the Crown (Borrows 2015, 739). Having said that, Borrows notes that reconciliation with First Nations still has a long way to go because the Crown still possesses underlying title and retains paramount sovereignty over the land (Borrows 2015, 740–1). This decision, along with others, illustrates that the McLachlin Court has continued to move in a postmaterialist, equality-oriented direction in the area of First Nation rights.

Aside from the clear parallel pattern found in the qualitative analysis of pollution rulings, the results of this chapter are more complex than the empirical results catalogued in the prior chapter. Empirical data gleaned from the logistic models there indicated that a consistent, increasing level of postmaterialist support took place across all the environmental cases decided by the Laskin, Dickson, Lamer, and early McLachlin Courts. That pattern appears to be replicated in the language of the landmark opinions of pollution cases, and the First Nation fishing cases reflect a postmaterialist tendency as early as the 1980s cases of *Jack* and *Elk*. What the qualitative analysis helps uncover is that postmaterialist language began taking root in particular environmental opinions as early as the 1970s and 1980s, resulting in tests that make it fairly difficult for materialist claims to prevail, especially in fishing and pollution cases. What the quantitative analysis helps document is the overall growth of a postmaterialist environmental ethic across the outcomes of all the cases over a 40-year period. Each level of analysis provides a contribution to the development of a pro-environmental narrative and win rates for environmental claims, and the unique perspectives they bring provide ammunition to support not only Inglehart's thesis but also the need for other scholars to take a multifaceted approach to the study of judicial behaviour.

Chapter Four

Postmaterialist Outcomes in Free Expression Disputes

Introduction

Ronald Inglehart's research indicates that post-industrial value changes are not only occurring in the environmental area but also emerging in other quality-of-life issues, such as the realm of individual self-expression (see Inglehart, Nevitte, and Basanez 1996, 53–5; Inglehart 1997, 35; Inglehart and Welzel 2005, 27–31). In his 1990 World Values Survey, Inglehart found that the desire to protect free speech, to give people more say in important government decisions, and more say on their jobs and in their communities collectively, provided some of the strongest-loading response items on a 12-item index of postmaterialism (1997, 242; Inglehart, Nevitte, and Basanez 1996, 53–5). These findings, along with others, suggest that the values of free speech and expression serve as core components of the emerging post-industrial values structure.

The recognition of speech and expression as a fundamental value is inherent in the founding documents of many democratic societies. In the United States, free expression finds its sanctuary in the First Amendment, and in Canada, it is enshrined in s. 2(b) of the Charter of Rights and Freedoms. Although Canada's expansive constitutional protection of free expression is relatively recent, the Supreme Court did hand down a series of rulings well before the Charter's adoption that are worth noting. In the 1938 *Alberta Press* case, the Supreme Court struck down Alberta's attempt to require newspapers to give the government the right to reply to critical coverage (*Reference re Alberta Statutes,* [1938] S.C.R. 100). This ruling was followed by several in the 1950s guaranteeing free expression rights in a series of Quebec civil liberties cases involving Jehovah's Witnesses, starting with *Boucher v. The King,* [1951]

S.C.R. 265 (Baar 1976, 370–1; Berger 1981; Russell 1987, 342; Ostberg 1995, 3; Hogg 2011, s. 34-2). Subsequently, in 1957, the court struck down a provincial law authorizing the padlocking of any home used to advocate communism (*Switzman v. Elbling*, [1957] S.C.R. 285). These rulings emanated from the belief that there was a Bill of Rights implicit in various contours of the British North America Act (Hogg 2011, s. 34-4c; *Reference re Alberta Statutes*, [1938] S.C.R. 100).

In the wake of those rulings, Parliament passed the statutory Canadian Bill of Rights in 1960 that guaranteed citizens many of the same freedoms found in the US. Bill of Rights. However, scholars have noted that the Canadian statutory Bill of Rights had minimal impact on judicial rulings, with the individual rights claimant winning only 5 of the 34 cases decided between 1960 and 1982 (see Russell 1987, 343; Morton, Russell, and Withey 1991, 61–2). In addition, there were no consistent majorities supportive of an expansion of civil liberties and civil rights until the 1980s (Baar 1976, 371; Epp 1998, 168). Given this unique history, it is worth examining whether attitudinal changes have occurred on free speech issues among the mass public and the justices of the Supreme Court of Canada.

Support for the notion of free expression as a key priority in society is something that is easily found in modern Canadian public opinion polls. For example, in the 2011 Canada Election Survey, Canadians were asked to rank the most important governmental priority among four possible selections. While ranking it below economic considerations, a full 31 per cent said that protecting freedom of speech was their top priority. Similar types of questions with different wording were used in 1988, 1992, and 1993, yielding similar levels of support for free expression as a top priority (Johnston et al. 1988, 1995). In the World Values Survey, Inglehart included a similar question, asking respondents on a scale of 1 to 10 to evaluate the freedom they had to make choices (with 10 reflecting a great deal of freedom). In the 2000 wave of the survey, nearly 60 per cent of Canadians gave a score of 8 or higher, and in 2005, that score was virtually identical. Moreover, Inglehart found that postmaterialists were more likely than materialists to give a score of 8 or higher on this question (66 versus 58 per cent) (World Values Survey 2000). This notion is further exemplified by data from a 1987 poll reported by Sniderman et al. (1996, 20), indicating that 98 per cent of Canadians supported freedom of expression in the abstract. Another barometer of Canadian support for free expression is shown in a 2013 cross-national Gallup Poll, in which 87 per cent of Canadians thought the media in their country had a lot of freedom. These findings ranked

Canadians 11th among 132 countries and situated them three places ahead of US respondents (English and Becker 2013). Collectively, these data suggest that support for freedom of expression, a hallmark of post-materialist thinking, has taken root in modern Canadian society.

While support for freedom of expression is an easy call for Canadians in the abstract, support for this value becomes more questionable when it is juxtaposed against protecting people from the harm caused by free expression in specific circumstances. For example, what if an extreme group wants to speak at a public rally? Alternatively, what if a movie theatre wants to show a film depicting sexually explicit material? According to Sniderman et al. (1996, 22, 74), support within the Canadian mass public for free expression eroded to 61 and 48 per cent, respectively, in these situations. This movement points to the tricky problem of confronting free expression in a particular context. Yet it is remarkable that 61 per cent of Canadians are willing to support the rights of extreme groups to hold public rallies, and such a finding would not have occurred in more materialist periods like the 1930s and 1940s. Ironically, Sniderman et al. (1996, 22) found that political and legal elites in Canada were far more likely to support the right of extreme groups to hold public rallies, at 87 and 92 per cent, respectively. This gap between the mass public and elite attitudes points to the importance of examining trends in Supreme Court rulings over time. Since the data imply that a more postmaterialist orientation may have emerged among politicians and lawyers when it comes to free expression claims, it is certainly worth examining whether these types of attitudes actually emerged in the outcomes of free expression cases decided by the Supreme Court.

Critics might argue that any movement in the postmaterialist direction is simply a reflection of the Charter of Rights and Freedoms' impact on the Supreme Court. While we believe that the Charter's very existence is emblematic of a broader postmaterialist mindset coming into bloom in Canada, it is important to note that both materialist and postmaterialist values are embedded in the Charter's language. For example, s. 1 contains language that allows for limits to be imposed on rights and freedoms as long as they are "justified in a free and democratic society." This safeguard allows the court to take a more nuanced position on freedom of expression than in the US context. It can endorse the postmaterialist notion of free speech, while also taking a materialist stance rooted in the desire to prohibit or punish harmful forms of expression or an equality stance that ensures that Canadians are not marginalized by free expression (Hiebert 1996, chap. 4). The duelling language of the Charter suggests that opposing socio-attitudinal forces can influence justices in a free expression case since interested parties can advocate for either an expansive interpretation of free expression or legitimate restrictions to protect society from harm or to promote egalitarian treatment of citizens.

This tension in the Charter points to the importance of tracking who wins and loses in these cases and which value priority (materialist) or which postmaterialist value (freedom or equality) takes precedence over time in the final rulings of the court. Put simply, if the s. 1 analysis results in a postmaterialist, libertarian outcome more often than not, this evidence would support the notion that the court is moving in the most pure, libertarian, postmaterialist direction. Moreover, the confounding problems posed by the duelling Charter language demonstrates the value of assessing the impact of a Charter variable within a larger logistic regression model. In such an empirical examination, researchers can control for the impact of s. 1 analysis as an independent variable and tease out its apparent materialist influence from a host of many other rival explanatory variables in a socio-attitudinal model of decision making.

Readers should be aware that there is a critical difference in Inglehart's postmaterialist value shift thesis when one examines free expression cases as opposed to environmental disputes, and there is inherent complexity in categorizing some of the cases in each area of law. In the environmental area, cases often feature a tension between materialist and postmaterialist value claims in the economic realm. These disputes can pit a company's or individual's interest in developing or harnessing natural resources for exploitative purposes against government or First Nation interests in maintaining the environment in its pristine or natural state for future generations. Yet it is important to acknowledge that some environmental disputes, especially those involving First Nation individuals, have legitimate equality arguments that are advanced on behalf of the litigants.

In contrast, disputes in the free expression area involve tensions in the social rather than the economic sphere. Disputes decided in this area often pit an individual's or group's desire to express its views about an issue or injustice against the government's interest in protecting the community from perceived social or physical harm. Yet free expression cases can also juxtapose the right to free expression against equality concerns, which, Inglehart would acknowledge, feature tensions between two postmaterialist values. While we agree, we contend that there is a continuum, or hierarchy, of postmaterialist values, with freedom occupying the most libertarian end of the continuum, followed closely by equality, while order occupies the furthest, materialist end of the spectrum. We classify equality as occupying a position that is slightly "less pure" in its postmaterialist orientation because it has communitarian elements that advocate for political and social equality at the expense of the absolute right to free expression. Ultimately, Locke (1689), Emerson (1963, 1970), and other theorists would argue that a democracy can exist without equality, albeit not ideally, but it cannot exist for long without freedom of expression among its citizenry.

It is important to understand that we identify the free expression case outcomes as postmaterialist only if they endorse the purest support for individual liberty or free speech, while equality and order concerns are labelled as materialist when juxtaposed against freedom. This means that our coding scheme identifies postmaterialist outcomes in the following way: judicial votes to support free expression claims, to endorse the right to engage in hate speech, to support obscenity, to allow press access to records, to endorse media coverage of trials, to support the right to picket, and to bargain or strike in collective bargaining disputes. Case votes endorsing equality rights at the expense of free expression, along with those suppressing free speech in the name of order, are coded as materialistic.

We recognize that this coding scheme works against our effort to validate Inglehart's theory because it fails to classify some equality case outcomes that embody postmaterialist value judgments, such as votes restricting hate speech that marginalizes various minority groups. Yet we contend that one must always code cases based on the specific value conflicts in a dispute, and when equality concerns are pitted against freedom arguments, we believe that equality is a postmaterialist value slightly less essential to the maintenance of a democratic system. Thus, we characterized the complex obscenity case of *R. v. Butler*, [1992] 1 S.C.R. 452 as a materialistic decision because it upheld restrictions on the dissemination of obscene materials and sexual paraphernalia. We acknowledge that many Canadians would see *Butler* as endorsing the postmaterialist value of treating women equally and the materialistic value of protecting society from harm (*R. v. Butler*, [1992] 1 S.C.R. 452). While we agree with the *Butler* outcome and acknowledge that the case seeks to promote the critical equality rights of women, given the continuum of postmaterialist values we have outlined, unfettered expression constitutes the most libertarian postmaterialist position.

While we acknowledge that equality constitutes a critical postmaterialist value, we have placed it in a *slightly* lower-priority position when it comes into conflict with free speech, given its essential role in maintaining a democratic system. As a result, we coded the court's hate speech decision in *R. v. Keegstra*, [1990] 3 S.C.R. 697 as a materialistic outcome because it is a case that pitted the unfettered right to express hateful views against society's interest in checking the harmful and marginalizing effects of that speech. Once again, we concede that *Keegstra* is a complex decision that in some ways pits two postmaterialist values against each other (equality and freedom) and that the egalitarian outcome is an important societal value worth promoting in the context of hate speech. However, our characterization of the postmaterialist value dimension suggests that the Supreme Court's decision is one that favoured equality and order over freedom (and rightfully so, in our view), and thus, this specific context embodies a case in which the court favoured a more materialistic outcome, given the value priorities being weighed.

In light of this description of our coding scheme, as mentioned earlier, our approach actually works to our disadvantage in validating Inglehart's theory when looking at cases that pit freedom versus equality concerns. Moreover, these cases, while comprising an equality element, are not presented as s. 15 Charter cases; rather, they are identified as s. 2(b) free expression cases, which is why our coding scheme focuses on the centrality of free speech concerns in these disputes. Ultimately, we remain faithful to our reading of traditional democratic theory, which stresses the importance of both liberty and equality, yet recognizes the core principle of freedom as being more central to the maintenance of a democratic political structure. As we have indicated, a democracy can exist with structural inequalities in place, but it cannot exist for long without the free exchange of ideas. In this chapter, we focus on the social tension and the empirical patterns that appear in the outcomes and voting records of the Supreme Court justices in free expression cases decided between 1973 and 2010.

Data and Methods for Descriptive Statistics and Judicial Voting Patterns

The data for this segment of the study, like those in the previous environmental chapter, were drawn from published reasons for judgment in the *Canadian Supreme Court Reports* from 1973 to 2010, and they were included in our analysis if a free expression issue was a central component of a case (N = 85).[1] As mentioned earlier, we decided to study rulings handed down during the 1973–2010 time period because this allows us to chart how the four most recent Canadian courts resolved free expression disputes, which naturally involved a fundamental postmaterialist concern during an era that witnessed the rise of legal mobilization by groups and the addition of the Charter of Rights and Freedoms into the Canadian Constitution. Moreover, it allows us to assess the degree to which Inglehart's shifting postmaterialist values thesis has taken place in the decision-making process of Canadian judicial elites over time in a post-industrial society where democratic principles, such as free expression, remain a principle core value.

Our analysis of the free expression rulings mimics that taken in the environmental area. We begin by providing basic descriptive statistics on 85 cases handed down between 1973 and 2010, such as identifying the types of free expression issues and the percentage of liberal rulings that were handed down in each sub-issue area and under different court tenures, along with an analysis of the different kinds of appellants, respondents, and interveners in these disputes. One should remember that assessing the percentage of postmaterialist rulings across the modern courts and the possible growth in interest group activity constitutes our first two tests of Inglehart's value change thesis. In the second stage of our analysis, we assess the voting patterns of the justices in the free expression area in terms of the percentage of pro–free expression rulings each handed down, their majority and dissent voting activity, and the percentage of times they penned a majority or dissent. As in the environmental chapter, we also provide scatterplots of the percentage of liberal rulings in the free expression area by year of birth across the Laskin, Dickson, Lamer, and McLachlin Courts; this constitutes our third assessment of Inglehart's postmaterialist values change thesis.

1 In the appendix, we provide a full list of the cases included in the study. Although we initially identified 133 cases as having a free expression element, we excluded many of them because they were more readily identified as cases involving religion, press access to records, the right to an interpreter in one's own language, the right to protect confidential sources, voting rights, mobility rights, language claims, and purely free association. However, we did include cases in which free speech and association claims were intertwined in the same dispute, with many of these featuring union claims for the right to collective bargaining. Several press cases were included in the data set as well because they turned on key issues of expression, such as spoken defamation, libel, and the silence or non-silence of reporters. Cases were excluded if they did not feature written reasons for judgment or motions for stays, hearings, and/or legal costs. In all, we included 85 cases in the analysis.

In the last stage of our quantitative analysis, we present three logistic regression analyses to assess the degree to which different case- and judge-level independent variables influence the liberal voting patterns of Canadian Supreme Court justices in free expression cases. As mentioned earlier, assessing judicial voting behaviour using logistic regression analysis provides a more sophisticated test of Inglehart's postmaterialist values thesis than the scatterplot analysis because it allows one to take into consideration possible rival variables that might influence the postmaterialist voting behaviour of the justices. In other words, it allows scholars to assess the impact of each independent variable in the equation, while holding the others constant, to assess the relative impact of each independent variable on the dependent variable in the equation. Overall, we believe that the last set of analyses provides the most comprehensive view of the patterns of judicial behaviour that have taken place on the Canadian Supreme Court in the free expression area over the last four decades. Moreover, the analysis provides the fourth and last quantitative test of the veracity of Inglehart's postmaterialist value shift thesis among legal elites in the free expression area.

Descriptive Statistics and Judicial Voting Patterns

The results found in the first seven tables provide an overview of various descriptive trends that are evident in the free expression cases decided by the Canadian Supreme Court between 1973 and 2010. Table 4.1 indicates that the court heard a range of cases, which fit into three distinct issue categories: free speech, free press, and free association. Since many of the free expression cases heard also featured a criminal charge or required the court to engage in s. 1 analysis under the Charter of Rights and Freedoms, these elements were included as separate categories in the table as well. Although the court heard only 85 distinct cases across the five categories during this period, many of the cases fell into two or more categories; this explains why the number of cases listed across the five categories is larger than the actual number handed down during this period. Not surprisingly, the largest percentage of cases heard was found in the free speech area, which collectively represented over 74 per cent of the docket. The free speech cases, in turn, could be further divided into the categories political speech, commercial advertising, obscenity, and hate speech. Surprisingly, the largest free speech subcategory, obscenity, constituted almost 20 per cent of the cases heard in this area, while at the opposite extreme, hate speech made up only 8 per cent of the free speech docket.

Table 4.1. Canadian Free Expression Cases by Issue Area, 1973–2010

Issue area	Cases (*N* = 85)	
	No.	%
Free speech	**63**	**74.1**
Political speech	13	15.3
Commercial advertising	14	16.5
Obscenity	16	18.8
Hate speech	7	8.2
Free association	**16**	**18.8**
Right to bargain	10	11.8
Right to strike	6	7.1
Free press	**13**	**15.3**
Libel/defamation	6	7.1
Press access to information	7	8.2
Seizure of materials	7	8.2
Fair trial concerns	7	8.2
Criminal cases	**27**	**31.8**
Charter s. 1	**45**	**52.9**

Note: Readers should be careful when interpreting this table. One should not expect that the subcategory totals or counts of cases will equal the total number of cases found in the three larger categories. For example, the free speech subcategories do not add up to the total for that category (63 cases) because several types of free speech cases are omitted from the table, either because they fall into areas of law that are too small to report here (such as solicitation of prostitution) or because they are captured in the free press area (such as defamation cases). In contrast, the sum of cases in the free press subcategories is larger than the total for that category because several of the cases feature more than one category of law. This also explains why the number of cases found in the criminal and Charter areas is so large. In short, criminal and Charter characteristics are featured in many of the cases, whether they deal with free speech, press, or association.

Commercial advertising and political speech were found in the middle, constituting 17 and 15 per cent of the free speech docket, respectively.

The next largest category in the free expression area dealt with cases raising free association claims, which constituted 19 per cent of the cases heard. Since we included only free association cases that also contained a free expression element, it is not surprising that 12 per cent of all cases analysed involved union claims featuring the right to collectively bargain, while the other 7 per cent focused on disputes relating to the workers' right to strike. Cases in the free press area constituted 15 per cent of the free expression docket over the last four decades, with 8 per cent of the cases involving the seizure of materials, access to information, and fair trial concerns, respectively. The free press cases were included in our study to specifically capture libel and slander disputes, which constituted 7 per cent of the free expression docket.

Table 4.1 indicates that over half the cases in the free expression area featured s. 1 analysis, while 32 per cent of them contained a criminal charge. It is not surprising that the Supreme Court engaged in s. 1 analysis in over half the free expression cases in the table, in light of the addition of the Charter of Rights and Freedoms to the Canadian Constitution in 1982. In essence, s. 1 of the Charter provides a built-in textual restriction on substantive guarantees, which allows the government to place "reasonable limits" on individual rights if they can be "demonstrably justified in a free and democratic society." This provision, as Knopff and Morton (1992) noted early on, has become an important element in the court's interpretative framework for resolving Charter cases, including those in the free expression area.

The court grappled with what would constitute reasonable limits on protected rights and liberties in two early cases – namely, *R. v. Big M Drug Mart*, [1985] 1 S.C.R. 295 and *R. v. Oakes*, [1986] 1 S.C.R. 103 – in which it established a two-stage analytical framework for assessing future Charter disputes (Peck 1987, 2). The interpretative approach the court discussed in these two disputes led some scholars to dub this the "Charter Two-Step" (Knopff and Morton 1992, 35). In the first stage of the analytic process, the court must define the scope of the right at issue and determine whether the challenged statute violates a protected Charter right. If so, the court subsequently moves to the second stage of analysis to determine whether it is reasonable to limit the fundamental right to advance other societal values, such as the maintenance of order, security, equality, or individual dignity. The fact that the Charter contains various built-in textual restrictions, such as s. 1, is a unique feature of the Canadian Constitution, and it indicates that Canadians realized that no guarantee deserves absolute protection (Hiebert 1996).

Thus, in the course of balancing competing interests in society, the Supreme Court has the power to restrict expressive guarantees that are violated under the Charter to advance other important community values in society. *Keegstra* represents an example of this interplay of values. In our categorization of cases, it is "scored" as both a criminal case and a s. 1 Charter case (in addition to being labelled a hate speech case; see *R. v. Keegstra*, [1990] 3 S.C.R. 697). In *Keegstra*, the court upheld the Criminal Code restrictions on hate speech because they passed s. 1 analysis and were justifiable in a free and democratic society. Readers should note that these textual limitations on rights found in the Canadian Constitution set it apart from the US Constitution and simultaneously enshrine conflicting value priorities that are central to Inglehart's

Table 4.2. Liberal Rulings in Canadian Free Expression Cases by Broad Issue Area, 1973–2010

Issue area	Cases, no. (*N* = *85*)	Liberal rulings, %
Free speech	63	44.4
Free press	13	30.8
Free association	16	25.0
Criminal case	27	22.2
S. 1 issue	45	48.9

postmaterialist thesis. Indeed, the Charter enshrines contrasting value priorities found at opposite ends of the social values spectrum, with fee expression counterbalanced by the notion that government can sometimes infringe substantive rights and liberties to promote security and maintain order in Canadian society or protect equality interests. We devote more discussion to these themes in chapter 5.

Table 4.2 highlights the pattern of liberal rulings handed down by the Canadian court across the five broad categories of free expression claims between 1973 and 2010. It is not surprising that the lowest level of support for free expression claims came in cases in which criminal charges had also been levelled against the defendant and in which only 22 per cent of the 27 cases heard were handed down in the liberal direction. This indicates that the justices were least sympathetic to individuals advancing a free expression claim in situations where a Criminal Code provision had been violated. In short, when order and freedom were most directly in conflict in these kinds of cases, the justices often sided with the government to protect order over free expression rights.

In contrast, the largest category of liberal rulings occurred in cases in which the Canadian court engaged in the Charter Two-Step analysis. Once the court determined that a free expression right had been violated, it subsequently determined that the violation was not justified in 49 per cent of the free expression claims under s. 1 analysis. In other words, individuals that brought free expression claims to the court after 1984 had roughly a 50-50 chance of having their rights upheld under the Charter Two-Step approach. Although some might wonder whether this represents decent odds, one must keep in mind that the Canadian court had favoured the rights claimant in only 5 of the 34 Canadian Bill of Rights cases it handed down between 1960 and 1982 (Morton, Russell, and Withey 1991, 61–2). Moreover, this constituted exactly twice as many liberal rulings as had been handed down in the free expression area under the Laskin tenure, just before the Charter was adopted (1974–1984). Although some scholars, such as MacKay (1983), suggested that the court would initially maintain a weak civil liberties record after the Charter was adopted, it is clear from a comparative perspective that the court breathed strong, healthy life into free expression claims once it determined that a violation of a free expression right had occurred. This rise in post-Charter liberalism suggests that as society became more accepting of free expression rights, the justices exhibited voting patterns that were in line with the mass public.

When one turns to the three discrete categories in the free expression area, the highest level of liberal postmaterialist rulings is found in the free speech area, at 44 per cent. This finding is not surprising given that Canada is a democratic society that places a high value on the participation of all citizens in the political process and the freedom of citizens to express their personal beliefs. The level is below 50 per cent because some of the free speech cases involved hate speech and slander, areas of law where expression received its lowest levels of support by the justices. The cases involving free press claims had the second-highest percentage of liberal rulings (31 per cent), followed by the free association area, where only 25 per cent of the rulings the court handed down were in the postmaterialist direction.

One explanation for why the justices might not have been as supportive in the free association area as they were in the other two areas might be because many of the disputes that in this area dealt with right-to-strike and right-to-bargain claims in union collective-bargaining disputes; the justices wanted to steer clear of these because they had historically favoured employers in labour relations cases. Having said this, they are no longer hesitant in this area. Indeed, the McLachlin Court has shown more favouritism towards unions in the free association realm since 2010, especially in the trilogy of decisions handed down in January 2015 endorsing the constitutional right to form a union and to strike (see *Mounted Police Association of Ontario v. Canada*, [2015] 1 S.C.R. 3; *Meredith v. Canada*, [2015] 1 S.C.R. 125; and *Saskatchewan Federation of Labour v. Saskatchewan*, [2015] 1 S.C.R. 225).

Table 4.3 breaks down the percentage of liberal rulings in the free expression area by decade and court period and constitutes the first direct assessment of Inglehart's shifting values thesis in the free expression area. With the exception of the 1980s, when only 23 per cent of the 26 free expression cases heard were handed down in the postmaterialist direction, Inglehart's thesis seems to be largely confirmed by the data. Indeed, the increase in the percentage of liberal free expression rulings,

Table 4.3. Liberal Rulings in Free Expression Cases by Decade and Court in the Supreme Court of Canada, 1973–2010

Court	Cases, no.	Liberal rulings, %
Decade		
1970s (1973–79)	11	36.4
1980s	26	23.1
1990s	30	50.0
2000s (2000–10)	18	50.0
Period		
Laskin Court (1974–84)[a]	12	25.0
Dickson Court (1984–90)	28	28.6
Lamer Court (1990–99)	26	50.0
McLachlin Court (2000–10)	18	50.0

[a]We excluded one case from the second half of the table because it was argued under the leadership of Chief Justice Fauteux (before 1974).

from a mere 36 per cent in the 1970s to 50 per cent in the 1990–2010 time period, coincides with the adoption of the Charter of Rights and Freedoms and the mobilization of rights advocates, documented by Epp (1998) and others in Canadian society. In other words, the court's movement in a postmaterialist direction in free expression cases occurred as a response to the adoption of the Charter and the rise of rights litigation, but it is also part and parcel of a larger and more significant postmaterialist value change taking place in Canada among both the citizenry and the political elites. The shifting postmaterialist value change that Inglehart has documented among the citizenry in advanced industrial societies seems to be reflected in a similar shift in attitudes by Canadian justices in free expression cases.

The second half of Table 4.3, which breaks down the percentage of liberal rulings in the free expression area across the four most recent court tenures, also highlights the impact that the Charter has had on the decision-making process of the justices on the Canadian court. Note, for example, that the justices on the Laskin and Dickson Courts, before the Charter came into full bloom, handed down only 25 and 29 per cent liberal rulings in the free expression area, while those on the Lamer and McLachlin Courts, after the Charter's rise in prominence, handed down 50 per cent liberal rulings. The table also indicates that the Charter helped trigger a rise in the number of free expression cases heard by the court, with over twice as many heard under the Dickson and Lamer tenures (28 and 26 cases) as heard during the Laskin tenure

(12 cases). However, readers should note that the number dropped down to 18 cases in the first 10 years of the McLachlin Court. Collectively, these data suggest that as Charter analysis became more commonplace and routine, the court became more emboldened in its protection of postmaterialist liberal values; this is evident in the free expression area under the Lamer and McLachlin tenures.

Table 4.4, in turn, assesses the Supreme Court's free expression docket in terms of the number of cases heard over time across the five sub-areas of law. Looking at the three discrete free expression areas first, one finds that free speech cases dominated the agenda of the court across the last four decades, constituting 63 of the 85 cases heard. Moreover, the cases heard in the free speech area were evenly divided across all four decades. Similarly, the Canadian court heard a steady, but low, rate of cases in the free association area starting in the 1980s, with four to six cases heard in each of the last three decades.[2] In contrast, the number of cases heard in the free press area seemed to peak in the 1990s during the Lamer Court tenure, only to drop to zero in the first 10 years of the McLachlin Court. Obviously, s. 1 issues do not appear until after the Charter's adoption in 1982, but the Charter Two-Step was a steady presence in the court's free expression jurisprudence after its adoption, featuring in 15 cases in each of the three post-Charter decades.

The high concentration of criminal charges in the free expression cases of the 1980s may help explain why the Dickson Court handed down only 29 per cent liberal rulings during that time (see Table 4.3). As mentioned earlier, when a free expression case includes a criminal violation, the justices on the court tend to look less favourably on those rights claimants, possibly because they are encroaching on other important values in Canadian society.

Table 4.5 captures the pattern of appellants and respondents that appear in free expression cases over the period from 1973 to 2010. The data reveal that the most frequent disputes in the 85 cases occur between an individual and the federal or provincial government (30 of 85 cases, 35 per cent; note that the total of 30 is arrived at by adding the 18 + 4 cases in the appellant row, titled "Individual," to the 7 + 1 cases in the respondent column, titled "Individual"). In almost three-fourths

---

2 One must keep in mind that we did not include all free association cases, but only those that had a free expression element in them. Thus, free association claims pertaining to religious groups or linguistic groups were omitted from our analysis.

Table 4.4. Number of Free Expression Issues Decided by the Supreme Court of Canada by Decade, 1973–2010

Issue area	1970s	1980s	1990s	2000s	Total
Free speech	10	18	20	15	63
Free press	2	3	8	0	13
Free association	1	5	4	6	16
Criminal case	3	13	6	5	27
S. 1 issue	0	15	15	15	45

of those cases, the individual is seeking to appeal a lower court ruling upholding the federal or provincial government's power to restrict the individual's free expression rights. There is a significant drop-off to the second most prominent litigant pairings: cases featuring either corporations or the media against the federal or provincial government, representing 11 and 10 of 85 cases, respectively, for each sector (13 and 12 per cent). In corporate disputes, companies petition the court for review in just under half the cases (9 of 19), most frequently to review a lower court ruling restricting their commercial expression rights in the marketplace. In contrast, when the government seeks review of pro-corporate rulings, at either the federal or the provincial level, it is primarily seeking to uphold restrictions on corporate advertising. In 80 per cent of the media cases that make it to the Supreme Court, the news organizations are taking a postmaterialist position by seeking to overturn lower court restrictions on the right to publish or broadcast, while the government seeks to restrict press rights in those claims.

One should note that while the federal and provincial governments play a large role in litigation in the free expression area (61 cases overall), city governments play a much more limited role, appearing in only 7 cases as either the appellant or the respondent across the last four decades. This makes sense because cities are rarely going to use their limited financial resources to fight against advocates of free expression in the legal system. Table 4.5 indicates that disputes between unions and all levels of government constitute 10 of the 85 cases, or 12 per cent of the free expression docket. However, unlike the bulk of disputes between the individuals or corporations and government, 8 of 10 of the union claims were fought at the provincial level. This makes sense because most of the regulation of labour activity in a federal system takes place at the provincial level.

Table 4.6 provides a breakdown of the appearances of the various litigants in free expression cases, along with the stance they took in the

Table 4.5. Appellants and Respondents in Canadian Free Expression Cases, 1973–2010

Appellant	Respondent								
	Federal government	Provincial government	City government	Individual	Union	Media	Corporation	Other	Total
Federal government	0	0	0	7	0	1	2	1	11
Provincial government	0	0	0	1	1	1	3	0	6
City government	0	0	0	2	1	0	2	0	5
Individual	18	4	2	3	1	1	0	2	31
Union	1	7	0	0	0	0	3	0	11
Media	5	3	0	2	0	0	0	0	10
Corporation	4	2	0	2	1	0	0	0	9
Other group	0	0	0	2	0	0	0	0	2
Total	28	16	2	19	4	3	10	3	85

Table 4.6. Litigant Free Expression Stances and Victories, 1973–2010

Party	Appellant	Respondent	Total	Took conservative position, no.	Took free expression position, no.	Conservative wins, %	Liberal wins, %
Federal government	11	28	39	39	0	69.2	–
Provincial government	6	16	22	22	0	68.2	–
City government	5	2	7	7	0	28.6	–
Individual	31	19	50	10	40	40.0	42.5
Union	11	4	15	0	15	–	33.3
Media	10	3	13	0	13	–	30.8
Corporation	9	10	19	5	14	20.0	50.0
Other group	2	3	5	2	3	100.0	33.3
Total	85	85	170	85	85	60.0	40.0

case (liberal or conservative) and the percentage of liberal or conservative victories they achieved across the last four court tenures. One must keep in mind that while the government always takes a conservative stance when facing free expression defenders, individuals and corporations may take either a liberal or a conservative stance in free expression cases, depending on the nature of the dispute. For example, an individual might file a libel action against a media company or slander action against a corporation, placing the individual on the conservative side of these disputes. Likewise, corporations are sometimes lined up against unions seeking to establish collective bargaining rights, while in other disputes, they might seek to advance the right to advertise to the public without government regulation. It is important to note that this latter position represents a postmaterialist stance because the company is advocating for freedom of expression and the right of individuals to receive its message. Some might argue that the profit motive is driving the corporation, thus making its stance a materialistic one. Although all companies are interested in making a profit, this is a fundamental misunderstanding of the corporate argument in the free expression area, which is founded on the notion of ensuring the free exchange of views in a marketplace of ideas and that individuals have the right to hear messages without government interference. This is a core principle that resides at the heart of a democratic society.

With this in mind, we turn to Table 4.6 to highlight the number of times each litigant takes a liberal (free expression) or conservative position and the frequency of liberal or conservative wins in those cases. Not surprisingly, media firms always take the liberal position when litigating disputes in the free expression area, and unions do so as well. Both types of litigants achieve approximately the same level of postmaterialist, pro–free expression victories, with unions winning 33 per cent of the time, while media firms win 31 per cent of the time. These data indicate that unions seeking the right to collectively bargain or strike have about the same chance of winning at the Supreme Court level as the media does in seeking to publish material freely, without government encroachment. Individuals, in contrast, have a better winning percentage in the 40 cases in which they advance a free expression argument, winning 43 per cent of the time. In one sense, this win rate is surprising because, clearly, both the media and unions have far more resources and time to devote to litigation efforts than individuals do. Yet one may counter that the higher individual win rate over unions and media makes sense given the adoption of the Charter in 1982 and the elevated status of individual rights obtained within the constitutional framework. Since corporations, on average, have the most resources to muster in the litigation process, it is not surprising that in the 14 cases in which they pursue a free expression outcome, they win half the time. This finding is in line with party capability theories of litigant behaviour (Galanter 1974, 2003; McCormick 1993), and while companies are interested in promoting their own economic interests, their focus in these cases is necessarily to promote the free exchange of ideas.

When turning to the results for government litigants, both federal and provincial government lawyers are highly successful in restricting free expression claims, with a 69 and 68 per cent track record, respectively. As mentioned in the environmental chapter, high win rates for governments fall in line with litigant resource theory, which postulates that since government counsel participate repeatedly in legal disputes and have more resources than many other lawyers, they develop compelling expertise and, thus, are more likely to convince justices to uphold restrictions on free expression rights (Galanter 1974, 2003). It is interesting to note that, unlike the federal or provincial government, when city governments participate in free expression claims, they do not fare well and, indeed, achieve the lowest conservative win rate of all levels of government and most other litigants as well (29 per cent). One explanation for this disparity between the failures of city government lawyers to restrict expressive rights and the high success rates of provincial and federal lawyers might also be explained by the repeat player theory. Since city government lawyers participate in many fewer free expression cases, they may not have developed the expertise that federal and provincial lawyers have achieved. Moreover, the fact that they do not possess the same level of resources that are available to higher-level lawyers also undermines their ability to restrict expressive rights. The upshot of Table 4.6 is that if you are a union, individual, corporation, or media firm advancing free expression rights, you want to be fighting at the municipal level because when facing a federal or provincial lawyer, the odds of a postmaterialist free expression victory decrease dramatically.

Table 4.7 identifies the different types of intervener activity that occurred in the free expression area (found at the top half of the table), and it highlights the number of times seven types of interveners supported the rights claimant over the last four decades (found at the bottom half of the table). The totals in the top half of Table 4.7 indicate that the number of interveners in the free expression area increased significantly between the 1970s and 1990s, moving from a low of 13 interveners in the 1970s to a high of 117 and 113 in the two succeeding decades. However, the number of interveners dropped off a bit, to 100, in the 2000s. If one looks more closely at the different kinds of interveners, one can see that different patterns emerge. While the number of interventions made by labour, media, and other groups increased over the four decades, the number of interventions made by the federal and provincial governments in free expression cases peaked in the 1980s, but fell significantly after that time period. Intervention activity by civil rights and liberties groups increased significantly up until the 1990s, but also fell off a bit in the last decade. One explanation for the rise and decline of cases and interventions might be a "Charter maturation effect" – namely, that activity was bound to be more intense right after the Charter's enactment and that a decline was inevitable as one moved to a more mature phase of Charter interpretation.[3] Recent work by Alarie and Green (2010) has also tabulated the intervener appearance and success rates of various groups during the first nine years of the McLachlin Court. They note that public interest groups and unions had an 87 per cent success rate in being granted leave to intervene, although unions sought to intervene in only 45 cases, as opposed to 249 for public interest groups. However, the success rate on the final merits of a case was 16 per cent higher for public interest groups: 63 per cent versus 47 per cent for unions (Alarie and Green 2010, 398–9).

To understand more readily what is going on in the free expression area, one must turn to the figures in the bottom half of the table, which clearly indicate that the number of interveners that favoured the rights claimant in free expression cases increased over the past four decades among labour, media, and, to a certain extent, civil rights/liberties and

3 Peter McCormick argues that the Charter "revolution" is essentially over and that Charter jurisprudence has entered a mature phase. In his words, "the 'heavy lifting' is over, the major battles have been fought, the governing principles are clearly established, the concern now is with the subtle details" of Charter interpretation (McCormick 2015, xx). While we agree that Charter jurisprudence in some areas of law has entered a mature phase, we think his characterization of the end of the Charter revolution is premature and myopic because the judicialization of politics and the nature of judicial review in Canada's parliamentary system ensures that the court will continue to play a central role in dealing with high-profile policy issues. For evidence of this point, see the court's recent rulings pertaining to the right to die, prostitution, indigenous land rights, and the freedom of association trilogy of 2015.

Table 4.7. Intervener Activity and Positions Favouring Free Expression Rights, 1973–2010

Intervener	1970s	1980s	1990s	2000s	Total
Federal government	2	14	9	3	28
Provincial government	11	70	39	29	149
Corporation/trade association	0	0	6	4	10
Civil liberties/rights group	0	12	21	16	49
Labour group	0	0	10	10	20
Media/news organization	0	4	11	13	28
Other group	0	17	17	25	59
Totals	**13**	**117**	**113**	**100**	**343**
Position favouring free expression rights[a]					
Intervener	1970s	1980s	1990s	2000s	Total
Federal government	0	0	0	0	0
Provincial government	0	0	0	0	0
Corporation/trade association	0	0	0	0	0
Civil liberties/rights group	0	3	16	14	33
Labour group	0	0	10	10	20
Media/news organization	0	4	4	13	21
Other group	0	3	14	7	24
Totals, pro–free expression	**0**	**10**	**44**	**44**	**98**
Proportion pro–free speech	0.0	8.5	38.9	44.0	28.6
Proportion anti–free speech	100.0	91.5	61.1	56.0	71.4

[a]We coded the direction of the interveners in reference to whether they had favoured free expression or a civil liberties interest, based on our reading of the Supreme Court cases.

other groups as well. While it is not surprising that government and corporate entities did not intervene on behalf of the free speech claimant during any of the decades, it seems that their intervention on behalf of other societal interests, such as order and security, steadily declined after the 1980s (see the top of Table 4.7). In line with these data, the proportion of pro–free speech interveners across the four decades studied went up from zero per cent in the 1970s to 44 per cent in the 2000s (see the bottom of the table). In contrast, anti–free speech intervention activity declined from 100 per cent of all interveners in the 1970s to 56 per cent in the 2000s, and one should note that some postmaterialist interveners favoured equality and would have opposed free expression from time to time. This clearly occurred in the legal rights field, where women's groups supported the suppression of free speech in favour of the equality interests of female victims of crime.

Collectively, these intervener data provide some evidence that there was a mobilization effort by various groups, outside the governmental

Table 4.8. Canadian Supreme Court Justices' Free Expression Voting Records, 1973–2010

Justice	Cases, no.	Free expression votes, no.	Liberal ruling, %
Binnie	20	15	75.0
McLachlin	*47*	*32*	*68.1*
Major	30	19	63.3
Laskin	*13*	*8*	*61.5*
Iacobucci	31	17	54.8
Arbour	11	6	54.5
Wilson	28	15	53.6
Cory	30	16	53.3
LeBel	17	8	47.1
Sopinka	30	14	46.7
Bastarache	21	9	42.9
Gonthier	42	17	40.5
Lamer	*37*	*15*	*40.5*
L'Heureux-Dubé	52	21	40.4
Dickson	*38*	*15*	*39.5*
Ritchie	11	4	36.4
Beetz	23	8	34.8
La Forest	41	14	34.1
McIntyre	18	6	33.3
Martland	10	1	10.0

Note: The table includes voting records for all justices participating in 10 or more cases. Eighteen justices were excluded from the table because they participated in fewer than 10 cases in the free expression area during the 1973–2010 period. The omitted individuals were Justices Abbott, Abella, Charron, Chouinard, Cromwell, de Grandpré, Deschamps, Estey, Fauteux, Fish, Hall, Judson, Le Dain, Pigeon, Pratte, Rothstein, Spence, and Stevens.

or corporate sphere, to actively participate in and support the rights claimants in free expression cases. These trends coincide with Epp's (1996, 1998) and Inglehart's (1997) evidence of growing support for postmaterialist values that place a greater emphasis on self-expression and democratic participation.

Judicial Voting and Authorship Patterns

In the next stage of our statistical analysis, we assess the career voting patterns of 20 Canadian Supreme Court justices in the free expression area between 1973 and 2010. More specifically, Table 4.8 ranks the justices from high to low in terms of their overall support of rights claimants in free expression cases during their tenure on the court.

The justices that stand out as the most supportive of expressive rights claims are Justices Binnie and McLachlin, both of whom supported them over two-thirds of the time. (The true outlier in this area is Justice Binnie, who supported free expression claims 75 per cent of the time.) These two justices were followed by a second tier of justices – namely, Justices Major and Laskin – who voted on behalf of expressive rights advocates between 63 and 62 per cent of the time. However, one must interpret the career scores of Justice Laskin cautiously since he heard only 13 cases in this area. At the other end of the spectrum sit Justices Beetz, La Forest, McIntyre, and Martland, all of whom supported the rights claimant less than 35 per cent of the time, with Justice Martland achieving a 10 per cent support score in the 10 cases that he heard in this time period. Readers should be aware that the more contemporary justices tend to congregate at the top of Table 4.8, indicating that there is a stronger pattern of postmaterialist voting among the justices born later and serving more recently on the Supreme Court of Canada.

If one looks at the four chief justices on the court, both Chief Justices McLachlin and Laskin stand out as relative leaders in the free expression area, supporting rights claimants 68 and 62 per cent of the time, respectively. In contrast, Chief Justices Dickson and Lamer favoured expressive claims only 40 and 41 per cent of the time. These figures fall just below the median for justices in the free expression area, Justices Sopinka and Bastarache, who supported free expression claims at a 47 and 43 per cent rate. Ironically, the two strongest supporters of free expression rights among the chief justices served before and well after the Charter's adoption, whereas the first two post-Charter chiefs provided more lukewarm support for free expression claims.

We subsequently reorganized the data in Table 4.8 into a figure that plots the career voting scores of the justices in the free expression area with their newspaper ideology scores at the time of their appointment to assess whether there is a correlation between the expected ideology of the justices and their career voting record across the four judicial tenures. The graph allows us to determine whether reports of the justices' ideological leanings at the time of their appointment are a good barometer of their voting track record in free expression cases. Obviously, we expected that justices who have more liberal newspaper ideology scores would have higher career support scores for rights claimants in the free expression area than their more conservative colleagues. If one recalls, we used the newspaper ideology scores for the justices based on our analysis of newspaper commentary made by journalists and

Figure 4.1. Free Expression Voting by Ideology Score

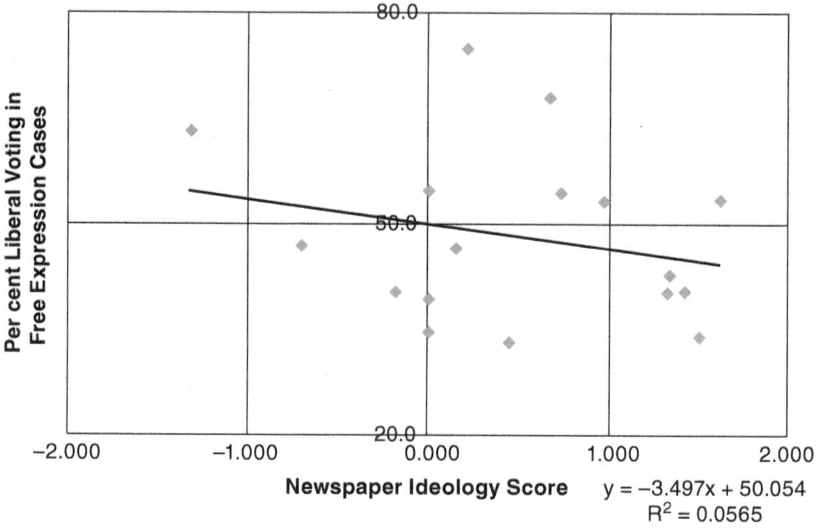

Per cent Liberal Voting in Free Expression Cases

80.0

50.0

20.0

−2.000 −1.000 0.000 1.000 2.000

Newspaper Ideology Score

$y = -3.497x + 50.054$

$R^2 = 0.0565$

Note: This figure includes the liberal voting record of only 17 of the 20 justices because we were unable to calculate newspaper ideology scores for Chief Justice Laskin and Justices Martland and Ritchie; journalists did not provide ideological commentary on these justices at the time of their appointment.

political reporters at the time they were elevated to the Supreme Court (Ostberg and Wetstein 2007).[4]

The findings in Figure 4.1 reveal surprising results. The data suggest that, contrary to expectations, there is no real correlation between newspaper ideology scores at the time of the justices' appointment to the Canadian Supreme Court and their subsequent career support score for pro–free expression rulings. In fact, the slope is in a slightly negative direction, indicating that a one-unit movement in the positive or liberal direction on the 5-point newspaper ideology scale yields a 3.5 per cent *decrease* in support for a free expression claimant. Yet because R-square for the equation is only .06, one should realize that there is very little explanatory power in the news ideology measure. The R-square value indicates that the perceived ideological leanings of the justices, whether in the liberal or the conservative direction, appears to have little impact

4 For a more complete review of how we coded each justice, consult Ostberg and Wetstein (2007, chap. 3).

Figure 4.2. Free Expression Voting by Year of Birth

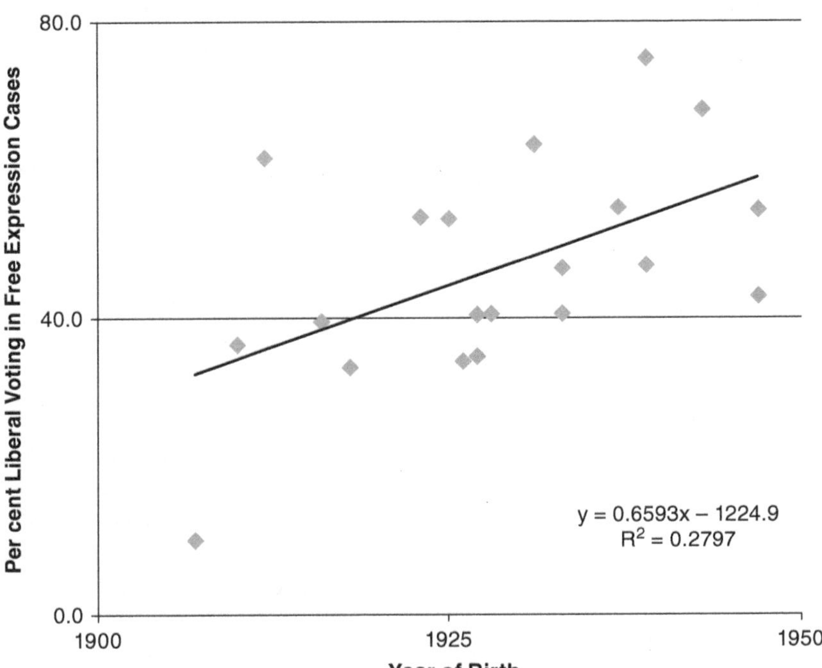

on their career support for free expression claims over the last 40 years; thus, other factors must be more relevant in the voting behaviour of the justices on the Canadian Supreme Court.

Perhaps one of the best ways to visualize the veracity of Inglehart's thesis is by placing all the justices in a scatterplot that pinpoints their respective career support score in the free expression area in relation to their year of birth. In short, Figure 4.2 allows us to assess whether, in keeping with Inglehart's shifting values thesis, there is an upward trajectory of support scores for rights claimants in free expression cases across 20 justices spanning a 40-year period. The evidence in Figure 4.2 clearly vindicates Inglehart's shifting values thesis over time among legal elites in Canadian society. The data reveal that as one moves through time from the older justices to the more recent appointees, the average justice becomes more supportive of free expression arguments. For example, the slope of the regression line (b = .659) indicates that a justice who was born in 1950 would be 20 per cent more supportive of free expression claims than a justice who was born in 1920 (.659 × 30 = 19.77). The fact that the equation garners a Pearson's r, or correlation coefficient of .59, suggests that there is a strong positive relationship between the birth year of a justice on the Canadian Supreme Court and his or her likelihood of supporting postmaterialist, expressive values.[5] The data from this scatterplot provide strong confirmation of the thesis that the time period in which the justices developed their world view and came of age as young adults has a strong impact on their career voting support for postmaterialist value positions in free expression cases. As subsequent appointees came to the court, they appear to have been increasingly in step with the postmaterialist shifts in favour of free expression rights that were occurring in the mass public.

We next provide a detailed account of the voting patterns and majority and minority authorship activity that the Canadian justices took in the free expression area over the 1973 to 2010 period. While the Canadian court generated a high rate of consensus over those 40 years, exhibiting a 70 per cent rate of unanimity across all the cases it generated written reasons for judgment between 1973 and 2010 it produced a much lower rate of consensus in the free expression area, handing down unanimous rulings in only 49 per cent of the cases. This low rate of agreement reflects the difficult and contentious nature of free expression disputes. Table 4.9 indicates that Chief Justice Dickson stands out as one of the decisive task leaders of the Canadian court in free expression cases, acting as majority author in 37 per cent of the cases that he heard in this area (14 of the 38 cases). His leadership in this area of law reflects his leadership in the environmental cases discussed in the two prior chapters. If one recalls, task leaders are individuals who possesses the intellectual ability and leadership skills to sway others on the court to embrace their point of view, and they often take on difficult cases (Danelski 1989; Ostberg, Wetstein, and Ducat 2004). Although Justice Ritchie acted as the majority-opinion author in 46 per cent of the

5 Pearson's r is the measure of association that identifies the strength and direction of the relationship between two interval-level indicators. It ranges between 0 and 1 (or −1) and is calculated by taking the square root of R-square, which measures the goodness of fit of the data points around the regression line (Manheim and Rich 1991, 272–3). If there is a perfect 1–1 relationship between the two variables, all the data points fall on the regression line. A relationship of .5 or higher identifies a fairly strong relationship between the two variables.

Table 4.9. Canadian Supreme Court Justices' Opinion Authorship Patterns in Free Expression Cases, 1973–2010

Justice	Cases, no.	Voting in majority, %	Majority author, %[a]	Voting in dissent, %	Dissenting author, %[b]
Ritchie	11	100.0	45.5	0.0	0.0
Dickson	*38*	*84.2*	*36.8*	*15.8*	*7.9*
Bastarache	21	90.5	23.8	9.5	4.8
McLachlin	*47*	*74.5*	*23.4*	*25.5*	*19.1*
Cory	30	83.3	23.3	16.7	13.3
Sopinka	30	83.3	23.3	16.7	3.3
Martland	10	90.0	20.0	10.0	10.0
McIntyre	18	94.4	16.7	5.6	5.6
Lamer	*37*	*94.6*	*13.5*	*5.4*	*2.7*
Beetz	23	87.0	13.0	13.0	4.3
LeBel	17	88.2	11.8	11.8	0.0
Binnie	20	80.0	10.0	20.0	5.0
Arbour	11	90.9	9.1	9.1	0.0
Laskin	*13*	*69.2*	*7.7*	*30.8*	*30.8*
La Forest	41	85.4	7.3	14.6	12.2
Iacobucci	31	90.3	6.5	9.7	3.2
L'Heureux-Dubé	52	80.8	1.9	19.2	3.8
Major	30	83.3	0.0	16.7	6.7
Gonthier	42	85.7	0.0	14.3	7.1
Wilson	28	75.0	0.0	25.0	17.9

Note: The table includes voting records for all justices participating in 10 or more cases.
[a]Majority authorship is calculated by dividing the number of majority opinions authored by the total number of cases heard by a justice.
[b]Dissenting authorship is calculated by dividing the number of dissenting opinions authored by the total number of cases heard by a justice.

cases he heard during this time period, since he participated in only 11 free expression cases between 1973 and 2010, his leadership in this area must be questioned, especially since he was not perceived to be a leader on the court.

A tier of four justices sits right below Chief Justice Dickson's task leadership: Justice Bastarache, who authored majority opinions 24 per cent of the time, followed by Justices McLachlin, Cory, and Sopinka, all of whom authored majority opinions in 23 per cent of the free expression cases they heard. Collectively, the top six justices have a much higher majority authorship rate than that of the court as a whole, which averaged 13 per cent across all 20 justices in Table 4.9. Similarly, three of the four chief justices authored more majority opinions than the mean majority authorship rate of 13 per cent, although Chief Justices Dickson and McLachlin authored far greater reasons for judgment in the free expression area than the other two chiefs, authoring 37 and 23 per cent of the cases they heard. Chief Justice Lamer wrote the majority opinion in 14 per cent of the free expression cases he heard, which is just above the mean of 13 per cent, while Chief justice Laskin wrote the majority opinions in only 8 per cent of the cases he heard (1 of 13). The main reason for Chief Justice Laskin's low output of majority opinions in this area was that he was so frequently in the liberal minority in his own court.

The majority-opinion authorship records of each chief justice in this area of law are slightly different from those found in the environmental area, where all four chiefs authored majority reasons for judgment at rates above the mean of 13 per cent. Having said this, when one compares the majority-opinion authorship rates in the two areas of law, one should note that it goes down by 4 per cent or more for Chief Justices Dickson, Lamer, and Laskin when one moves from environmental cases to the free expression area, while it goes up for Chief Justice McLachlin by 6 per cent. This demonstrates that Chief Justice McLachlin has emerged as an important task leader in the field of free expression.

At the other extreme of majority authorship sit Justices Major, Gonthier, and Wilson, who authored no reasons for judgment. In the case of Justice Wilson, she joined the second-fewest number of majority opinions (21 of 28 cases) and authored the second-highest proportion of dissents (18 per cent, or 5 cases). Justices Major and Gonthier, unlike Justice Wilson, constitute the judicial followers in the free expression area because they joined a fair amount of majority opinions without ever taking a leadership role.

The five big dissenters in the free expression area were Chief Justice Laskin, Chief Justice McLachlin, Justice Wilson, Justice Binnie, and, not surprisingly, Justice L'Heureux-Dubé, who is often identified as one of the great dissenters on the Canadian Supreme Court (McCormick 2000; Ostberg and Wetstein 2007). These justices dissented in 31, 26, 25, 20, and 19 per cent of the free expression cases they heard throughout their tenures, respectively. Yet since Chief Justice Laskin participated in only 13 cases in the free expression area during his tenure on the court, one must keep in mind that his 31 per cent dissent rate amounts to four of these 13 cases. Three of the five justices, with the exception of Justices L'Heureux-Dubé and Binnie, also authored the most dissents in this area, with Chief Justice Laskin authoring dissents in all the cases in which he cast a minority vote. Many of Chief Justice McLachlin's dissents are in the libertarian direction, something we highlight in the next chapter. Overall, one should note that the first three women on the Canadian court were three of the most prolific dissenters in the free expression area between 1973 and 2010.

Data and Methods for the Logistic Regression Analysis

In the last stage of our statistical analysis, we conducted logistic regression analysis at the judge-vote level to assess the impact that various independent variables had on the voting behaviour of the 36 justices in the free expression area.[6] If one remembers, the strength of logistic regression analysis is that it allows us to assess the relative impact of various judge- and case-level factors on judicial voting behaviour, while keeping other possible rival variables constant in the equation. This approach allows us to test the veracity of a socio-attitudinal model of judicial decision making. As in the environmental section, we developed three different model equations in the free expression area: the first examines the impact of judge-level variables on 574 judge-vote outcomes, the second tests the impact of case-level variables on 643 voting outcomes, while the third model combines all the independent variables into one equation, again using only 574 case votes. We conduct logistic regression because the dependent variable in the equation is a dichotomous variable, identifying whether a justice ruled in favour of a rights claimant or not in free expression cases (1 = liberal postmaterialist ruling, 0 = conservative materialist ruling).

We label the following types of case votes as either liberal or postmaterialist in the data set: votes to uphold free expression claims in the political arena or involving more controversial speech, such as obscenity or hate speech; votes supporting commercial advertising in the marketplace; votes striking down libel or defamation claims; votes allowing press access to information; votes against the seizure of materials from reporters; votes invoking the right of the media to cover trial proceedings; votes endorsing the right to engage in secondary picketing; and votes favouring the right to bargain and/or strike in a collective bargaining dispute. The coding of cases in the free expression area

---

6 For the judge-level model and the combined model (which includes both judge- and case-level data), we assessed the voting behaviour of only 26 justices because we had no newspaper ideology scores for 10 of the justices (Ostberg and Wetstein 2007). However, the model featuring case characteristics uses the voting records of all 36 justices.

is a straightforward process and follows intuitively from Inglehart's postmaterialist changing values thesis, assuming that liberty resides at the most postmaterialist end of the value spectrum, followed by equality and order at the opposite end.

Some might question why support for commercial advertising in the marketplace is labelled as postmaterialist, especially if the advertising involves tobacco or marketing toys to children. However, as we noted earlier, although companies engaged in commercial advertising are indeed trying to sell products, their ultimate argument is in favour of a free exchange of ideas for all to hear and consume in an unfettered manner, which is a hallmark of a liberal democratic system. Alternatively, others might contend that allowing hate speech and obscenity violates the equality rights of others. While we agree with that contention, if you are an advocate of pure free speech, as Justice Oliver Wendell Holmes would contend, you must allow speech, no matter how hateful, to be unregulated unless it presents a "clear and present danger" of immediate substantive harm. This is justified so that the best ideas and "truth" can claim victory in the rough-and-tumble of political and social debate (*Abrams v. United States*, 250 U.S. 616 [1919]). In his words, it is essential that "we should be eternally vigilant against attempts to check the expression of opinions that we loathe" (quoted in Ducat 2004, 784). Thus, a pure postmaterialist view of free speech envisions the support of companies seeking to advertise even tobacco and toys to children because it involves an exchange of ideas and does not represent an imminent threat to society's safety. If Inglehart's thesis is correct, that a postmaterialist value shift is taking place among the mass public of advanced industrial societies, we would expect that, in keeping with his thesis, elite Canadian Supreme Court justices would hand down more libertarian pro–free expression rulings in these cases over time.

The independent variables in the equations consist of a host of judge- and case-level variables that allow us to assess the following critical question: Are judicial rulings in the free expression area principally driven by judge-level variables, such as ideology, gender of the justice, and region of country, or do the facts of a case, such as whether it involves political speech or commercial advertising or whether the Canadian Civil Liberties Association (CCLA) intervenes in a case, play a more prominent role in influencing voting behaviour among Canadian justices? Moreover, the inclusion of different chief justice tenures allows us to also assess the veracity of Inglehart's shifting values thesis among judicial elites in the free expression area, while simultaneously controlling for other important variables in the equation. Ultimately, our holistic logistic model is designed to construct a set of variables that are rooted in a socio-attitudinal model of judicial behaviour: one that examines personal traits of the justices, individual-level attitudes, changing world views over time, legal characteristics, and litigant and intervener influences on the justices.

We included 6 judge- and court-level variables and 13 case-level variables in the logistic analysis. We also created models that mirror, as much as feasible, the equations developed in the environmental area for comparative purposes. The first three judge-level variables that appear in the free expression area – namely, gender, newspaper ideology, and academic teaching experience – replicate ones found in the environmental area, although each would support different hypotheses. The gender variable is a dichotomous variable that was included in the equations (1 = female, 0 = male) to test whether gender differences appear in the free expression area, although, as in the environmental area, one might posit different hypotheses regarding gender difference. For example, some prior research has found that women are more supportive of vulnerable groups and individuals in society (see Ostberg, Wetstein, and Ducat 2002). Thus, one might hypothesize that female justices would be more willing to vote for a rights claimant because they want to ensure that the have-nots, or those that are underdogs, are heard in the political system and the marketplace of ideas.

If this hypothesis is accurate, one would expect that the female justice coefficient will be positive. Yet since the type of speech in question matters, female justices might be less likely to support rights claimants in cases involving obscene activity, hate speech, or a company trying to advance advertisements aimed at harming children or vulnerable groups in society. Our argument here is rooted in the ethic of care literature, which suggests that women are much more interested in promoting the welfare of others in the community and are more committed to protecting vulnerable individuals from harm (see Gilligan 1982, 1987; Lyons 1988; West 1991; MacKinnon 1993; Ostberg, Wetstein, and Ducat 2002; Ostberg and Wetstein 2007, 120, 127). Thus, we included in the model some variables that assess the type of speech in question to tease out whether female justices are more supportive of free speech claims, all other things being equal. If they are less supportive than male justices, the coefficient for the gender variable should be negative.

As in the environmental area, we included a measure of ideology based on our journalistic assessments of the ideological leanings of the justices at the time of their appointment to the Supreme Court (Ostberg and Wetstein 2007). The scores range from −2 for the most conservative comments to +2 for the most liberal comments. In the free expression area, we use scores for 26 of the 36 justices, with Justice Chouinard receiving the most conservative score (−1.375) and Justice Wilson the most liberal score (+1.618). Despite our earlier scatterplot (see Figure 4.1), it is hypothesized that justices who obtain more positive liberal newspaper scores are more likely to rule in favour of free expression claims because they are supportive of various groups and individuals having an equal opportunity to be heard in the political and social arenas. Similarly, for the third judge-level variable, it is expected that justices who have spent time teaching in academia or as a law professor (1 = spent time teaching in a law school, 0 = no time teaching) would be more likely to favour expressive rights claimants given the relationship that has been shown between academic teaching and liberal voting behaviour by justices (Tate and Sittiwong 1989; Songer at al. 2012). The fourth judge-level variable is a dichotomous variable that tests whether the region a justice comes from impacts how he or she votes in free expression cases (1 = Quebec, 0 = non-Quebec). It is hypothesized that justices from Quebec will be more likely to rule against rights claimants because they come from a more conservative, Catholic culture, which has traditionally been more deferential to authority and community norms (Tate and Sittiwong 1989; Songer et al. 2012).

The last two judge-level variables in the equations are dichotomous variables that identify the justices that voted during the Chief Justice Lamer or McLachlin tenure (1 = vote under the Lamer or McLachlin Court, 0 = otherwise). Although we included an independent variable for the Dickson Court in the environmental area, we could not do so in the free expression area because the Laskin Court handed down few free expression claims. Thus, we combined the rulings of the two earlier courts in this area and kept them out of the equations for comparative purposes.[7] These variables provide us with the ability to test whether Inglehart's postmaterialist transformation thesis has taken place among

7 There were 40 free expression cases heard during the Laskin and Dickson Courts. The rulings in these two courts were combined because there were not enough Laskin Court decisions to look at them separately in the analysis.

elite Canadian justices in the free expression area, in line with changing attitudes in the mass public. If it has, we expect justices in the Lamer and McLachlin Courts to hand down progressively more libertarian, postmaterialist rulings in free expression cases than justices under the Laskin and Dickson tenures. As such, the coefficients for the Lamer and McLachlin indicators should be positive.

The 13 case-level variables test whether various case facts, including issue areas, parties in a suit, and interveners, had a decisive impact on judicial voting behaviour in the free expression area. As in the environmental area, we included four interveners that seemed to make theoretical sense to include in the subsequent models. First, we calculated the number of pro–free expression interveners across all the cases; these ranged from 0 to 13. Relying on litigant resource theory, which we discussed in the environmental section, it was hypothesized that the more pro–free expression interveners that appeared in a case, the greater the likelihood that the justices would pick up on various important intervener cues and hand down rulings favouring a free speech claimant (Galanter 1974, 2003; Brodie 2002; Manfredi 2004; Alarie and Green 2010). We next included a dichotomous variable that assessed whether the CCLA participated as an intervener in a case (1 = yes, 0 = no), and it was hypothesized that if the CCLA intervened, its arguments would signal to the justices that this was an important free expression case, and they would be more likely to hand down a liberal ruling than otherwise.

We included two other types of intervener in the logistic regression equations: one that identified the number of provincial interveners (ranging from 0 to 8) and another that assessed the number of unions that had intervened in collective bargaining cases (ranging from 0 to 4). We decided to examine the impact of government interveners at the provincial level, versus the federal one, because they participated in more free expression cases, and multiple provinces often participated in a single case. We hypothesized that the greater the number of provincial interveners there were in the case, the greater the likelihood that the justices would rule against the rights claimant in favour of the community values and safety interests. Last, we hypothesized that the greater the number of union interveners that participated in a case, the more likely it would be that the justices would pick up on important pro-union arguments and thus be more likely to hand down rulings in favour of those seeking collective bargaining agreements.

We included six issue characteristics in the logistic models; they made theoretical sense for explaining judicial voting behaviour in free expression cases, and they would provide a substantive advancement in the research on free speech disputes by extending the time frame of analysis over a 40-year period and increasing the number of independent variables that prior researchers have analysed (see Ostberg and Wetstein 2007; Songer et al. 2012). Since the number of cases in the subcategories of the free press and free association area discussed in Table 4.1 were too small to include separately in the analysis, we decided to compare the impact that these two broad categories would have on judicial voting relative to free expression cases, which we excluded for comparative purposes. Each of these variables was included as a dichotomous variable in the equations (1 = free association or free press, 0 = otherwise). In keeping with Emerson's theory that free speech is the most critical type of expression in the political process and in maintaining a democratic society, it was hypothesized that both of the coefficients for free association and free press would be in the negative direction (since the free speech category is not in the equation).[8] However, since free association is also necessary to ensure that citizens have the opportunity to share and express their views collectively, we hypothesized that the negative coefficient for free press cases would be greater than the one for free association cases. Thus, we expected a hierarchy to emerge in which the justices would provide the greatest support for free speech cases, followed by free association and free press, in that order.

Since there were sufficient numbers of cases in the different subfields of the free speech category, we also decided to test whether Emerson's hierarchy existed in the free speech category itself. We included a dichotomous variable in the equation for political speech (1 = political speech, 0 = not political speech), commercial advertising (1 = advertising, 0 = not advertising), and obscenity (1 = obscene activity, 0 = not obscene activity), with hate speech and libel/defamation kept out of the equation for comparative purposes. Obviously, we expected that all three variables would have positive coefficients relative to hate speech and defamation, yet political speech should have the largest coefficient, followed by commercial advertising and then obscenity. One might quibble over whether justices should protect obscene expression more than hate speech given that both are clearly at the bottom level

8 We discuss the theoretical foundations of Emerson's arguments regarding the rationale for protecting free speech in a democratic society in chapter 5.

of First Amendment or Charter s. 2(b) protection. However, a credible argument could be made that obscene behaviour does provide more value to society than hate speech or defamation in that it might feature expressive activity that supplies important educational, artistic, or social values to Canadian citizens.

Two additional case features that were unique and necessary to assess in the free expression area were whether there was a criminal charge in the case (1 = yes, 0 = no) and whether the court engaged in s. 1 analysis, or the Charter Two-Step, when assessing the free expression claim (1 = s. 1 analysis, 0 = no s. 1 analysis). All things being equal, it was expected that when a criminal charge was filed in a case, the justices would be less likely to rule in favour of an expressive rights claimant because the individual had engaged in unlawful activity to advance their expressive interests. In contrast, it was expected that in cases in which the court engaged in the Charter Two-Step and found that an underlying s. 2(b) expressive right had been violated under the Charter, it would be more likely to find that such an infringement was not justified under s. 1 analysis because free expression had obtained constitutional protection under the Charter and constituted a fundamental right for all Canadian citizens.

The last two dichotomous independent variables in the logistic equations related to the parties that were involved in a suit. The first assessed whether or not the federal or provincial government was a party in the suit (1 = federal or provincial government was a party in the suit, 0 = not a party in the suit), while the second pertained to whether an individual was seeking the expressive right in the case (1 = individual seeking right, 0 = individual not seeking right). In line with litigant resource theory, discussed earlier, we expected that when the federal or provincial government was a party in the suit, the justices would be more likely to rule in its favour because it had honed its litigating skills through repeat activity in the courts and often had more resources at its disposal than municipal litigators. (The latter were kept out of the equation for comparison purposes.)

Likewise, we anticipated that, all other things being equal, litigators representing individuals seeking expression rights would have lower rates of appellate success than those representing unions or corporations, in part because of the resource disadvantages they had relative to these better-funded litigants. Overall, the logistic regression models provide a more detailed account of what kinds of independent variables play a critical role in influencing judicial voting behaviour in the free expression area over the last 40 years, whether they are at the judge level or involve case facts, the parties, intervener activity, or different court tenures. Moreover, the final overarching model allows us to test the impact of all the variables on Canadian judicial voting behaviour and assess the impact of Inglehart's shifting postmaterialist values thesis in free expression cases in a more comprehensive manner. Ultimately, we are interested in assessing whether a better developed socio-attitudinal model, which takes into consideration values that justices acquire in their formative years, can help explain shifts in the decision-making patterns of justices on the Canadian Supreme Court over time, while controlling for a host of other variables in the equation.

Explaining Liberal Free Expression Rulings Using Logistic Regression

In Table 4.10, the first model, found at the far left of the table, examines the impact of the six judicial-level variables on voting behaviour, while the second looks at the impact that the 13 case-level variables have on judicial outcomes. The third model, in turn, examines the impact that all 19 variables have, while simultaneously controlling for all other variables in the equation over the 1973–2010 time period. Our goal, as stated earlier, was to identify the different kinds of variables that play a critical role in explaining liberal, post-materialist votes in the free expression area. Although most of the independent variables that emerge as being statistically significant in the first two equations do prove statistically significant in the comprehensive model, the fact that one critical variable – namely, the McLachlin Court, fails to emerge as statistically significant in the final equation is worth noting and will be discussed in greater detail below.

A quick look at the summary goodness-of-fit statistics at the bottom of Table 4.10 indicates that while all three models achieve statistical significance, the judge-level model explains only 58 per cent of the votes correctly and is statistically significant at the 99 per cent confidence level. The 13-variable case-level model correctly predicts 70 per cent of the voting activity and has a reduction in error of 49 per cent, while the combined model, with 19 variables, correctly predicts 68 per cent of the voting outcomes and has a reduction in error of 44 per cent. Like the environmental area, there is a slight dip in the overall explanatory power between the case-level model and the overall combined model. This is essentially due to the inclusion of several judicial-level variables

Table 4.10. Estimating the Odds of a Liberal Vote in Canadian Supreme Court Free Expression Cases, 1973–2010

Variable (min., max.)	Judge-level model			Case-level model			Combined prediction model		
	Coefficient	Standard error	Change in probability	Coefficient	Standard error	Change in probability	Coefficient	Standard error	Change in probability
Female justice (0, 1)	.259	.219	.064				.281	.234	.070
Ideology score (–1.375, 1.618)	–.094	.122	–.070				–.088	.131	–.065
Academic (0, 1)	–.091	.192	–.023				–.097	.208	–.024
Quebec justice (0, 1)	–.490*	.192	–.120				–.613**	.207	–.149
Lamer Court (0, 1)	.350*	.202	.087				.510*	.248	.126
McLachlin Court (0, 1)	.487*	.226	.121				–.054	.270	–.013
Press case (0, 1)				–1.214***	.299	–.270	–1.295***	.337	–.286
Association case (0, 1)				–.624*	.284	–.149	–.417	.307	–.101
Political speech case (0, 1)				–.121	.247	–.030	.069	.269	.017
Commercial advertising (0, 1)				–.342	.285	–.083	–.112	.336	–.028
Obscenity (0, 1)				.061	.286	.015	.149	.321	.037
Criminal charge (0, 1)				–.762***	.239	–.183	–.589*	.265	–.143
S. 1 assessment (0,1)				1.043***	.220	.252	1.195***	.257	.284
Federal or provincial party (0, 1)				–.692**	.240	–.171	–.782**	.269	–.193
Individual seeking right (0, 1)				–.522**	.204	–.129	–.652**	.227	–.160
Number of free expression interveners (0, 13)				–.020	.042	–.063	–.002	.045	–.006
CCLA intervenes (0, 1)				–.266	.268	–.065	–.444	.289	–.108
Number of union interveners (0, 4)				–.011	.120	–.011	–.026	.122	–.026
Number of provincial interveners (0, 8)				–.225***	.050	–.381	–.204***	.053	–.353
Constant	–.238	.217		1.126	.308		1.027	.391	
Number of cases	574			643			574		
Chi-square –2 log likelihood	15.703**			83.174***			89.372***		
Pseudo R-square	.036			.162			.193		
Per cent correct predictions	58.4			69.5			68.3		
Reduction in error	9.6			48.5			43.8		

Note: Nine justices are omitted from the logistic regression model because newspapers did not provide ideological commentary on their appointment: Justices Abbott, Fauteux, Judson, Laskin, Martland, Pigeon, Pratte, Ritchie, and Spence.

*Significant at 95% confidence level; **significant at 99% confidence level; ***significant at 99.9% confidence level.

that have minimal explanatory power in the large equation, although they make theoretical sense to include in the analysis given our overall interest in developing a comprehensive socio-attitudinal model of judicial behaviour. In short, while this is not the most parsimonious model, all the variables are necessary because there is a theoretical explanation for their inclusion. Despite this slight dip in explanatory power, both the case-level and combined equations provide robust, model-fit statistics and explain a good deal of the variance in the dependent variable.

If one looks at the judge-level model, only three of the six variables are important in the equation – namely, the Quebec justice variable and the Lamer and McLachlin Court variables. As expected, when Quebec justices hear a free expression case, the change in probability score tabulated in the third column indicates that they are 12 per cent less likely to hand down a ruling in favour of the rights litigant as their fellow colleagues (*b* = –.490, statistically significant at the 95 per cent confidence level). This finding demonstrates that Quebec justices, as a group, are more conservative than their colleagues and had a greater propensity to side with the claims for order and security in the free expression area over the last 40 years. The positive parameter estimates for the two court variables in the equation were statistically significant and in the expected direction (*b* = .350 for the Lamer Court, and *b* = .487 for the McLachlin Court). While the odds-ratio analysis shows that the Lamer Court justices were 9 per cent more likely to rule in favour of free expression claims than their Laskin and Dickson counterparts, the McLachlin Court justices were 12 per cent more likely to do so. The data in this initial model seem to support the idea that Inglehart's shifting values thesis is taking place among legal elites in Canadian society and that as one moves closer in time to the present court period, justices demonstrate a greater propensity to hand down liberal postmaterialist rulings in the free expression area.

The newspaper ideology measure did not achieve statistical significance in either the judge-level or the combined model. Indeed, the coefficients in both equations were virtually identical (*b* = –.094 in the judge model, *b* = –.088 in the combined model), and the probability of producing a liberal ruling in the free expression area among the justices was negligible in both models. This finding is in line with prior research on the Canadian court showing that the ideology did not matter much in judicial decision making in free speech cases (see Ostberg and Wetstein 2007; Alarie and Green 2008, 85). Yet the fact that this finding holds up across a longer time span and larger swathe of cases in the free expression area has important ramifications for comparative scholars of high courts around the world. Indeed, quantitative scholarship on US appellate courts has touted the pre-eminence of the attitudinal model over other models of the decision-making process for over the past 60 years (see Segal and Spaeth 1993, 2002; Segal, Spaeth, and Benesh 2005). Its dominance might lead one to believe that the attitudinal model necessarily provides the most compelling explanation of judicial voting behaviour in other advanced industrial countries as well.

Yet ideology does not play a critical role in the voting behaviour of the Canadian justices in free expression cases, despite the fact that Canada has a similar culture and structure to the United States, and this highlights the need for scholars to systematically assess the veracity of the attitudinal model in top courts outside the United States for comparative purposes. Although previous studies have demonstrated that ideology does influence the voting behaviour of Canadian justices in some important areas of law (see Ostberg and Wetstein 2007; Songer et al. 2012), the fact that its impact is not as consistent or as pervasive as in the Unites States continues to be a compelling and worthwhile finding. Moreover, the fact that it was not found to be important in the free expression area is significant for comparative scholars because one would think that ideology would matter when deciding on a right that is fundamental to maintaining a democratic system.

As in the environmental area, many more variables in the case-level model of free expression disputes achieved statistical significance than in the judge-level model. Indeed, 7 of the 13 independent variables were critical in the equation, and all but one achieved statistical significance at the 99 per cent confidence level. This, in turn, explains the 11 per cent increase in case votes correctly predicted in the model over the judge-level one. Looking more closely at the case results in Table 4.10, only one of the four intervener variables achieved statistical significance – namely, cases in which provincial governments took a stance ($b = -.225$). As expected, the negative coefficient suggests that in cases in which provinces intervened, the justices were 38 per cent less likely to hand down a ruling favouring the free speech claim. This finding suggests that when provinces intervene in free expression cases, the justices are more likely to pick up on important public safety and security cues put forth by the government and hand down rulings that meet those concerns. It is worth noting that the coefficients for the CCLA and union interveners, although insignificant, were in the unexpected direction. Thus, the rise in intervener activity by these two pro-rights groups over the last several decades has not had a decisive pro-rights impact on the Canadian justices in the free expression area.

Only two of the parameter estimates for the five issue characteristics included in the case-level model were statistically significant, although all of them were in the expected direction. The negative coefficient for the free press variable (*b* = −1.214, statistically significant at the 99.9 per cent confidence level) indicates that when the justices heard disputes related to media publications or free press rights, they were 27 per cent less likely to hand down a liberal ruling than in free speech cases. In addition, the parameter estimate for free association cases was statistically significant and in the correct direction, albeit smaller than the one in the free press area (*b* = −.624). As a result, in cases featuring a free association claim, the justices were 15 per cent less likely to hand down a liberal, postmaterialist ruling than in free speech cases. These findings suggest that in the case-level equation, the Canadian justices did exhibit a behaviour that followed Emerson's hierarchy of judicial protection for the three broad areas of free expression, in which the justices provided the greatest protection to free speech claims, followed by association and, last, press concerns. In contrast, none of the three parameter estimates were significant in our test for a hierarchy of protected values solely in free speech cases. The small magnitude of the changes in probability for obscenity, commercial advertising, and political speech indicate that when controlling for other case facts, parties, and interveners, the justices failed to differentiate between the form and type of free expression at issue when reaching their decision in this area of law. Put simply, other case characteristics appeared to be more prominent in driving the decision-making outcome, a finding that parallels earlier scholarship in this area (see Ostberg and Wetstein 2007).

The two unique case characteristics and two party variables in the equation achieved statistical significance, and all were in the expected direction. As anticipated, in free expression cases in which a criminal charge was filed against a litigant (*b* = −.762), the justices were 18 per cent less likely to rule in favour of the free speech claimant who broke the law. In contrast, when the justices engaged in s. 1 analysis after determining that a Charter violation had occurred (*b* = 1.043, statistically significant at the 99.9 per cent confidence level), they were 25 per cent more likely to determine that the violation was not justified in a democratic society than in cases in which s. 1 analysis was not involved. This finding indicates that when the Charter was added to the Constitution in 1982, the justices on the Supreme Court began taking the free expression mandates found in s. 2(b) seriously despite the qualifying provisions that were included in the document.

Turning to the party variables in the case-level equation, one finds that when the federal or provincial government was a party in a suit ($b = -.692$, statistically significant at the 99 per cent confidence level), the rights claimant had a 17 per cent lower chance of winning the case. This finding suggests that rights claimants had a much better chance of winning free expression victories against city or local government officials than their federal or provincial counterparts. Meanwhile, when a litigator sought expressive rights on behalf of individuals ($b = -.522$, statistically significant at the 99 per cent confidence level), as opposed to those representing corporations or unions, they were 13 per cent less likely to win the case, all other things being equal. The fact that these variables achieved statistical significance makes sense and gives further credence to Galanter's (1974) claim that federal and provincial governments have more practice honing their skills in appellate court than city governments. Moreover, it supports the notion that individuals have fewer resources to fight in court than those advocating corporate and union interests.

The third logistic equation in Table 4.10 provides a holistic model that includes the six judge-level variables and 13 case-level variables in one large equation. As in the environmental area, this third model produces results that are virtually identical to those found in the previous two equations, with one major exception. As discussed earlier, the 19-variable model correctly predicted 68 per cent of the cases and had a 44 per cent reduction in error over the modal guessing strategy. Although there were small shifts in the coefficients and slight changes in the probabilities as one moves from the first two models to the third one, 8 of the 10 variables that proved statistically significant in the first two equations were also significant in the combined model and in the expected direction. As in the environmental area, the bulk of the variables that provided explanatory power in the combined equation were at the case level, while only two of the three judge-level variables remained prominent.

The one judge-level variable that did not achieve statistical significance in the full model is the one for the McLachlin Court ($b = -.054$), and, unlike its coefficient in the judge-level model, it is now in the unexpected direction, albeit small in magnitude. Indeed, the change in probability for this variable in the equation is negligible (roughly 1 per cent). This outcome is an important finding that might appear puzzling given our earlier statistical results. Even though Inglehart's shifting postmaterialist values thesis seemed confirmed during the descriptive stage of our analysis, when we assessed judicial-career, liberal voting scores in the free expression area in relation to year of birth and additionally in the first judge-level logistic equation, it loses some of its power once we introduce case-level and litigant variables into the equation. The fact that the Lamer Court variable (b = .510) is statistically significant and in the expected direction in the combined model lends credibility to the idea that a value shift has indeed taken place among some judicial elites in the free expression area over time. The change in probability for this variable shows that justices under the Lamer tenure were 13 per cent more likely to hand down liberal rulings in the free expression area than their colleagues on the earlier Laskin and Dickson Courts, even when controlling for other factors.

However, the fact that the McLachlin Court variable is not significant in the combined model shows the importance of incorporating case-level variables when developing regression models for top-level courts. We also note that this finding vis-à-vis the McLachlin Court squares with some of the research on the fading power of the Charter revolution in recent years (see McCormick 2015). Moreover, it makes sense that, after the initial flurry of first-order Charter rulings in favour of free expression claimants, disputes have become more difficult to decide in this area of law. Another explanation for these McLachlin Court findings is that the justices of the more contemporary period are far more interested in promoting equality interests in free expression cases than in endorsing unfettered free expression. This stance is understandable in light of the heightened need for ensuring that all voices are heard, especially in the political realm, where the elites and political parties have an oversized voice in the election process; see *Harper v. Canada (Attorney General)*, [2004] 1 S.C.R. 827. Indeed, the traditional postmaterialist value of endorsing free expression has been supplanted in many cases by the protection of equality interests to promote a healthier, more vital democracy. The absence of a strong coefficient for the McLachlin Court is indicative of a gradual tectonic shift of values in the postmaterialist framework, with greater emphasis on equality over libertarian notions of unregulated speech. We focus more explicitly on this theme in the political speech cases in the following chapter.

For justices on the Canadian Supreme Court, case facts relating to issue characteristics, parties in a suit, and intervener activity seem to have a profound impact on their voting behaviour in the free expression area. Ironically, the changes that took place for the McLachlin Court variable in the free expression area were almost the mirror opposite of what occurred in the environmental area. If we simply relied on the descriptive statistics in the first stage of our analysis and the results from the judge-level model, we would have concluded that there was a steady upswing in the percentage of liberal rulings over time for the Lamer and McLachlin Courts from their earlier two predecessors and that it was the presence of the later judges that mattered most in promoting this shift (see Figure 4.2). Moreover, that upswing was subsequently verified using logistic regression with various judge-level variables.

However, when the case-level variables are introduced into the logistic equation, one finds that the McLachlin Court did not hand down any more liberal rulings in the free expression area than justices in the Laskin and Dickson Courts. Thus, unlike the environmental area, when case-level variables are added to the equation to take into account the possible impact that increasingly difficult case facts, parties, or interveners might have on the justices, the postmaterialist liberal shift that seemed to appear in the descriptive statistics and first regression equation seems to disappear. Overall, while the Canadian court moved in a decisive postmaterialist direction under the Lamer Court tenure, that trend seems to have moderated in the first 10 years of the McLachlin Court, at least in the free expression area. The recent decline in the postmaterialist trend might be attributed to the complex issues and litigant resources that repeat players have brought to bear in the modern free expression cases. In other words, it is possible that the complexity of recent free expression claims is forcing the justices to pay greater attention to the issues, factual circumstances, and briefs submitted by repeat players, thus making it more difficult for the justices to simply rely on their own world view, and current attitudes and values, to act as cues for resolving these complex disputes. Alternatively, the McLachlin Court may be more reluctant to hand down rulings in a libertarian direction in the free speech area because other postmaterialist values, such as equality, are considered to be more important than unfettered free speech for this court. As suggested earlier, this argument is more clearly laid out in the next chapter.

The complete logistic model featured in this chapter helps identify the relative weight of various factors in a socio-attitudinal explanation of free expression voting outcomes. There is evidence that specific individual background variables have an influence on the justices, such as their upbringing in Quebec and, to some degree, their socialization during the later period of economic security (as witnessed by the Lamer Court's positive and significant coefficient). Even so, stronger impacts are evident among specific case characteristics that tap the role of criminal charges in the case, social groups, repeat litigators, and presence of provincial government interveners. Missing from the analysis is consideration of the rationale used by the justices in support of their decisions. We will now take a closer look at some of the precedent-setting cases in two salient areas of free speech – namely, commercial advertising and political speech – to get a better idea of how the law has developed in these issue areas over the last 40 years. The legal trends that emerge help shed some light on why the McLachlin Court moved away from libertarian postmaterialist rulings in free expression disputes.

Chapter Five

Qualitative Analysis of Political Speech and Commercial Advertising Disputes

Introduction

In the previous chapter, we uncovered evidence of a postmaterialist value shift in the outcomes of free expression cases decided over the last 40 years, although there appears to have been a movement away from freedom and towards equality as a preferred postmaterialist value priority in the first 10 years of the McLachlin Court. Following the pattern established in chapter 3, this chapter turns to a detailed qualitative assessment of the reasons for judgment in landmark cases, this time focusing on disputes involving political expression and commercial advertising. To set the stage for this analysis, we outline why leading scholars think that free expression is central to a democratic society. In doing so, we draw some parallels between the theoretical and the philosophical defence of free expression and Inglehart's empirical documentation of a postmaterialist value shift in various advanced industrial societies.

A number of scholars have explored the philosophical foundations of a free and democratic society and articulated several reasons for protecting expression in this type of political system (see Locke 1689; Mill 1859; Meiklejohn 1960; Black 1968; Hogg 2011, s. 43-4; Ducat 2013, 802–9). Inglehart's recognition of self-expression as an essential postmaterialist value has distinctive parallels with Thomas Emerson's (1963, 1970) belief that freedom of expression is essential to a democratic polity because, in part, it enables people to reach their full potential as human beings, allowing them to develop their own views and express themselves in their own ways (Emerson 1963, 1970, 6; see also Nowak and Rotunda 1995, 991–2). A second justification for protecting free expression is that democratic societies cannot exist without the consent of the governed. Free expression at its most fundamental level allows individuals to have a voice in the democratic process by debating the merits of various policy choices and selecting those who make decisions for them, thus allowing citizens to have an indirect influence on the major decisions of the day (Locke 1689; Emerson 1963, 1970). Inglehart also documented this feature as being essential in a post-modern society and has noted a causal connection between mass self-expression and flourishing democratic institutions (Inglehart and Welzel 2005, 150–7; Inglehart et al. 2008, 266).

A third rationale for promoting freedom of expression is that it fosters the discovery of truth and the advancement of knowledge in a democracy (Mill 1859; Emerson 1963, 1970; Ducat 2013). Members of society must allow the free exchange of all ideas in the marketplace, no matter how caustic or far-fetched, so that the best ideas are heard and truth can prevail over falsehood. One of the clearest statements regarding the importance of the free exchange of contested ideas is expressed by Justice Oliver Wendell Holmes in his dissent with Justice Brandeis in *Abrams v. United States*, 250 U.S. 616 (1919), a case in which the Supreme Court was trying to grapple with setting limits on free expression in the midst of the First World War. In this dissent, he stated, "The ultimate good desired is better reached by the free trade in ideas – that the best test of truth is the power of the thought to get itself accepted in the competition of the market, and that truth is the only ground upon which" the wishes of the people "can be carried out" (*Abrams v. United States*, 250 U.S. 616 [1919], quoted in Ducat 2013, 812). Taken together, these three rationales for free expression are essential to developing and maintaining a democracy, and clearly, postmaterialist notions of individual self-expression, self-fulfilment, and the attainment of truth cannot exist without unfettered speech.

Postmaterialist and Materialist Charter Language

Assessing whether members of the Supreme Court of Canada use these concepts in their written reasons for judgment is the central focus of this chapter. Not long after the Charter of Rights and Freedoms was adopted, the Canadian Supreme Court echoed some of the same themes discussed by Emerson and other defenders of free expression. In *Irwin Toy v. Quebec*, [1989] 1 S.C.R. 927, the court's majority opinion, penned by Chief Justices Dickson and Lamer and Justice Wilson, summarized three key reasons for protecting freedom of expression.

> (1) seeking and attaining the truth is an inherently good activity; (2) participation in social and political decision-making is to be fostered and encouraged; and (3) the diversity in forms of individual self-fulfillment and human flourishing ought to be cultivated. (*Irwin Toy v. Quebec*, [1989] 1 S.C.R. 927, at 976)

The court majority in *Irwin Toy* provides the same justification for protecting expression as noted by earlier political theorists, and readers should take particular note that the same principles lie at the core of the postmaterialist value structure enunciated by Inglehart. Some critics might argue that any movement in the postmaterialist direction is simply a reflection of the Charter of Rights and Freedoms' impact on the court. As many scholars have noted, the addition of the Charter to the Canadian Constitution in 1982 ushered in a rights revolution that has played out in subsequent decades (see Manfredi 1993, 2001; Morton and Knopff 2000; Ostberg and Wetstein 2007; Songer et al. 2012). However, we believe that the Charter's very existence is emblematic of a broader postmaterialist mindset coming into bloom in Canada. Moreover, it is important to reiterate that both materialist and postmaterialist values are embedded in the Charter's language, and despite its prominent recognition of the right to freedom of expression, its adoption allowed justices of the modern Supreme Court to breathe strong life into the s. 2(b) protections, while simultaneously restricting expressive activity under s. 1.

The significance of s. 1 of the Charter cannot be ignored. The competing values within the interpretive framework of the Canadian Constitution, and the tension that plays out on the judicial stage, allow the justices to engage in the Charter Two-Step and justify restrictions on repugnant forms of expression, such as obscenity, pornography, hate speech, and untruthful advertising, in an effort to secure the materialist outcomes of order, safety, and security or to promote equal treatment of Canadians (Knopff and Morton 1992, 35). When justices give substantive rights such as free expression a broad purposive interpretation in a particular case, they necessarily support postmaterialist values because they elevate that right to fundamental status and recognize its importance in maintaining the democratic process, fostering the search for truth, and ensuring individual self-fulfilment. In contrast, when justices on the court determine in a case that a regulation that violates expressive rights is justified under s. 1, they necessarily give priority to the materialist concern for ensuring order and security and that individuals are protected from harm in the marketplace of ideas. Alternatively, justices can use s. 1 analysis to buttress the equal treatment of individuals in society and allow postmaterialist equality concerns to trump the unfettered free expression arguments of litigants. This unique Canadian compromise, which is absent from the US Constitution, brings an element of complexity to the Canadian Constitution and gives justices the leeway to promote values at different points on the freedom-equality-order continuum. This complexity also provides a unique opportunity to study Inglehart's thesis in the Canadian context.

Why Support for Free Expression Reflects Postmaterialist Values

Before turning to an examination of landmark cases, we want to reiterate how our conception of postmaterialist values informs our discussion of them. In short, free expression cases present a tension between the values of freedom and order on the one hand and freedom and equality on the other hand. Cases that juxtapose freedom versus order provide the most natural fit with Inglehart's postmaterialist-materialist dichotomy because they pit an individual's right to free expression against society's interest in protecting the community from the harmful effects of some forms of speech. For example, such cases may include an individual's expressive right to engage in hate speech or slander and a union member's right to strike pitted against the government's materialist interest in protecting society from such potentially harmful expression. Inglehart would label defenders of pure free speech as advocating postmaterialist values because the ability to freely express one's thoughts is a core value that dates back to philosophical thinkers since the Enlightenment (Locke 1689; Mill 1859; Meiklejohn 1960; Emerson 1963, 1970; Ducat 2013, 802–9). Put simply, hard-core postmaterialists are likely to be the most vocal defenders of an absolute right to free expression, whereas hard-core materialists are likely to be the most ready to suppress expression if it causes harm to individuals and the community.

As we indicated in the prior chapter, free expression cases also counterbalance the right to free expression against equality interests. While Inglehart sees both as postmaterialist values – at least in reference to order – we reiterate that there is a continuum of postmaterialist values, with freedom occupying the most libertarian end of the postmaterialist

Table 5.1. Postmaterialist-Materialist Values: Examples of Value Conflicts in Cases

Type of dispute	Postmaterialist value priority		Materialist value
	Freedom	Equality	Order
Campaign finance restrictions	Allow unlimited campaign expenditures	Restrict wealthy campaign expenditures to promote fairness	
Political advertising	Allow individuals to place political advertisements to sway voters	Restrict political advertisements to promote fairness and balance in politics	
Commercial advertising	Allow advertising that targets children		Restrict ads that target children because of their vulnerability and inability to make informed decisions

continuum, followed closely by equality, and order at the farthest, materialist end. Cases that present a tension between free expression and equality interests can include arguments over the right of government workers to participate in election campaigns, disputes over campaign finance laws, and laws restricting the rights of individuals to place political advertisements. In such cases, justices can either side with the liberty claims of the individuals to engage in unlimited campaign expenditures, and allow political advertising, or take a stance in favour of fair treatment or equality in the political process by restricting wealthy campaign expenditures.

While Inglehart would argue that a pro-equality outcome is postmaterialist in nature, such an outcome needs to be seen in an even broader value context and in light of the alternative possibility – namely, that a more forceful, postmaterialist outcome would endorse pure liberty interests over equality because freedom is essential to the maintenance of a democratic system. While the restriction of campaign expenditures in the name of political fairness and equality has become a modern democratic touchstone, we argue that it is a slightly "less pure" postmaterialist position because ensuring the free exchange of ideas lies at the bedrock of a democratic polity. Having said this, we acknowledge and are sympathetic to the difficulties that emerge when unfettered political speech and unlimited campaign expenditures become a problem for modern democratic elections. Our depiction of the postmaterialist-materialist continuum of values in a few specific free expression contexts is presented in Table 5.1.

We contend that justices envision these legal disputes as lying along a value spectrum that generally pits freedom concerns against equality or order demands, in part because the parties arguing the cases before the court tend to frame the disputes in the context of fundamental rights on the one hand and the need for limits on rights on the other. From Inglehart's theory, we postulate that the justices are in some respect a product of their formative years, with more contemporary justices being more inclined to endorse the postmaterialist spirit of free expression and, to a lesser extent, equality principles at the expense of order and safety concerns. Inglehart's theory of value change helps us comprehend how justices situate disputes in a changing landscape of value priorities and provides shorthand cues for how to decide the cases. If Inglehart's theory is correct, as attitudes towards free expression and equality change with generational replacement in the mass public, so too should the decisions of the Supreme Court. If correct, evidence of this change over time should be found in the language and word choices of the justices in their opinions.

Following the pattern set in chapter 3, we use qualitative content analysis to assess the value structure the justices bring to the process of writing reasons for judgment. The approach starts from the assumption that we can draw inferences about the values that are important to the justices based on the meaning of the words they choose to highlight in their legal rationale. In the context of political speech and commercial expression cases, whenever justices seek to emphasize a postmaterialist, pro–free expression stance, we expect them to imbue their rationale with words like *fundamental freedoms, liberty, the pursuit of truth, self-expression, self-actualization, self-fulfilment*, and *individual autonomy*. These words reflect a prioritization of freedom as the most important value along the freedom-equality-and-order continuum. Alternatively, justices who hand down rulings highlighting words such as *ensuring equality, egalitarian, fairness, balance*, and *avoiding favouritism* are far more focused on promoting equal access to the democratic process, and they are highlighting a commitment to securing the postmaterialist value of political equality over political liberty. Such language reflects a keener interest on the part of the justices in protecting equality interests at the expense of unfettered expression. At the other end of the spectrum, when justices seek to highlight the value of order and safety, they are likely to use words like *harm, order, protecting the vulnerable, injury to society*, and *placing reasonable limits on expression*. Moreover, justices at the materialist side of the continuum will be more interested in quelling breaches of the peace or barring demonstrations to protect citizens from potential riots and to ensure community safety.

As we suggested in the prior chapter, our reading of the cases is designed to look for nuance and directional value statements that reflect the central rationale for a justice's reasons for judgment. Overall, we suggest that a content analysis of the judgments and the word choices at the core of a ruling reflect the legal value priorities in the minds of the justices. This is a recognition that the language and tone used in the written reasons for judgment matter. All things considered, we are concerned with the content of the language and values at the heart of the rationale, which dictates the future direction of the law. If Inglehart's theory of value change is relevant, we expect to see more contemporary justices of the Supreme Court using postmaterialist language more frequently than justices who served 20 or 30 years ago. In light of the findings in chapter 4, we also suspect that the form of that postmaterialist language will reflect a greater emphasis on equality concerns in the first decade of the McLachlin Court, and we believe that this is reflective of a court and society that support equality norms to a greater extent than unfettered free expression rights.

Since two critical rationales for protecting free expression in a democratic society include fostering political participation and individual self-fulfilment, we decided that it would be prudent to assess the language and rationale of cases in the areas of political speech and commercial advertising. Moreover, these cases often highlight a materialistic-postmaterialist tension between the freedom to engage in political discourse, campaigning, or campaign financing and the government's desire to invoke restrictions that reduce the apparent harms of unfair competition or to place rational limits on the political activities of government employees. In many of these cases, political participation is linked with expressive activity, and the question boils down to whether government limitations are allowable.

Commercial advertising, in turn, presents a unique set of dynamics when materialist and postmaterialist claims come into conflict. In many of these cases, the question turns on a company's freedom to advertise a product in a certain way versus a materialistic sentiment advocated by government to protect individuals in society from the harm of certain forms of advertising. Here the government becomes the paternalistic protector of individuals in the marketplace of ideas, seeking to ensure that corporate advertising is not targeting the uninformed, such as children, or does not make disingenuous claims about a product. Moreover, in some instances, government has gone so far as to require certain forms of advertising to ensure that the truth about a product comes out (i.e., tobacco advertising restrictions). Readers should note that a postmaterialist viewpoint, and one advocated by hard-core free speech advocates, would allow the advertising to go unfettered in most circumstances and let the discourse in the marketplace allow consumers to make their own informed choices. Those on the materialist side of this debate believe that consumers are bound to make faulty choices in their freedom to consume or not consume certain products, and, therefore, government must protect them from unscrupulous activity.

In the end, these forms of expression lie at the heart of what it means to live in a democracy. Moreover, political speech and commercial advertising cases represent two of the largest subsets of free expression disputes handed down during the 1973–2010 period, with 15 per cent of the cases invoking political speech and 17 per cent featuring commercial advertising ($N = 13$ and 14, respectively).

Political Speech Cases

Political Speech – Landmark Decisions of the Laskin and Dickson Courts

One prominent area of contested free speech law has been the realm of political expression. These cases raise issues about the ability of Canadians to participate in political processes and to voice their dissent and critical views of government. In some cases, the definition of speech is stretched to include symbolic protest or assembly for parades, but in all cases, the pivotal concerns highlighted by Emerson are in play: the notion that free speech is central to the pursuit of truth, the pursuit of democratic engagement, and, in many cases, the pursuit of individual self-fulfilment.

There were three significant political speech cases heard by the Laskin and Dickson Courts, and the earliest leading case featured an individual seeking to overturn an ordinance placing a 30-day ban on public assemblies in Montreal (*Attorney General (Canada) and Dupond v. Montreal*, [1978] 2 S.C.R. 770, hereafter *Dupond*). The court ultimately ruled (6–3) to endorse the city's actions, with Justice Beetz arguing that the ordinance fell within the province's power because the British North America Act (BNA Act) granted it the power to make laws pertaining to "matters of a merely local or private nature." *Dupond* is part of a long line of cases that involve the federal criminal law power and provincial efforts to suppress the conditions that foster crime (for other examples, see *Bedard v. Dawson*, [1923] S.C.R. 681; *Westendorp v. R.*, [1983] 1 S.C.R. 43; and *Rio Hotel Ltd. v. New Brunswick (Liquor Licensing Board)*,

[1987] 2 S.C.R. 59). Since the actions here were related to the use of local public spaces in Montreal under exceptional circumstances, the ordinance was seen as preventative and designed to suppress conditions that had fostered crimes in earlier protests (*Dupond*, [1978] 2 S.C.R. 770, at 792). Justice Beetz directly rejected the argument that the ordinance violated fundamental freedoms, noting that it "prohibits the holding of all assemblies, parades or gatherings for ... thirty days, irrespective of religion, ideology or political views" (*Dupond*, [1978] 2 S.C.R. 770, at 795). The language used by Justice Beetz is clearly materialistic in nature, promoting security and safety over any free speech arguments.

As a final materialistic coda, Justice Beetz took a parting shot at the argument that the ordinance and by-law were in conflict with fundamental freedoms found in either the BNA Act or the 1960 statutory Canadian Bill of Rights. He noted that "demonstrations are not a form of speech but of collective action. ... They are of the nature of a display of force rather than of appeal to reason; their inarticulateness prevents them from becoming a part of language and from reaching the level of discourse" (*Dupond*, [1978] 2 S.C.R. 770, at 797). These statements suggest that such demonstrations ran contrary to the democratic discourse or pursuit of truth and, therefore, were unworthy of absolute constitutional protection. In this manner, the materialist pole of safety and order held sway in Justice Beetz's majority opinion over the post-materialist argument for liberal free expression.

Chief Justice Laskin, writing in dissent, advanced the libertarian free expression argument, claiming that Montreal had enacted a "mini-Criminal Code" to quell breaches of the peace and ensure public order and, in doing so, had infringed the federal government's criminal law power (*Dupond*, [1978] 2 S.C.R. 770, at 775). He pointed out that there were sufficient federal laws on the books to punish and prevent violence associated with protests and demonstrations, including the power to make arrests without warrants and to disperse assemblies (*Dupond*, [1978] 2 S.C.R. 770, at 779). Chief Justice Laskin took issue with the majority's justification for placing a ban on all assemblies for 30 days. He wrote, "Here persons who might seek to associate or gather for innocent purposes are to be barred ... because of a desire to forestall the violent or the likely violent. This is the invocation of a doctrine which should alarm free citizens" (ibid.). Chief Justice Laskin's argument demonstrates the overreach that he saw in the Montreal ordinance: it threw the "baby" of free assembly and dissent out with the bathwater simply because of past problems with violent protesters.

The *Dupond* case nicely demonstrates the dual positions that exist in the realm of political expression. On the postmaterialist side of the argument, free expression is worthy of protection, and if things get out of hand, government can punish the offenders without shutting down the vehicle of expression. The other side of the argument is clearly rooted in the maintenance of order and safety, and the desire to protect society and its citizens from the harms that can befall property owners and other citizens when protests get out of hand, a position that clearly carried the day in the *Dupond* case. As Hogg (2011, s. 43-5) has pointed out, Montreal's ordinance would have certainly come under intense Charter scrutiny had it been adopted in the wake of the Charter.

In 1987, the Dickson Court turned its attention to a different form of political speech. In *OPSEU v. Ontario (Attorney General)*, [1987] 2 S.C.R. 2 (hereafter *OPSEU*), the focus was on the rights of public servants and union employees to run for office and engage in electioneering activities like canvassing and soliciting donations for political parties. The union and individuals believed the law should not prohibit individuals from running for federal office without taking a leave from their public service jobs; it should also not prohibit them from engaging in political support of candidates for federal office (*OPSEU*, [1987] 2 S.C.R. 2, at 9–10). Ultimately, the Supreme Court upheld the province's efforts to restrict political activities by government workers.

While the decision in *OPSEU* resulted in a 6–0 materialist, anti–free speech outcome, the justices split into three camps in reaching their decision. Justice Lamer issued a brief, narrow opinion that would have simply upheld the provincial restriction because s. 92(4) of the Constitution Act granted provinces exclusive authority over the establishment of the tenure of office and the "appointment and payment of provincial officers" (*OPSEU*, [1987] 2 S.C.R. 2, at 58). Justice Dickson, writing a more lengthy solo concurrence, upheld the law, concluding that the province could enact restrictions on the political activities of employees because they pertained to civil rights. In short, labour regulations like those envisioned in the law, which required government employees to take a leave of absence to run for office, were essentially labour laws that were justifiable when balancing free speech interests against the need for an impartial public service. The broadest opinion for upholding the law came from Justice Beetz's majority opinion (signed by three others), which endorsed the law under the province's power to amend, "from Time to Time … the Constitution of the Province" (s. 92, Constitution Act, 1867; *OPSEU*, [1987] 2 S.C.R. 2, at 37–8).

The free speech arguments advanced by OPSEU and the three individual employees were undercut by two important facts in this case. First, the inability to make arguments on Charter grounds under s. 2(a) or 2(b) of the Charter left the attack on the regulations in the realm of a question of federalism: did the law overstep provincial power by encroaching on the regulation of federal election rights? That question left the playing field of discourse largely to principles of governmental power and an interpretation of the law as a valid labour law, regulating the employment rights of public servants. Second, because the employees had not faced disciplinary proceedings, the controversy had not yet ripened to the point of actual harm to the employees, a point raised by Chief Justice Dickson in his judgment (*OPSEU*, [1987] 2 S.C.R. 2, at 26).

In the face of these hurdles, the arguments advanced by the appellants pointed to libertarian, postmaterialist language from prior rulings by the court. For example, the court had acknowledged in *RWDSU v. Dolphin Delivery*, [1986] 2 S.C.R. 573 that freedom of speech and expression was recognized as an essential feature of Canadian democracy even before the adoption of the Charter (*RWDSU v. Dolphin Delivery*, [1986] 2 S.C.R. 573, at 584). Given these recognitions, the union sought to extend the purview of free expression to the political activities of the employees in question. Despite these arguments, both Chief Justice Dickson and Justice Beetz claimed that no right was absolute and that reasonable limits were prudent. Justice Dickson pointed out that the prior ruling in *Fraser v. Public Service Staff Relations Board*, [1985] 2 S.C.R. 455 had called for a balancing of free speech interests against other competing values; he added that the case stood for the proposition that freedom of expression "is a fundamental value but that certain reasonable abridgements, motivated by other competing values, may validly be authorized by a legislature" (*OPSEU*, [1987] 2 S.C.R. 2, at 25).

While Chief Justice Dickson spent little time articulating the competing values in play, the competition was manifestly evident in the opinion of Justice Beetz. For him, the free speech rights of the appellants were stacked against the rights of the citizens of Ontario to expect impartiality and political neutrality from their public servants (*OPSEU*, [1987] 2 S.C.R. 2, at 41–6). In short, when balancing the interests, regulations are sometimes necessary to ensure that an impartial government staff is at work for society. The fair-minded tenor of *OPSEU* reflects a postmaterialist concern for political fairness, which stands in contrast to the materialist, security-minded ruling handed down by the Laskin Court majority in the *Dupond* case. Yet both are contrasted against unrestrained freedom of expression. The communitarian leaning of the 1970s and 1980s would begin to fade away in some of the Lamer Court rulings of the 1990s, but there is no doubt that, in the interplay among freedom, equality, and order, *Dupond* and *OPSEU* reflected the values of a court not yet ready for the full flowering of free expression claims.

Political Speech – Landmark Decisions of the Lamer Court

The introduction of Charter rights helped accelerate the number of political speech cases that reached the Supreme Court's docket. In total, six separate cases invoking important political speech claims made it to the court between 1991 and 1999. In one of them, the court relied on the Charter to reverse the decision in *OPSEU* by striking down blanket prohibitions on government employees that were engaging in work for the benefit of federal candidates for office or federal parties (*Osborne v. Canada*, [1991] 2 S.C.R. 69).[1] While political campaigns remained a central focus of this area of law for the Lamer Court, so did access to public property to engage in communication. In the paragraphs that follow, two pivotal rulings are analysed to explore their contribution to the materialist-postmaterialist debate and because they foreshadow similar controversies that would be present in the first decade of the McLachlin Court in the 2000s.

In *Committee for the Commonwealth of Canada v. Canada*, [1991] 1 S.C.R. 139 (hereafter *Committee for the Commonwealth*), the court addressed whether a public airport authority could ban political solicitation in Montreal's Dorval Airport – a question that brought the court squarely into the debate of public forum regulations. On appeal, the Supreme Court framed the issues around whether the regulations violated the Charter and, if so, whether they were justified under s. 1 analysis. The court, voting 9–0, sided with the postmaterialist, free speech claim, but a set of fractured opinions indicated a wide variety of views on the subject of protecting free speech in public spaces.

Justice McLachlin, who authored the plurality opinion, laid out the distinctions that divided her moderate view from the more extreme

1 In *Osborne*, the court struck down the Ontario provisions that prohibited any work on behalf of federal parties or candidates during an election campaign. While restrictions on political activities might be justified under s. 1 of the Charter to advance the interest of maintaining an impartial public service, the restrictions in question were too broad and all-encompassing and did not present a narrower means to achieve that objective (*Osborne v. Canada*, [1991] 2 S.C.R. 69; Hogg 2011, 43–57).

ones advanced by Justice L'Heureux-Dubé and Chief Justice Lamer. She characterized Justice L'Heureux-Dubé's opinion as the most liberal, suggesting that it advocated for protecting all expression on public property under s. 2(b) of the Charter and called for an assessment of the appropriate time, place and manner restrictions on such expression under s. 1 analysis. At the other extreme was Chief Justice Lamer, who contended that s. 2(b) protection should extend to expression in public spaces only if it did not unduly impair the function of government property. As he put it, "The fact that one's freedom of expression is intrinsically limited by the function of a public place is an application of the general rule that one's rights are always circumscribed by the rights of others" (*Committee for the Commonwealth*, [1991] 1 S.C.R. 139, at 156–7). By taking such an interest-balancing position, Chief Justice Lamer was endorsing materialist values at the expense of a postmaterialist view of free speech. What troubled him were the actions of the RCMP and airport officials, who had invoked commercial regulations to prohibit political speech that was incompatible with an airport facility. On those grounds, then, Chief Justice Lamer upheld the free speech claims of the Committee, but his particular position on s. 2(b)'s application suggested a narrow approach to free speech rights in this context.

Justice L'Heureux-Dubé, joined by Justice Cory, dispatched the public space question by finding that airport zones provided spaces for political engagement where many people have "time to kill and little to do" (*Committee for the Commonwealth*, [1991] 1 S.C.R. 139, at 193). Her reasons for judgment contained the flowery language of postmaterialist, liberal free expression, citing authors like Emerson (1963) and others in defence of political expression. At one point she stated, "Freedom of expression cannot be jettisoned in any system which values self-government" (*Committee for the Commonwealth*, [1991] 1 S.C.R. 139, at 170). At another turn, she wrote, "Free debate has often been perceived as the optimal means to discover 'truth' – through the 'marketplace of ideas' in which truth will ultimately prevail" (*Committee for the Commonwealth*, [1991] 1 S.C.R. 139, at 173). Ultimately, Justice L'Heureux-Dubé used the *Irwin Toy* test to conclude that the actions of the officer and the regulations themselves served to infringe Charter s. 2(b) rights and that they could not be saved under s. 1 scrutiny (*Irwin Toy*, [1989] 1 S.C.R. 927). The open-ended nature of the language contained in the regulations, which prohibited anyone from conducting "any business or undertaking, commercial or otherwise," left much to the imagination and could include just about any free speech activity imaginable. For vagueness and overbreadth, the regulation was constitutionally invalid. Had the law been tied in some way to problems of airport ingress and egress, or security, the story might have been different (*Committee for the Commonwealth*, [1991] 1 S.C.R. 139, at 222–3).

If Justice L'Heureux-Dubé's opinion stood for the proposition that virtually all speech on public property was worthy of s. 2(b) protection, Justice McLachlin's could be summarized as claiming that *some speech* is subject to s. 2(b) protection on *some public property*. Using principles from the *Irwin Toy/Oakes* test, she contended that if the government's purpose in enacting a regulation was to restrict the content of expression by limiting the forums in which it occurred, then s. 2(b) would apply and the regulation would be an unconstitutional infringement. If, however, the regulation was content neutral, it may not infringe s. 2(b) at all. In the face of content-neutral regulations, the individual claimant would have to show that the expression in question, including its time, place, and manner, would promote one of the purposes underlying the guarantee of free expression: "(1) the seeking and obtaining of truth; (2) participation in social and political decision-making; and (3) the encouragement of diversity in forms of individual self-fulfillment and human flourishing by cultivating a tolerant, welcoming environment for the conveyance and reception of ideas" (*Committee for the Commonwealth*, [1991] 1 S.C.R. 139, at 238–9). Note that the language of Justice McLachlin emanates from a postmaterialist perspective, yet for her, the onus was squarely on the individual to demonstrate a link between the core values of free speech and the need to conduct it in a public space.

The application of *Irwin Toy* and *Oakes* principles led Justice McLachlin, in turn, to take a middle-of-the-road position and conclude that the regulation was content neutral, but that the effect of the law was clearly to limit free expression, which was worthy of protection.[2]

---

2 The *Oakes* test is somewhat similar to the *Irwin Toy* test. In *Irwin Toy*, the majority claimed that one must turn to the analysis laid out by Justice Dickson to guide the court's s. 1 analysis in the case at hand (*Irwin Toy*, [1989] 1 S.C.R. 927, at 987). Both tests required the justices to assess whether the objective of the law was significant and important, and whether the means chosen were proportionate to the legislative objective. To make the latter assessment, the court had to consider three things: whether the law was rationally connected to the objective, whether the means chosen caused a minimal impairment of free expression, and whether there was proportionality between the harmful effects of the law and its benefits (*R. v. Oakes*, [1986] 1 S.C.R. 103). For a discussion of the significance of *Oakes* and *Irwin Toy*, and Chief Justice Dickson's contribution to the cases, see Cameron (1997).

In her view, the government had failed to identify an objective of sufficient importance to justify the infringement on free expression, nor were the means chosen in any way proportionate or rationally connected to any government objective (*Committee for the Commonwealth*, [1991] 1 S.C.R. 139, at 250–1). As a result, Justice McLachlin's "middle road" decision reached the same conclusion on the merits of the case as the other two opinions. What is intriguing about the three main opinions in this case is how they reflect three different value positions on the materialist-postmaterialist dimension of where and how free speech can flourish, with Justice L'Heureux-Dubé taking the most libertarian, postmaterialist position and Chief Justice Lamer taking a more materialist stance.

In a subsequent ruling by the Lamer Court in *Libman v. Quebec (Attorney General)*, [1997] 3 S.C.R. 569 (hereafter *Libman*), the focus of the court went back to regulations on political campaign expenditures. The regulations in question had the effect of providing equal public funding to "yes" and "no" national committees that would organize in support of, or opposition to, a referendum question. Public spending restrictions on "regulated campaign expenses" essentially guaranteed equal access to the media to advocate for and against the referendum. Robert Libman and the Equality Party objected to the restrictions, particularly those on so-called unregulated activities, maintaining that they violated both freedom of expression and freedom of association (s. 2(b) and 2(d) of the Charter). The Supreme Court, using s. 1 analysis, voted 9–0 to strike down Quebec's campaign finance law.

The structure of the *per curiam* opinion followed the contours of the *Oakes* test and the principles laid out in *Irwin Toy*. As a threshold question, the regulations clearly infringed both freedom of expression and freedom of association. Thus, the court was in no doubt that the campaign finance restrictions violated the Charter. Turning to the s. 1 analysis, the court expressed a favourable view of the objective of the Quebec regulations – to promote fairness and equal access and participation in the democratic process – an objective that lay at the core values of free expression (see *Libman*, [1997] 3 S.C.R. 569, at 596–7). The court went on to conclude that the means were rationally connected to the objective of promoting democratic equality because the law equalized access to financial resources for the opposing sides and ensured that election discourse was not dominated by those with more money (*Libman*, [1997] 3 S.C.R. 569, at 599). The laws had the effect of equalizing access to financial resources for the opposing sides in a referendum or election and ensured that election discourse was "not dominated by those with access to greater financial resources" (ibid.).

Thus, the postmaterialist value of equality emerged to counter unregulated speech rights as an important touchstone for this rationale in support of campaign finance limits. Even so, the law in question failed miserably on the minimal impairment test. The nature of the unregulated restrictions outlined in the law were "so restrictive that they came close to being a total ban" on expression (*Libman*, [1997] 3 S.C.R. 569, at 616). For example, third-party individuals were essentially not allowed to purchase media ads or programs under the law, and this left them at the mercy of editors and producers if they were to get their message out at no cost. The restrictive third-party measures were struck down as an unjustifiable infringement on free expression and association. Yet the court's obiter dicta at the end of the ruling opened the door for legislative changes that might save the regulation. By citing the finance restrictions in the Canada Elections Act favourably, and by referencing the federal Lortie Commission report on campaign expenditures, the court signalled a "less restrictive" approach that might pass constitutional muster (*Libman*, [1997] 3 S.C.R. 569, at 619–20). Such an approach might allow individual citizens to make limited individual campaign expenditures that could be pooled for a particular cause. Subsequent to the court's clear message, the Quebec National Assembly enacted a $1,000 limit on independent third-party expenditures (Hogg 2011, s. 43-60).

The court's ruling in *Libman* walked the line of two value positions typically seen at the postmaterialist end of the value spectrum. While endorsing the importance of political expression as a core value in a democracy, the ruling also recognized the unfairness that flowed from the influence of big money in election campaigns. The opinion's language balanced the liberal, purposive defence of unencumbered political expression, while recognizing government's authority to place restrictions on independent political expenditures that might weaken the equitable access to information that Canadians expected from their election campaigns. By overturning the law, the language of the pro-free expression values ruled the day in *Libman*, but the unmistakable seeds were sown for campaign finance laws that restricted unlimited spending to endorse equality norms.

Political Speech – Landmark Decisions of the McLachlin Court

The problems surrounding campaign expenditures that had been debated by the Lamer Court resurfaced in a subsequent McLachlin Court ruling pertaining to independent, third-party expenditures (*Harper v. Canada (Attorney General)*, [2004] 1 S.C.R. 827, hereafter *Harper*). This case featured a complex array of spending limits on political contributions, including a regulation prohibiting advertising on election day, requirements for third parties to register with the Chief Electoral Officer, and a law requiring third parties or individuals to identify themselves in all ads. In a 6–3 decision, the court majority upheld all the laws as being constitutionally justifiable under s. 1 of the Charter or as not being in violation of the Charter at all. The minority, led by Chief Justice McLachlin and Justice Major, would have struck down the spending restrictions found in the Canada Elections Act. As such, the court's majority reasons for judgment appeared to reflect a materialist endorsement of efforts to limit free expression in the political realm – especially in support of equality norms – while the minority position embodied a more literal, postmaterialist reading of free expression as a fundamental right that should remain unfettered.

The main area of disagreement in *Harper* turned on the spending restrictions imposed on individuals, or so-called third parties, in national elections. The law called for a spending limit of $3,000 per individual in an electoral district during the election cycle and a limit of $150,000 across the country. The restrictions had the practical effect of leaving the political playing field almost entirely to the major political parties, which operated under much more liberal spending guidelines (see Hogg 2011, s. 43-59). Both sides of the court found the restrictions to violate the free expression right in s. 2(b) of the Charter. However, the dissenting opinion by Chief Justice McLachlin and Justice Major (joined by Justice Binnie) would have thrown out the law under s. 1 analysis because it did not minimally impair the right to free expression and had a severe impact on an individual's ability to communicate during an election (*Harper*, [2004] 1 S.C.R. 827, at 847–9). The concern here was that by setting the spending limits so low, the government had made it difficult for an individual to mount a truly effective advertising campaign at either the local or the national level (*Harper*, [2004] 1 S.C.R. 827, at 837–8). The dissenting view was rooted in a libertarian, postmaterialist vision of political communication.

The opinion echoed the language of Emerson (1963) and promoted the significance of unfettered debate in promoting a democratic system (Manfredi and Rush 2007, 2008).[3] Chief Justice McLachlin and Justice Major wrote that "the ability to engage in effective speech in the public square means nothing if it does not include the ability to attempt to persuade one's fellow citizens through debate and discussion" and that "freedom of expression must allow a citizen to give voice to her vision for her community and nation, to advocate change through the art of persuasion in the hope of improving her life and indeed the larger social, political, and economic landscape" (*Harper*, [2004] 1 S.C.R. 827, at 841). Left unsaid in this perspective of political communication was the recognition that money was the lifeblood of modern political discourse. The minority was indicating that with such great restrictions placed on the use of money in elections, political discourse would in effect be harmed, leaving the playing field essentially in the hands of the major political parties.

The majority opinion by Justice Bastarache laid out the value conflict in a distinctive way, drawing the line between a libertarian notion of free expression (advocated by the dissenting justices) and an "egalitarian model of elections" advocated by scholars and parliamentary officials concerned about the pernicious effect of big money in elections (*Harper*, [2004] 1 S.C.R. 827, at 868; see Manfredi and Rush 2008). Justice Bastarache wrote, "The state can restrict the voices which dominate the political discourse so that others may be heard," resulting in a better informed democracy in which "no one voice is overwhelmed by another" (*Harper*, [2004] 1 S.C.R. 827, at 868). Justice Bastarache argued that campaign finance limits were rational in their connection to the objectives of promoting *equality* in political discourse, in their protection of the integrity of the campaign finance system, and in their power to ensure that voters had confidence in elections (*Harper*, [2004] 1 S.C.R. 827, at 881–8). On the question of minimal impairment, he indicated that deference was owed to Parliament's efforts to balance the competing interests of political expression and meaningful participation during an election period (*Harper*, [2004] 1 S.C.R. 827, at 888–90). He noted that people were free to spend political money as they wished outside the dates set aside for an election contest, a position that would provide

3 Manfredi and Rush (2007) argue that there has been an interesting convergence in thinking in campaign finance cases decided by the US and Canadian Supreme Courts, most notably between Chief Justice McLachlin and Justice Stephen Breyer.

little comfort for an individual wanting to persuade people about the best outcome during an election cycle.

It is interesting to note that the value positions that are in play in both *Libman* and *Harper* are twin values typically associated with postmaterialist thinking. One side promotes the significance of equal participation in politics as a significant value for government to uphold. Here, the government is seen as the protector of lower-income, common-person interests in society, and the language of some of the justices begins to trumpet an egalitarian notion of postmaterialist thought. The idea is that society should regulate wealthy interests so that all people can have equal access to the political marketplace as informed voters (Dawood 2006, 271). On the other side, we see the libertarian argument of postmaterialist views: the idea that the political marketplace should remain largely unchecked and that political spending should be allowed to take place so ideas can be disseminated throughout the body politic – what Dawood calls the liberty view of freedom of speech (ibid.). In this way, the postmaterialist language of equality can be used to advance an argument restricting the traditional postmaterialist value of unencumbered free expression.

The tension between the values of equality and liberty mentioned above were also at stake in the case of *Baier v. Alberta*, [2007] 2 S.C.R. 673, in which the McLachlin Court ruled on whether it was lawful for a province to prohibit school employees from running for school board offices. Adopted on the heels of labour strife in 2004, Alberta's School Trustee Statutes Amendment Act was designed to prohibit school employees from serving on *any* district school board in the province (in prior years, the law had prohibited employees only from seeking election to the school board in which they worked). The appellant school employees argued that the new law was unconstitutional because it infringed Charter rights to political free expression and s. 15 notions of equality and could not be saved under s. 1 analysis. The court, voting 6–1, rejected those arguments.

Justice Rothstein's reasons for judgment pointed out that the teachers were arguing that denying their ability to run for office was tantamount to denying their ability to speak out on education issues, an argument that failed to recognize that s. 2(b) rights had traditionally been conceived as "negative rights," preventing government from encroaching on the right to free speech, and not as "positive rights," which required government to allow for and provide a platform for free expression (*Baier v. Alberta*, [2007] 2 S.C.R. 673, at 686). According to

Justice Rothstein, the proper test in this case for examining the alleged constitutional infringement was a blend of the *Irwin Toy* test and one the court had established in another ruling (*Dunmore v. Ontario (Attorney General)*, [2001] 3 S.C.R. 1016). The court had to first determine whether an activity invoked a form of expression protected by the Charter (a threshold question drawn from *Irwin Toy*). Next, the question was whether the claimant was seeking a "positive entitlement to government action or simply the right to be free from government interference" (*Baier v. Alberta*, [2007] 2 S.C.R. 673, at 691). If the rights claimant was seeking a positive right, then the factors outlined in *Dunmore* need to be validated: (1) that the claim was "grounded in a fundamental freedom of expression rather than in access to a particular statutory regime"; (2) that the claimant had demonstrated a "substantial interference" with fundamental freedoms, or that the statutory regime had "the purpose of a substantial interference with s. 2(b) freedoms"; and (3) that the "government was responsible for the inability to exercise the fundamental freedom" (*Baier v. Alberta*, [2007] 2 S.C.R. 673, at 691). If the above components were true, s. 2(b) would be violated, and the court would need to engage in s. 1 analysis.

Applying the modified *Dunmore* test to the case at hand, Justice Rothstein indicated that the right to free expression was in play but that the appellants were seeking access to the "statutory platform of school trustee candidacy," and thus, they were seeking a positive right (*Baier v. Alberta*, [2007] 2 S.C.R. 673, at 694). As such, the appellants had to demonstrate the last three elements of the *Dunmore* test, which, in this case, they could not. Justice Rothstein pointed out that their core claim was to essentially assert "the right to run for election and serve as trustees," a claim that was not grounded in the fundamental freedom of expression (*Baier v. Alberta*, [2007] 2 S.C.R. 673, at 697). He pointed out that the appellants were free to engage in a host of free expression activities despite not running for office, such as writing letters to newspapers and engaging in lobbying efforts (*Baier v. Alberta*, [2007] 2 S.C.R. 673, at 698).

If the opinion of Justice Rothstein emanated from a restrained, materialist vision of s. 2(b) rights, then Justice Fish's dissent represented the polar opposite – namely, taking an expansive view of free expression and equality interests. His opening line signalled his postmaterialist perspective. "This case concerns political expression and the issue is whether its *deliberate suppression* by Alberta violates s. 2(b) of the *Canadian Charter of Rights and Freedoms*. With respect …, I believe that it does" (*Baier v. Alberta*, [2007] 2 S.C.R. 673, at 709; emphasis added). For Justice Fish, the change in law removed a critical platform for the appellants to engage in free expression, and it was done without any need for Alberta to show that the restriction could be saved by s. 1 of the Charter as "justified in a free and democratic society" (*Baier v. Alberta*, [2007] 2 S.C.R. 673, at 710–11). For him, free expression was central to the case; he noted that "the appellants' claim is grounded in the fundamental, constitutionally protected freedom to express oneself meaningfully on matters related to education. … By excluding school employees from the ability to run for and serve as trustees, Alberta has substantially interfered with their ability to exercise this freedom" (*Baier v. Alberta*, [2007] 2 S.C.R. 673, at 716). Note that Justice Fish's language conveyed his intention to side with the appellants in any kind of *Dunmore* analysis (a fundamental freedom was at stake, not a statutory platform). For Justice Fish, it was cold comfort to tell teachers that they could still express themselves on education matters using other means. As he put it, "Active participation in an election and service as a trustee are *qualitatively* different means of expression than simply shouting from the sidelines" (*Baier v. Alberta*, [2007] 2 S.C.R. 673, at 717; emphasis in original. In the end, Justice Fish stood alone in advocating a purely libertarian, postmaterialist vision of the dispute.

The dispute in *Baier* echoes earlier rulings in the Lamer and Dickson Courts pertaining to public employee participation in the political process. Whereas Justice Fish believed it was unfair to prevent school employees from running for office, other justices across various courts believed public employees should not have sway over government decisions. One side of the argument values the right of public employees to participate in a meaningful way in the political process, reflecting a postmaterialist vision of free expression and political engagement. The other side sees the need for an impartial corps of public employees, untainted by their engagement in politics. This is the perspective that favours the touchstone value of fairness over the free expression arguments of rights claimants. When surveying the landmark political speech rulings across the last 40 years, it is clear that the postmaterialist flowering that was evident in the Lamer Court was subsequently tempered with a set of less libertarian and more egalitarian rulings in the first decade of the McLachlin Court.

The two landmark rulings from the contemporary court have upheld restrictions on political spending and have upheld a law preventing school employees from running for school boards (*Harper* and *Baier*).

In that sense, the qualitative content analysis identifies a steady march towards postmaterialist, pro–free expression values in landmark political speech cases in the 1980s and 1990s and a tendency to endorse the slightly more moderate postmaterialist equality value in the McLachlin Court. Yet it is important to note that the egalitarian leaning of the recent political speech cases elevates the postmaterialist value of equal participation in politics over the unfettered-liberty interests of speech in the marketplace of ideas. This suggests that the apparent value shift of the McLachlin Court is really replacing one postmaterialist value with another – namely, endorsing the notion of equal participation in the political process, a hallmark of a society founded on democratic values (for a contrary argument rejecting the egalitarian approach of the McLachlin Court, see Boland [2013]).

Commercial Advertising – Landmark Decisions of the Laskin and Dickson Courts

A second prominent area of free speech disputes pertains to commercial advertising. These cases raise issues about the importance of advertising for economic gain and the tension that emerges when government sees some of that advertising as being harmful to certain groups in society. During the 1973–2010 period, the Canadian Supreme Court handed down 14 rulings in the commercial advertising area. Seven of the cases juxtaposed the government's interest in protecting consumers from the harmful effects of advertising against corporate interests seeking the right to market their product or service without government regulation. Five other cases featured government or professional associations against individuals, and in four of those cases, the individual was advancing the postmaterialist, liberal argument. The last two cases in this area pitted a union and a media corporation against the government, with both the union and the media organization advancing the liberal right to advertise. In each of these disputes, key principles from Emerson can be identified, with the pursuit of truth and individual self-fulfilment subject to the whims of marketers and companies seeking to make a profit.

In one of the early cases heard during the Laskin tenure, *Attorney General (Que.) v. Kellogg's Co. of Canada et al.*, [1978] 2 S.C.R. 211 (hereafter *Kellogg's*), the court addressed whether Quebec could restrict a manufacturer from advertising cartoons on television intended to influence children. The Supreme Court, in a 6–3 vote, found the provincial restriction to be a constitutionally legitimate exercise of its power to regulate commerce within its borders (*Kellogg's*, [1978] 2 S.C.R. 211, at 220). Justice Martland's majority opinion indicated that the provision was part of a general provincial regulation aimed at *all* advertisers who used cartoons directed at children, regardless of the medium they used. As such, Quebec was not trying to regulate the operation of television broadcasts, as the respondent company contended, but Kellogg's ads themselves, so the federal government's power to regulate broadcasting was only indirectly implicated (*Kellogg's*, [1978] 2 S.C.R. 211, at 224–5). For Justice Martland, it was clear that Quebec had adopted the law to protect children from the harmful effects of cartoon advertising. Justice Martland's willingness to support a blanket ban on cartoon advertising struck a materialist chord aimed at protecting children in society.

Chief Justice Laskin, writing in dissent, took issue with Justice Martland's focus on the object of the injunction and the limited nature of the regulation's impact. According to him, and the two other dissenters, just because the provincial statute was directed at the advertiser, and not a television station, did not mean there was "no intrusion" on the federal government's power in relation to television programming (*Kellogg's*, [1978] 2 S.C.R. 211, at 215). Since prior rulings by the court had established that the federal government had exclusive power to regulate the content of television programming, the province could not acquire "ancillary power" over this medium by simply claiming that it had the right to control advertising by companies doing business in the province (*Kellogg's*, [1978] 2 S.C.R. 211, at 216). Ultimately, Chief Justice Laskin concluded that Justice Martland and the majority had wrongly extended provincial power beyond its legitimate confines.

This dispute, at its crux, largely pivoted on a concern over federalism, with both the majority and dissenting opinions squarely focused on which level of government had the authority to regulate and control commercial advertising on television aimed at children. While the majority argued that the province should have the power to regulate the sale of goods and services by companies within its own borders, the minority suggested that the federal government should have exclusive control over the content of television broadcasts. Yet within this federalist framework, Justice Martland used language on the materialist side of the spectrum when he asserted, "The object of the regulation … is clear. It is sought to protect children in Quebec from the harmful effect of the kinds of advertising therein prohibited" (*Kellogg's*, [1978] 2 S.C.R. 211, at 223). This passage recognized the need to allow provincial governments the right to protect the safety and well-being of their citizenry, especially those most vulnerable to manipulative advertising. Meanwhile, Chief Justice Laskin, in his dissent, did not advance a directly postmaterialist argument discussing the possible detrimental effect that the provincial regulation might have on the market value of products sold by Kellogg's or the value, if any, that cartoon commercials might provide the Quebec consumer. Not only did such arguments not fit within the federalist dispute, but Chief Justice Laskin would also have been hard pressed to argue convincingly that Quebec citizens would benefit from cartoon ads promoting processed, sugary cereals, such as Kellogg's Sugar Snaps or Frosted Flakes (for a similar argument about commercial advertising that targets children, see Pomeranz [2010]).

Ten years later, the Dickson Court heard another case that echoed some of the themes of the *Kellogg's* case. In *Irwin Toy*, [1989] 1 S.C.R. 927, the court analysed a Quebec regulation restricting commercial advertising aimed at children under the age of 13. Yet this time, the court evaluated the statute under the Charter of Rights and Freedoms and heard it on the heels of two cases striking down laws that had required businesses to use only the French language on public signs, posters, and commercial advertising (*Ford v. Quebec*, [1988] 2 S.C.R. 748 and *Devine v. Quebec*, [1988] 2 S.C.R. 790). However, in *Irwin Toy*, the focus returned to advertising products aimed at children, introducing an obvious post-Charter parallel with the *Kellogg's* case. Ultimately, the court ruled that this type of commercial expression was entitled to protection under s. 2(b) because Irwin Toy had intended the activity to "convey a meaning" and the purpose of the Quebec restriction directly prohibited citizens from hearing the message (*Irwin Toy*, [1989] 1 S.C.R. 927, at 931–2). However, the court went on to conclude that the regulation was justified under s. 1 because it served the pressing and substantial concern of protecting vulnerable children from manipulative advertising techniques and the ban was rationally connected to achieving that overall objective (*Irwin Toy*, [1989] 1 S.C.R. 927, at 986–7, 991).

Irwin Toy achieved landmark status because it established a two-step test for examining whether an activity conveyed a meaning and whether the purpose or effect of the government restriction was to curtail that freedom of expression (*Irwin Toy*, [1989] 1 S.C.R. 927, at 931). Ultimately, the two-step test developed in *Irwin Toy* ensured that the court gave a broad, liberal interpretation to expressive rights and reflected the purposive approach laid down in earlier Charter rulings. Yet this was possible because the court could subsequently justify the impugned restriction under s. 1 if the legislation advanced a pressing substantial interest and if the means chosen were proportional to its objective (Ostberg 1998, 496). In making this latter assessment, the court had to consider whether the regulation was rationally connected to the overall objective, whether it impaired the right as little as possible, and whether the deleterious effects were outweighed by the abridgment of the right (*Irwin Toy*, [1989] 1 S.C.R. 927, at 991–1000).

Applying the two-step analysis to the facts in *Irwin Toy*, the court concluded that cartoon advertising aimed at children was a protected form of speech. Justice Martland stated that a broad and liberal interpretation of free expression was necessary because it "ensure[s] that everyone can manifest their thoughts, opinions, beliefs, indeed all expressions of the heart and mind, however unpopular, distasteful or contrary to the mainstream." Borrowing principally from the thinking of Thomas Emerson (1963, 1970), the majority suggested that this right must be given fundamental status because "in a free, pluralistic and democratic society we prize a diversity of ideas and opinions for their inherent value both to the community and to the individual" (*Irwin Toy*, [1989] 1 S.C.R. 927, at 968).

These statements illustrate an expansive postmaterialist interpretation of the freedom of expression, which is not surprising given its importance to Canadian democratic society. However, the majority could provide a broad interpretation of this right in the abstract because it could subsequently restrict cartoon ads under s. 1 of the Charter. The justification for the regulation flowed from the persuasive force of advertising on young minds. The majority highlighted the need to protect a "group which is particularly vulnerable to the techniques of seduction and manipulation abundant in advertising." Evidence also showed "a generalized concern in Western societies with the impact of media, and particularly but not solely televised advertising, on the development and perceptions of young children" (*Irwin Toy*, [1989] 1 S.C.R. 927, at 987). Clearly, this two-stage analysis provided the justices with a unique mechanism that allowed them to "have their cereal and eat it too." They could broadly interpret free expression in the first stage, only to restrict it under s. 1 analysis because the materialist concerns for the safety and well-being of young minds could trump any postmaterialist argument in favour of manipulative ads.

If *Kellogg's* and *Irwin Toy* shone the spotlight on advertising aimed at children, a case heard late in the Dickson Court, *Rocket v. Royal College of Dental Surgeons of Ontario*, [1990] 2 S.C.R. 232 (hereafter *Rocket*), shone the light on professional advertising targeted at adults. In this case, the court addressed the legal question of whether a restriction on commercial advertising by dentists violated the right to free expression and, if so, whether it was justified under s. 1 analysis. In the case at hand, two dentists had participated in a commercial campaign, advertising that they stayed at Holiday Inn hotels when they travelled on business. Justice McLachlin, writing for the court, applied the *Irwin Toy* test to determine that the law violated freedom of expression because it purposely prohibited normal and acceptable forms of professional advertising aimed at conveying a message that was not obscene through radio, television, and newspapers (*Rocket*, [1990] 2 S.C.R. 232, at 244–5). However, unlike its ruling in *Kellogg's* and *Irwin Toy*, the court went on to rule that the complete ban on dental advertising was not justified under s. 1 of the Charter. Justice McLachlin argued that although Ontario had a sufficiently compelling interest in trying to maintain high standards in the dental profession and protect the public from misleading advertising, the restrictions chosen were not reasonable or justified. The crux of her argument was that the government could have chosen less restrictive controls on advertising. Instead, the law was a blanket ban on all dental advertising, and thus, it necessarily curtailed the transmission of valuable information that the public might find useful, even if it was in the unlikely format of promoting Holiday Inn as the hotel of choice while travelling (*Rocket*, [1990] 2 S.C.R. 232, at 250).

In reaching her conclusion, Justice McLachlin argued that what set this case apart from *Irwin Toy* was that here they were dealing with adults, instead of children, and thus the protection of consumer choice became more salient. She pointed out that the majority in *Irwin Toy* had decided not to emphasize that aspect of advertising because it had realized that protecting children from commercial exploitation necessarily outweighed any consumer interests put forth (*Rocket*, [1990] 2 S.C.R. 232, at 247–8). In this case, Justice McLachlin could more easily advance the liberal, free expression argument than the majority could in *Irwin Toy* or *Kellogg's* because the ads in *Rocket* were aimed at adults rather than children. Indeed, at one point she stated, "It cannot be denied that expression of this kind does serve an important public interest by enhancing the ability of patients to make informed choices. Furthermore, the choice of a dentist must be counted as a relatively important consumer decision" (*Rocket*, [1990] 2 S.C.R. 232, at 247). In another passage, Justice McLachlin speculated on the type of professional advertising that might benefit consumers. She stated, "Dentists should be able to advertise their hours of operation and the languages they speak, information which would be useful to the public and present no serious danger of misleading the public or undercutting professionalism" (*Rocket*, [1990] 2 S.C.R. 232, at 250).

In contrast to *Irwin Toy*, this case presented a scenario in which consumer interest in making informed economic choices necessarily outweighed upholding principles of professional integrity that were apparently safeguarded by a complete ban on ads by dentists. Readers should note that woven throughout Justice McLachlin's opinion were threads of Emerson's defence of the free exchange of relevant ideas for the advancement of knowledge.

Commercial Advertising – Landmark Decisions of the Lamer Court

While the Dickson Court cases settled several questions about commercial ads, left unsettled was the status of a growing body of laws setting limits on cigarette advertisements. This became the central issue of the Lamer Court in *RJR-MacDonald Inc. v. Canada*, [1995] 3 S.C.R. 199 (hereafter *RJR-MacDonald*), in which, in a fractured ruling, a majority of justices struck down legislation dealing with commercial activity pertaining to tobacco advertising, promotion, and labelling. More specifically, the court addressed the principal question of whether elements of the Tobacco Products Control Act, which placed a complete ban on advertising and promotion of tobacco products and required manufacturers to place unattributed health warnings on those products, violated the free expression guarantee in the Charter and whether the restrictions were justified under s. 1 of the Charter. All members of the court agreed, and the Attorney General conceded, that the ban on advertising and promotion violated s. 2(b) of the Charter.

Yet Justice McLachlin, with four of her colleagues, took issue with the constitutional legitimacy of the warning label restrictions. She maintained that, as Justice Lamer had pointed out in an earlier case, freedom of expression included the right to express, or not express, oneself (*Slaight Communications Inc. v. Davidson*, [1989] 1 S.C.R. 1038). Thus, the government's health warning requirement, along with the inability of manufacturers to write other information they might want to include on their packages, infringed the Charter (*RJR-MacDonald*, [1995] 3 S.C.R. 199, at 326). Critics might contend that Justice McLachlin's allowance of companies to have the right to advertise reflects a materialist sentiment because it aligns with the profit motive of the company. However, this is a misunderstanding of these disputes and of her stance, which is evident from her statement above – namely, that a company should have the right to express or not express itself in a democracy.

Recognizing that the law fell within Parliament's criminal law power and that the regulation violated s. 2(b), the court went on to apply the *Oakes* reasonableness test (*RJR-MacDonald*, [1995] 3 S.C.R. 199, at 201). Five justices agreed that the restrictions did not pass s. 1 Charter justification. Justice McLachlin argued that the aim of the advertising ban and mandated health warnings were to persuade Canadians not to buy and use tobacco. She concluded that both of these aims were sufficiently important to justify overriding free expression because "even a small reduction in tobacco use" would make a difference in the health of the Canadian citizenry (*RJR-MacDonald*, [1995] 3 S.C.R. 199, at 336). However, the legislation did not meet the proportionality prong of the *Oakes* test because the complete ban and unattributed health warnings were not a minimal impairment on expressive rights.

Second, Justice McLachlin found no causal connection between decreasing tobacco consumption and an absolute ban on the use of cigarette trademarks and brand logos on things like lighters and belt buckles (*RJR-MacDonald*, [1995] 3 S.C.R. 199, at 342). Third, in her view, government must show why it could not develop less intrusive bans, such as ones aimed at children or lifestyle ads (*RJR-MacDonald*, [1995] 3 S.C.R. 199, at 344). These less intrusive measures might achieve the same reduction in tobacco use as the more intrusive measures established by the government. Thus, the majority struck down the legislation, placing it on the postmaterialist side of the value conflict, at least in relation to tobacco advertising and the brand image of products. Even with this postmaterialist outcome, there was a materialist undertone to the opinion, highlighting the significant health concerns related to tobacco consumption.

In dissent, Justice La Forest argued that a common sense approach indicated that the government had met the first prong of the *Oakes* test. Given the vast amount of money spent on tobacco ads by the tobacco industry, concern over its harmful effects, and recent jurisprudence of the court, a rational connection existed between the prohibitions and the goal of reducing tobacco use (*RJR-MacDonald*, [1995] 3 S.C.R. 199, at 292). Justice La Forest also pointed out that government needed to institute a complete ban on this type of expression after experiencing the failure of a variety of partial bans over two decades (*RJR-MacDonald*, [1995] 3 S.C.R. 199, at 213). Last, Justice La Forest concluded that Parliament's interest in reducing the number of direct inducements for Canadians to consume tobacco outweighed any negative effects on the companies' right to advertise (*RJR-MacDonald*, [1995] 3 S.C.R. 199, at 320).

Throughout his dissenting opinion, Justice La Forest emphasized that a more flexible and nuanced approach to s. 1 analysis would enable the court to weigh free expression rights more readily against other social values, like government's interest in protecting the safety and security of the community. His materialistic tenor comes through when he states that although the government could not provide definitive proof regarding the causes of tobacco consumption, it had introduced overwhelming evidence of the harmful effects that it had on Canadians, including causing various deadly diseases and tobacco addiction. For him, this made the law valid because it addressed a pressing and substantial concern (*RJR-MacDonald*, [1995] 3 S.C.R. 199, at 272–4). Justice La Forest went on to argue that given the underlying profit motive behind the tobacco ads and the harm caused by tobacco consumption, this type of expression fell "far from the core values" of truth, individual self-fulfilment, and political participation. As a result, government needed to provide only a "rational basis" for enacting the legislation (*RJR-MacDonald*, [1995] 3 S.C.R. 199, at 279–84). There is a clear materialistic undertone evident in Justice La Forest's analysis of the tobacco regulations.

In contrast to the materialist tone of the dissenting opinion, Justice McLachlin's majority decision provided several notable examples of a postmaterialist orientation towards commercial free expression. For instance, when she discussed why companies might object to the requirement of placing unattributed health warnings on tobacco products, she pointed out that they resented not only being forced to say something "but also to being required to do so in a way that associates them with the opinion in question" (*RJR-MacDonald*, [1995] 3 S.C.R. 199, at 348); for a critique of Justice McLachlin's position, see Moon (1995). This language indicates that Justice McLachlin stood at the postmaterialist end in this critical commercial advertising case. She also took issue with Justice La Forest's hierarchical approach when he concluded that tobacco ads deserved a much lower degree of protection because they supported values on par with "prostitution, hate mongering, or pornography" (*RJR-MacDonald*, [1995] 3 S.C.R. 199, at 282–3). According to Justice McLachlin, Justice La Forest's hierarchical approach failed to appreciate the important role tobacco ads played by providing consumers with valuable information, such as the "price, quality and even health risks associated with different brands," all of which related to lawful activity in Canadian society (*RJR-MacDonald*, [1995] 3 S.C.R. 199, at 347). She nicely summed up her position when she stated, "Freedom of expression, even commercial expression, is an important and fundamental tenet of a free and democratic society. If Parliament wishes to infringe this freedom, it must be prepared to offer good and sufficient justification for the infringement and its ambit. This it has not done" (*RJR-MacDonald*, [1995] 3 S.C.R. 199, at 350).

Justice McLachlin's position in *RJR-MacDonald* was widely criticized, and as Parrish points out, the majority should not have engaged in the dismantling of the regulatory action, which was rightly aimed at protecting the health of Canadians, most notably the young (Parrish 1995). Justice McLachlin took a postmaterialist stance in this commercial expression case, but she opened the door to the possibility that a future, less intrusive restriction on tobacco companies might be constitutionally valid.

Commercial Advertising – Landmark Decisions of the McLachlin Court

The Supreme Court's treatment of tobacco laws came back into play in 2007, when the McLachlin Court voted to uphold a revised version of the Tobacco Products Control Act that the Lamer Court had previously struck down in *RJR-MacDonald* (*Canada v. JTI-MacDonald Corp.*, [2007] 2 S.C.R. 610, hereafter *JTI-MacDonald*). The interplay between the Canadian Supreme Court and Parliament in the tobacco advertising area over the 1995–2007 period exemplifies the "Charter dialogue" that leading constitutional scholars claim has emerged during the post-Charter period (see Manfredi and Kelly 1999; Morton and Knopff 2000; Roach 2001; Kelly 2005; Hogg, Bushell Thornton, and Wright 2007; Hogg 2011). After the Lamer Court ruling in *RJR-MacDonald*, Parliament enacted new legislation that allowed tobacco manufacturers to provide information and engage in brand-preference advertising. However, it outlawed a series of activities, including lifestyle advertising and promotion, advertising aimed at young people, and false or misleading advertising and promotion, and it also required tobacco companies to include health warnings on tobacco products that constituted 50 per cent of the display surface (*JTI-MacDonald*, [2007] 2 S.C.R. 610, at 611). The companies challenged various aspects of these restrictions and contended that the Tobacco Act also prohibited the publication of scientific work funded by the tobacco industry. Ultimately, the McLachlin Court rejected all the challenges made by the tobacco industry, principally because Parliament had made a concerted effort to revise the statute and limit its scope, so that it more readily met the three-pronged *Oakes* test.

At the beginning of her reasons for judgment, Chief Justice McLachlin, writing for a unanimous court, determined that, contrary to the manufacturer's contention, when one read the "scientific work" provision in light of the Tobacco Act as a whole, it did not prevent the publication of serious scientific work sponsored by manufacturers. Rather, it simply prevented them from using scientific work in commercial ads aimed at consumers and thus did not violate their free expression rights (*JTI-MacDonald,* [2007] 2 S.C.R. 610, at 612). Although Chief Justice McLachlin went on to find that the remaining six contested provisions violated the expressive rights of tobacco manufacturers, she concluded that they could all be justified. She argued that s. 20 of the Tobacco Act, which prohibited "false, misleading or deceptive" promotion, as well as promotion that was "likely to create an erroneous impression," met the first prong of the *Oakes* test because government had a pressing and substantial concern in preventing misleading advertising from encouraging tobacco consumption and this concern was rationally connected to Parliament's overarching public health objectives (*JTI-MacDonald,* [2007] 2 S.C.R. 610, at 612–13). Chief Justice McLachlin concluded that the provision met the proportionality test because banning misleading advertising might reduce smoking, thereby outweighing expressive rights in this context because of the "lower value" such ads had for society (ibid.).

Chief Justice McLachlin used similar arguments to justify the ban on advertising to children, lifestyle ads, and sponsorship promotions found in other sections of the act. However, she concluded that the provisions met the minimal impairment requirement because the statute allowed tobacco companies to provide information and brand-preference advertising (*JTI-MacDonald,* [2007] 2 S.C.R. 610, at 613–15). She also concluded that the warning requirements found in the Tobacco Products Information Regulations passed s. 1 scrutiny because Parliament had a pressing and substantial interest in informing potential buyers of the health hazards associated with smoking. As in the case of the deceptive ad provision, Chief Justice McLachlin concluded that the size of the warning labels fell within the range of reasonable requirements and that the benefits obtained through larger warning labels outweighed the prejudicial effects of limiting the expressive rights of manufacturers (*JTI-MacDonald*, [2007] 2 S.C.R. 610, at 615).

The arguments advanced by Chief Justice McLachlin reflect a materialistic concern for the health, safety, and welfare of Canadian citizens, and they demonstrate a remarkable change in her thinking from the *RJR-MacDonald* case just 12 years earlier. Throughout her ruling, she continually hammered home the point that any detrimental effects from curtailing "low value" expressive speech in society must give way to the government's overwhelming interest in protecting Canadian citizens from the hazardous effects of smoking. The language she invoked throughout her opinion is telling: it reflects a court and a justice that had become more comfortable with restricting free expression arguments advanced by tobacco manufacturers now that Parliament had provided "detailed and copious evidence in support of its contention." Moreover, new scientific evidence had shown "that half of smokers will die of tobacco-related diseases and that the costs to the public health system are enormous" (*JTI-MacDonald*, [2007] 2 S.C.R. 610, at 620). She believed that these restrictions were in step with the changes made in other countries, some of which were more restrictive than Canada's (*JTI-MacDonald*, [2007] 2 S.C.R. 610, at 621). These passages indicate that the McLachlin Court was much more willing to restrict liberal expressive rights than the Lamer Court. This swing back toward the materialist position was justified in light of the new scientific evidence provided by the government, the court's concerted efforts to embrace narrower restrictions, and the growing international recognition that restricting manipulative promotional tobacco ads campaigns constituted a legitimate policy objective.

The McLachlin Court addressed advertising in a very different venue in *Montreal (City) v. 2952-1366 Quebec Inc.*, [2005] 3 S.C.R. 141 (hereafter *Montreal*), in which it upheld a restriction on commercial advertising by a nightclub owner. The case also clarified the standard for assessing s. 2(b) violations on public property. In this case, the owner of a strip club had tried to attract business by playing music and commentary from the show at the entrance of the club in downtown Montreal. The city had subsequently charged the owner with violating a municipal law that prohibited businesses from amplifying noise through loudspeakers to pedestrians on the street (*Montreal*, [2005] 3 S.C.R. 141, at 149). After determining that Montreal had the power to regulate nuisances within the city, the majority addressed the issue of whether the city had violated the business owner's free expression rights and, if so, whether it was justified under s. 1 analysis.

The majority applied the principles laid out in *Irwin Toy* to conclude that the noise emanating from inside the club did have "expressive content" because the owner was trying to convey a message over the loudspeaker that would entice people to come into the club to watch the show. Although some people might find the message offensive, since it was expressed in a non-violent manner, it fell under s. 2(b) protection (*Montreal*, [2005] 3 S.C.R. 141, at 166–7). However, the majority went on to argue that in *Irwin Toy* and *Committee for the Commonwealth*, [1991] 1 S.C.R. 139, it had acknowledged that the "method or location" of the expressive activity may also exclude it from s. 2(b) protection. In the *Montreal* case, the McLachlin Court streamlined two tests it had embraced in *Committee for the Commonwealth* for assessing speech on public property into one cohesive test that combined the two approaches (*Montreal*, [2005] 3 S.C.R. 141, at 167–9). According to the majority in *Montreal*, one had to first assess whether the public property either historically or functionally was a place where one would expect to have a right to free expression. Second, one had to assess whether allowing free expression in that location would conflict with the underlying values that free expression promoted – namely, democratic discourse, individual self-fulfilment, and the search for truth (*Montreal*, [2005] 3 S.C.R. 141, at 172). When the *Montreal* majority applied this test to the case at hand, it concluded that the club owner had a right to express his message on the street because people have historically done so, and allowing it would not undercut the underlying values protected by freedom of expression (*Montreal*, [2005] 3 S.C.R. 141, at 174). Since the club owner's expressive activity on public property deserved protection under s. 2(b), the city by-law necessarily violated his expressive rights.

The majority went on to apply the three-part *Oakes* test to assess whether the by-law could be justified under s. 1 analysis. Chief Justice McLachlin and Justice Deschamps concluded that the restriction was valid because the city had a pressing and substantial interest in reducing noise pollution in downtown Montreal and had created a proportionate regulation. First, the limited ban on noise was rationally connected to the goal of maintaining "peace and quiet" for citizens walking along the city streets. Moreover, the law impaired the rights of club owners in a reasonably minimal way because the city had claimed that it could not devise a more "practical way" to deal with this complex urban issue and the idea of regulating noise using sound-level meters seemed unrealistic. Last, the beneficial effects of reducing noise pollution on

Montreal's streets outweighed the negative effects of the regulation because citizens had a right to live in a healthy and relatively peaceful urban environment free from noise transcending normal city sounds (*Montreal*, [2005] 3 S.C.R. 141, at 179–80).

The language used by Chief Justice McLachlin and Justice Deschamps in the *Montreal* case clearly reflects a court that falls on the materialist side of the values spectrum. Although the city by-law did eliminate all noise emanating from sound equipment, with a few exceptions, the majority argued that the city had sufficiently tailored the restriction to deal with an important quality-of-life issue in an urban environment. Moreover, it argued that elected officials must have flexibility to deal with these complex social issues and the court should not substitute its views "simply because it can think of a better, less intrusive way to manage the problem" (*Montreal*, [2005] 3 S.C.R. 141, at 178). The majority's stance is indicative of a court that is more concerned with establishing civic order and maintaining a peaceful urban environment than with protecting the expressive rights of Montreal nightclub owners. Only Justice Binnie, the lone dissenter, argued that the regulation failed to meet the minimal-impairment requirement. He argued that the statute was overbroad because it would "inhibit free expression in many circumstances where alternative modes of expression are not available, and where the use of such sound equipment in no way bothers the neighbours or adversely affects the quality of urban life" (*Montreal*, [2005] 3 S.C.R. 141, at 207). In contrast to Justice Binnie, the majority's interest in upholding Montreal's by-law in the name of protecting innocent, unsuspecting pedestrians from the harmful effects of amplified advertising seems reminiscent of earlier rulings, like *Irwin Toy* and *Kellogg's*, in which the court had struck down statutes in the interest of protecting vulnerable children from misleading advertising.

If one were to step back and look at the six advertising cases holistically, it seems that the Supreme Court has come full circle in the commercial advertising area in terms of Inglehart's values thesis. Initially, the Laskin and Dickson Courts upheld restrictions on commercial advertising that were aimed at children in *Kellogg's* and *Irwin Toy*, which seemed justified since children are more susceptible to manipulative advertising campaigns than adults. This materialistic stance seemed to give way to a more libertarian, postmaterialist stance taken by the Lamer Court in the commercial advertising area. In *Rocket*, the Lamer Court took a libertarian stance when it struck down a statute limiting advertising by dentists. Yet this ruling stands in sharp contrast to the materialist stance taken eight years earlier by the Dickson Court when it upheld a remarkably similar statute banning commercial advertising by lawyers. Subsequently, in *RJR-MacDonald,* the Lamer Court seemed willing to support postmaterialist, expressive rights in the commercial advertising area, even though the interests it supported involved the promotion and sale of a toxic product to Canadian citizens. However, in the first 10 years under the McLachlin Court, the liberal stance taken under the Lamer tenure in the commercial advertising area seemed to give way to a more materialist approach reminiscent of the earlier Laskin and Dickson Courts. This was illustrated by the modern court's willingness to uphold restrictions in the landmark cases of *Montreal* and *JTI-MacDonald,* the latter of which provided the court with the opportunity to uphold marketing restrictions on tobacco products akin to the ones that had been struck down under the Lamer Court.

Part of the court's retrograde response in this area of law stems, in part, from Parliament's effort to narrow its tobacco restrictions in line with prior court rulings. This evolution of the arc of law is emblematic of an ongoing Charter dialogue between the courts and the Canadian Parliament (Manfredi and Kelly 1999; Morton and Knopff 2000; Roach 2001; Kelly 2005; Hogg, Bushell Thornton, and Wright 2007; Hogg 2011). The overall picture that one should take away from the six landmark cases heard by the Canadian court over the last four decades is that the judicial elites have intentionally moved in an increasingly libertarian, postmaterialist direction, as hypothesized during the Lamer Court, but have swung back in the materialist direction during the first 10 years of the McLachlin Court. This retrograde movement in the commercial speech area is juxtaposed to the McLachlin Court's postmaterialist stance in the political speech area, which is indicative of a court that is interested in ensuring that fairness and equality are maintained in a modern democracy, where wealthy interests are increasingly playing an outsized role in the polity. The McLachlin Court's rulings in this area are reflective of a society and culture that is far more supportive of equality concerns than other democracies, where unfettered free speech rights reign supreme.

The findings in the qualitative analysis of commercial and political speech cases dovetail nicely with the overarching quantitative examination of judicial outcomes across all free expression cases over the last 40 years. As in the qualitative area, the most sophisticated logistic regression model in the prior chapter confirmed that the Lamer Court had ruled in favour of a free expression claimant at a significantly higher rate than the Laskin/Dickson Courts, but the McLachlin Court had not. While the McLachlin Court moved back in a materialist direction in the commercial speech area, it embraced the postmaterialist value of equality in the political speech area. Taken together, the findings from the qualitative and quantitative perspectives provide a more robust picture of the extent to which Inglehart's postmaterialist value change thesis played out in the free expression area. Indeed, the complementary results presented in the last two chapters validate and reinforce each set of findings. Although the Lamer Court took strides in developing the right to unfettered expression, the first 10 years of the McLachlin Court seem to have documented a greater preference for materialist and egalitarian values. Only time will tell whether this value shift will have a lasting impact.

Chapter Six

Postmaterialist Outcomes in Discrimination Disputes

Introduction

At the heart of Ronald Inglehart's shifting value priorities thesis is the contention that as populations of advanced industrial societies move into a postmodern phase of societal development, they move away from materialistic concerns of economic advancement and security in favour of a new set of postmaterialist value priorities that promote individual self-fulfilment, well-being, and quality-of-life concerns. One component of this transformation process is that the postmodern citizenry becomes increasingly concerned with ensuring that individuals are treated equally under the law so that all members of society achieve a better quality of life and become more individually self-fulfilled. In Canada, the political realization of this notion is most evident in the language of s. 15(1) of the Charter of Rights and Freedoms, which prohibits discrimination on the basis of "race, national or ethnic origin, colour, religion, sex, age or mental or physical disability." The inclusion of equality rights in the Canadian Constitution in 1982 highlights Canada's commitment to recognizing equality as a fundamental right in society and, on its face, reflects a significant movement towards embracing postmaterialist values on a grand scale.

The adoption of a non-discrimination clause in the Charter was a development that coincided with a rise in significant levels of support for equality rights among Canadians over the last 35 years. This shift in public opinion can be seen in survey results tapping public attitudes in two prominent areas of concern – namely, gay rights and equality for women. Although gay rights are not explicitly recognized in the Charter, readers familiar with post-Charter history are aware that the

Supreme Court took the historic step of reading the protection of homosexuals from discrimination into s. 15(1) of the Charter in *Egan v. Canada*, [1995] 2 S.C.R. 513. We discuss this case more fully in chapter 7, but its significance suggests that, at first blush, the Canadian court was attentive to the changing attitudes of the public in this area of equality. For evidence of this public opinion shift, consider the results from the World Values Surveys of 1981, 1990, 2000, and 2005, which had asked Canadians "whether homosexuality can always be justified, never be justified, or something in between" (respondents were asked to use a 10-point scale, with 1 = never justifiable and 10 = always justifiable). The findings document a gradual shift in a postmaterialist direction on this question, with 52 per cent of Canadians in 1981 saying homosexuality is never justifiable, while only 19 per cent gave the same response in 2005 (Inglehart 1997, 279; World Values Survey 2005). This shift downward was also accompanied by a rise in the percentage of respondents that were neutral on the question. Between 2000 and 2005, there was a 9 per cent jump in the percentage of respondents that gave a neutral score of 5 on the 1–10 scale: 13 and 22 per cent, respectively (World Values Survey 2000, 2005).

Moreover, when the 2005 data from the World Values Survey are broken down into different age cohorts, the younger cohorts of Canadians are far more likely to believe that "homosexuality is always justifiable," a finding that supports Inglehart's thesis of intergenerational value change. Indeed, respondents aged 29 and younger were twice as likely to agree that "homosexuality is always justifiable" than respondents 50 and older (35 and 15 per cent, respectively) (World Values Survey 2005). A similar gap appeared at the opposite end of the continuum for these two age cohorts (with 12 and 24 per cent saying that "homosexuality is never justifiable") (ibid.). These data provide compelling evidence that an intergenerational shift in attitudes towards gay rights has been taking place in Canada in recent years.

Surveys by Inglehart and others provide similar evidence documenting changing public attitudes towards equality rights for homosexuals. For example, in 2000 and 2005, the World Values Survey asked Canadians "if they would not like to have homosexuals as neighbours." Overall, the percentage saying they would not like to have homosexuals as neighbours dropped from 17 per cent in 2000 to 14 per cent in 2005. Significantly, the 3 per cent decline in this response rate occurred evenly across postmaterialists and materialists alike, falling from 11 to 8 per cent for postmaterialists and from 26 to 23 per cent among materialists

(World Values Survey 2000, 2005). Moreover, in the 2000 Canadian Election Survey (Blais et al. 2004), 49 per cent of Canadians endorsed the position that gays and lesbians should be allowed to get married – a full four years before the Canadian Supreme Court endorsed this position in *Reference re Same-Sex Marriage*, [2004] 3 S.C.R. 698. Research by Lehman (2006) using the Canadian National Elections Study series of the 1990s and 2000s suggested that recent levels of public support for same-sex marriage and gay rights in general were directly related to the degree of traditional moral values that were espoused by individuals and the effect they had on LGBT individuals more than demographic factors such as age, sex, income level, and education. For example, data from 1997 indicated that, among individuals with very traditional moral values, only 6 per cent supported gay marriage, while those espousing very progressive views supported gay marriage at 77 per cent. Yet Lehman's research showed that there was movement by all groups over time and that, by 2004, the number of very traditional Canadians supporting gay marriage had jumped to 21 per cent, while those at the other extreme had jumped to 94 per cent (Lehman 2006, 22). These data provide further evidence that a postmaterialist shift has been taking place in attitudes towards gay rights in modern Canadian society.

The type of postmaterialist value shift that has occurred towards gay rights can also be seen in the area of sexual equality, another salient battleground for discrimination disputes in recent decades. For example, between 1981 and 2005, public approval in Canada for women to have a child as a single parent rose from 35 per cent to 45 per cent. Moreover, in recent editions of the World Values Survey, Inglehart has documented that Canadians are less likely to think of men as "better political leaders than women" and that the degree of confidence in the women's movement has increased over time. For instance, between 2000 and 2005, the percentage of Canadians indicating that they had "a great deal" or "quite a lot of" confidence in the women's movement jumped from 57 per cent to 67 per cent (World Values Survey 2000, 2005). Interestingly, during that five-year period, the gap between materialists and postmaterialists on this response item disappeared, with materialist support catching up to the level of postmaterialist supporters. Thus, both groups in the 2005 survey expressed equal confidence in the women's movement in Canada. Finally, the Canadian Election Survey has frequently asked whether "we have gone too far in pushing equal rights in this country." If a postmaterialist shift has truly taken place, as Inglehart suggests, the percentage of Canadians agreeing with that statement should have declined. Indeed, between 1993 and 2000, the percentage that agreed that "we have gone too far in pushing equal rights" dropped from 46 to 37 per cent (Johnston et al. 1988, 1995; Blais et al. 2004). This general equality-rights question, along with the others presented above, provides strong evidence that a broad-based attitudinal shift has taken hold in Canada, endorsing equality rights in general and women's rights in particular.

Although the data above suggest that a decisive postmaterialist shift has taken place among the Canadian public, it is an open question whether the same pattern has appeared among political and legal elites in Canada. From a political perspective, one would expect that as the public becomes more supportive of equality rights, legal and political elites should be in step with that movement. Prior research by Sniderman et al. (1996, 106) shows that, in a 1987 survey, legal elites in Canada were far more likely to support equal child custody rights for lesbian mothers than the mass public (87 and 72 per cent, respectively). Similarly, when asked about the specific context of allowing homosexuals to teach in provincial schools, 69 per cent of legal elites were supportive, while 51 per cent of randomly selected Canadians endorsed this view. Research also indicates that legal elites were 18 per cent less likely than the mass public to agree that "we have gone too far in pushing equal rights in this country" (Sniderman et al. 1996, 86). Collectively, these data document that legal elites, or the population from which judges are drawn, were far more likely to embrace postmaterialist, pro-equality stances than the average Canadian in the late eighties. Subsequent research by Matthews (2005) indicates that public support for same-sex marriage spiked after a series of legal challenges resulted in pivotal rulings by the Supreme Court, with, for example, *M. v. H.*, [1999] 2 S.C.R. 3 generating a rapid shift in attitudes on this issue. Regardless of whether elites are more supportive of equality rights than the public or vice versa, the movement by both groups in the postmaterialist direction points to the importance of testing Inglehart's thesis in the context of the Supreme Court of Canada over a four-decade period.

Even though scholars have documented more supportive attitudes in the equality area among the mass public and legal elites over time, it is important to remember that s. 1 of the Charter provides a significant textual limitation that allows Supreme Court justices to limit equality claims in favour of materialist and communitarian values. As we indicated in earlier chapters, s. 1 guarantees rights subject only to "reasonable limits prescribed by law" that "can be demonstrably justified in a free and democratic society." As in the free expression area, this language provides a legitimate rationale for justices to recognize expansive equality rights under s. 15(1), but to subsequently restrict those rights if government has enacted reasonable laws. In practice, this tension can result in the court ruling that while an individual rights claimant has a right to be protected from sex discrimination (under s. 15), that right can be superseded by government's power to allow some reasonable distinctions among people within the law (under s. 1). The dualistic tension in the Charter, which parallels the dichotomy that Inglehart posits between materialist and postmaterialist value dimensions, provides a compelling reason to tease out the empirical patterns of judicial decisions in equality cases.

Given that seven women have been elevated to the Canadian court since 1982, a natural question that arises is whether female justices approach equality disputes differently than their male colleagues. Research by Ostberg and Wetstein (2007) and Songer et al. (2012) has found that female justices on the modern Canadian Supreme Court have been decisively more postmaterialist in their resolution of discrimination suits than their male counterparts. Indeed, Ostberg and Wetstein (2007, 133) documented that the likelihood of a liberal vote in a host of equality cases decided between 1984 and 2003 was 73 per cent for female justices but only 47 per cent for their male counterparts when controlling for a variety of explanatory variables. Songer et al., in turn, found that gender splits within the Canadian Supreme Court are evident across criminal, civil rights, and liberties cases as well as economic cases during the same time frame (2012, 145–50).

Although these findings provide some compelling evidence that a gender gap exists in the resolution of equality disputes, most of the scholarly analysis has been focused on post-Charter cases over a 20-year period. Recent work on the contemporary court by Alarie and Green (2009a, 491–2) suggests that equality cases have a tendency to drive up liberal voting patterns for justices of the McLachlin Court who are Liberal Party appointees. Our research seeks to expand the analysis of equality cases to a 40-year horizon. Moreover, simply because female justices as a group are more supportive of equality claims than their male colleagues does not mean that the court as a whole has necessarily moved in a postmaterialist direction in the equality area over the last 40 years. As a result, there is still a need to test the applicability of Inglehart's postmaterialist thesis of intergenerational value change in a setting like the Supreme

Court of Canada. In this chapter, we focus on the empirical patterns that emerge in the outcomes and voting records of the justices in equality cases decided between 1973 and 2010, while in chapter 7, we examine the language and rationale used by the justices in a subset of landmark cases dealing with gay rights and sex discrimination.

It is important to remind readers that, in equality cases, like the free expression area, the postmaterialist-materialist concerns fall on a social rather than economic value dimension. In short, these cases present a social tension between equality claims on the one hand and government interests in protecting traditional societal values on the other. For example, when a lesbian brings an equality suit seeking equal access to a child in a child custody dispute, it pits postmaterialist notions of equality before the law against the desire by governments and others to protect gender norms and the "sanctity" of the traditional family unit. Similarly, when a woman brings a suit trying to gain access to an all-male organization, the dispute pits a gender-equality claim against traditional arguments for maintaining all-male clubs and the freedom of men to create them. Thus, it is important to highlight that, in the equality area, the social tension is one that typically pits the value of equality versus order and the freedom to discriminate.

However, there is an inherent complexity to these cases that must be noted because many equality claims involve monetary concerns, whereby an individual is seeking lost income and/or benefits. For instance, some cases involve the denial or extension of social service benefits, raising the issue of whether justices might be more deferential to government interests when public money is involved. As James has pointed out, when minority groups such as First Nation individuals and women seek equal treatment under the principles of the Charter or other legal frameworks, they are necessarily pursuing materialistic outcomes for themselves, leading him to note that they are "misrecognized materialists" (James 2006, 12). As such, the claim for equality has the effect of also invoking an economic dimension on behalf of a rights claimant, and, therefore, the pursuit of equality can also contain a materialist component that advances the economic interest of the rights claimant if they win. While this economic component is relevant, we believe it is not the predominant line of enquiry in these cases. Rather, the legal core of these disputes is principally framed and analysed by the justices through the prism of fostering social equality rather than economic equality and, thus, we believe that this dimension is the central focus of these disputes.

Data and Methods for Descriptive Statistics and Judicial Voting Patterns

The data for this segment of the study, like the environmental and free expression sections of the book, were drawn from published opinions of the *Canadian Supreme Court Reports* between 1973 and 2010 and were included in our analysis if a discrimination claim was a central component of the case ($N = 106$).[1] The cases in this area feature a mixture of disputes raising claims of unequal treatment on the basis of sex, disability, age, religion, marital status, sexual orientation, race, ethnicity, citizenship, and status as a prisoner. We begin this section by analysing the 106 discrimination claims from a quantitative perspective, following much the same format as we used in the prior two sections of the book by providing various descriptive statistics, followed by analysing the voting behaviour of the justices, and ending with logistic regression models that control for various judge- and case-level variables in the equation.

Descriptive Statistics and Judicial Voting Patterns

The data in the first seven tables provide descriptive statistics on various trends in equality cases handed down by the Canadian Supreme Court over the past 40 years. Table 6.1 indicates that the court heard a wide variety of discrimination claims and that they fell into two distinct issue categories, those dealing with different types of discrimination claims and those pertaining to benefits and job loss. Since many of the equality cases also involved the Canadian Human Rights Commission (CHRC) or required the court to engage in Charter analysis, under s. 15 or some other Charter provision, these separate categories were included in the table as well. Thus, as in the previous two sections of the book, since some of the cases fell into two or more issue categories, the number of cases listed across the four categories *is greater* than the 106 distinct cases that the court heard during this period. Across the 106 cases, the court heard a total of 112 discrimination claims, with almost two-thirds of the legal disputes heard involving sex, disability, and age discrimination claims. While 23 per cent of the cases heard by the court involved some type of sex discrimination, 22 and 21 per cent pertained

1 The list of cases included in the data set is provided in the appendix.

Table 6.1. Canadian Discrimination Cases by Issue Area, 1973–2010

Issue area	Cases (*N* = *106*)	
	No.	%
Type of discrimination	**112**	**100.1**
Sex	24	22.6
Disability	23	21.7
Age	22	20.8
Religion	11	10.4
Marital status	10	9.4
Gay	9	8.5
Race/ethnicity	7	6.6
Citizenship	4	3.8
Prisoner	2	1.9
Benefits/job loss	**52**	**49.1**
Government benefits	17	16.0
Private benefits	8	7.6
Job loss/forced retirement	27	25.5
Human rights commission		
Human rights commission	35	33.0
No human rights commission	71	67.0
Charter	**80**	**75.5**
S. 15 issue	53	50.0
Other substantive Charter issue	27	25.5
No Charter issue	50	47.2

Note: Readers should be careful when interpreting this table. One should not expect that the subcategory totals or counts of cases will match up with the total number of cases found in the discrimination category (106 cases) because more than one type of discrimination may appear in a case. This also explains why the numbers of cases found in the Charter areas are so large. In short, Charter characteristics are featured in many of the cases, and some cases have more than one Charter provision at issue in the dispute.

to disability and age discrimination. A second tier of discrimination claims heard by the court dealt with religion, marital status, and gay rights, which collectively constituted 28 per cent of the disputes heard in this area of law. While 10 per cent of these claims involved religious discrimination, 10 per cent related to marital status, and 9 per cent dealt with gay rights. The smallest percentage of cases fell into race/ethnicity, citizenship, and prisoner rights categories, and collectively, they constituted only 12 per cent of the discrimination claims heard by the court over the four decades studied.

Over the last 40 years, 52 of the cases addressed issues pertaining to benefits or job loss, a number that constituted 49 per cent of all cases heard in this area of law. More specifically, while 16 per cent of the cases involved government benefits, 8 per cent dealt with benefits relating to corporations or other private entities. Moreover, 26 per cent of the cases heard in this category involved disputes pertaining to job loss or forced retirement. Clearly, discriminatory treatment in relation to benefits and job loss constituted a salient issue in Canadian society over the four decades in our study. Table 6.1 suggests that the CHRC or a provincial human rights commission was involved in almost a third of the cases dealing with discrimination claims (33 per cent), which is not surprising since many citizens are required to seek a ruling from a commission before entering litigation. Since an equality provision was written into the Charter of Rights and Freedoms, one would expect that a large percentage of the cases heard in the discrimination area would trigger a Charter review. Indeed, 50 per cent of the cases in our data set raised a s. 15 issue, while 26 per cent of the discrimination claims raised other substantive Charter issues, and 47 per cent raised no Charter issues because many were heard before the Charter was enacted. As mentioned in previous chapters, the reason the court did not hear more cases involving a Charter claim in this area of law stems from the fact that the first Charter equality cases were not handed down until 1989. Overall, it seems that the Canadian Supreme Court has heard a large swathe of discrimination cases over the last 40 years, although a bulk of these disputes fall into only a few select areas.

Table 6.2 provides an account of the percentage of liberal, pro-equality rulings handed down by the court in nine of the most numerous types of discrimination that were identified in the first table.[2] The data reveal that the largest percentage of pro-equality rulings were handed down in the private benefits and gay rights areas (63 and 56 per cent, respectively); however, since so few cases were heard by the court in these two areas, the number amounts to five of the pro-equality rulings in each of these areas of discrimination law. The two other areas that featured over 50 per cent liberal rulings included religious and disability discrimination, where the court handed down 55 and 52 per cent liberal

2 Although we usually want the court to hand down 10 or more rulings in a subcategory before calculating the percentage of liberal rulings handing down in that category, since gay rights constitutes such an important issue area and the court heard nine cases in this category, we decided to include the findings in this subcategory as well. Moreover, since the percentage of liberal rulings relating to private benefits and government benefits were at the two ends of the spectrum, we decided to keep the findings from these two categories separate, even though only eight cases were handed down in the private benefits subcategory.

Table 6.2. Liberal Rulings in Canadian Discrimination Cases by Broad Issue Area, 1973–2010

Issue area	Cases, no. (*N* = *106*)	Liberal rulings, %
Private benefits	8	62.5
Gay	9	55.6
Religion	11	54.5
Disability	23	52.2
Job loss/forced retirement	27	48.1
Sex	24	41.7
Marital status	10	30.0
Government benefits	17	29.4
Age	22	27.3

Table 6.3. Liberal Rulings in Discrimination Cases by Decade and Court in the Supreme Court of Canada, 1973–2010

Court	Cases, no.	Liberal rulings, %
Decade		
1970s (1973–79)	2	0.0
1980s	28	53.6
1990s	41	36.6
2000s (2000–10)	33	54.5
Period		
Laskin Court (1974–84)[a]	10	40.0
Dickson Court (1984–90)	21	52.4
Lamer Court (1990–99)	40	37.5
McLachlin Court (2000–10)	33	54.5

[a]We excluded two cases from this period because they were argued under the leadership of Chief Justice Fauteux; however, they were handed down in 1974 and 1975, so they were included in the data set.

rulings, respectively. In contrast, the lowest levels of postmaterialistic, pro-equality liberal rulings were found in the areas of age discrimination and marital status, where the court handed down only 27 and 30 per cent liberal rulings, respectively. One possible explanation for why members of the court might be least sympathetic to disputes involving age discrimination is that they themselves are required to retire from the bench at the age of 75.

Table 6.3 highlights the percentage of liberal rulings handed down in discrimination cases in each of the last four decades and by court period. The data reveal a steady increase in the number of discrimination cases heard between 1970 and 1990, with the court hearing only two discrimination claims in the 1970s and 41 cases in the 1990s. However, in the first decade of the twenty-first century, there was a slight drop in the number of discrimination cases heard by the court, and only 33 of these claims were heard during the first 10 years of Chief Justice McLachlin's tenure. This relatively steady rise in the number of discrimination cases heard by the court is indicative of a society that is more conscious of the saliency of this issue and the rise of grass-roots organizations devoted to taking these kinds of policy issues through the legal system. If one looks at the percentage of pro-equality rulings handed down under the last four judicial tenures, there has been a steady trend upward, with the exception of the Lamer Court. The percentage of pro-equality rulings handed down in the discrimination area do increase by 12 per cent as one moves from the Laskin tenure (40 per cent liberal) to the Dickson tenure (52 per cent liberal), where the court began deciding the first discrimination claims under the Charter in 1989. This liberal, postmaterialist trend in the discrimination area dips to 38 per cent under the Lamer tenure, yet rises to a high of 55 per cent in the first 10 years of the McLachlin Court.

Overall, Table 6.3 provides support for Inglehart's shifting values thesis in the discrimination area over the past 40 years. Not only have more individuals and organizations brought more discrimination claims to court, but the justices of the Dickson and McLachlin Courts have also become more sympathetic towards these claims. The apparent retrograde shift of the Lamer Court justices is similar to the findings in chapter 2, where the justices exhibited a retrograde pattern of reduced postmaterialist voting in environmental cases. These data point to the complexity of decision patterns across time and across multiple issue areas, with postmaterialist movement within the court sometimes subject to the increasing difficulty in fact patterns and the mitigating legal interpretations that emerge in the cases over time. In addition, the "human dignity" factors articulated in *Law v. Canada (Minister of Employment and Immigration)*, [1999] 1 S.C.R. 497 have posed a significant impediment to achieving successful pro-equality outcomes, and thus, they may have necessarily dampened the enthusiasm of claimants to bring forward such claims (Hendry 2002; Ryder, Faria, and Lawrence 2004; Hogg 2011, s. 55-8). Despite these important caveats, the data in the discrimination area over the past 40 years, like the free expression area, do support a general movement in the postmaterialist direction.

Table 6.4 presents a breakdown of the number of discrimination issues decided by the court in seven of the substantive subcategories identified in Table 6.2 (benefits/job loss, gay, religion, disability, sex,

Table 6.4. Number of Discrimination Issues Decided by the Supreme Court of Canada by Decade, 1973–2010

Issue area	1970s	1980s	1990s	2000s	Total
Sex	1	6	11	5	23
Disability	1	3	11	8	23
Age	0	10	7	4	21
Religion	0	3	4	4	11
Marital status	0	1	6	3	10
Gay	1	0	4	4	9
Benefits/job loss	0	15	21	14	50
Human rights commission	1	13	12	9	35
S. 15 issue	0	7	27	19	53

marital status, and age). We decided to combine the three subcategories in the benefits and job loss sections for the purposes of this table since they measure similar data. During the 1970s, the court handed down three rulings pertaining to gay rights, and sex and disability discrimination. The small number of decisions reflects the period before constitutional protections had been enshrined and illustrates the weak nature of the statutory Canadian Bill of Rights in Canadian society. Table 6.4 also shows that in six of the seven substantive areas, there was a steady increase in the number of discrimination cases heard between the 1970s and 1990s, which encompassed the Laskin, Dickson, and Lamer Court tenures. This increase is not surprising given that the Charter of Rights and Freedoms was added to the Constitution in 1982. The one exception to this rule pertained to cases heard in the area of age discrimination, where the number of cases heard by the court peaked at 10 in the 1980s, only to fall off to 7 and then 4 in the following two decades.

The one interesting finding is that there was a decline in the number of cases heard by the court in the first 10 years of the McLachlin Court in five of the seven areas, with the numbers staying level with the 1990s for age and gay discrimination. One possible explanation for the fall-off in discrimination disputes under the McLachlin tenure ties back to the Charter maturation argument and the notion that many of the key principles in discrimination law had been settled and could be situated in a comprehensive framework by the close of the 1990s (McCormick 2015, 88–90, 134). As a result, after the flurry of rulings in this area in the 1990s, the number of discrimination cases was bound to decrease in the first 10 years of the subsequent Chief. A quick perusal of the totals at the end of the table indicates that the court heard the highest number of issues in the benefits and job loss area (50), followed by claims of sex and disability discrimination, which constituted less than half as many claims as heard in the benefits and job loss category (23 cases each). The court heard the fewest number of cases involving gay rights and marital status (9 and 10 cases, respectively), possibly because these areas of discrimination only recently gained sufficient prominence in Canadian culture.

Table 6.5 documents the different types of appellants and respondents that typically appeared in discrimination suits at the Supreme Court level. The data reveal that, as in the free expression area, the most common pairing occurred between an individual and the federal or a provincial government (46 of 106 cases, 43 per cent). Also similar to the free expression area, an individual sought to appeal a lower court finding in favour of the government's policy in almost three-fourths of these disputes. It is not surprising that the largest share of claims was brought by an individual against the federal and provincial levels of government, given the large number of individuals that are employed by the government and the large number who receive government services or benefits. Moreover, individual litigants would be motivated to eliminate discriminatory practices by government officials, especially in light of the explicit governmental protections secured in the Charter of Rights and Freedoms.

The limited nature of disputes between an individual and municipal governments is even more pronounced in the discrimination area than in the free expression area, with the individual seeking to appeal a lower court ruling upholding a supposedly discriminatory municipal policy in one instance over the past 40 years. One reason for such a low volume of cases at the municipal level is the emergence of human rights commissions and tribunals, which serve as a specialized forum to resolve many of these disputes and eliminate the need for higher-level appeals. Another reason emanates from party capability theory, which suggests that municipalities are far less likely than provincial and federal governments to advance an appeal all the way to the Supreme Court (Galanter 1974, 2003; McCormick 1993; Kritzer 2003).

As in the free expression area, a substantial drop-off exists in the first and second most prominent litigant pairings in the discrimination area, with those taking place between individuals and educational institutions (10 of 106 cases, 9 per cent). In 7 of these 10 cases, an individual appealed a ruling by the lower court that restricted equality rights in educational institutions. Litigation pairings between individuals and corporate entities followed a close third (9 of 106, 8 per cent), with two-thirds of the

Table 6.5. Appellants and Respondents in Canadian Discrimination Cases, 1973–2010

Appellant	Respondent								
	Federal government	Provincial government	City government	Individual	Union	Corporation	Educational institution	Other	Total
Federal government	0	0	0	10	1	2	0	3	16
Provincial government	0	0	2	3	0	3	0	0	8
City government	0	5	0	0	1	1	0	0	7
Individual	19	14	1	3	1	6	7	1	52
Union	1	4	0	0	0	1	1	0	7
Corporation	1	0	0	3	1	0	0	0	5
Educational Institution	0	0	0	3	2	0	0	0	5
Other group	2	1	0	1	1	1	0	0	6
Total	23	24	3	23	7	14	8	4	106

Table 6.6. Litigant Equal Rights Stances and Discrimination Victories, 1973–2010

Party	Appellant	Respondent	Total	Took conservative position, no.	Took equality position, no.	Conservative wins, %	Liberal wins, %
Federal government	16	23	39	36	3	66.7	33.3
Provincial government	8	24	32	22	10	63.6	50.0
City government	7	3	10	10	0	30.0	–
Individual	52	23	75	3	72	0.0	43.1
Union	7	7	14	2	12	100.0	58.3
Corporation	5	14	19	17	2	35.3	50.0
Educational institution	5	8	13	13	0	53.8	–
Other group	6	4	10	3	7	66.7	42.9
Overall total	106	106	212	106	106	55.7	44.3

appeals brought by individuals against corporate entities. One explanation for why individuals appealed more cases against educational institutions than corporations over the past 40 years may be increasing concern over mandatory retirement. While it is not surprising that the bulk of the pairings involved individuals and federal and provincial governments, it *is* surprising that the litigant pairing between individuals and educational institutions edges out those involving corporations, especially given the bad reputation corporations have obtained in the popular culture in the area of equality and discrimination. One should note that individual-versus-corporation cases are not about the Charter but rather about statutory human rights code complaints. In these disputes, corporations have such a financial and litigation edge over the lone individual that settlements may be more common, and thus petitions to the Canadian Supreme Court are likely to be few in number.

Table 6.6 highlights the number of appearances of various litigants, the number of times they took a liberal or conservative position in discrimination cases over the last 40 years, and the percentage of victories they obtained in those cases. Unlike the free expression area, where the government always took the conservative position, while unions and the media always took the liberal position, the stances taken by six of the eight types of litigants identified were far more mixed in the discrimination area. More specifically, in the discrimination area, only municipal governments and educational institutions took a conservative stance in all the cases in which they participated. Although both the federal and the provincial governments did advocate on behalf of equality interests in some disputes, they predominantly took the conservative stance in the discrimination area (36 of 39 appearances for the federal government, 22 of 32 appearances for a provincial government). As in the free expression area, the federal and provincial governments achieved the two highest conservative win rates, outside the Other Group category (67 and 64 per cent, respectively). Although these two levels of government experienced a slightly lower win rate in discrimination cases than in the free expression area, the win record in both areas, as mentioned earlier, fits nicely with party capability theory, which posits that litigants with deep pockets and proficiency in the litigation process will have much more success in the legal system (Galanter 1974, 2003; McCormick 1993; Kritzer 2003). The government's stance in these two areas of law stands in direct contrast to the overwhelmingly liberal stance it took in the environmental area over the past four decades, although its win rate across all three areas of law is impressive regardless of what stance it took. The government's win record at the municipal level in discrimination cases is less than half that found at the federal and provincial levels (30 per cent), and this disparity mimics the one found in the free expression area. Clearly, municipal governments do not have the same deep pockets or litigation expertise as the other two levels of government.

Except for governmental litigants, educational institutions always took the conservative position in discrimination cases, while corporations did so in 17 of the 19 cases they participated in. However, their win rates stood in stark contrast with each other, with educational institutions winning 54 per cent of the time, while corporations won only 35 per cent of the time. One possible explanation for this disparity is that since public education falls under the purview of governmental power, these institutions are far more careful about adhering to policies that ensure fair treatment in the school setting than corporate entities, which lie outside the confines of government authority. Moreover, many of the cases in the education area pertained to retirement disputes, an area of law that has not been favourable to plaintiffs. One should also note that the win rates of both of these litigants were well short of the win rates of federal and provincial governments in discrimination cases.

Not surprisingly, the two litigants that overwhelmingly took the liberal, postmaterialist stance in discrimination cases were individuals and unions (72 of 75 cases for individuals and 12 of 14 cases for unions).

Table 6.7. Intervener Activity in Discrimination Cases, 1973–2010

Intervener (no. of cases)	1970s	1980s	1990s	2000s	Total
Federal government	0	11	13	10	34
Provincial government	1	26	43	68	138
Civil liberties/rights group (27)	0	0	29	29	58
Disability group (22)	0	5	23	19	47
Indigenous group (6)	16	0	10	14	40
Religious group (11)	0	1	19	17	37
Union (5)	0	2	8	18	28
Female group (17)	4	3	13	5	25
Other group	3	2	24	37	66
Totals	**24**	**50**	**182**	**217**	**473**
Position favouring equal rights, 1973–2010[a]					
Intervener	1970s	1980s	1990s	2000s	Total
Federal government	0	0	2	3	5
Provincial government	0	8	9	14	31
Civil liberties/rights group	0	0	28	29	57
Disability group	0	5	23	19	47
Indigenous group	16	0	10	0	26
Religious group	0	1	4	7	12
Union	0	1	8	18	27
Female group	4	3	11	4	22
Other group	3	1	14	27	45
Totals, pro-equality rights	**23**	**19**	**109**	**121**	**272**
Proportion, pro-equality	95.8	38.0	59.9	55.8	57.5
Proportion, anti-equality	4.2	62.0	40.1	44.2	42.5

[a]We coded the direction of the interveners in reference to whether they favoured equality or a civil liberties interest based on our reading of the Supreme Court cases.

The win rate for unions was the highest of all the liberal-oriented litigants, at 58 per cent, while individuals had the fourth-highest win record, behind the provincial government and corporations, at 43 per cent. One explanation for this lower winning record is that individuals tend to have fewer resources at their disposal and are bound to have less success than repeat players in the legal system.

Table 6.7 documents the eight specific types of intervener activity in discrimination cases and the number of times they favoured equality rights over the 1970–2010 time period. The totals found at the bottom of the top half of the table indicate that intervener activity in discrimination cases, like the environmental area, increased steadily across all four decades, ranging from a low of 24 and 50 interventions across all eight types of interveners in the 1970s and 1980s to a high of 217 interventions in the 2000s. Unlike the free expression area, overall intervener activity in the discrimination area did not decline during the first decade of the McLachlin tenure, but increased by 35 interventions. When one looks more closely at the different types of intervener activity, there is a notably steady rise across the first three decades for seven of the eight groups, while provincial government and union intervener activity peaked in the 2000s, and civil rights and liberties group activity remained steady during the last two decades of the study. Only First Nation and female groups did not quite fit this pattern. This distinctive feature, which often plays out in high-profile cases, is illustrated by First Nation groups and unions, which engaged in 40 and 28 interventions but only in 6 and 5 cases, respectively, across the four decades.

Provincial government was the one group that dwarfed the rest in its overall intervention rates in discrimination cases, having over four times the number of interventions as the federal government. This same trend occurred in the free expression cases. However, this large rate of interventions can be partially explained by the fact that multiple provincial governments often intervene in a given suit. This fact aside, one should note that the intervention activity by the provincial governments has grown the most across numerous cases over the past 40-year period. Collectively, these data reinforce the findings in the environmental and free expression areas that interest group activity has increased significantly over time for most groups, reinforcing Epp's (1996, 1998) notion that legal mobilization by various groups has become entrenched and a force to be reckoned with in the judicial system of established democracies like Canada.

In the second half of Table 6.7, one can get a better idea of whether Inglehart's postmaterialist values thesis has played out among intervener groups in the discrimination area over the past 40 years. The totals at the bottom of the second half of the table indicate that, in general, there is a similar trajectory of growth in pro-equality interventions over time as in the intervention activity that occurs in the top half of the table. Moreover, these findings mirror the pattern that was found in the environmental and free expression areas of law. Except for the 1970s data, which was inflated by the fact that 16 First Nation representatives intervened in support of the equality claim advanced in a single case, the findings indicate that interventions in favour of equality claims moved from a low of 19 in the 1980s to a high of 121 in the 2000s. From a proportional perspective, pro-equality intervening activity went from a level of 38 per cent in the 1980s to 60 and 56 per cent in the 1990s and 2000s. A reverse trend appeared for anti-equality interveners. This suggests that, in the discrimination area, as in the free expression area, there has been a rise in interest group activity, in both the volume and the proportion of postmaterialist-seeking interveners. This is not surprising because of the emergence of the Charter. Nonetheless, it does lend credence to Inglehart's theory of an intergenerational change taking place as more grass-roots efforts are made on behalf of postmaterialist values. The cumulative findings across these two distinct areas of law lend support to Inglehart's contention that a postmaterialist value transformation has occurred among the attitudes of the mass public over time and that this transformation has impacted the judicial system, partly because of the pressures brought on justices through intervener activity by various grass-roots groups in Canadian society.

Judicial Voting and Authorship Patterns

In the second stage of our analysis, we assess the career voting behaviour of 23 Canadian Supreme Court justices that participated in 10 or more discrimination cases during the 1973–2010 period. Table 6.8 provides a ranking of the career voting record of the justices, from high to low, in terms of the percentage of time they supported discrimination claims during their tenure on the court. The findings reveal that the top two justices that supported discrimination claims were two of the earliest female justices on the court: both Justices L'Heureux-Dubé and Wilson favoured equality claimants 72 and 70 per cent of the time, respectively. Justice McIntyre also supported such claims over two-thirds of the time, with a support score of 67 per cent. We are confident in these findings since all three justices heard a robust number of cases in this area of law. Readers should note that five of the top seven pro-equality voting records emanate from female justices, reflecting a clear tendency for most female justices to have a decisively liberal perspective on discrimination disputes; this makes sense since they themselves are likely to have faced some form of discrimination throughout their careers and lifetimes. In contrast, Justice Sopinka was the lowest supporter of equality claimants, favouring them only 29 per cent of the time. The next-lowest justice to favour equality claims was Justice Gonthier, who provided 7 per cent more support for these rights than Justice Sopinka, at 36 per cent. The two justices found in the middle of the pack, Justices LeBel and Chouinard, both supported equality claims 50 per cent of the time.

The pro-equality support records by the chief justices in the discrimination area are fairly similar to those found in the free expression area,

Table 6.8. Canadian Supreme Court Justices' Discrimination Voting Records, 1973–2010

Justice	Cases, no.	Pro-equality votes, no.	Liberal ruling, %
L'Heureux-Dubé	58	42	72.4
Wilson	23	16	69.6
McIntyre	18	12	66.7
Abella	14	9	64.3
McLachlin	*72*	*46*	*63.9*
Fish	19	12	63.2
Arbour	18	11	61.1
Estey	17	10	58.8
Binnie	44	25	56.8
Beetz	20	11	55.0
Dickson	*31*	*17*	*54.8*
LeBel	30	15	50.0
Chouinard	12	6	50.0
Bastarache	44	21	47.7
Iacobucci	54	25	46.3
Cory	41	19	46.3
Lamer	*48*	*22*	*45.8*
Charron	11	5	45.5
Major	51	21	41.2
Deschamps	22	9	40.9
La Forest	43	17	39.5
Gonthier	56	20	35.7
Sopinka	34	10	29.4

Note: Fifteen justices were excluded from the analysis in the equality area because they had fewer than 10 votes: Justices Abbott, Cromwell, de Grandpré, Fauteux, Hall, Judson, Laskin, Le Dain, Martland, Pigeon, Pratte, Ritchie, Rothstein, Spence, and Stevenson.

with Chief Justice McLachlin providing the most support for these claims at 64 per cent, while Chief Justice Lamer falls below the mean level of support with a score of 46 per cent. Unlike the free expression area, where Chief Justice Dickson joins Chief Justice Lamer by providing a support score just below the mean at 40 per cent, in discrimination claims, his score is slightly above the median, at 55 per cent. It is interesting to note that Chief Justice McLachlin provides the lowest level of support in the environmental area, while Chief Justice Laskin provides the highest level of support in the environmental area and the second highest in free expression claims. However, his record could not be tabulated for equality cases because he heard too few claims in this legal area. Collectively, it seems that the three most recent chief justices have provided different levels of support for discrimination claims, with the most recent, Chief Justice McLachlin, a woman, taking the most liberal stance in equality claims.

If one looks comparatively across the three areas of law analysed in this study, the justices collectively provided the highest level of support for postmaterialist values in the environmental area, with the median justices providing 58 per cent support, whereas the median justices in the equality and free expression area provided only 50 and 45 per cent support, respectively. These findings indicate that the Canadian Supreme Court justices have embraced postmaterialist values to the greatest extent in the environmental area, which is not surprising given the grave impact that various pollutants are having on our fragile ecosystem. The increase in global warming, ozone depletion, acid rain, and a host of other environmental concerns point to the need for elite citizens in advanced industrial societies, such as top justices in Canada, to take a leadership role in protecting the environment for the well-being of future generations and the survival of humanity as a whole. One explanation for why support for postmaterialist values is lowest in the free expression area is that these cases often deal with expression at the margins of social acceptability, such as hate speech, pornography, and obscenity. In addition, they present a complex intersection of values, and many of the disputes are imbued with a postmaterialist equality element that is not categorized as postmaterialist in our scoring of the votes. As we indicated earlier, modern Canadian justices are more concerned with elevating postmaterialist equality over unfettered free expression, something that sets them apart from their US counterparts. These findings are reflective of a culture that, while not perfect, prioritizes the value of equality in an effort to ensure that cultural diversity flourishes and that individuals are treated with equal dignity in political and social affairs.

If one looks at which justices provide the highest and least amount of support for postmaterialist values in the three areas of law, one is struck by the fact that no clear, consistent support pattern emerges. In fact, the justices that provide the highest level of support are different in each of the three areas of law, as are the justices providing the median and lowest levels of support. These findings suggest that the justices on the Canadian Supreme Court do not exhibit consistent voting patterns across different areas of law, and justices that exhibit libertarian patterns in one area of law do not necessarily do so in another area of law, which is primarily the case in the US context. This lower level of consistency across issue areas makes the Canadian justices stand out from their US counterparts and suggests, as we have pointed out in earlier research, that the Canadian justices exhibit a more complex, nuanced

Figure 6.1. Pro-equality Voting by Ideology Score

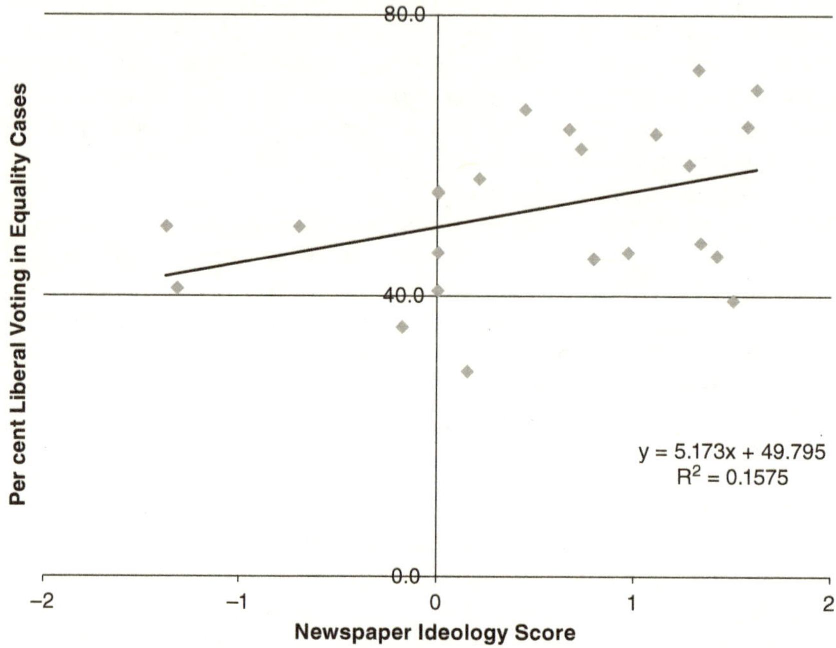

ideological approach to their decision making; this is understandable because they are not as ideologically polarized as their US counterparts (see Ostberg and Wetstein 2007; Songer et al. 2012).

Following our approach in the previous two areas of law, the data in Table 6.8 were converted into a figure that plots the justices' career-liberal voting scores in equality cases by their newspaper ideology scores at the time of their appointment to the bench (see Figure 6.1). As discussed in the earlier chapters, the newspaper ideology scores were borrowed from our earlier work, which tabulated scores based on journalistic assessments at the time of a justice's appointment to the Supreme Court (see Ostberg and Wetstein 2007). Unlike the free expression area, but like the environmental area, newspaper ideology scores seem to constitute a good barometer of the career-voting behaviour of the Canadian justices in equality cases across the four judicial periods. There is a positive correlation between the two measures, indicating that a one-unit increase in the positive or liberal direction on the 5-point newspaper ideology scale is accompanied by a 5 per cent increase in support for the rights claimant in discrimination claims (slope = 5.17). The R-square value indicates that almost 16 per cent of the variance in voting behaviour in the equality area can be explained by the newspaper ideology scores of the justices; this is almost identical to the variance found in the environmental area. Thus, in both discrimination and environmental claims, the apparent ideological leanings of the justices do appear at first blush to impact the career support for discrimination claims over the last 40 years. The equality findings are amplified by other research indicating that the ideal preference points of justices in the McLachlin Court equality cases can be partially explained by the ideological leanings of the justices (see Alarie and Green 2009a, 501).

Figure 6.1 excludes 13 justices because they participated in fewer than 10 cases in the discrimination/equality area during the 1973–2010 period – namely, Justices Abbott, Fauteux, Hall, Judson, Laskin, Le Dain, Martland, Pigeon, Pratte, Ritchie, Rothstein, Spence, and Stevenson. In addition, Justices Cromwell and de Grandpré were excluded because they did not participate in any discrimination cases during the period studied. Since Justices Dickson and Beetz have nearly identical scores on the two indicators, the figure appears to graph 22 justices instead of the actual total of 23 justices.

One way of assessing Inglehart's postmaterialist values thesis against the Canadian Supreme Court is to create a scatterplot that assesses the relationship between the justices' career-support scores in the discrimination area and their year of birth. As we have mentioned in earlier chapters, it is expected that the justices who are born later are more likely to exhibit higher liberal, career-support scores in discrimination cases because they are more likely to embrace postmaterialist values and therefore support the pro-equality values put forth by rights claimants. The findings in Figure 6.2 illustrate that, contrary to expectations, there is no real correlation between year of birth of the justices and their subsequent liberal-support score for rights claimants in discrimination cases. Ironically, these findings mirror those found in the environmental area, but are contrary to the results found in the free expression area. As in the environmental area, the regression line in Figure 6.2 is slightly negative, indicating that a justice born 10 years later is 1.5 per cent less likely to support the rights claimant in equality cases (slope = –.150). However, the dispersion of justices around the regression line and the fact that the R-square is .019 suggests that there is virtually no relationship between the year of birth of a justice and his or her likelihood

Figure 6.2. Pro-equality Voting by Year of Birth

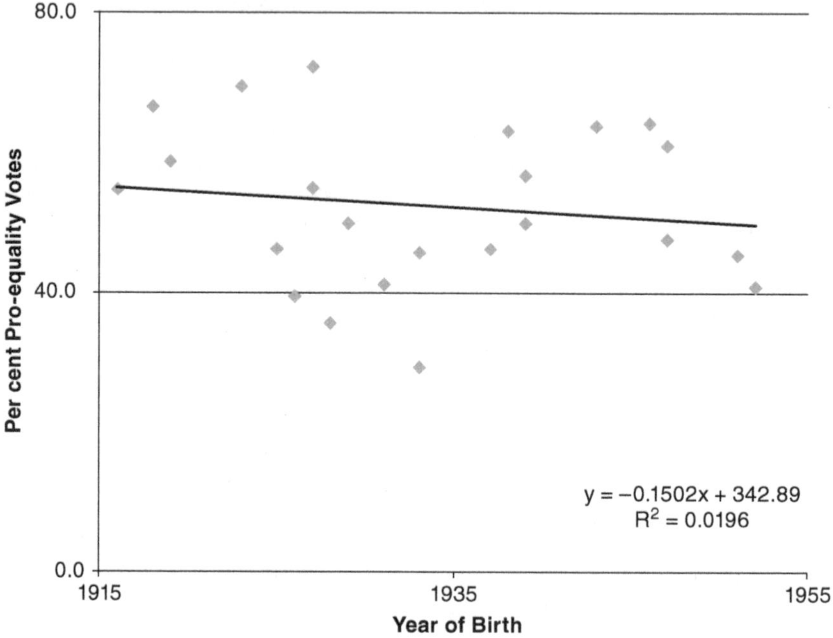

of providing liberal career support for equality claims. Thus, at first glance, it seems that, in the equality area, like the environmental area, Inglehart's shifting values thesis over time is not in play among top-level justices in Canadian society.

An alternative way of testing Inglehart's shifting values thesis on the Canadian Supreme Court over time is to assess the percentage of career pro-equality voting among justices who were appointed after the Charter was adopted into the Constitution in 1982. The rationale behind assessing the correlation between the year of birth of the 17 justices who were appointed after the Charter's adoption and their respective career-voting record is that it allows one to assess whether there is a shifting values thesis at play among the youngest, most recent cohort of Supreme Court justices. The findings in Figure 6.3 *do not* support this thesis. Instead, they reveal that the post-Charter justices who were born 10 years later than their post-Charter colleagues are no more likely to support the rights claimant in discrimination claims (slope = .033). The fact that the equation yields an R-square value of zero suggests that

Figure 6.3. Pro-equality Voting by Year of Birth, Post-Charter Justices

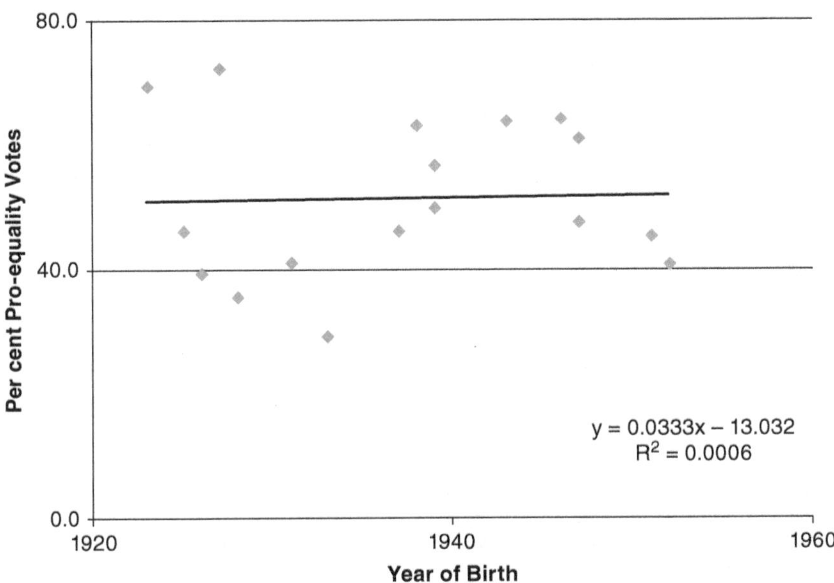

there is no support for Inglehart's contention that the value changes taking place in the population at large are also occurring among the younger judicial elites, at least in regard to discrimination cases.

The justices represented in Figure 6.3 are Justices Abella, Arbour, Bastarache, Binnie, Charron, Cory, Deschamps, Fish, Gonthier, Iacobucci, La Forest, LeBel, L'Heureux-Dubé, Major, McLachlin, Sopinka, and Wilson.

As in the previous two sections of the book, we next provide a detailed account of the voting behaviour and authorship pattern of the justices in the equality area over the past four decades (see Table 6.9). One should note that the justices exhibit a rate of unanimity in the discrimination area that falls in between the low rate found in the free expression area (49 per cent) and the high rate found in the environmental area (78 per cent), handing down unanimous rulings in 59 per cent of the cases (62 of 106 cases). This rate is also 11 per cent lower than the court's overall unanimity record of 70 per cent, which suggests that equality issues, like free expression ones, generate more conflict among the justices on the Canadian high court. The data in Table 6.9 indicate that Justice McIntyre served as the task leader in the discrimination

Table 6.9. Canadian Supreme Court Justices' Opinion Authorship Patterns in Discrimination Cases, 1973–2010

Justice	Cases, no.	Voting in majority, %	Majority author, %[a]	Voting in dissent, %	Dissenting author, %[b]
McIntyre	18	94.4	33.3	5.6	5.6
Sopinka	34	97.1	29.4	3.9	2.9
La Forest	43	95.3	25.6	4.7	0.0
McLachlin	*72*	*81.9*	*22.2*	*18.1*	*15.3*
Iacobucci	54	92.6	20.4	7.4	3.7
Deschamps	22	81.8	18.2	18.2	13.6
Dickson	*31*	*90.3*	*16.1*	*9.7*	*6.5*
Abella	14	92.9	14.3	7.1	7.1
Cory	41	87.8	12.2	12.2	12.2
Bastarache	44	90.9	11.4	9.1	6.8
Binnie	44	84.1	11.4	15.9	9.1
Lamer	*48*	*91.7*	*10.4*	*8.3*	*2.1*
Beetz	20	95.0	10.0	5.0	0.0
LeBel	30	83.3	10.0	16.7	6.7
Charron	11	90.9	9.1	9.1	9.1
Estey	17	94.1	5.9	5.9	0.0
Wilson	23	82.6	4.3	17.4	13.0
Gonthier	56	92.9	3.6	7.1	7.1
Major	51	88.2	2.0	11.8	5.9
L'Heureux-Dubé	58	65.5	1.7	34.5	25.9
Fish	19	78.9	0.0	21.1	10.5
Chouinard	12	91.7	0.0	8.3	0.0
Arbour	18	77.8	0.0	22.2	11.1

Note: The table includes voting records for all justices participating in 10 or more cases.
[a]Majority authorship is calculated by dividing the number of majority opinions authored by the total number of cases heard by a justice.
[b]Dissenting authorship is calculated by dividing the number of dissenting opinions authored by the total number of cases heard by a justice.

area, acting as majority author in 33 per cent of the cases that he heard in this area of law (6 of 18 cases). His leadership activity in this area stands in stark contrast to his record in the other two postmaterialist areas of law. In the free expression area, he fell into the middle of the pack, authoring only 3 of the 18 cases he participated in, while in the environmental area, he authored no majority opinions despite participating in 16 cases in this area of law. The next two notable leadership writers in the discrimination area, both of whom participated in many more cases than Justice McIntyre, are Justices Sopinka and La Forest, authoring 29 and 26 per cent of the cases they heard, respectively (10 of 34 cases for Justice Sopinka, 11 of 43 cases for Justice La Forest). While Justice Sopinka provided fairly strong leadership in the free expression area by writing majority opinions in 23 per cent of the cases he heard (7 of 30 cases), Justice La Forest, like his colleague Justice McIntyre, did not stand out as a task leader in either of the other two fields of law.

Overall, it seems that different task leaders have emerged on the Canadian Supreme Court in each of these three postmaterialist areas of law over the last 40 years. While Chief Justice Dickson served as task leader in both the environmental and the free expression areas, he was accompanied by Justices Martland and Beetz in environmental claims and Justices Ritchie and Bastarache in free expression ones. The task leaders in the discrimination area, however, include Justices McIntyre, Sopinka, and La Forest. These findings mirror prior research by Ostberg and Wetstein (2007), which suggested that judicial behaviour is far more nuanced and differentiated across discrete areas of law. The findings also fit nicely with the notion that justices rely on intra-court norms that promote specialists to be more frequent writers of reasons for judgment in their particular area of expertise.

At the other end of the equality spectrum sit Justices Fish, Chouinard, and Arbour. Although none of these justices authored a majority opinion in the discrimination area, Justice Chouinard's activity demonstrates that he acted as the ultimate judicial follower in the equality area because he joined the majority opinion in 11 of the 12 cases he heard. In contrast, the record of both Justices Arbour and Fish indicate that they serve as the two judicial outliers in the discrimination area because they issued two of the three highest rates of dissent (22 and 21 per cent, respectively). It is interesting to note that these same three justices fall at the bottom of the majority authorship table in the environmental area as well, although in this area, both Justices Arbour and Chouinard acted as judicial followers because they joined the majority opinion in all the cases that they heard. Since Justice Fish joined a few environmental dissents (15 per cent, or two cases), he was not as much of a follower as the other two justices. The justice that had the highest proportion of dissents in the equality area, not surprisingly, was Justice L'Heureux-Dubé, who dissented in 35 per cent of the cases that she heard (20 of 58 cases). She also penned more dissents than any other justice, writing the dissent in three-fourths of those cases (15 of 20). Two other justices that engaged in high rates of dissent in the equality area were Justices McLachlin and Deschamps, both dissenting in 18 per cent of the cases they heard. Although they came in third and fourth in dissenting votes, just behind Justices Arbour and Fish, they came in second and third in authoring dissents in the equality area, with Justice McLachlin authoring in 15 per cent of the cases she heard (11 of the 72 cases) and Justice Deschamps authoring in 14 per cent (3 of 22 cases).

Last but not least, one should note that five of the six top dissenters in the equality area were women, which is remarkable given that only seven women served on the Canadian Supreme Court over the period of our study. This finding lends credence to the contention by some scholars that gender differences do matter, especially when Canadian Supreme Court justices grapple with disputes in the discrimination area (for further discussion, see Ostberg and Wetstein [2007]; Hausegger, Hennigar, and Riddell [2009]; Songer et al. [2012]).

Looking across all three areas of law, it is not surprising that the chief justices tend to serve as relative task leaders, authoring majority opinions well above average, in most cases. For example, Chief Justice Dickson was among the top two majority-opinion writers in the environmental and free expression cases, and his rate of authorship in discrimination cases placed him well above the mean (16 per cent). Similarly, Chief Justice McLachlin was in the top four among majority-opinion authors in discrimination and free expression cases, and she was well above the mean authorship rate in the environmental area (17 per cent). While Chief Justices Laskin and Lamer were majority-opinion leaders in environmental cases (22 and 19 per cent, respectively), Chief Justice Lamer was in the middle of the pack in discrimination and free expression cases (10 and 14 per cent, respectively). Only Justice Chief Laskin was below the mean in free expression cases, in which he was a frequent dissenter in his own court.[3] Clearly, the data suggest that chief justices do feel a responsibility to take a leadership role on their own courts, at least in prominent postmaterialist areas of law.

Data and Methods for the Logistic Regression Analysis

In the last stage of our statistical analysis, we conduct logistical regression analysis at the judge-vote level to determine whether the 1–1 correlations that seemed to exist between judicial ideology and liberal, postmaterialist voting behaviour hold up when other independent

3 Since Chief Justice Laskin participated in fewer than 10 cases in the discrimination area, he was not included in our analysis of voting and authorship patterns in those cases.

variables are controlled for in the equation. Likewise, we are interested in looking more closely at the impact that various independent variables have on the voting behaviour of 26 justices in the equality area over the past 40 years.[4] As in the previous two legal areas of analysis, we develop three logistic models that assess the relative impact that various judge- and case-level factors have on judicial voting behaviour. While the first model tests the impact that 6 judge-level variables have on 795 judge vote outcomes, the second model analyses the impact that 15 case-level variables have on 833 vote outcomes. The third model, in turn, places all 21 independent variables into one equation to test the impact of various factors on 795 judge votes in discrimination cases. Logistic regression analysis was conducted for all three models because the dependent variable in the equation is a dichotomous variable identifying whether or not a justice ruled in favour of a rights claimant in equality claims (1 = liberal ruling, 0 = conservative ruling).

As in the free expression area, the coding of the case outcomes in the equality area is a relatively straightforward process, and it naturally follows Inglehart's postmaterialist value change thesis. We labelled a vote as liberal or postmaterialist if a justice voted in favour of a rights claimant in numerous areas of discrimination, including gay rights, disability, sex, religion, and marital status claims. We also considered votes cast to prevent job loss or forced retirement as liberal or postmaterialist, and votes upholding rights to employment or government benefits in the private or public realm. If Inglehart's changing values thesis is correct – namely, that a value shift is taking place among the citizens of advanced industrial societies – we would expect that the voting behaviour of Canadian Supreme Court justices would run in the same direction and result in more liberal rulings over time. Our test for such changing degrees of postmaterialist support is captured by the Lamer and McLachlin Court indicators that are included in the equations. If the value change argument is accurate, the coefficient for these

4 As mentioned in the other areas of analysis, we are able to assess the voting behaviour of a total of only 26 justices in the judge-level and the combined model (which includes both judge- and case-level data) because we are unable to create newspaper ideology scores for the 10 earliest justices in our study. The justices we were unable to create newspaper ideology scores for were Justices Abbott, Fauteux, Hall, Judson, Laskin, Martland, Pigeon, Pratte, Ritchie, and Spence. However, the model dealing with case characteristics used the voting records of all 35 justices that heard cases in the discrimination area.

two court variables should be positive and the values should be largest for the most recent period – namely, the McLachlin Court.

As in the previous two legal sections, the independent variables included in the three models are aimed at assessing whether judicial rulings in the equality area are principally driven by judge-level variables, such as gender, ideology, and academic background, or whether case-level characteristics play a more important role in influencing the voting behaviour of the justices. We also included variables for different chief justice tenures to assess whether Inglehart's shifting values thesis plays out among judicial elites over the last 40 years in equality claims, while also controlling for 19 other important variables in the equation. We omit discussion of the various hypotheses for each variable because at this point, readers are familiar with our regression models from the prior two quantitative chapters. Instead, we highlight some of our hypotheses for particular, new variables of interest in discrimination cases.

We included 15 distinct case-level characteristics in the logistic regression models that test the degree to which various case facts, parties in the suit, litigants, or interveners play a decisive role in judicial voting behaviour by Canadian justices in the equality area. More specifically, we entered six types of discrimination issues in the logistic models as dichotomous variables that made theoretical sense for explaining judicial voting behaviour in the discrimination area and would build on prior work conducted in this area of law (see Ostberg and Wetstein 2007). Each of these variables is dichotomous and tapped whether discrimination involved in the case related to disability (1 = yes, 0 = no), age (1 = yes, 0 = no), sex (1 = yes, 0 = no), and/or religion (1 = yes, 0 = no). Each of these forms of discrimination are outlawed in s. 15 of the Charter of Rights and Freedoms, as is discrimination on the basis of race and national or ethnic origin. In our regression equations, we omitted race, ethnicity, and national origin because they were not addressed as frequently by the court as the other areas of discrimination. Having said this, we expected that the coefficients in the model for age, sex, disability, and religion would not be radically different from each other because they all have heightened protection in the Constitution, and we surmised that the coefficients would not be large when compared with the omitted categories because they also are protected rights under the Constitution.

Although gay rights were not protected in the original text of the Charter, over the last 20 years, gay rights issues have come to play an increasingly prominent role in contemporary Canadian society (Ostberg and Wetstein 2007, 129; Songer et al. 2012). Evidence of this can be found in the rise of various interest groups litigating on behalf of gay and lesbian causes and the growing prominence of gay and lesbian issues in the media, social discourse, and political institutions. The emergence of the gay rights movement culminated in two significant achievements. First, the court made the historic decision in *Egan v. Canada*, [1995] 2 S.C.R. 513 to "read" sexual orientation into the fabric of the Charter. This and other rulings in the area of gay rights have ensured that the rights of gays and lesbians have received constitutional protection. Second, the federal government, after much political wrangling, recognized the rights of gays to marry in *Reference re Same-Sex Marriage*, [2004] 3 S.C.R. 698. In light of these historic developments, we expected that the voting behaviour of Supreme Court justices in Canada would reflect a significant postmaterialist tendency in the area of gay rights and that this tendency would be stronger and more positive than the rulings in the omitted categories of race and ethnic or national origin cases.

The sixth discrimination issue referenced in the models is marital status, which is not protected in s. 15 of the Charter, but rather was read into the Charter as an "analogous ground" for protection from discrimination in *Miron v. Trudel*, [1995] 2 S.C.R. 418. In line with the scoring scheme mentioned above, this is a dichotomous variable that equals 1 if a claim of marital status discrimination was brought and 0 otherwise. Since marital status is not protected in the original text of the Charter, we expected that the justices would be less likely to rule in favour of a rights claimant, at least in comparison to the three issue traits left out of the equation (race, ethnicity, and national origin). As such, we expected the coefficient for this variable to be negative.

Two other discriminatory elements that we took into consideration were whether a case concerned a job loss or forced retirement (1 = yes, 0 = no) or whether a rights claimant was seeking some sort of job, government, or private benefits. Since individuals can work for either a private company or a government entity in Canadian society, and we were interested in testing whether the justices treat cases involving these two types of benefits differently, we coded the benefits variable as a three-pronged measure (0 = no benefits, 1 = private benefits, and 2 = government benefits). Although we expected the justices to embrace the postmaterialist values of seeking equality among the Canadian citizenry and to protect rights claimants, we anticipated that the justices would react most negatively to government deprivations of benefits. The logic behind this claim stems from the belief that government discrimination is anathema to postmaterialist values in a representative democracy and would be less tolerable in the eyes of the justices than private acts of discrimination in the marketplace.

The job loss variable, in turn, was included to test the hypothesis that the justices would be more sympathetic to litigants who were facing the prospect of losing their economic livelihood or being forced into retirement. All other things being equal, we expected that this coefficient would be positive, at least in relation to cases that did not feature a potential job loss or forced retirement. Ironically, the advancement of equality arguments and the validation of the equality interest in these cases, which represent a hallmark postmaterialist stance, simultaneously allow an individual to secure their material well-being. Thus, in job loss and forced retirement cases, the normal juxtaposition between the competing poles of materialist and postmaterialist values blend into one effort to secure both the economic livelihood and the equality interests of an individual who has suffered from discrimination.

Two other case features that we wanted to assess in the discrimination area included the degree to which a ruling by a human rights commission had influenced the voting behaviour of the justices and whether a case included other Charter issues beyond the s. 15 equality right. In the first instance, it was expected that if a human rights commission had handed down a ruling in favour of a rights claimant (+1), the justices on the Supreme Court would be likely to defer to that ruling because the arbitrators that serve on these commissions are experts in the field. However, in view of the deference to human rights commission decisions, if a commission handed down a conservative ruling (−1), the justices would be more likely to uphold the ruling. If a human rights commission was not involved in a case, it was coded as 0. The coefficient, then, was expected to be positive for this variable: pro-equality votes by a human rights commission would prompt pro-equality voting by the Supreme Court justices, while anti-equality votes would prompt similar votes in the high court.

In the second instance, we hypothesized that if a discrimination case raised additional Charter issues beyond s. 15 (+1), the justices would be less likely to hand down a ruling in favour of the individual than in cases in which only s. 15 (0) or no Charter issue (−1) was raised. We reached this hypothesis because individuals who raise multiple Charter claims are often perceived as "pushing the legal envelope" too far for the comfort level of the justices. If no Charter issues were raised in a case – for example, in marital status cases and suits heard before the Charter era – the case was scored with a −1.

Three types of intervener were included in the regression models that seemed to make theoretical sense to examine in the discrimination area. First, we tabulated the number of pro-equality interveners that were included in each case, and it ranged between 0 and 15 across the cases included in the analysis. We hypothesized that the more pro-rights interveners there were in a case, the more likely it was that the justices would hand down a ruling in favour of the rights claimant. As was mentioned in the two other sections of the book, previous scholarship on litigant resource theory suggests that justices often rely on the specialized legal briefs brought forward by interveners because they provide important cues to guide them when handing down rulings in a given area of law (see Galanter 1974, 2003; Brodie 2002; Manfredi 2004; Langer 2005). Thus, we expected this variable to yield a positive coefficient in the logistic regression models.

We also included a variable, unique to the discrimination area, that identified whether or not the Women's Legal Education and Action Fund (LEAF) had intervened in a suit (1 = yes, 0 = no), and we obviously expected that, in such a case, there would be a greater tendency for the justices to hand down a pro-equality ruling because the presence of LEAF would highlight the salience of the discrimination claim for the justices (Brodie 2002; Manfredi 2004). Last, we included a government variable, for comparative reasons, that tallied the number of provincial governments that had intervened in a given case; this number ranged from 0 to 7 across all the cases. It was expected that since rights claimants often bring discrimination claims against government entities at the local, provincial, or national level, it made sense to include a government variable in the equation. As in the free expression area, we decided to focus on the provincial level instead of the other two because more of those governments had participated in discrimination claims; as a result, we anticipated that where provincial interventions were most frequent, the justices would react to those case cues and tend to vote against equality interests, thus resulting in a negative coefficient.

The last two independent variables in the logistic equations pertain to the parties that were involved in the cases. While the first captures whether or not a corporation was involved in a dispute (1 = corporation is a party in the case, 0 = not a party in the suit), the second assesses situations where the federal or provincial government is a party in the case and takes a pro-equality position. In the first instance, it is hypothesized that when corporations are involved in a discrimination case, the justices will be more likely to hand down a ruling in favour of the discrimination claimant because these cases most clearly exemplify a materialist-postmaterialist rift between the parties involved, even more so than when government entities are involved as litigants.

In the second instance, it is expected that in situations where the federal or provincial governments take a pro-equality stance as parties in a dispute, the justices are more likely to rule in favour of the rights claimant than not. This variable is scored on a continuum ranging from –1 (when the federal or provincial government takes an anti-equality stance) to 0 (when no government party is involved) to 1 (when the federal or provincial government defends the equality interest). In cases where the federal or provincial government stands up for equality interests, it sends a powerful postmaterialist signal to the justices, and as such, the coefficient in the equation should be positive.

Taken as a whole, the three logistic regression models allow us to analyse the relative impact that judicial characteristics and a myriad of case facts have on judicial voting behaviour in the equality area. Moreover, they allow us to compare and contrast the three areas of law to determine whether the same types of variable that are statistically significant in one area of law prove statistically significant in the other two areas as well. Last, the final overarching model enables us to test the relative impact that Inglehart's postmaterialist shifting values thesis has in the equality area and compare it to those found in the environmental and free expression areas. We can then reach some overall conclusions about the veracity of his thesis across three distinct and prominent postmaterialist issue areas.

Explaining Liberal Discrimination Rulings Using Logistic Regression

In Table 6.10, we begin by examining the impact of a judge-level model, containing the same six variables found in the other two legal areas, on vote outcomes, followed by assessing the impact of a 15-variable case-level model. We ultimately observe the effects of 21 variables on Canadian judicial voting behaviour, while simultaneously controlling for all other variables in the equation. A quick review of the summary and goodness-of-fit statistics found across the bottom of the table indicates that all three models achieve statistical significance at the 99.9 per cent

Table 6.10. Estimating the Odds of a Liberal Vote in Canadian Supreme Court Discrimination Cases, 1973–2010

Variable (min., max.)	Judge-level model			Case-level model			Combined prediction model		
	Coefficient	Standard error	Change in probability	Coefficient	Standard error	Change in probability	Coefficient	Standard error	Change in probability
Female justice (0, 1)	.565***	.181	+.139				.601***	.191	+.147
Ideology score (–1.375, 1.618)	.165*	.098	+.123				.189*	.104	+.140
Academic (0, 1)	–.174	.168	–.043				–.282	.179	–.070
Quebec justice (0, 1)	–.044	.16	–.011				–.098	.169	–.024
Lamer Court (0, 1)	–.400*	.186	–.100				–.259	.242	–.065
McLachlin Court (0, 1)	–.067	.201	–.017				.159	.261	+.040
Gay discrimination (0, 1)				.781**	.302	+.187	.842**	.348	+.199
Disabled discrimination (0, 1)				–.112	.212	–.028	–.218	.231	–.054
Age discrimination (0, 1)				–.411*	.233	–.102	–.388	.250	–.097
Sex discrimination (0, 1)				–.093	.219	–.023	–.212	.231	–.053
Religious discrimination (0, 1)				.653**	.277	+.158	.689**	.284	+.166
Marital status discrimination (0, 1)				–.817**	.278	–.197	–.864**	.294	–.209
Benefits (0, 2)				–.076	.115	–.038	.007	.125	+.003
Job loss/forced retirement (0, 1)				–.023	.216	–.006	–.301	.233	–.075
Human rights commission ruling (–1, 1)				–.304*	.156	–.151	–.283*	.168	–.140
Charter beyond s. 15 (–1, 1)				–.358**	.124	–.177	–.541***	.144	–.264
Interveners pro-equality (0, 15)				.041*	.024	+.223	.072*	.038	+.252
Provincial government intervenes (0, 7)				.055	.061	+.095	–.030	.069	–.052
LEAF intervenes (0, 1)				.794***	.257	+.191	.907***	.283	+.214
Corporate party (0, 1)				.517*	.246	+.127	.405	.258	+.100
Federal or provincial government pro-equality (–1, 1)				.312*	.162	+.154	.272	.172	+.134
Constant	.140	.202		–.104	.210		.031	.296	
Number of cases	795			833			795		
Chi-square –2 log likelihood	26.042***			79.496***			111.961***		
Pseudo R-square	.043			.121			.175		
Percentage correct predictions	57.2			62.7			64.5		
Reduction in error	12.1			24.8			27.1		

Note: Nine justices are omitted from the logistic regression model because newspapers did not provide ideological commentary on their appointment: Justices Abbott, Fauteux, Judson, Laskin, Martland, Pigeon, Pratte, Ritchie, and Spence.

*Significant at 95% confidence level; **significant at 99% confidence level; ***significant at 99.9% confidence level.

confidence level. Although the judge-level model correctly predicts only 57 per cent of the discrimination cases correctly, the 15-variable case-level model increases that prediction rate to 63 per cent and has a reduction in error of 25 per cent. The combined 21-variable model, in turn, correctly predicts 65 per cent of the cases correctly and reduces the error by 27 per cent. Although there is a steady rate of improvement in forecasting postmaterialist voting across the three models, the explanatory power of the case-level and combined models in the discrimination area are far below what they were in the free expression (70 per cent for the case model, 68 per cent for the combined model) and environmental areas of law (74 per cent for the case model, 71 per cent for the combined model). Having said that, the three models in the discrimination area provide robust model-fit statistics and effectively explain a considerable amount of the variance in the dependent variable.

Turning to the judge-level model, one finds that, as in the other two areas of law, only three of the six variables in the equation achieve statistical significance – namely, indicators for the female justices, the Lamer Court variable, and newspaper ideology. As expected, when female justices on the Canadian Supreme Court hear discrimination cases, the change in probability score calculated in the third column of the judge-level model indicates that they are 14 per cent more likely than their male counterparts to rule in favour of the postmaterialist rights claimant ($b = .565$, statistically significant at the 99.9 per cent confidence level). This variable had the strongest change in probability score in the model, which indicates that gender is a driving force in influencing liberal voting patterns among the justices in discrimination cases. This finding provides fodder for individuals who argue that more women need to be elevated to the high court in Canada, especially in light of the judicial differences found in discrimination cases over the last 40 years. Although this variable was also statistically significant in the environmental area, one should note that, in that model, the coefficient was in the negative direction ($b = -.530$), indicating that the female justices, as a group, were more likely to side with the material interests of fishing advanced by First Nation individuals over environmental claims. Yet one could argue that the different voting patterns are actually in alignment if the votes in the environmental area are viewed through the prism of female justices being more sensitive to the interests of vulnerable individuals who have suffered some economic inequality in society. In both areas of law, the female justices are more attuned than their male brethren to the plight of the downtrodden or those seeking equal recognition under the law, suggesting that the emphasis on equality as a postmaterialist value transcends all other value positions in the minds of the female justices.

Unlike the other two areas of law, the newspaper ideology score is statistically significant in the expected direction, and it suggests that the Canadian justices who are ranked more positively, or liberally, by journalists at the time of their appointment to the top court handed down 12 per cent more liberal, postmaterialist rulings in the discrimination area than their more conservative colleagues (*b* = .165, statistically significant at the 95 per cent confidence level). This finding makes sense because one would expect the liberal justices on the court to be more inclined to embrace pro-equality, postmaterialist arguments, which ensure that all individuals are treated equally under the law and in society. This finding also matches with prior research, which found that newspaper ideology was critical to liberal voting patterns on the Canadian Supreme Court in discrimination cases (see Ostberg and Wetstein 2007; see also Alarie and Green 2009a), and it provides additional evidence across a broader span of cases and time periods that attitudinal voting plays a role in resolving cases in the discrimination area. The findings in support of ideological voting behaviour also fits nicely with the patterns found on the US Supreme Court, where ideological polarization is much more apparent (Segal and Spaeth 1993, 2002; Segal, Spaeth, and Benesh 2005).

The last variable in the model that was statistically significant was the Lamer Court variable; however, it was in the unexpected direction (*b* = –.400, statistically significant at the 95 per cent confidence level). Contrary to expectations, justices on the Lamer Court were 10 per cent less likely than their Laskin and Dickson Court colleagues to rule in favour of those who brought forward discrimination claims. This finding is at odds with the statistically significant, positive findings for this variable in the other two areas of law, and it suggests that, at first blush in the discrimination area, Inglehart's shifting values thesis does not seem to hold up. The fact that the coefficient for the McLachlin variable is also negative, although not statistically significant, suggests that maybe Inglehart's shifting values thesis has occurred among elite justices in only certain areas of law. The other possibility to consider is that a brief, postmaterialist burst of activity in this area of law occurred during the Dickson Court and has been tempered in recent years, at least when considering the other judge-specific variables like gender.

As in the other two areas of law, many of the case characteristics in the second regression model achieve statistical significance at a greater rate than in the judge-level model. Indeed, 10 of the 15 variables included in the equation were statistically significant, although 5 of them were only at the 95 per cent confidence level. Four of the six types of discrimination traits in the model were statistically significant, and three of them were in the anticipated direction. The two variables that achieved the greatest change in probability were gay rights and marital status, although the swings in each were in opposite directions. As expected, the Canadian justices are 19 per cent more likely to rule in favour of gay rights than in discrimination claims relating to race, ethnicity, and national origin, the three issue categories left out of the equation (*b* = .781, statistically significant at the 99 per cent confidence level). This result makes sense given the prominence of gay rights issues in Canadian society over the last 20 years and given that the Supreme Court gave it constitutional status in *Egan v. Canada*, [1995] 2 S.C.R. 513. This finding suggests that, all other things being equal, the justices on the Canadian court think that discrimination on the basis of sexual orientation is a more salient and problematic issue than discrimination based on the three omitted categories. In contrast, when the justices on the Canadian court heard cases involving marital status discrimination, they were 20 per cent less likely to rule in favour of the rights claimants than in the three omitted categories (*b* = –.817, statistically significant at the 99 per cent confidence level). This finding was in the expected direction, and it makes intuitive sense since marital status, unlike race, ethnicity, and national origin, does not have protection under the Charter of Rights and Freedoms, and the court has not subsequently read this right into the Constitution.

Two other issue traits achieved statistical significance: religious discrimination (*b* = .653, significant at the 99 per cent confidence level) and age discrimination (*b* = –.411, significant at the 95 per cent confidence level). In the first instance, the findings reveal that the justices were 16 per cent more likely to rule in favour of a rights claimant in cases pertaining to religious discrimination compared to those involving to race, ethnicity, or national origin. In the second instance, the justices were 10 per cent less likely to rule in favour of age discrimination claims than those relating to the omitted categories. One explanation for why the justices might be less sympathetic to age discrimination claims stems from the fact that they themselves are required to retire from the top bench at the age of 75. Regardless of the viability of this explanation, one must keep in mind that we expected the justices to treat age, sex, disability, and religion no differently than the excluded categories of race, ethnicity, and national origin because all of them have obtained a heightened protection under the Constitution. The fact that both religion and age discrimination are treated statistically differently than the omitted categories, albeit in opposite directions, indicates that while religious discrimination engenders greater sympathy on the part of the justices than the omitted categories, age discrimination engenders less.

Two other unique case features that we wanted to test in the discrimination area were statistically significant, although the coefficient for a human rights commission was in the unanticipated direction. As expected, in cases that involved Charter issues beyond the s. 15 equality right, the justices were 18 per cent less likely to rule in favour of a litigant than in cases in which the court addressed only a s. 15 equality claim ($b = -.358$, statistically significant at the 99 per cent confidence level). This finding indicates that the justices do not look kindly on individuals who try to push the legal envelope by raising numerous Charter issues in a single dispute. However, contrary to expectations, the coefficient for a human rights commission was negative ($b = -.304$, statistically significant at the 95 per cent confidence level), indicating that the justices were 15 per cent less likely to rule in favour of a rights claimant if a human rights commission had handed down a ruling in their favour in lower court. Although this finding seems counterintuitive, it makes sense once one realizes that appellate courts tend to select cases whose lower court ruling they disagree with, given the costs associated with those appeals and the time constraints on their dockets (Flemming and Krutz 2002).

Two of the three intervener variables included in the case-level model were statistically significant, and both were in the expected direction. The positive coefficient for the number of pro-equality interveners suggests, for example, that when 15 interveners join a case supporting the rights claimant, the justices are 22 per cent more likely to hand down a ruling in his or her favour than in cases in which they do not join a suit ($b = .041$, statistically significant at the 95 per cent confidence level). Similarly, when LEAF intervened in cases, the justices, as expected, were 19 per cent more likely to rule for a litigant raising an equality claim ($b = .794$, statistically significant at the 99.9 per cent confidence level). The findings for these two variables makes sense given that the justices often rely on cues from the briefs submitted by various interest groups to help them resolve salient disputes. Thus, when groups supporting the equality claim appear in a given case, not only does it highlight the claim as a critical controversy for Canadian citizens, but the briefs may also provide key information for the justices to consider. Ultimately, both kinds of information provide critical cues to help the justices resolve disputes in discrimination cases.

The last two variables to achieve statistical significance in the case-level model were the two party variables, and both variables were in the expected direction. The corporate party variable indicates that the justices are 13 per cent more likely to hand down a liberal, postmaterialist ruling in the equality area when a corporation is a party in the case (b = .517, statistically significant at the 95 per cent confidence level). This makes intuitive sense because justices in a postmaterialist age are more likely to sympathize with a litigant who is fighting a large corporate entity that seeks to obtain more materialist goods at the expense of the individual. Similarly, when either the federal or a provincial government takes a pro-equality stance, the justices are 15 per cent more likely to rule in favour of the rights claimant (b = .312, statistically significant at the 95 per cent confidence level). This finding indicates that when government opposes discrimination, it can swing the odds decisively in favour of pro-rights litigants. Both of these variables suggest that, in the case-level model, at least, the role that the parties play in discrimination cases can influence how the Canadian justices vote in this issue area.

The third regression results, found at the far right of Table 6.10, are derived from a combined model that includes all 21 variables from the first two equations. This is the most important regression equation in the table because it assesses the relative impact of all the independent variables, while simultaneously controlling for all other variables in the equation. Like the other areas of law, the third model yields nearly identical results as those found in the other two equations. As mentioned earlier, the 21-variable equation is the best model of the three, correctly predicting 65 per cent of the cases and generating a 27 per cent reduction in error over the modal guessing strategy.

One should note that four of the variables that achieved statistical significance in the initial two models are no longer statistically significant in the combined model. Most noteworthy for the Inglehart shifting postmaterialist values thesis is the fact that the Lamer Court indicator is no longer statistically significant, although the coefficient is still in the unexpected direction (b = –.259). The findings suggest that the justices on the Lamer Court are 7 per cent less likely to rule in favour of a rights claimant than justices on the Laskin and Dickson Courts.

Meanwhile, the McLachlin Court indicator has an even smaller impact of 4 per cent, although its coefficient is in the expected positive direction (*b* = .159). Ultimately, the findings for both the Lamer and the McLachlin Court variables in the combined model suggest that Inglehart's shifting values thesis does not seem to hold up in the discrimination area, as it did in the environmental area. Since the Lamer and McLachlin Court variables are insignificant in the final regression equation, the results actually demonstrate that, all other things being equal, the justices have been consistent in their voting behaviour in discrimination cases across all four chief justice tenures during the 1973–2010 period. One explanation for this finding is that, in the discrimination area, the justices on the Canadian court might have shifted towards a liberal, postmaterialist stance at a much earlier stage than in environmental claims. Alternatively, the overwhelming statistical significance that the two judge-level variables have in the combined model – namely, gender and ideology – may diminish or wash out any difference that might exist across the different court tenures.

This possibility is exemplified in the large swing in odds in favour of a pro-rights litigant that occurs for each of these judge-level variables in the combined model. Specifically, female justices are 15 per cent more likely than their male colleagues to rule in favour of a litigant in discrimination cases (*b* = .601, statistically significant at the 99.9 per cent confidence level), while those scoring the most liberally on the newspaper ideology score were 14 per cent more likely to rule in favour of a claimant (*b* = .189, statistically significant at the 95 per cent confidence level). Alternatively, the power of other variables may be diminished because of the so-called Charter maturation effect, which implies that the justices may be less prone to advance pro-equality arguments because key constitutional principles were already settled in this area of law by the mid-to late 1990s (McCormick 2015). A connected possibility for explaining fewer pro-equality rulings in recent years is that the justices might be concerned by the rising government expenditures pursued by rights claimants and public criticism of a perceived rise in activism by the court. This notion is exemplified in *Auton v. British Columbia*, [2004] 3 S.C.R. 657, in which the court rejected the equality claim by families seeking the right to expensive health care therapies for autistic children. Despite these caveats, it is clear that ideology and gender go a long way to explaining the postmaterialist voting behaviour of the Canadian justices in equality claims over the four most recent chief justice tenures.

The fact that the newspaper ideology measure achieved statistical significance in the combined model in the discrimination area, but failed to have a decisive impact in either the free expression or the environmental area of law, is also worthy of commentary. The disparate findings for the ideology variable in these three areas of law highlight an important feature of the modern Canadian court and one that sets it apart from its US counterpart. Scholarship on the US Supreme Court over the last 40 years has decisively shown the pre-eminence of ideology in influencing the decision-making process of top-level justices across all areas of law (see Segal and Spaeth 1993, 2002; Segal, Spaeth, and Benesh 2005). Attitudinal studies have become so pervasive in the US context that many scholars, and laypeople alike, might come to believe that ideology necessarily explains the decision-making process of all common law appellate courts in advanced industrial societies. However, the findings of this study, along with prior research conducted on the Canadian Supreme Court, demonstrate that all common law top courts are not cut from the same ideological cloth (see Ostberg and Wetstein 2007; Alarie and Green 2008, 2009a, 2009b; Songer 2008; Songer et al. 2012). Indeed, the justices on the Canadian Supreme Court are far less ideologically polarized in their decision-making process than their southern colleagues, and this is exemplified by the results from the combined regression equations across all three areas of law included in this study. Ultimately, the findings in the three distinct areas, like our prior research, illustrate that the Canadian justices are far more nuanced in their decision-making process and that other factors, such as issue traits, case facts, interveners, and parties in a suit, also play a critical role in how the justices resolve complex legal issues in Canadian society.

Turning to the case-level characteristics in the full regression model, 7 of the 10 variables remain statistically significant in the combined model, and all of them feature nearly identical coefficients and produce comparable swings in the odds ratio of pro-equality voting as those in the case-level model. The three variables that no longer achieved significance in the combined equation were age discrimination and the two litigant or party variables; this is not surprising since all three variables achieved significance only at the 95 per cent confidence level in the case-level model. Although the roles played by the two parties included in the combined equation did not seem to influence judicial decision making in the discrimination area, they did significantly impact the justices in the expected direction in the other two areas of law. The fact that a party variable failed to sway the justices in discrimination claims might also be due to the overwhelming influence that both gender and ideology play for members of the high court in the equality area of law.

Looking across the three empirical chapters, it seems that Inglehart's shifting values thesis has had a decisive impact in the environmental area, a result that is captured in the final combined regression model. The court also moved in a decisive postmaterialist direction in the free expression area under the Lamer Court, although that trend was tempered in the first 10 years of the McLachlin Court, which placed a greater emphasis on postmaterialist equality concerns. This transformation was best exemplified in the McLachlin Court's effort to ensure that all voices were heard equally in the political process and that campaigns were not hijacked by any one group (see *Harper v. Canada (Attorney General)*, [2004] 1 S.C.R. 827). In the discrimination area, while the Lamer and McLachlin Court indicators are not statistically significant in our overall model, the power of these court periods is really reflected through the overwhelming impact of the gender variable in our regression model. We believe that this indicator is indicative of a postmaterialist awakening among the female justices of the court in discrimination cases. Put simply, the female justices have had a profoundly different, more liberal voting pattern than the male justices. Their growing and strengthening presence through the late Dickson, Lamer, and early McLachlin Courts has sparked a pro-equality revolution in discrimination cases over the last four decades. The next chapter highlights this movement using the language and rationale embedded in the written reasons for judgment in gay rights and sex discrimination cases, two of the most significant areas of equality litigation in modern Canadian society.

Chapter Seven

Qualitative Analysis of Gay Rights and Sex Discrimination Disputes

Introduction

The results of the prior chapter suggest that the ascendance of female justices on the Supreme Court of Canada helped accelerate a pro-equality, postmaterialist value shift across the late 1980s and 1990s and early 2000s. Of course, our conclusion about such a value shift up to this point is dependent solely on voting patterns across all discrimination disputes. The case for this argument is more robust and complete if the written reasons for judgment support this quantitative finding. With that in mind, this chapter, like those found in the prior two sections of the book, provides a qualitative assessment of the language and rationale in key discrimination disputes over four decades of the Canadian Supreme Court. If the language and tone of the opinions become more equality oriented over time, it lends credence to the contention that the shift in public values Inglehart documented has transpired to a certain degree among the judicial elites in discrimination cases as well. When examining these cases, we pay particular attention to the role of the female justices to tease out their influence on any substantive values changes. Before discussing landmark equality disputes, it is helpful to understand the theoretical foundation for examining Inglehart's value change thesis in the context of equality disputes.

A key principle of British, French, and US political thought of the seventeenth and eighteenth centuries was that all individuals are created equal in society, even though, in reality, we all know that some are more equal than others. Leading political philosophers of the time, such as Locke (1689), Montesquieu (1748), Rousseau (1762), and Madison (1788), introduced the idea that states were not above reproach and that citizens of these societies had the inalienable right to dissolve unfair or rogue governments. A cornerstone of their thinking was that governments existed to serve the people and that all citizens should be protected equally under the law. The ideas of these philosophers were so powerful that they were subsequently woven into the founding documents of many advanced democracies. Despite the ideals professed in the founding documents of these countries, minority groups in the United States and Canada have struggled to secure equal rights under the law, with the most recent battleground of equality occurring in the area of gay rights and gender discrimination (L'Heureux-Dubé 2000). Although the principles put forth by these philosophical thinkers have yet to be fully realized, the desire for equal treatment lies at the crux of postmodern democracies, which cherish the idea that all groups should be treated fairly, equally, and honestly in society.

On a more practical level, the analysis of discrimination cases is important because Inglehart's theory of postmodern social change indicates that postmaterialist societies tend to embrace quality-of-life concerns that value the equal treatment of others, and he has successfully documented this trend among the Canadian public over time (Inglehart 1997; Inglehart and Welzel 2005). As mentioned in the prior chapter, Inglehart's findings indicate that Canadians have increased their support for women having a child as a single parent, having homosexuals as neighbours, and seeing homosexuality as justifiable. Since equality lies at the centre of a postmaterialist democracy, and since Inglehart's findings show that the Canadian mass public has moved in a postmaterialist direction in recent years, it makes intuitive sense to explore equality cases from both a quantitative and a qualitative perspective.

Scholars who have pondered the nature of equality are quick to point out that those who discuss equality are often at odds with each other because there are two distinct notions of equality – namely, equality of opportunity and equality of outcome (see Morton and Knopff [2000, 66–73] for a similar discussion). Those who support equality of opportunity are interested in ensuring that all individuals have an equal chance to succeed in society. These individuals believe that government should pass laws ensuring that everyone has, for example, the same chance to obtain an education, housing, and job opportunities, or obtain admission into a social club. In contrast, those who advocate for equality of outcome are more interested in government passing laws to ensure that wealth and resources are redistributed in society so that individuals have more equal standards of living. This distinction is important for the study of postmaterialist judicial behaviour because justices might take fundamentally different stances on cases raising these issues. For example, a judge might favour an equality-of-opportunity argument put forth by a claimant seeking recognition and inclusion in a fraternal organization, but be less favourable to a claim advocating equality of outcome to secure benefits or restitution. Although both positions will have the potential to move the court in a postmaterialist direction, how justices approach equality rights will have important implications for the resolution of these types of claims.

Critics might contend that equality-of-opportunity assertions are woven from postmaterialist cloth, while equality-of-outcome arguments are more legitimately materialistic in nature. For instance, Michael Mandel (1994) discussed the connection between judicial rulings that advance equality-of-outcome interests and the materialistic advantages that flow from those decisions in his assessment of equality rights litigation. Mandel was critical of pro-equality Charter litigants who obtained rulings that simply cemented the existing status quo power structure in society (Mandel 1994, 460). From his perspective, much Charter litigation "takes for granted basic power relations," and he maintained that equal rights cases tend to focus on equal access to existing institutions, rather than the need to revamp institutions that have sustained discriminatory practices in the past (ibid.). We believe that Mandel's emphasis on changing the power structure of society reflects both a materialistic and a postmaterialist goal in a larger postmaterialist context, and as such, it blends the postmaterialist lens of equality with the materialist intent of more equal economic power structures for all in society.

Other critics argue that social groups seeking equality are interested in pursuing both materialist and postmaterialist types of goals. Matt James (2006) has made this point in his discussion of the role that social movements have played in the recent history of Canada's constitutional debates. He contends that women and various other marginalized groups have not only sought recognition and inclusion in the constitutional debates and text but also sought to advance a materialist agenda to correct for past economic harms caused by discrimination (James 2006, 10–12; see also Smith 2002). As such, James argues that scholars such as Inglehart may have oversimplified or "misrecognized" the aspirations of modern equality-seeking movements. James rightly argues that scholars may misunderstand the fact that modern social movements ultimately aspire to advance postmaterialist goals of respect and equal recognition, while also seeking materialist interests relating to correcting issues such as poverty, repression, and unemployment.

For many scholars, it does not matter how the language of equality is advocated; what matters is that more groups are recognized as "Charter Canadians," who have secured an avenue for participating in politics and pursuing equal status for perhaps the very first time. Alan Cairns (1991, 109) has argued that the Charter brought "new groups into the constitutional order," allowing a host of minority groups the opportunity to challenge past inequities and repression by prior governmental regimes. These Charter Canadians have included women, indigenous peoples, minority language groups, ethnic minorities, and the disabled, and their use of s. 15 as an instrument of social change has been profound (Cairns 1991; Brodie and Nevitte 1993; L'Heureux-Dubé 2000; Morton and Knopff 2000). Whenever Charter Canadians pursue equality claims, they are bound to be seeking some kind of materialistic gain in their pursuit of more equal treatment in society. However, Inglehart might respond that democratic courts that aspire to more fully advocate for and advance the equality interests of previously disadvantaged minority groups, regardless of whether these concerns are materialistic or intrinsic, will be committed to a higher postmaterialist calling than more materialist courts, which might deny these claims altogether.

For the purposes of this book, we, like Inglehart, believe that, at its intrinsic core, seeking the equality interests of previously disenfranchised groups in society is a value position that tends to fall on the postmaterialist side of the values conflict continuum, regardless of whether it falls into the equality-of-opportunity or equality-of-outcome camp. Litigants may find greater purchase from an equality-of-opportunity point of view, but we believe that both equality-of-opportunity and equality-of-outcome claims emanate from a higher, postmaterialist platform of elevating and promoting equality concerns over other values in society, such as the desire to maintain order or the freedom to discriminate against groups one does not like.

Given the different types of equality arguments that litigants might raise, it is important to examine the language used by the justices in resolving equality disputes. It is our belief that the language that justices use in their written opinions will convey the value priority that they seek to advance, whether they support postmaterialist values or not. In fact, justices can use statements that seek to promote equality of opportunity, equality of outcome, both, or neither. Indeed, s. 1 of the Charter provides justices with the flexibility to describe equality rights expansively, yet decide to limit rights in the particular case at hand.

Alternatively, justices who are of a materialistic mindset might deny that an equality right exists at all. Thus, looking at the language used in landmark equality cases is critical because it provides insights into the tone and degree to which a justice supports equality rights, whether it be none at all, only in small measure, in limited circumstances, or as a sweeping embracement of them. Examining the language used, in turn, provides us with further insight into the degree to which Inglehart's intergenerational values thesis has been incorporated by the Canadian Supreme Court over time in the equality area.

Since it is unrealistic to review all 106 cases that the Canadian court handed down in the discrimination area over the 1973–2010 period, we decided to review one or two landmark cases in gay rights and sex discrimination cases during the Laskin/Dickson and Lamer Courts and the first 10 years of the McLachlin tenure. These two areas of law were selected because they address highly contentious political and social issues that have fostered considerable debate and controversy among the justices, the media, and the public at large. Moreover, these cases are commonly considered the most significant discrimination cases that the Canadian Supreme Court has handed down in the modern era. They are cases that naturally pit materialistic concerns for maintaining traditional notions of marriage and social hierarchy against post-materialist interests of groups and individuals who hope to achieve equal status under the law. In addition, discussion of these hallmark cases makes sense given the vast political-mobilization efforts that have been launched on behalf of women's issues and gay rights in the post-Charter era (Epp 1998; Brodie 2002; Manfredi 2004; Langer 2005). Last, we decided to study these cases because Inglehart collected survey data in the equality area by asking questions specifically related to gay rights and gender discrimination (World Values Survey 2011). Since he and others have documented changes in attitudes among the Canadian public in these two areas over time, it makes intuitive sense for us to look for changing attitudes among the judicial elites in these two sub-fields of discrimination law. Although some might argue that selecting the gay rights and sex discrimination cases represents "the low-hanging fruit" for testing Inglehart's transformation theory, if we do not find a shift in judicial values in two of the most prominent areas of discrimination, we are unlikely to find it in other areas of equality law.

One other important reason for conducting the qualitative analysis in the equality area is to examine the particular writing patterns of the female justices since the quantitative findings indicated that they were casting postmaterialist votes at a far higher rate than their male colleagues (Ostberg and Wetstein 2007; Songer et al. 2012). This suggests that the female justices might be leading the postmaterialist charge in the discrimination area, and if this is true, the gender gap is likely to play out in the language of the written opinions as well. Ultimately, we believe that conducting both a quantitative and a qualitative assessment of discrimination cases strengthens the assessment of Inglehart's values thesis because a qualitative assessment of the actual decisions allows the reader to grasp the subtle nuances that occur in individual cases and across a subcategory of law, features that are often masked by holistic quantitative analysis.

As in the previous sections of the book, we took into consideration what a leading constitutional expert has identified as landmark cases to help dictate the cases we selected to analyse under the different court tenures.[1] Gay rights disputes typically pit homosexuals seeking equal treatment under the law, in relation to issues such as marriage, housing, or spousal benefits, against the materialist interests of government or others in maintaining traditional patterns of social behaviour. Thus, if the justices hand down rulings that move in a postmaterialist direction over time, we expect that they will use language that identifies gay rights as a "fundamental right" or "essential to the value of human dignity" that society must protect. Moreover, they might create a more stringent standard that government officials or others must meet to restrict such rights. Similarly, sex discrimination cases often highlight a tension between a woman's effort to obtain equal treatment in a variety of guises, such as workplace benefits, child custody, or other social situations, and the materialistic interests of others in maintaining the traditional patriarchal value structure in society. If justices are shifting in a postmaterialist direction, we expect them to use language suggesting that gender discrimination is an "affront to human dignity" or that women deserve "the same treatment" as men in society. Phrases like these, along with any stringent standards that the justices might develop, help provide an overarching understanding of whether they are moving in a postmaterialist

1 Specifically, we looked at the major cases that Peter Hogg reviewed in his 2011 text, *Constitutional Law of Canada*, to help guide what gay rights and gender discrimination cases we chose to analyse. Readers should note that our cases are not solely constitutional; some of them involve disputes based on provincial and federal human rights laws.

direction in these two issue areas over time. In light of these remarks, we devote the rest of this chapter to analysing key rulings in the gay rights and sex discrimination areas.

Landmark Gay Rights Cases of the Laskin and Dickson Courts

There have been nine rulings handed down by the Canadian Supreme Court in the gay rights area between 1973 and 2010. While only one case was heard under the Laskin/Dickson tenure, four were heard under the Lamer and McLachlin Courts, respectively. We plan to examine six of the nine cases. Although these rulings comprise only 9 per cent of the cases in the discrimination area, several of them address some of the most salient, cutting-edge rulings by the Canadian court in the discrimination area to date.

During the Laskin/Dickson tenure, the only gay rights case the Supreme Court heard was *Gay Alliance Toward Equality v. Vancouver Sun*, [1979] 2 S.C.R. 435 (hereafter *Gay Alliance*), in which the court addressed the legality of a newspaper's refusal to publish an advertisement for a homosexual periodical. Justice Martland, writing for a six-member majority of the Laskin Court, ruled that a board of enquiry had misapplied s. 3 of British Columbia's Human Rights Code because the service involved – namely, publishing advertising – should give newspaper editors the right to control the material they chose to publish as well as the right to refuse to publish materials they did not wish to print (*Gay Alliance*, [1979] 2 S.C.R. 435, at 455). Moreover, s. 3 of the Human Rights Code was not applicable because the newspaper did not refuse to publish the ad based on the "personal characteristic" of the individual seeking to place it, but rather did so based on the "content or text" of the ad itself. In essence, Justice Martland concluded that s. 3 did not dictate the scope of the content that newspapers must make available to the public, but simply required that the service the newspaper provided be made available to all citizens that wanted to use it (*Gay Alliance*, [1979] 2 S.C.R. 435, at 456).

The language used by Justice Martland is indicative of his support for newspapers having the freedom to promote whatever values they choose, even ones that might discriminate against a group of citizens in society. At one point, Justice Martland stated that the newspaper had simply "adopted a position on the controversial subject of homosexuality. It did not wish to accept an advertisement seeking subscription to a publication which propagates the views of the Alliance" – namely, one that promoted a homosexual lifestyle (*Gay Alliance*, [1979] 2 S.C.R. 435, at 455–6). Indeed, the newspaper had indicated that it had "reasonable cause" for denying the advertisement because "homosexuality is offensive to public decency" and "the appellant newspaper had a duty to protect the morals of the community" (*Gay Alliance*, [1979] 2 S.C.R. 435, at 443). There were clear materialistic undertones to these comments, and they highlight the Laskin Court majority's strong support for traditional societal values. Since Justice Martland endorsed the moral stance taken by the newspaper, he was clearly siding with a value position rooted in the notion that corporations have the freedom to take stances against groups they do not like, such as denying ads that advance a homosexual lifestyle. This is a hallmark element of a materialist world view.

Chief Justice Laskin, writing in dissent, contended that s. 3 of the Human Rights Code sought to prevent discrimination unless reasonable grounds were provided for denying services that were customarily available to the public (*Gay Alliance*, [1979] 2 S.C.R. 435, at 446–7). According to Chief Justice Laskin, the local board of enquiry had been entitled to determine that the denial of the advertisement was grounded in unacceptable personal bias on the part of the newspaper and that "bias against homosexuals" did not constitute a reasonable cause for refusing to publish the ad (*Gay Alliance*, [1979] 2 S.C.R. 435, at 448). Justice Dickson, in a separate dissent, concluded that the whole point of human rights legislation was to prevent businesses and institutions from adopting biased policies that allowed them to refuse to provide a class of citizens with a service that they provided to the public at large (*Gay Alliance*, [1979] 2 S.C.R. 435, at 472). Clearly, the language and rationale used by both dissenting justices reflected a desire to advance the postmaterialist values of ensuring that equal rights in advertising were provided to all citizens, including homosexuals.

Landmark Gay Rights Cases of the Lamer Court

After the 1979 *Gay Alliance* case, there was a significant gap in time before another case raising gay rights issues reached the Canadian Supreme Court. The introduction of the Charter of Rights and Freedoms spurred the new cases, and the Lamer Court was asked in 1995 to explore the scope of the equal rights provision found in s. 15(1) of the Charter in relation to various gay rights issues. Although the original text of s. 15(1) explicitly protects individuals in Canadian society from discrimination on the basis of race, sex, colour, religion, age, national or ethnic origin, or disability, the founders of the Charter had failed to include sexual orientation as a listed category that was protected under the Constitution. As a result, in the landmark cases of *Egan v. Canada*, [1995] 2 S.C.R. 513 and *Vriend v. Alberta (Attorney General)*, [1998] 1 S.C.R. 493, the Supreme Court began to grapple with whether s. 15(1) of the Charter also protected gays and lesbians from discrimination in the public and private spheres.

In *Egan v. Canada*, [1995] 2 S.C.R. 513 (hereafter *Egan*), the court handed down a highly fragmented 5–4 ruling that highlighted the divergent views the justices had taken on the appropriate approach to use in s. 15(1) analysis and in regard to whether gay rights deserved protection in the case at hand. Here, a gay couple had alleged that the Old Age Security Act violated their equality rights because it limited spousal benefits to heterosexual couples that had lived together for a year or more (*Egan*, [1995] 2 S.C.R. 513, at 514). Although a plurality of five justices agreed that the Old Age Security Act violated the appellants' s. 15(1) equality rights, Justices L'Heureux-Dubé and McLachlin wrote separate concurrences because both took issue with the approach used by Justice Cory to reach this outcome. Meanwhile, Justice Sopinka agreed that a s. 15(1) violation had occurred, for the reasons articulated by Justice Cory, but he joined four of the justices to determine that the violation was justified under s. 1 analysis. The number of opinions written in this case exposed the fragmentation of the court on key issues of constitutional interpretation, resulting in a clear materialist-postmaterialist schism on the court.

Justice Cory, writing for three members of the court, argued that the court should adopt the two-step approach in the gay rights area that it had laid out in *Andrews v. Law Society of British Columbia*, [1989] 1 S.C.R. 143 and *R. v. Turpin*, [1989] 1 S.C.R. 1296. The approach involved first determining whether the statute created a distinction between the appellant and other individuals in society and whether it resulted in a denial of equal protection or benefits of the law. The second step required the justices to assess whether the denial of equality rights was based on personal characteristics that were enumerated in s. 15(1) of the Charter or on analogous grounds and whether that distinction imposed a disadvantage or burden on the appellant in relation to others in society (*Egan*, [1995] 2 S.C.R. 513, at 517).

When Justice Cory applied the first prong of the test to the case at hand, he concluded that the plain wording of the Old Age Security Act created a clear distinction between heterosexual common law couples, who were eligible for benefits, and homosexual common law couples, who were not. This resulted in a denial of equal economic benefits that was significant because it "may have a serious detrimental effect upon the sense of self-worth and dignity of members of a group because it stigmatizes them" (*Egan*, [1995] 2 S.C.R. 513, at 594).

Turning to the second prong, Justice Cory concluded that the distinction in the Old Age Security Act was clearly based on a personal characteristic. He concluded that sexual orientation was analogous to the other types of discrimination prohibited under s. 15(1). In doing so, he highlighted the social, economic, and political disadvantages suffered by gays and lesbians throughout history, the growing consensus among legislatures that sexual orientation constituted an analogous form of discrimination, and the numerous rulings that supported this conclusion (*Egan*, [1995] 2 S.C.R. 513, at 600–3). Moreover, it placed this group at a disadvantage, and he pointed out that "the discriminatory impact can hardly be deemed to be trivial when the legislation reinforces prejudicial attitudes based on such faulty stereotypes" (*Egan*, [1995] 2 S.C.R. 513, at 604). Since the federal statute failed both prongs of the two-step analysis, Justice Cory concluded that it violated s. 15(1) of the Charter.

Both Justices L'Heureux-Dubé and McLachlin agreed with Justice Cory's outcome, but wrote separate concurrences because they thought the court should use another approach for assessing whether discrimination occurred within the meaning of s. 15(1) in the last phase of the two-part analysis. Justice L'Heureux-Dubé argued that instead of focusing on the grounds or reason for the distinction, the court should focus on the discriminatory *effects* of the law (*Egan*, [1995] 2 S.C.R. 513, at 552–3). She backed this point up with the statement that discrimination occurred whenever a distinction was "promoting or perpetuating the view that the individual adversely affected ... is less capable, or less worthy of recognition or value as a human being or as a member of Canadian society" (*Egan*, [1995] 2 S.C.R. 513, at 552–3). Justice McLachlin, in contrast, argued that, to establish discrimination, the court should assess not only the reason for the distinction in the statute but also whether it was grounded in stereotypical beliefs about the group or its personal characteristics (see *Miron v. Trudel*, [1995] 2 S.C.R. 418, at 419). Although these justices took different paths in the last stage of s. 15(1) analysis, since their stances did not affect the overall outcome of forcefully supporting gay rights, one can largely ignore the subtle distinctions between them.

In contrast to the justices in the majority, the four justices who dissented in *Egan* did not believe that the Old Age Security Act violated equality rights under the Charter. Unlike Justice Cory, Justice La Forest applied a slightly different, three-part analysis that focused on whether the law created a distinction between the appellant and others, whether that distinction resulted in a disadvantage, and last, whether the distinction was based on an irrelevant personal characteristic enumerated or analogous to those found in s. 15(1) of the Charter (*Egan*, [1995] 2 S.C.R. 513, at 514). Applying these standards, Justice La Forest concluded that the law drew a distinction and that the distinction resulted in a disadvantage for the appellant under the law. Moreover, he agreed with the majority that sexual orientation was indeed a personal characteristic that was analogous to those protected under s. 15(1) because it was unchangeable or changed only at great personal cost (ibid.). However, in the last phase of his analysis, Justice La Forest concluded that the distinction made by Parliament in the Old Age Security Act between the appellant and others was relevant because it ensured that the heterosexual social unit remained intact in society. Although society could define marriage to include homosexual couples, he clearly believed that heterosexual couples alone would ensure that procreation and traditional child-rearing practices were maintained in society. However, Justice La Forest concluded that even if s. 15(1) had been violated, it would be saved under s. 1 analysis (*Egan*, [1995] 2 S.C.R. 513, at 515–16).

Justice Sopinka, who agreed with the majority that s. 15(1) had been violated, constituted the swing vote in this case because he subsequently agreed with Justice La Forest, and three others, that the distinction embedded in the Old Age Security Act was justified under s. 1 analysis. In short, he concluded that the law passed the *Oakes* test because Parliament had taken an incremental and flexible approach that slowly extended social benefits to different minority groups in society. Justice Sopinka concluded that, in doing so, Parliament had taken a substantial step in trying to alleviate poverty for those in the greatest need of financial assistance due to retirement or loss of a spouse (*Egan*, [1995] 2 S.C.R. 513, at 516–17). It is important to note that, despite the highly fragmented ruling in *Egan*, all the justices on the Lamer Court recognized the need to include sexual orientation as a prohibited form of discrimination listed in the text of s. 15(1) of the Charter. In doing so, the court made substantial strides in moving the law in a postmaterialist direction by recognizing that same-sex couples deserved the same level of protection under the Charter as other disadvantaged groups in Canadian society.

Three years later, the Lamer Court addressed the similar issue of whether Alberta's Individual's Rights Protection Act (IRPA) violated s. 15(1) of the Charter because it omitted sexual orientation as a protected category against discrimination (*Vriend v. Alberta (Attorney*

General), [1998] 1 S.C.R. 493, hereafter *Vriend*). In this case, the court not only solidified the overarching analytic framework to use in analysing gay rights claims but also shored up its movement in a postmaterialist direction by making explicit the values it sought to promote under s. 15(1) of the Charter. The appellant, Vriend, had been fired from a full-time position at a college because he was gay, despite receiving positive annual performance evaluations and steady pay raises over the tenure of his employment (*Vriend*, [1998] 1 S.C.R. 493, at 507). Vriend and gay and lesbian groups filed suit, seeking a declaration that Alberta's IRPA violated equality rights under the Charter. Unlike its earlier ruling in *Egan*, the Lamer Court unanimously ruled that Alberta's human rights statute did violate s. 15(1) of the Charter and could not be saved under s. 1 analysis, and seven of the eight justices ruled that sexual orientation must be read into the Alberta statute. While Justice L'Heureux-Dubé wrote a concurrence that continued to take issue with the court's approach for evaluating gay rights under s. 15(1), only Justice Major dissented from having sexual orientation read into Alberta's IRPA because he thought the Alberta legislature had a right to decide this issue (*Vriend*, [1998] 1 S.C.R. 493, at 499–500).

In handing down their majority ruling, Justices Cory and Iacobucci pointed out that the Supreme Court had used a myriad of approaches when assessing equality rights violations under the Charter, yet they followed the same overarching two-step framework that they had applied in *Egan*, which entailed assessing whether the law at issue created a distinction that resulted in inequality under the law and whether that denial constituted discrimination under the law (*Vriend*, [1998] 1 S.C.R. 493, at 539).[2] When Justice Cory applied this test to the case at hand, he concluded that the exclusion of sexual orientation in the IRPA violated s. 15(1) of the Charter because neither prong of the test had been met. According to Justice Cory, the exclusion of sexual orientation from the IRPA created a distinction between homosexuals and other disadvantaged groups because other groups were formally protected from discrimination, while homosexuals were not. More important, the statute's under-inclusiveness also created a distinction because gays and lesbians had been historically discriminated against in a way that heterosexuals had not. At one point Justice Cory stated, "It is, of course,

2 The majority opinion featured one part written by Justice Cory and another part written by Justice Iacobucci.

true that discrimination against gays and lesbians exists in society. The reality of this cruel and unfortunate discrimination was recognized in *Egan*" (*Vriend*, [1998] 1 S.C.R. 493, at 543). Justice Cory went on to conclude that the IRPA also failed to meet the second prong of the test because sexual orientation was based on personal characteristics that were analogous to those explicitly recognized under s. 15 of the Charter. Justice Cory argued that the effect of the law discriminated against gays and lesbians because they were unable to seek recourse under the mechanisms established under the law, and this sent the message that discrimination of this type was not as important as other types of discrimination. Collectively, these features dictated that the IRPA violated s. 15(1) of the Charter.

Even if a statute violated equality rights under s. 15(1) of the Charter, the court had to also assess whether the government's infringement was reasonably justified under s. 1 of the Charter using the test established in *R. v. Oakes*, [1986] 1 S.C.R. 103. Justice Iacobucci, who wrote this part of the majority ruling, concluded that the law violated three key elements of the *Oakes* test because there was no pressing and substantial objective that justified overriding this analogous, constitutionally protected right; there was no rational connection between the exclusion of sexual orientation from the act and the overarching goal of trying to protect the dignity of all Albertans; and the law did not minimally impair the rights of gays and lesbians (*Vriend*, [1998] 1 S.C.R. 493, at 557). Last, Justice Iacobucci concluded that any benefits in excluding sexual orientation from the statute were outweighed by the "numerous and clear" harmful effects of excluding sexual orientation from the statute.

The language used by Justices Cory and Iacobucci throughout the majority reasons for judgment indicated that, eight years into Chief Justice Lamer's tenure, the Canadian Supreme Court had decisively moved in a postmaterialist direction in terms of protecting gay and lesbian rights under the Charter of Rights and Freedoms. The fact that the court unanimously ruled that Alberta's human rights provision violated s. 15(1) and could not be saved under s. 1 analysis, and also agreed on the overarching stringent framework the court should use to assess such violations, was remarkable given the highly fragmented ruling the court had handed down three years earlier in *Egan*. *Vriend* represents a consolidation of postmaterialist views in this area, and it is noteworthy that it was penned by two male, centrist justices. The court's remedy of reading sexual orientation into the statute was also noteworthy since the Alberta legislature had rejected the inclusion of such a provision numerous times, a point that triggered Justice Major's partial dissent in the case. The degree to which the Lamer Court embraced the importance of protecting gays and lesbians from discrimination is highlighted at the beginning of the ruling, when Justice Cory discussed the importance and rationale behind s. 15(1) of the Charter. At one point he stated, "So soon as we say any enumerated or analogous group is less deserving and unworthy of equal protection and benefit of the law all minorities and all of Canadian society are demeaned. … It can never be forgotten that discrimination is the antithesis of equality and that it is the recognition of equality which will foster the dignity of every individual" (*Vriend*, [1998] 1 S.C.R. 493, at 536).

Ultimately, the *Vriend* case represented a decisive movement away from the Dickson Court's materialist stance in protecting the morality and order of Judaeo-Christian values in the *Gay Alliance* case. The language of *Vriend* indicated that the court, as a whole, had largely embraced postmaterialist values in the realm of equality rights for gays. In our view, this transformation reflects a broader societal change in tandem with the changing membership of the court during that period.

In light of its ruling in *Egan*, it was not surprising that, four years later, the Lamer Court addressed a similar landmark issue, this time regarding spousal support in *M. v. H.*, [1999] 2 S.C.R. 3, in the context of Ontario's Family Law Act. After a 10-year, intimate relationship between two women had deteriorated, M. sought a claim for support under the law; she challenged its constitutional validity under s. 15(1) of the Charter because it extended spousal benefits to unmarried heterosexual couples who had lived together for three or more years, but not to similarly situated same-sex couples (*M. v. H.*, [1999] 2 S.C.R. 3, at 28). Justice Cory, writing for six members of the court, applied a refined set of equality guidelines, which had been outlined by Justice Iacobucci earlier that same year in *Law v. Canada*, [1999] 1 S.C.R. 497. In the *Law* case, Justice Iacobucci had argued that future equality claims under s. 15(1) should entail the following three broad enquiries: (1) whether the law created a distinction between the claimant and others based on personal characteristics or failed to take into consideration his or her disadvantaged position in society, (2) whether the claimant had been treated differently based on either enumerated or analogous grounds under s. 15(1) of the Charter, and (3) whether the differential treatment discriminated in a substantive way (*Law v. Canada*, [1999] 1 S.C.R. 497, at 499–500).

According to Justice Iacobucci, the crux of the analysis was determining whether substantive discrimination had occurred, which was assessed in light of the overall purpose of s. 15(1) and various contextual factors that might help determine whether an individual's dignity had been violated in a given case. He argued that the general purpose of s. 15(1) was to alleviate various ills, such as prejudice, stereotyping, and historical discrimination, in an effort to uphold human dignity for all (*Law v. Canada*, [1999] 1 S.C.R. 497, at 500–1). Justice Iacobucci identified four factors that could be assessed regarding the legislation: (1) whether the claimant or group had experienced pre-existing disadvantages, vulnerabilities, or stereotyping; (2) whether the law actually valued and respected the claimant's situation in society; (3) whether the purpose or effect of the law was to improve the lot of a more disadvantaged person or group in society; and (4) whether the nature and scope of the interest affected by the law was serious and fundamental (*Law v. Canada*, [1999] 1 S.C.R. 497, at 501–2). In many ways, the standards outlined by Justice Iacobucci in the *Law* case provided hallmarks of a postmaterialist framework of analysis, an approach that recognized the dignity and fundamental importance of every individual in Canadian society. Even so, some have criticized *Law* because the very contextual factors it established to make a discrimination claim have proven to be confusing and an impediment to equality rights seekers (see Ryder, Faria, and Lawrence 2004; Fyfe 2007; Froc 2010; Koshan and Hamilton 2013; MacKay 2013).

When Justice Cory subsequently applied this revised equality approach in *M. v. H.*, [1999] 2 S.C.R. 3, at 28), he concluded that Ontario's Family Law Act violated s. 15(1) of the Charter and could not be justified under s. 1 analysis. He argued that the first two prongs of the equality enquiry had been met because the act granted spousal benefits to unmarried opposite-sex couples, while failing to extend such rights to similarly situated same-sex couples. Thus, it created a formal distinction based on sexual orientation, a personal, unchangeable characteristic that the court had recognized as analogous to those found in the text of s. 15(1) of the Charter (*M. v. H.*, [1999] 2 S.C.R. 3, at 26). Justice Cory also concluded that the differential treatment constituted a form of substantive discrimination because it withheld spousal benefits from M., thus undermining her dignity under Canadian law. When he took into consideration various economic contextual factors facing same-sex couples, along with the overall purpose of s. 15(1), Justice Cory concluded that the legislation violated M.'s rights.

Justice Iacobucci, writing for the majority regarding the s. 1 issue, concluded that s. 29 of the Family Law Act failed the second prong of the *Oakes* test. Although he argued that the statute addressed a pressing and substantial objective, he did not think that the law passed constitutional muster because, among other things, excluding same-sex couples from receiving spousal support under the act did not meet the overall objectives of reducing the burden of the public purse or ensuring the equitable resolutions of economic family law disputes (*M. v. H.*, [1999] 2 S.C.R. 3, at 26–7). According to Justice Iacobucci, this shortcoming, along with others, dictated that s. 29 should be excluded from the Family Law Act, but given the profound impact that this ruling would have on legislation throughout Canada, the court postponed implementation of the ruling for six months to allow legislatures across Canada to modify similar discriminatory statutes (*M. v. H.*, [1999] 2 S.C.R. 3, at 10). Professor Peter Hogg (2011) pointed out that, aside from provincial legislation, 68 federal provisions needed to be changed, including the Canada Pension Plan (CPP), which became the subject of a class action suit in *Canada v. Hislop*, [2007] 1 S.C.R. 429. We discuss the *Hislop* case later in this chapter, but there is no denying that the *M. v. H.* case was a clearly postmaterialist ruling that had a wide-ranging impact across the Canadian political and legal landscape.

Landmark Gay Rights Cases of the McLachlin Court, 2000–2010

In *Reference re Same-Sex Marriage*, [2004] 3 S.C.R. 698, the federal government sought guidance from the Supreme Court regarding the constitutional validity of a proposed parliamentary act that would allow marriage between same-sex couples, while also allowing religious officials to refrain from performing those marriages if they so choose. Specifically, s. 1 of the proposed legislation stated, "Marriage, for civil purposes, is the lawful union of two persons to the exclusion of all other," while s. 2 of the act allowed "… officials of religious groups to refuse to perform marriages that are not in accordance with their religious beliefs" (*Reference re Same-Sex Marriage*, [2004] 3 S.C.R. 698, at 699). Given the significance of the proposed legislation, the court was asked to address four questions: (1) whether the proposed provisions fell within the exclusive legislative authority of the federal government; (2) whether same-sex marriage for civil purposes was consistent with the Charter of Rights and Freedoms; (3) whether freedom of religion, found in s. 2(a) of the Charter, protected religious officials from having to perform same-sex marriages that ran counter to their religious tenets; and (4) whether the opposite-sex requirement for civil marriage, articulated in the common law and in Quebec's Federal Law-Civil Law Harmonization Act, were consistent with the Charter (*Reference re Same-Sex Marriage*, [2004] 3 S.C.R. 698, at 705–6). Although a unanimous court thought it unwise and inappropriate to answer the last question, in part because Parliament sought to achieve uniformity regarding civil marriages throughout Canada, it handed down an affirmative ruling favouring gay marriage on the first three legal issues, with one small caveat.

According to the court, to determine whether the proposed act fell within the exclusive power of the federal government, one had to apply the two-part test articulated in *R. v. Hydro-Québec*, [1997] 3 S.C.R. 213, which required an assessment of the "dominant characteristic of the law" as well as which level of government possessed the authority over marriage under s. 91(26) and s. 92(12) of the Constitution Act, 1867. According to the court, the establishment of same-sex civil unions fell exclusively within the power of the federal government because the dominant characteristic of s. 1 of the proposed law pertained to the "capacity to marry" or the establishment of same-sex civil unions, and s. 91(26) of the Constitution Act, 1867 gave this authority exclusively to the federal government. However, the court went on to reason that s. 2 of the proposed legislation, allowing religious officials to opt out of performing such marriages, fell within the power of the provincial governments because it dealt with the performance, or "solemnization," of marriage once the capacity to marry had been recognized, and s. 92(12) of the act conferred responsibility over that matter to the provincial governments (*Reference re Same-Sex Marriage*, [2004] 3 S.C.R. 698, at 708–9, 716). Thus, while Parliament could expand the establishment of marriage to include civil unions between same-sex couples under s. 91(26), it had to concede that power over the performance of marriage rituals belonged to the provincial legislatures under s. 92(12).

In handing down its ruling, the court rejected the contention that marriage was a concept rooted in Christian tradition and was "fixed in time." This moralistic argument envisioned marriage as a heterosexual institution that preceded the development of legal institutions and structures and, therefore, could not be altered by law. Instead, the court adopted an approach that could change with the times and reflected a liberal interpretation of the powers enumerated in the Constitution Act. At one point, the court stated, "Our Constitution is a living tree which, by way of progressive interpretation, accommodates and addresses the realities of modern life" (*Reference re Same-Sex Marriage*, [2004] 3 S.C.R.

698, at 710). In essence, the court recognized the need to embrace a Constitution that could evolve and adapt to changing values so that it could continue to effectively govern successive generations of Canadian citizens. In taking this stance, the court was clearly aligning itself with the postmaterialist value changes that had occurred in society at large.

Turning to the second and third legal questions in the case, the court concluded that extending marriage to same-sex couples was consistent with the Charter and that the freedom of religion, found in s. 2(a) of the Charter, did protect religious officials from performing same-sex civil unions against their faith. In the first instance, the court argued that, contrary to assertions, the underlying purpose of the preamble and substance of s. 1 of the proposed law aimed to further the government's interest in extending equality rights to same-sex couples and thus it was consistent with the principles articulated under the Charter's equality provision. In the second instance, the court simply summarily concluded that given the expansive protection given to religion under s. 2(a) of the Charter, it necessarily protected religious officials from a statutory provision requiring them to perform same-sex civil unions that ran counter to their religious tenets (*Reference re Same-Sex Marriage*, [2004] 3 S.C.R. 698, at 710, 722–3). Despite this materialistic caveat, the McLachlin Court's approach in this seminal case illustrates that the justices had overwhelmingly embraced postmaterialist values in discrimination cases relating to gay rights in modern Canadian society. This shift in values put forth by elite judicial policymakers was remarkable since, only 16 years earlier, the court had embraced a much different stance in the area of gay rights.

Three years later, in *Canada v. Hislop*, [2007] 1 S.C.R. 429, the court addressed several legal issues surrounding spousal survivor benefits that emanated from the Lamer Court's landmark ruling in *M. v. H.*, [1999] 2 S.C.R. 3. In *M. v. H*, the court had held that same-sex couples were entitled to the same level of spousal support obligations as divorced heterosexual couples.

In the wake of the ruling in *Canada v. Hislop*, the federal government amended the CPP to extend survivor benefits to same-sex partners, although there were several limits placed on eligibility and the payment of benefits. After the new CPP went into effect, a class action suit was brought by same-sex survivors, challenging the constitutionality of several sections of the CPP. The most important challenge pertained to whether benefit eligibility should extend back to April 1985, when s. 15(1) of the Charter had gone into effect. Another major challenge to the law was its seemingly arbitrary selection of July 2000 as the starting date for same-sex survivors to begin receiving benefits. On this question, the court was asked to address whether the amended CPP discriminated against same-sex survivors and, if so, what kind of retroactive remedy should be imposed.

Justices LeBel and Rothstein, writing for a six-judge majority, ruled that both the eligibility and the payment-start restrictions of the CPP violated s. 15(1) of the Charter because they limited same-sex survivors to being eligible for benefits only on or after January 1998, while opposite-sex survivors faced no such limitation. The court majority concluded that the eligibility of gay survivors should begin when the s. 15(1) equality provision of the Charter took effect (*Canada v. Hislop*, [2007] 1 S.C.R. 429, at 452). Second, one of the payment restrictions violated equality principles because it allowed payments to heterosexual survivors retroactively 12 months from application, while gay survivors could receive payments only after July 2000. Justices LeBel and Rothstein concluded that neither of these provisions could be justified under the s. 1 *Oakes* test because the federal government had failed to provide suitable evidence to show a pressing and substantial interest for limiting the benefits in the way it had. Moreover, neither provision met the rational-connection and minimal-impairment prongs of the *Oakes* test for similar reasons (*Canada v. Hislop*, [2007] 1 S.C.R. 429, at 452–8). Put simply, the court reasoned that the same rules should apply for gay survivors and heterosexuals alike and that the starting point for benefit payments should be extended back to April 1985 for everyone. One of the problems with this ruling, as noted by Hogg (2011), is that while survivors were eligible for pension benefits by virtue of the Charter back to 1985, they were able to collect payments under the new law only for 12 months before 2000, when the CPP amendments had gone into effect. As Hogg pointed out, this occurred "despite the fact that homosexual CPP contributors had paid exactly the same premiums as heterosexual contributors" for years (Hogg 2011, s. 55-80).

When looking at the landmark gay rights cases as a whole, the development of law in this area provides some of the best evidence of a qualitative evolution towards postmaterialist values by the Canadian Supreme Court. While the court in the 1970s had produced a decision quite sceptical of gay equality claims, its rulings in the late 1990s and 2000s regularly expounded the virtue of recognizing gay rights under the Constitution and ensuring that fundamental principles of human dignity and equal protection were extended to homosexuals under the law. The anti-gay animus in the *Gay Alliance* case gave way to the legalization of marriage and the extension of a host of equal benefits to gay citizens in Canadian society by 2010. No doubt the Charter's adoption helped accelerate this evolutionary process, but this transition would not have occurred if the justices had not breathed strong, healthy life into the pro-equality arguments in gay rights cases. It is clear that the modern justices of the Canadian Supreme Court have adopted a value framework in concordance with Inglehart's theory that traditional arguments of morality and order will necessarily be trumped by notions of equality and fair treatment for homosexuals in a post-modern society.

As suggested by the work of Sniderman et al. (1996) and Matthews (2005), in many ways the court's justices and legal elites helped to promote greater value change within the mass public by being in front of these issues and framing the debate in ways that shifted mass attitudes between the early 1990s and 2004. An additional point that emerges from the reading of the written opinions is that while female justices were more ready to advance postmaterialist arguments in the early Lamer Court, the majority opinions of most of the gay rights cases came from the pens of centrist male justices (Justices Cory and Iacobucci) or, frequently, from a unanimous court. Thus, the impact of gender is less prominent in the sub-field of gay rights cases, at least when analysing the language of these written opinions. Our next discussion turns to the issue of sex discrimination, and it provides a field of litigation ripe for assessing gender differences between the male and female justices.

Landmark Sex Discrimination Cases of the Laskin Court

Our review of the sex discrimination disputes highlights eight important cases handed down between 1974 and 2010. Early cases in this area of law centred on disparate treatment of First Nation women and pregnant women. For instance, in a pair of cases that were consolidated in *Attorney General of Canada v. Lavell*, [1974] S.C.R. 1349 (hereafter *Lavell*), the Supreme Court addressed the legality of a provision of the Indian Act that allowed First Nations to deny native women Indian status and land rights for having married non-natives.[3] Since there was no comparable

3 Even though *Lavell*, [1974] S.C.R. 1349 was technically handed down under the Chief Justice Fauteux tenure, since it was an important sexual discrimination case that bridged the gap between the Fauteux and Laskin Courts, we decided to include it in our analysis.

provision regarding male Indians, the legal question was whether the statute violated the women's right to equality under the 1960 Canadian Bill of Rights. In a 5–4 plurality opinion, Justice Ritchie, writing for four justices in the majority, concluded that the Canadian Bill of Rights could not render a provision of the Indian Act inoperable because it was not designed to alter or change the terms of the British North America Act (BNA Act), which delegated First Nation issues exclusively to Parliament (*Lavell*, [1974] S.C.R. 1349, at 1358–9). According to Justice Ritchie, the disparate treatment the different sexes found in the Indian Act could be changed only by statutory language expressly enacted for that purpose (*Lavell*, [1974] S.C.R. 1349, at 1359–60). Thus, for him, the equal protection clause in the statutory Canadian Bill of Rights could not be used by Parliament to overturn "legislation treating Indians on reservations differently than other Canadians" (*Lavell*, [1974] S.C.R. 1349, at 1359).

Justice Ritchie went on to differentiate this case from the court's earlier ruling in *The Queen v. Drybones*, [1970] S.C.R. 282 and, in doing so, eviscerated the scope of equal protection under the Canadian Bill of Rights by interpreting "equality before the law" as requiring only that officials provide equal treatment in the application and enforcement of the law in Canadian courts. Justice Ritchie went on to argue that the *Lavell* case differed from *Drybones* because here the court was dealing with a provision of the Indian Act that had created disparity in the treatment of First Nation individuals *on reserve*, whereas the *Drybones* case dealt with criminal behaviour *off reserve*, which could not be administered without treating intoxicated natives differently than non-natives. In other words, Justice Ritchie thought that *Drybones* represented a clear example of a case that presented unequal treatment in the enforcement and application of laws in Canadian courts. The *Lavell* case, however, was confined to the behaviour and legal status of native Indians on reserve; thus, the statutory Canadian Bill of Rights was not applicable, and only Parliament had the power to adapt and change it, if it so desired (*Lavell*, [1974] S.C.R. 1349, at 1372).

Readers should note how Justice Ritchie's argument appears to undercut the postmaterialist spirit of the 1960 Canadian Bill of Rights. This is exemplified when he stated, "'Equality before the law' ... is not effective to invoke the egalitarian concept exemplified by the 14th Amendment of the U.S. Constitution as interpreted by the courts of that country" (*Lavell*, [1974] S.C.R. 1349, at 1365). Justice Ritchie maintained that unlike the broad notion of equality rights recognized in the United States, the court's ruling in *Drybones* was narrow and applied simply to the equal application of the law to natives and non-natives alike in ordinary courts found off reserve. For many, this was an unconscionable narrowing of the effect of the equality provisions found in s. 1(b) of the Canadian Bill of Rights.

This point was not lost on Justice Laskin. Writing for three of the justices in dissent, he indicated that the majority written reasons for judgment eviscerated the scope and application of the 1960 Canadian Bill of Rights and amounted to an "oblique appeal for the overruling of the *Drybones* case" (*Lavell*, [1974] S.C.R. 1349, at 1382). A postmaterialist tone is evident throughout Justice Laskin's written dissent. According to him, the history of discrimination against First Nation women embodied in a provision of the Indian Act could not stand against the clear meaning of the Canadian Bill of Rights, which explicitly prohibited *any Canadian law* from discriminating on the basis of sex. For Laskin, the application of the Canadian Bill of Rights was clear and should be applied to all "pre-existing Canadian legislation as well as subsequent Canadian legislation" that engaged in some form of discrimination on the basis of sex (*Lavell*, [1974] S.C.R. 1349, at 1388). Moreover, Justice Laskin contended that this very principle had been established in *Drybones* even though it had dealt with discrimination on the basis of race and not sex. From his perspective, the majority reasons for judgment condoned continuing historical patterns of discrimination against First Nation women under Parliament's historical power to govern Indian relations in the BNA Act (*Lavell*, [1974] S.C.R. 1349, at 1388–9). Justice Laskin's postmaterialist vision of the 1960 Canadian Bill of Rights stands in stark contrast to the majority's willingness to disregard the protections of equality for all Canadians announced in *Drybones*.

Five years later, the Laskin Court heard a case dealing with sex discrimination under the 1960 Canadian Bill of Rights in *Bliss v. Attorney General of Canada*, [1979] 1 S.C.R. 183 (hereafter *Bliss*). In that case, the Laskin Court addressed whether s. 46 of the Unemployment Insurance Act, which denied a pregnant woman the right to receive ordinary unemployment benefits during her pregnancy, violated her right to equality. Although Parliament had enacted a second provision, s. 30(1), that allowed pregnant women to receive *special* benefits during pregnancy, *Bliss* did not meet the "ten weeks of insurable employment" qualifications, and therefore, the woman was not eligible for *any* benefits, special or ordinary, under the newly amended act. In court, she argued that her "pregnancy status" in effect prevented her from receiving ordinary unemployment benefits – the very benefits that she was seeking – that were extended to both men and women who were not pregnant.

Justice Ritchie, writing for a unanimous court, argued that if one read both provisions in conjunction with each other, it was clear that Parliament was trying to develop a comprehensive scheme that enabled women to receive special unemployment benefits during their pregnancy (starting eight weeks before the week of childbirth and extending six weeks beyond). Yet he argued that Parliament had to place limitations on those entitlements and that those limitations were a valid and integral part of a comprehensive scheme that met a valid federal purpose. At the core of his argument was the contention that even though the legislation treated one segment of the population differently from another, it did not constitute sex discrimination because the goal was to provide additional benefits to pregnant women, not to degrade them as a group (*Bliss*, [1979] 1 S.C.R. 183, at 191). Moreover, the legislative scheme was not aimed at promoting inequality between the sexes, but rather reflected a real biological distinction that existed between the sexes. At one point Justice Ritchie stated, "Any inequality between the sexes in this area is not created by legislation but by nature" (*Bliss*, [1979] 1 S.C.R. 183, at 190). He concluded that the limitations on unemployment benefits during pregnancy were relevant and important conditions to the entitlement and that the differential treatment was aimed at achieving an overall valid federal objective (*Bliss*, [1979] 1 S.C.R. 183, at 192–3). As such, the law did not violate the right to equality under the 1960 Canadian Bill of Rights.

Since this ruling disadvantaged pregnant women from receiving regular unemployment benefits in relation to their male counterparts, the Laskin Court ruling set a materialist tone in this area of law. In essence, this ruling allowed patriarchal sex discrimination to continue in the area of unemployment benefits to a group that many would argue could least afford it. Although this ruling was subsequently overruled in *Brooks v. Canada Safeway Ltd.*, [1989] 1 S.C.R. 1219, the materialistic tone of the written reasons for judgment could be seen in its paternalistic attitude, which endorsed a law that maintained long-standing stereotypes about the "inability" of pregnant women to work late into their pregnancy. It also reflected a materialist, traditional stance in the patronizing way it described the legal distinction as one flowing from "nature" and not from the law itself. As constitutional law scholar Peter Hogg pointed out, any disadvantage created by pregnancy necessarily constitutes discrimination on the basis of sex because only women can become pregnant (Hogg 1997, 1233). The court's classification scheme based on differences in nature constituted a thinly disguised form of sex discrimination.

Landmark Sex Discrimination Rulings of the Dickson Court

Ten years later, the Dickson Court addressed a similar issue in *Brooks v. Canada Safeway Ltd.*, [1989] 1 S.C.R. 1219 (hereafter *Brooks*). In this landmark case, the court addressed two questions: first, whether Safeway's health benefits plan discriminated against pregnant women and, if so, whether the exclusion constituted sex discrimination in violation of Manitoba's Human Rights Code. Turning to the first issue, Chief Justice Dickson, writing for a unanimous court, concluded that since Safeway's health plan failed to provide *any* accidental and sickness benefits to women during a 17-week period of pregnancy, regardless of their reason for missing work, the employer had singled out a particular group for much less favourable treatment than other employees under the plan (*Brooks*, [1989] 1 S.C.R. 1219, at 1236). Although Chief Justice Dickson agreed with the respondent that pregnancy could not be classified as either "a sickness or an accident," he determined that given the "fundamental importance" of pregnancy in society, the conditions associated with procreation constituted a "valid health-related reason" for missing work. He went on to argue that the employer's health plan singled out one group to bear the social and financial burden of pregnancy and that the differentiation was discriminatory. At one point he stated, "It cannot be disputed that everyone in society benefits from procreation. The Safeway plan, however, places one of the major costs of procreation entirely upon one group in society: pregnant women" (*Brooks*, [1989] 1 S.C.R. 1219, at 1238). Thus, he concluded that Safeway's benefits plan was discriminatory towards pregnant women.

Turning to the second issue in the case, Chief Justice Dickson contended that discrimination against pregnant women also constituted sex discrimination because, as we all know, pregnancy is "unique to women." Relying on arguments made by Peter Hogg, 10 years of jurisprudence arising from claims of human rights discrimination and changes taking place in the workforce, he concluded "that *Bliss* was wrongly decided or, in any event, that *Bliss* would not be decided now as it was decided then" (*Brooks*, [1989] 1 S.C.R. 1219, at 1243). Continuing his earlier theme, he concluded that it was unfair to put pregnant women at an "economic and social" disadvantage in relation to others, and thus, a company health benefits package could not exclude compensation for pregnant women (ibid.). The act of overturning a precedent-setting case just 10 years after its holding provides some of the strongest evidence of a court making an about-face in line with promoting postmaterialist value changes.

In *Janzen v. Platy Enterprises Ltd.*, [1989] 1 S.C.R. 1252 (hereafter *Janzen*), a second sex discrimination case handed down the same day as *Brooks*, the Dickson Court ruled that the type of sexual harassment experienced by two female waitresses from a fellow male employee in the workplace constituted sex discrimination in violation of Manitoba's Human Rights Code. Chief Justice Dickson rejected the lower court's contention that sexual harassment and sexual discrimination were fundamentally different concepts. He determined that a long line of judicial rulings in Canada and the United States had acknowledged that certain types of sexual harassment did constitute sex discrimination (*Janzen*, [1989] 1 S.C.R. 1252, at 1278). He stipulated that the persistent, unwelcome sexual advances and verbal abuse experienced by the waitresses from the male employee, who had the authority to fire them, constituted sexual harassment. Moreover, he argued that it represented sex discrimination because it limited the opportunities for advancement by the victims of the sexual harassment based on their gender (*Janzen*, [1989] 1 S.C.R. 1252, at 1279). In talking about the effects of such activity on women, Chief Justice Dickson invoked postmaterialist language when he concluded, "Sexual harassment is a demeaning practice.... By requiring an employee to contend with unwelcome sexual actions or explicit sexual demands, sexual harassment in the workplace attacks the dignity and self-respect of the victim both as an employee and as a human being" (*Janzen*, [1989] 1 S.C.R. 1252, at 1284).

After Chief Justice Dickson defined the terms, he subsequently rejected the lower court's contention that the unwelcome sexual activity did not constitute sex discrimination because it was based on sexual attraction and not gender. He also rejected the idea that the Canadian Human Rights Act was designed only to eradicate categorical discrimination of an entire group. On the first point, the chief justice noted that since only women could be subject to harassment by heterosexual males, it made no sense to contend that gender had nothing to do with the type of discriminatory treatment that took place in this case (*Janzen*, [1989] 1 S.C.R. 1252, at 1288–91). He also indicated that even if sexual harassment was directed at one or two individuals in a specific group, discrimination still occurred (ibid.). Thus, the Court of Appeal had relied on faulty reasons to reach an unjust conclusion.

Both of these cases illustrate that the Dickson Court had moved in a decisive postmaterialist direction on the issue of sex discrimination in relation to the Laskin Court. The paternal and patronizing tone of the rulings in the two sex discrimination cases heard in the 1970s seemed to have given way under the Dickson tenure to a court that was unanimous in its intent to protect the financial and social well-being of women in the workforce along with maintaining their dignity in society as a whole. Readers should note that although the *Brooks* and *Janzen* decisions failed to invoke Charter s. 15 application (because they involved private actions), since they came to the court in the wake of the adoption of the Charter, they fostered considerable interest group activity, which probably played a role in moving the Supreme Court in such a decisive postmaterialist direction. In addition, the fact that these disputes were also heard by a court comprised of two female justices should not be overlooked. The full impact of the role of female justices in sex discrimination cases would come into full bloom during the subsequent Lamer Court tenure.

Landmark Sex Discrimination Rulings of the Lamer Court

In the landmark case of *Gould v. Yukon Order of Pioneers*, [1996] 1 S.C.R. 571 (hereafter *Gould*), the Lamer Court addressed the legal question of whether denying women membership in an all-male, private fraternal organization constituted discrimination under the Yukon Human Rights Act. Justice Iacobucci, writing for six of the justices in the majority, pointed out that it was not disputed that the Yukon Order of Pioneers' rejection of female members amounted to sex discrimination. However, the critical question was whether this *type* of discrimination was prohibited under s. 8(a) of the Yukon Human Rights Act, which specifically prohibited discrimination when services were provided to the public at large (*Gould*, [1996] 1 S.C.R. 571, at 583).

In answering this question, Justice Iacobucci claimed that it was well documented that courts should use a broad, liberal, purposive approach when assessing human rights legislation, which required justices to look at the exact wording of the statute to fully understand its meaning (*Gould*, [1996] 1 S.C.R. 571, at 585–6). Since sub-provision s. 8(c) specified that one could not discriminate in relation to membership in certain types of associations, Justice Iacobucci indicated that it was clear that the legislature had carefully considered the kinds of organizations that could and could not discriminate when granting membership. Moreover, the act addressed membership as a separate issue from discrimination in the offering of services to the public discussed in s. 8(a).

Justice Iacobucci subsequently concluded that s. 8(c) specified only that associations that had an economic or professional nature could not discriminate, and thus he reasoned that the legislature must have intended that other types of organizations could adopt restrictive membership rules (*Gould*, [1996] 1 S.C.R. 571, at 588). Applying this logic to the case at hand, he concluded that the Yukon Order of Pioneers fell at the social end of the organization spectrum and thus could adopt male-only membership policies. Justice La Forest reinforced the social emphasis of the order when he stated that it existed in part to provide a variety of male-bonding experiences for its members (*Gould*, [1996] 1 S.C.R. 571, at 620). Since s. 8(c) prohibited discrimination in economic and professional organizations and this organization had a social and fraternal focus, the majority concluded that the law did not forbid it from creating male-only policies. Justice Iacobucci also pointed out that the only services the order offered the public were historical data and documents produced by a select few individuals who collected and recorded Yukon historical materials. Since the order provided these "end products" to both men and women alike, the order did not discriminate in relation to the services that it provided to the public at large (*Gould*, [1996] 1 S.C.R. 571, at 589).

It is important to note that both of the female justices on the Canadian Supreme Court at the time wrote dissents taking issue with the majority ruling. Both justices agreed with the lower human rights tribunal that the order had engaged in a prohibited form of discrimination under s. 8 of Yukon Human Rights Act. While Justice McLachlin's dissent focused more narrowly on the problems embedded in the majority's ruling regarding services provided to the public in s. 8(a), Justice L'Heureux-Dubé's dissent took issue with numerous elements of the majority ruling, including the standard of review that the majority claimed the Court of Appeal should use when reviewing human rights tribunal decisions. Justice McLachlin argued that several factors had contributed to her conclusion that membership in the order *itself* constituted a service to the public under s. 8(a). Since the order took on a prominent public profile, embarked on numerous public functions, had a large roster of members, and promoted camaraderie that flowed from its public purpose and history as a group for pioneers, it conferred benefits that women should also enjoy (*Gould*, [1996] 1 S.C.R. 571, at 656). Indeed, to become a member of the order "is to seek and to gain a respect in the community," so she believed that membership in it should not be denied to half the Yukon population (*Gould*, [1996] 1 S.C.R. 571, at 657).

Justice L'Heureux-Dubé took issue with the standard of review that the majority had used, arguing that the appeal involved a question of fact, or application of the law to the facts. Since the disputed elements pertained to the tribunal's factual conclusion that the order's activities provided services to the public, the appellate court should show deference to the tribunal's factual conclusion, given its expertise. In Justice L'Heureux-Dubé's view, the reviewing court should not overturn the tribunal's findings unless they were patently unreasonable (*Gould*, [1996] 1 S.C.R. 571, at 634–5). In contrast, the majority had argued that less deference was required because this case involved a matter of law that needed correcting. Justice L'Heureux-Dubé determined that the tribunal could have interpreted s. 8 in its entirety to reasonably conclude that the order provided a single service to the public by collecting, preserving, and publishing the history of the Yukon. Moreover, like Justice McLachlin, she believed that the tribunal had made no error in concluding that discrimination had occurred when the order provided services to the public because it excluded women from membership and that membership itself constituted a service to the public within the holistic meaning of s. 8(a) (*Gould*, [1996] 1 S.C.R. 571, at 578–9).

The dissents from the two female justices on the Canadian court in this case are telling because they indicate that the women on the court viewed the exclusion of women from private organizations differently from their male colleagues. While the men focused on the brotherly environment and camaraderie such organizations offered men, the women highlighted the social status and economic benefits that these associations provided to the select few in society. It is interesting that it took individuals who had likely experienced discrimination at the hands of men – namely, women – to communicate how all-male organizations could impinge on the social and economic status of women. As a result, the postmaterialist perspective of Justices L'Heureux-Dubé and McLachlin makes sense precisely because they could relate more closely to the traditional discriminatory impact that women had historically faced in society. Readers should note how these themes juxtaposed in *Gould* echo the overarching quantitative findings of gender differences documented in the prior chapter.

In a subsequent landmark ruling, the Lamer Court shifted the focus away from social and fraternal organizations towards the effects of sex discrimination in the workplace. In *British Columbia (Public Service*

Employee Relations Commission) v. BCGSEU, [1999] 3 S.C.R. 3 (hereafter *BCGSEU*), the court grappled with the firing of a female firefighter who had performed well on the job, but had failed to pass one of four aerobic-fitness tests established for forest firefighters. The employee and union filed a grievance, alleging that the aerobic standard set by the government had the effect of discriminating against women. The case was significant because it set out a new, liberal, three-part test for the review of so-called bona fide occupational restrictions that resulted in discrimination against a certain class of employees.

Justice McLachlin, writing the opinion for a unanimous court, concluded that the two legal standards of review in cases pertaining to workplace discrimination – namely, "direct discrimination" and "adverse effect discrimination" – needed to be recast into one uniform test (*BCGSEU,* [1999] 3 S.C.R. 3, at 15–17). According to Justice McLachlin, the development of two tests had resulted in confusion in the lower courts and human rights tribunals. The fact that the arbitrator and Court of Appeal had applied the two tests in the case pointed to the difficulty in knowing which standard to apply. Justice McLachlin took up this task in *BCGSEU,* [1999] 3 S.C.R. 3.

Justice McLachlin established a new, three-part test that would help determine whether a prima facie discriminatory practice was an allowable, bona fide occupational restriction. First, an employer could justify an alleged discriminatory practice if the employer developed a standard that was "for a purpose rationally connected to the performance of the job." Second, the employer must show that the standard was adopted with an "honest and good faith belief" that it fulfilled a "legitimate work-related purpose." Third, the court must determine whether the standard was reasonably necessary to accomplish a "legitimate work-related purpose." To show that the standard was reasonable, Justice McLachlin concluded that one must demonstrate that it was not possible "to accommodate individual employees" similar to the claimant "without imposing undue hardship upon the employer" (*BCGSEU,* [1999] 3 S.C.R. 3, at 32–3). This new test was a difficult one for employers to meet because it required them to find ways to accommodate individual differences as long as it did not create an "undue hardship" (*BCGSEU,* [1999] 3 S.C.R. 3, at 33).

Applying the new test to the case at hand, Justice McLachlin easily found that the first two prongs had been met because the employer had a rational purpose in establishing an aerobic-fitness standard to ensure that all firefighters could perform safely and efficiently and there was a good-faith belief that the test was not designed to discriminate on the basis of sex (*BCGSEU*, [1999] 3 S.C.R. 3, at 39–40). However, the government had failed to pass the third prong of the new test. Although fitness experts had been used to establish the aerobic standard, and while it was reasonably necessary to identify physically fit firefighters, the government had not shown that it would suffer an undue hardship if a different standard was used for female firefighters (*BCGSEU*, [1999] 3 S.C.R. 3, at 40). Indeed, having a different aerobic standard was particularly relevant in the face of scientific evidence that women have a lower aerobic capacity than men (*BCGSEU*, [1999] 3 S.C.R. 3, at 39). Moreover, according to Justice McLachlin, setting a different standard for men and women did not result in "reverse discrimination" if both sexes were held to some minimum standard based on their different aerobic capabilities. Quoting Justice McLachlin,

> As this Court has repeatedly held, the essence of equality is to be treated according to one's own merit, capabilities and circumstances. True equality requires that differences be accommodated. ... A different aerobic standard capable of identifying women who could perform the job safely and efficiently therefore does not necessarily imply discrimination against men. (*BCGSEU*, [1999] 3 S.C.R. 3, at 44)

The upshot of this ruling was that the female firefighter in the case had suffered illegal discrimination when she was fired because the discriminatory job requirement could not be justified as a legitimate occupational requirement that could not be modified. The court restored the arbitrator's ruling and ordered back pay for the female firefighter (*BCGSEU*, [1999] 3 S.C.R. 3, at 45). In reaching its unanimous decision, the Lamer Court not only presented a forceful, postmaterialist justification for employment equity, but it also laid out new ground rules for cases raising discrimination claims in the workplace setting, rules that benefited women. Seen in this light, the language of the *BCGSEU* firefighter case mimics the dissenting arguments made by the female justices in *Gould*. Perhaps not surprisingly, the *BCGSEU* written reasons for judgment was the handiwork of a female justice, just as the postmaterialist language in *Gould* flowed from the pens of female justices. One year later, Justice McLachlin would become the first woman to be appointed Chief Justice of the Supreme Court of Canada, perhaps foreshadowing a historical flowering of pro-equality rulings during her tenure.

Landmark Sex Discrimination Rulings of the McLachlin Court, 2000–2010

If the Lamer Court decisions were about the direct examination of discriminatory practices, the important McLachlin Court decisions turned on questions of jurisdictional authority and the power of labour arbitration boards and human rights commissions. Take, for example, the issues in *Parry Sound (District) Social Services Administration Board v. O.P.S.E.U., Local 324*, [2003] 2 S.C.R. 157 (hereafter *Parry Sound*), in which the court had to determine whether the dismissal of a female probationary employee a few days after her return from pregnancy leave represented a potentially discriminatory act that was reviewable by a labour board. The majority of the Supreme Court said yes (7–2), but there was a divide on the court about how much power a labour board had in reviewing human rights law violations (like sex discrimination) and whether the provincial legislature had given it the authority to do so.

Justice Iacobucci wrote the majority written reasons for judgment in *Parry Sound*, and there is no escaping the sweeping power he gave to labour boards to review discriminatory acts. Since the woman who was fired after returning from pregnancy leave was still a probationary employee, the collective bargaining agreement gave the employer the right to lay someone off at the "sole discretion of and for any reason satisfactory to the Employer." Moreover, it stipulated that such a firing of a probationary employee could not be the subject of a grievance and arbitration hearing (*Parry Sound*, [2003] 2 S.C.R. 157, at 164–5). Despite the language in the contract, the employee had filed a grievance with her union, alleging that her discharge was "arbitrary, discriminatory, in bad faith and unfair" (*Parry Sound*, [2003] 2 S.C.R. 157, at 165). The employer objected to the Ontario Labour Relations Board hearing the arbitration.

When the labour board panel heard the dispute, it noted the bargaining agreement's exclusion of the dispute from its authority, but claimed that there was a statutory authority to hear the grievance. In its view, s. 48(12)(j) of Ontario's Labour Relations Act allowed the board to apply human rights and other employment-related laws, even if they conflicted with the contours of a collective agreement (*Parry Sound*, [2003] 2 S.C.R. 157, at 167). In short, the law required it to arbitrate disputes in which a claim of sex discrimination – or other acts of discrimination – had been alleged in a grievance. Justice Iacobucci claimed that the labour board's reasoning indicated that the standard of review of a board's decision was a stringent one. For a judge or court to overturn a labour board's decision, the ruling must be "patently unreasonable" (*Parry Sound*, [2003] 2 S.C.R. 157, at 171). Justice Iacobucci noted that the standard for overturning a decision was very high, and it was designed to provide a great deal of deference to the specialized expertise of labour boards and their efforts to resolve cases in an expeditious manner.

In siding with the labour board interpretation, Justice Iacobucci ensured that the potential application of postmaterialist values could take place in a unique, quasi-judicial setting. He saw the laws and statutes of the provinces, such as human rights codes that prohibit discrimination, as a "floor beneath which an employer and union cannot contract" (*Parry Sound*, [2003] 2 S.C.R. 157, at 176). This meant that a collective bargaining agreement was not the only thing that bound an employer and an employee, and Justice Iacobucci indicated that employers, after all, could not use the contract to violate laws (see *Parry Sound*, [2003] 2 S.C.R. 157, at 178). Moreover, he indicated that empowering labour boards to hear discrimination grievances fell within the plain meaning of the law and made for good public policy. Letting those grievances play out in a broader, more accessible forum for employees had the advantage of bolstering human rights safeguards in settings that were more informal, allowing for resolution of disputes in a manner that was good for both employers and employees (*Parry Sound*, [2003] 2 S.C.R. 157, at 187). While labour boards might not have special expertise in Human Rights Code grievances, Justice Iacobucci pointed out that they could develop that expertise quickly (*Parry Sound*, [2003] 2 S.C.R. 157, at 187–8). All in all, it was a win for the employee and her union's effort to allow her sex discrimination grievance to be heard by a labour board panel.

While Justice Iacobucci's reasons for judgment stood for the proposition of endorsing broad powers of authority for labour boards, the dissent by Justice Major stood for the exercise of judicial restraint in the face of legislative silence. For Justice Major, who wrote for himself and Justice LeBel, this case was about inappropriate judicial action by the labour board and Court of Appeal in reading statutory discrimination provisions into the contours of a collective bargaining agreement. Justice Major believed that the collective bargaining agreement explicitly prohibited grievances by a discharged probationary employee, and the mere existence of Ontario's Labour Relations Act and Human Rights Code could not change that fact. Instead, the female employee could pursue a remedy using the Human Rights Code. She could allege sex discrimination and bring her claim to the Ontario Human Rights Commission (*Parry Sound*, [2003] 2 S.C.R. 157, at 198, 203). Indeed, Justice Major is not wholly materialist in his value orientation because he encouraged the use of human rights legislation and tribunals for these types of claims.

The two sides of *Parry Sound* reflect an interesting wrinkle in the postmaterialist-materialist value conflict. Seen in the light of encouraging broader participation in democratic institutions, Justice Iacobucci's ruling not only endorsed equality-seeking behaviour but also the value of citizen engagement with government agencies that would review and uphold equality claims. Thus, he expressed an expansive vision of equality adjudication as an activity not only for courts but also for specialized administrative tribunals. Justice Major's opinion took a more traditional tack, representing a vision of old-style legislative power. It implied that if unions wanted grievances of discrimination to be reviewed by labour boards, they should use standard political channels to convince the legislature to change the law, not use the courts as a policymaking body. Thus, *Parry Sound* features an activist-restraint dimension of judicial behaviour that is overlaid on a discrimination case, one that raises fundamental questions about the appropriate forum for sex discrimination claims in union-management conflicts.

A similar sex discrimination case in the context of a labour-management dispute emerged as a critical issue three years later in *Canada (Human Rights Commission) v. Canadian Airlines International Ltd.*, [2006] 1 S.C.R. 3 (hereafter *Canadian Airlines*). This case involved a flight attendants' union and its pay discrimination claim on behalf of flight attendants, a predominantly female group of employees. The union claimed that the flight attendants were paid differently than the pilots and mechanics (predominantly men) working for Air Canada for work of "equal value" in the same establishment. Under provisions of the Canadian Human Rights Act (s. 11) and the Equal Wages Guidelines (s. 10) put in place to enforce the act, the flight attendants' union argued that this resulted in sex discrimination by the company (*Canadian Airlines,* [2006] 1 S.C.R. 3, at 9). The initial pay equity complaint was filed in 1991, and the Supreme Court's decision 15 years later focused on the narrow procedural question of how to interpret the meaning of the words "in the same establishment." If the pilots, mechanics, and flight attendants were all working in the same establishment, then the discrimination claim and analysis of pay inequity could go forward in front of the Canadian Human Rights Commission (CHRC). If not, the discrimination claim should be dismissed (*Canadian Airlines*, [2006] 1 S.C.R. 3, at 12).

Justices LeBel and Abella wrote the joint reasons for a unanimous court, and the outcome was decisively in favour of the flight attendants' union. Air Canada's position was that the three classes of employee were members of different collective bargaining agreements, with three different wage and personnel policy structures. From the company's standpoint, each group was working in separate establishments with separate personnel manuals within a single company, and this line of argument was endorsed initially by the CHRC (*Canadian Airlines*, [2006] 1 S.C.R. 3, at 10). In contrast, the Federal Court of Appeal had sided with the union, arguing that Air Canada treated all its employees using a single, integrated business strategy and under a "common personnel and wage policy" (ibid.). Justices LeBel and Abella took this same position. After reviewing the history of the statutory language and wage guidelines developed by the CHRC, they noted that limits on the geographic scope of "establishment" had long ago fallen out of the interpretation of the language. As a result, an employment establishment could span different locations, offices, and sites across the provinces (*Canadian Airlines*, [2006] 1 S.C.R. 3, at 14–19).

Justices LeBel and Abella were critical of Air Canada's interpretation of the law. Accepting a view of "establishment" as one where collective bargaining agreements essentially defined each establishment would prevent the very wage comparisons that were intended in the law. If each bargaining agreement distinguished each employment establishment as unique, then no wage equity analysis would ever occur, "thereby undermining the purpose of the Act, namely to determine whether wages paid to women reflect an undervaluation based on systemic discrimination resulting not only in occupational segregation, but also in diminished bargaining strength, and, likely, diminished wages and benefits" (*Canadian Airlines*, [2006] 1 S.C.R. 3, at 23). In short, Air Canada's approach would "turn collective bargaining into a tool to consolidate discriminatory practices" (ibid.). The justices found Air Canada's arguments disingenuous and concluded that management had adopted a common approach to collective bargaining, using similar methods of dealing with benefits, bargaining, and communication for all employee groups. As a result, the discrimination complaint could go forward, and the matter was referred back to the CHRC for a continuation of its pay equity investigation (*Canadian Airlines*, [2006] 1 S.C.R. 3, at 24–5).

Despite the court's ruling in favour of the flight attendants in the Air Canada dispute, it is important to remember that it came 15 years after the initial filing of the complaint. It is clear that the financial stakes for the company were significant. Unfortunately, such a long battle for pay equity is not uncommon. In 2013, female workers for Canada Post reached a settlement to end a 30-year-old pay-equity-discrimination claim when the government-funded agency finally decided to pay back lost wages in a dispute that had started in 1983 (Lu 2013). These two prominent cases relating to pay equity litigation demonstrate the long haul that women have faced in winning equal pay for work of equal value. The postmaterialist value of equal treatment is obviously important, and the recognition of equality could bring significant material benefits to workers who feel they have been wronged. But there is no mistaking the materialistic arguments advanced by companies that seek to avoid the costs of pay equity claims, and they have demonstrated a steadfast willingness to contest such claims in the interest of protecting their bottom line. The one shining feature of the McLachlin Court's rulings is that their decisions in *Parry Sound* and the *Canadian Airlines* dispute have provided specialized tribunals with the power and authority to review sex discrimination complaints in a meaningful way. Given that these cases addressed jurisdictional considerations, it is yet to be determined how much equality women will achieve under labour board and human rights commission rulings.

A holistic examination of the gay rights and sex discrimination written opinions reveals a clear postmaterialist shift over time. In both areas of law, the predominantly materialist tone of the written reasons for judgments of the 1970s eventually gave way to a pro-equality language, especially in the 1990s and 2000s. Indeed, the textual analysis of the opinions provides compelling evidence that a postmaterialist shift has occurred in these two sub-areas of equality dispute. No doubt, female justices have exhibited some of the most powerful postmaterialist tendencies: witness the dissenting opinions in *Gould* as primary examples of this trend. Yet even the male justices of the Lamer and McLachlin Courts adopted language in equality cases that recognized the value of equality for its intrinsic and extrinsic qualities. The written opinions of these later Canadian courts regularly endorsed equality principles because they promoted the "human dignity" of all people and because they compensated for the economic harms suffered by those who had been stigmatized in the past. By recognizing these twin features of equality, the modern Canadian justices have endorsed, more often than not, not only the value of equality of opportunity but also equality of outcome in these two issue domains.

However, it should be noted that, subsequently, the court has backed away from the human dignity standards because the approach has become unworkable. For example, in *R. v. Kapp*, [2008] 2 S.C.R. 483, at 504, the court acknowledged that the human dignity factors have "become confusing and difficult to apply" and proven to be a "burden on equality claimants" (see also Fyfe 2007; Froc 2010; Koshan and Hamilton 2013; MacKay 2013, 65). In the contemporary Lamer and McLachlin Courts, the adjudication of equality conflicts has been expanded to a broad realm of government bodies, most notably human rights commissions and labour boards. As noted by some of the justices, the accessibility of these forums and informality of their proceedings allow individuals an easier avenue to pursue claims if they have been treated unequally. As a result, the postmaterialist shift in these two equality areas have encompassed two important components: (1) a greater recognition of equality as a basic fundamental value and (2) a greater recognition of an individual's right to pursue recourse for unequal treatment in quasi-judicial bodies. These two patterns – gleaned from the written opinions of the justices – provide clear evidence that a postmaterialist value change has taken place in key sub-areas of discrimination law, a change that could not be revealed by an overarching quantitative analysis of judicial voting behaviour across all equality cases.

One of the important overarching findings of this chapter is that the qualitative analysis of judicial opinions amplifies the findings from the prior chapter. While the quantitative analysis of judicial voting patterns provides scholars with insight into how the Canadian Supreme Court has resolved discrimination disputes across a wide sweep of cases, illustrating that gender differences and case factors play a large, explanatory role, a detailed qualitative analysis provides deeper insight into the specific doctrinal direction the justices have taken in two key sub-areas of equality law. Each level of analysis is important because it allows scholars to examine judicial behaviour from different vantage points. Moreover, when those unique insights are taken together, they provide scholars with a deeper and more complete understanding of the postmaterialist changes that have been happening on the Canadian Supreme Court over time and in this area of law. In addition, this understanding highlights the powerful role that female justices have played in marshalling that value change.

Chapter Eight

The Impact of Value Change in the Supreme Court of Canada

One enduring question in the study of judicial behaviour is how well high court voting patterns and the written opinions of the justices reflect the evolving world view of the mass public. Judicial scholarship to date has shown that appellate court judges pay attention to legal factors like precedent and stare decisis, along with the strategic interplay among the justices, when making decisions. Research has also shown the dominant role that the attitudes and values of the justices have in their decision-making process (see Segal and Spaeth 1993, 2002; Ostberg and Wetstein 2007; Songer et al. 2012). To the extent that attitudes and values inform judicial opinions, the question becomes, how much and to what extent do the shifting views of the mass public become reflected in the written decisions of the justices? Inglehart's theory of intergenerational value change shows that public opinion in a range of advanced industrial societies has gradually evolved in a postmaterialist direction. His theory implies that the same postmaterialist forces at work in the mass public might also shape the long-term evolution of judicial decisions. Our study has tracked the degree to which the gradual postmaterialist shift in public opinion has been reflected in the shifting value priorities of judicial elites over time in three broad areas of law, recognizing that judicial decisions are in fact the by-product of legal, strategic, attitudinal, and social forces that influence the dynamics of any given case. In doing so, we have advanced a socio-attitudinal model of judicial behaviour, which provides a longer and broader framework to help explain why justices in modern democracies might be more postmaterialist in their value orientation over time.

The main chapters of the book have featured a core series of tests designed to unpack and tease out the specific evidence of postmaterialist value change in discrete areas of law. This chapter provides a brief summary of the findings from our quantitative and qualitative research strategies, and it situates those findings in a larger practical and theoretical context. As a guide to this effort, we provide a summary table that shows these tests, their findings, and whether Inglehart's thesis is confirmed by the results. We recognize from the start that correlation is not causation, but the number of tests that we have presented in our study reflects a rigorous research strategy that attempts to peel back successive layers of explanation of what is happening in the Canadian Supreme Court in key areas of law. Our analysis examined five core, independent hypothesis tests derived from Inglehart's thesis using quantitative methods and one qualitative hypothesis rooted in a deep reading of the language and rationales of the written opinions of the justices. The use of both quantitative and qualitative methods is unique and provides a more holistic and robust assessment of our socio-attitudinal model of judicial decision making. Our overall findings provide strong support for Inglehart's thesis, although there are important caveats in discrete areas of law that are noteworthy.

Our first direct test of Inglehart's thesis in free speech, discrimination, and environmental cases addressed the question of whether there was an observed increase in the percentage of postmaterialist outcomes across the Laskin, Dickson, and Lamer Courts and first 10 years of the McLachlin Court. The findings suggest that there was a decisive shift in the percentage of liberal rulings in the free expression area over time, providing the strongest confirmation of Inglehart's theory of value change (see finding 1 in Table 8.1). The dramatic shift in free speech support was heightened by the liberalizing impact that the Charter had on the court in the free expression area. In the discrimination area, the findings reveal an overarching rise in postmaterialist support for equality concerns across the Laskin and Dickson Courts and first 10 years of the McLachlin Court, yet the voting behaviour of the Lamer Court failed to meet the requisite pattern. Despite this anomaly, the findings provide fairly strong evidence of a postmodern, shifting value change in discrimination cases over time. In the environmental cases, the findings also provide some support for Inglehart's thesis, with the Dickson and Lamer Courts of the 1980s and 1990s issuing more pro-environmental rulings than the 1970s court. However, under the first 10 years of the McLachlin Court, it seems there was a movement away from protecting the environment, with the court providing even less support than under the Laskin Court tenure (see finding 1 in Table 8.1).

Table 8.1. Summary of Postmaterialist Value Change Hypotheses and Findings from the Qualitative and Quantitative Assessments

Question	Environment				Free speech				Discrimination			
	Laskin	Dickson	Lamer	McLachlin	Laskin	Dickson	Lamer	McLachlin	Laskin	Dickson	Lamer	McLachlin
1. Does the percentage of postmaterialist rulings trend in a positive direction across the four courts?	53%	71%	67%	50%	25%	29%	50%	50%	40%	52%	38%	55%
Findings	Somewhat confirmed				Confirmed				Somewhat confirmed			
2a. Was there an increase in postmaterialist intervener activity across the decades and courts studied?	2	36	60	121	0	10	44	44	23	19	109	121
Findings	Confirmed				Confirmed				Confirmed			
2b. Does the proportion of postmaterialist interveners increase across the decades and courts studied?	100%	88%	57%	50%	0%	9%	39%	44%	96%	38%	60%	56%
Findings	Not confirmed				Confirmed				Somewhat confirmed			
3. Is there a positive bivariate correlation between a judge's birth year and career postmaterialist voting record?	Slope = –.245				Slope = .659				Slope = –.150			

Findings	Not confirmed	Confirmed	Not confirmed
4. Are the regression coefficients for the Lamer and McLachlin Court eras positive and significant in relation to the Laskin/Dickson Court eras in judge-level logistic regression models?	.648* .768* .496 +13.4 +18.5 +12.1	.350* .487* +8.7 +12.1	−.400 −.067 −10.0 −1.7
Findings	Somewhat confirmed	Confirmed	Not confirmed
5. Are the regression coefficients for the Lamer and McLachlin Court eras positive and significant in relation to the Laskin/Dickson Court eras in the final, overall logistic regression models?	.724* 1.06** 1.80*** +16.7 +24.6 +39.9	.510* − .054 +12.6 −1.3	−.259 .159 −6.5 +4.0
Findings	Confirmed	Somewhat confirmed	Not confirmed
6. Do the written opinions and language of the justices suggest a postmaterialist shift in critical areas of law?	Pollution: **Confirmed** Energy: **Not confirmed** Fishing rights: **Somewhat confirmed**	Commercial ads: **Somewhat confirmed** Political speech: **Somewhat confirmed**	Gay rights: **Confirmed** Sex discrimination: **Confirmed**

Thus, at first blush, there seems to be only moderate support for Inglehart's thesis in this area of law. Collectively, across all three areas, there does appear to be a significant, broad rise in postmaterialist rulings as we move closer to the present.

Looking at the role of intervener activity, our findings overwhelmingly confirmed an increase in postmaterialist intervener activity across all three areas of law, with the rise in interveners being strongest in both the environmental and the discrimination areas and more modestly in free speech cases (see finding 2a in Table 8.1). The rise in intervener participation across all three areas has provided justices with insights and cogent arguments that help justify the protection of rights in these three areas of law. Moreover, our findings reinforce a larger pattern of widespread interest group mobilization documented by other scholars in the discipline (see Epp 1998; Hein 2001; Brodie 2002; Manfredi 2004; Langer 2005; Alarie and Green 2010).

The second component of interest group activity, assessing the proportion of postmaterialist interveners in contrast to their opponents, documented strong confirmation of Inglehart's thesis in two of the three areas of law. The strongest pattern emerged in the free expression cases, followed by a similar pattern in three of the four court periods in discrimination cases (the Laskin Court does not fit this pattern). However, the rise in the proportion of postmaterialist intervener activity was not shown in environmental disputes. In fact, the percentage of pro-environment interveners has successively declined in each of the four court periods studied (see the environmental data in finding 2b of Table 8.1). The reason for this reverse pattern is that the increased mobilization by environmental groups has been overwhelmed by a countermobilization by corporate interests on the one hand and First Nation representatives on the other hand. For corporations, there is a material incentive to intervene and pursue the development of natural resources for economic gain. For First Nation individuals, the intervening activity of First Nation groups is aimed at securing special access to hunting and fishing subsistence rights, which are often invoked in the name of historical treaties and long-held customs.

Our test of bivariate correlations between a justice's birth year and career postmaterialist voting record revealed a decisive relationship in only the free speech area of law (see finding 3 in Table 8.1). For instance, we found that a justice born in 1949 was 13 per cent more likely to support free speech arguments than a justice born in 1929. However, the same postmaterialist relationship was not found in either of the bivariate scatterplots for the environmental or discrimination cases. So the overall conclusion to be drawn from the simple bivariate analysis is mixed: strong support for Inglehart's thesis in free speech disputes, but no support in the two other areas of law.

When conducting a more sophisticated logistic regression analysis to assess the impacts of judge-level variables such as gender, ideology, law school teaching experience, and region on voting behaviour in relation to our main independent variable – namely, the court period indicators – a postmaterialist relationship emerged over time in the free speech cases (see finding 4 in Table 8.1). In other words, the later Lamer and McLachlin Court justices did exhibit a greater tendency to vote for postmaterialist outcomes than their colleagues from the earlier periods. The court period results proved more moderate in the environmental area, but the confirmation of a postmaterialist shift in discrimination cases did not appear, largely because we believe the value change was driven mainly by gender differences within the court.

The most rigorous test of Inglehart's thesis is illustrated in the final logistic regression models, when case characteristics are added to the judge- and court-level variables. Once the case facts were taken into consideration, the environmental cases provided the strongest confirmation that a postmaterialist shift has taken place over time (see finding 5 in Table 8.1). It is important to note that these shifts are evident, while controlling for rival explanatory variables, such as the types of litigants involved in disputes, interveners, constitutional and legal issues in play in the cases, to name a few, and they point to the importance of conducting logistic regression analysis when rival variables are included in the equation. Inglehart's intergenerational postmaterialist thesis was also confirmed in the free speech area; however, the behaviour of the McLachlin Court justices did not fit the expected pattern (see finding 5 in Table 8.1). We believe that the McLachlin Court findings are attributable to a court that was more interested in elevating postmaterialist equality concerns and principles of fairness in the political process over liberty interests in political speech cases. In contrast, the findings in the discrimination and equality cases did not fit the expected hypothesis of increasingly postmaterialist rulings over time (see finding 5 in Table 8.1). We believe that the small impact of the court-level variables in this model makes sense when realizing that the gender variable is one of the most important factors for explaining pro-equality outcomes. Taken as a whole, the full regression models document a strong confirmation of Inglehart's thesis in the environmental area, moderate confirmation in free speech disputes, and little confirmation in discrimination cases, although we believe that a gender split within the court documents a clearly postmaterialist movement in this area.

Taking a look across all the quantitative hypotheses advanced to test Inglehart's intergenerational values thesis, it seems there is a strong to moderate confirmation that a value shift has occurred in these prominent issue areas in the Supreme Court of Canada. Indeed, using 18 hypothesis tests across the three issue areas, we find strong confirmation of the thesis in eight tests and moderate confirmation in five of the tests, leaving only five situations in which there is no confirmation. Collectively, this quantitative evidence, gathered using a multi-pronged research strategy, suggests that the modern Canadian court justices are indeed moving in a postmaterialist direction in these three areas of law, although the pattern is more obvious in some areas than others.

The quantitative analysis yielded strong to moderate evidence of value change across the modern Supreme Court of Canada, but what about the qualitative findings? In the hallmark pollution cases, a definitively postmaterialist ethic appeared over time in the court, starting with its ruling in *Fowler* and *Northwest Falling* to allow government regulation of water pollution in the 1980s. By the 2000s, it had become commonplace for the court to recognize that all levels of government have authority to help control the blight of pollution. As a result, we reach the conclusion in finding 6 of Table 8.1 that the qualitative analysis of pollution cases confirms Inglehart's hypothesis of a postmaterialist shift over time. Unlike in the pollution area, the Canadian court issued a weak pro-environmental record in the five energy cases, despite the strong pro-environmental stance taken by the Lamer Court in *Oldman River*. These findings are not surprising given the extent that North Americans are dependent on energy production to fuel advances in economic and social development. Moreover, until Canadian society becomes less dependent on energy production, such rulings are likely to continue. Despite the complexity of many of the cases and the low environmental win rate across the five cases, there is still evidence in the language of these energy rulings that demonstrates that most of the justices understand and believe in the importance of recognizing environmental protection as a "fundamental value" in Canadian society. This language, along with the seminal postmaterialist ruling in *Oldman River*, lays the groundwork for further movement in the postmaterialist direction in future energy cases.

We believe that the fishing rights cases present a classic tension between materialist and postmaterialist interests. The language of the opinions throughout the period studied recognizes a hierarchy of interests that places environmental conservation foremost in the minds of the justices, followed by the interests of First Nation peoples to practise historically grounded fishing practices, and ranking the lowest hierarchical status to commercial and sport fishing. Yet the justices have struggled with the application of this hierarchy in light of the distinctive equality-based and cultural arguments advanced by indigenous groups, and some of their rulings, like *Marshall I*, have faced widespread criticism. While notable materialist, equality-oriented wins have been secured by First Nation individuals, the difficulty of establishing a factual record in support of traditional fishing practices helps ensure that postmaterialist environmental values remain prominent in the vernacular of the justices' opinions. Thus, our conclusion in Table 8.1 suggests moderate confirmation of the Inglehart thesis in the language and opinions of fishing rights cases.

Looking across the span of environmental cases that we studied, we find strong evidence of postmaterialist values in some sub-areas of environmental law, but less so in others. Indeed, one might view the value stances in the three sub-areas as though they are moving along an evolutionary course, with a prominent postmaterialist evolutionary trajectory in the pollution area, a slower trajectory in the First Nation fishing area, and the least movement in the small subset of energy cases. Yet when one supplements this textual analysis with the picture of aggregated voting patterns across all environmental disputes, a clearer image of a postmaterialist value shift becomes evident among the Canadian judicial elites. The qualitative approach has the advantage of shedding light on the language and legal rationales used by the justices in landmark cases. Yet the small sample size of this kind of analysis of high-profile cases has its drawbacks, including a tendency to foster a distorted, myopic view of what is taking place in the broader area of law. Thus, one needs to combine such analysis with a quantitative approach to collectively obtain a more holistic perspective of the overarching postmaterialist patterns that are emerging in the area of environmental law.

In the sweep of the six landmark commercial advertising cases reviewed, it seems the Canadian court has come full circle in terms of Inglehart's value change thesis. While the Laskin and Dickson Courts took a materialist stance when they upheld restrictions on commercial advertising in *Kellogg's* and *Irwin Toy*, the Lamer Court took a much more postmaterialist stance in this area in *Rocket* and *RJR-MacDonald*.

This marked postmaterialist shift in the Lamer Court was undercut in the first 10 years of the McLachlin Court, when the majority was more predisposed to the materialistic stance also evident in commercial advertising cases decided by the Laskin and Dickson Courts (see *JTI-MacDonald*). As a result, we conclude that a qualitative reading of the commercial speech cases provides moderate confirmation of the Inglehart hypothesis (see finding 6 in Table 8.1).

The political speech cases followed a unique pattern of postmaterialist value change. A materialistic law-and-order tone was set by the Laskin Court in *Dupond*, but that gave way to the Charter period, which spurred the Lamer Court to recognize and expand expressive rights in the realm of political speech. In the important area of campaign finance law, the Lamer Court struck a postmaterialist chord in *Libman*, yet the McLachlin Court subsequently moved away from this trend in *Harper*. Writing from a concern for political equality, the McLachlin Court abandoned the language of adherence to freedom for one that ensured that political speech was not dominated by the wealthy and that all individuals had equal opportunity to participate in the electoral process (*Harper*, [2004] 1 S.C.R. 827; Manfredi and Rush 2008, 104–5). Thus, the language of the McLachlin Court written reasons for judgment provide a key insight into the postmaterialist shift in the modern Supreme Court – namely, that the McLachlin Court is *not* abandoning postmaterialist tendencies in the political speech cases, but is rather substituting one postmaterialist value (equality) for another (free speech). Our reading of the landmark political speech cases leads us to conclude that there is moderate confirmation of the Inglehart postmaterialist hypothesis in the Supreme Court of Canada (see finding 6 in Table 8.1).

Despite the apparent negligent postmaterialist movement by the justices over time in the most advanced quantitative tests across all equality claims, the written reasons for judgment in the gay rights area provide some of the strongest evidence of a qualitative movement towards postmaterialist values by the modern Supreme Court justices. The arc of cases moved from the Laskin/Dickson Court's reluctance to recognize equality rights for gays in the late 1970s in *Gay Alliance* to subsequent rulings by the Lamer and McLachlin Courts that took a very different tack. Although the Lamer Court ultimately denied gay couples access to old age benefits in *Egan*, the real significance of the case is that all the justices believed that sexual orientation should be read into s. 15(1) of the Charter, thereby putting gay rights on the same level as other constitutional protections and providing the justices with a vehicle to expand protections to gay couples in the future. A full flowering of liberal gay rights rulings took root in the McLachlin Court, with the more modern court endorsing gay marriage and the extension of pension benefits to gay couples. Collectively, these cases demonstrate that the Canadian Supreme Court has indeed exhibited a decisive movement in the postmaterialist direction, at least in the area of gay rights, resulting in our conclusion of strong confirmation of the Inglehart hypothesis (see finding 6 in Table 8.1). Thus, in marked contrast to the quantitative findings across all discrimination cases, the language of the modern gay rights decisions reveals that, in this class of cases at least, the court has resoundingly endorsed postmaterialist values that promote the fundamental equality of gays in Canadian society. Granted, the gay rights cases, like the energy cases in the environmental area, amount to a small fraction of discrimination rulings, but their political clout cannot be overstated.

The trajectory of opinions in the sex discrimination area provides nice confirmation of the Inglehart thesis as well, with the Canadian court moving from a strong materialist and paternalistic tone, allowing disparate treatment of the sexes during the Laskin Court (see *Lavell* and *Bliss*), to embracing much more postmaterialist language that demands equality between the sexes under the first 10 years of the McLachlin Court tenure. Having said this, the landmark Lamer Court case of *Gould* exposed a clear divide between the male and female members of the court over gender discrimination. Despite the materialistic outcome of *Gould*, the Lamer Court set a new, progressive standard for assessing discrimination claims in the workforce that benefited women. This liberal stance continued during the first 10 years of the McLachlin Court, with two rulings endorsing labour board and human rights commission reviews of discrimination claims in *Parry Sound* and *Canadian Airlines*. Ultimately, the sex discrimination and gay rights cases present evidence that an evolutionary, postmaterialist movement of the kind Inglehart documented in the mass public has occurred among the modern judicial elites of Canada (see our conclusion regarding finding 6 in Table 8.1).

These findings stand in stark relief to the quantitative results, which showed that there has not been much movement in the postmaterialist direction across all discrimination cases, at least when controlling for other, rival explanatory variables like the gender of the justices. This points to the importance of delving into the language and rationales of the equality rulings to tease out impressive postmaterialist shifts in key sub-areas of law. It is important to realize that the arguments of the female justices stand out for their marked support for equality claims, putting them in the forefront of postmaterialist opinions. As a result, the gender variable's strength in the quantitative analysis receives overt validation when carrying out a detailed reading of the opinions. In short, the postmaterialist pioneers of equality in the Canadian Supreme Court were the female justices.

Conclusion

Our book was motivated by our interest in assessing whether there has been a rise in postmaterialist thinking evident in the rulings of Canadian Supreme Court justices over the four decades that mirrors Inglehart's documentation of changing opinions among the Canadian mass public. The triangulation of evidence from different methodologies points to some clear evidence of an increase in postmaterialist rulings, at least in the areas of environmental, free speech, and equality law. The data from the qualitative and quantitative chapters of our research identify some important overarching conclusions that scholars should take away from this work. First, it is too often the case that researchers pick one approach or the other to drive their analysis of judicial behaviour. This book takes a different tack and provides compelling evidence of the importance of using both quantitative and qualitative approaches in a single study. The beauty of quantitative analysis rests in its ability to provide an overarching synthesis of complex material, to tease out the impact of rival explanatory variables, and to numerically assess long-term trends and patterns within and across various areas of law. In other words, quantitative analysis helps us understand complex data in a relatively straightforward and holistic manner, while making sure that other factors are not explaining the results.

However, some critics have noted that one of the shortcomings of quantitative analysis is that it treats all cases equally and focuses principally on voting outcomes (see Macfarlane [2013] for this criticism). These weaknesses point to the strengths of qualitative enquiry, which allows researchers to track the doctrinal development of law over time through the language and tests featured in the opinions and to recognize that some cases are more important than others. A pivotal contribution of this book is that it provides critical evidence, from both a quantitative and a qualitative perspective, of Inglehart's theory of value change at work in the Canadian body politic and among Canadian judicial elites. Another advantage of the dual methodological approach is that it allows us to frame the justices' decisions and written work within a socio-attitudinal model of decision making; this approach provides a longer and broader framework of analysis that recognizes that the justices' decisions are derived from their social background experiences as teenagers and young adults, from prevailing attitudinal forces that shape generational thinking about issues, and from the collegial relations and norms that operate within the Supreme Court of Canada. This socially embedded, longer-term framework has been missing from too much of the literature. and it can help augment our understanding of how justices decide cases and shed light on the direction that judicial decision making is taking in key areas of law in Canada, and possibly elsewhere, in the foreseeable future.

A second important conclusion derived from the quantitative chapters is that the rise of legal mobilization, which occurred before and was accelerated after the Charter revolution, demonstrates that the justices have access to, and are responsive to, the postmaterialist claims brought forth in briefs and litigation by interest groups. In line with other earlier studies, our data demonstrate a clear increase in interest group activity across three prominent areas of law, with significant jumps in overall intervening activity between the 1970s and the 2000s. Indeed, the intervening activity in favour of postmaterialist claims jumped at least fourfold in each of the three areas of law between the 1980s and 2000s. The significance of this activity is that it helped provide the justices with the language and rationales necessary to endorse postmaterialist values at increased rates over time. This places the justices in the social orbit of groups in the mass public that are advocating for postmaterialist change, making their opinions the partial by-product of another element of the socio-attitudinal model of judicial behaviour. In short, recognition of the growing postmaterialist impact of interest groups on Supreme Court justices is simply recognizing that their opinions are the product of their own formative background experiences, their intra-court relationships and interactions, and their willingness to adopt the language and values of societal interests as they work to develop sound judgments and write good law. Thus, the importance of interest groups cannot be overstated in helping to shape the advance of postmaterialist judicial behaviour and in helping to further flesh out another side to the socio-attitudinal model of judicial decision making.

The increasing participation of postmaterialist interest groups in litigation strategies helps provide a long-running narrative of one of the mechanisms for value change within a Supreme Court. If Supreme Courts are seen as reactive institutions that can decide cases largely on the basis of appeals that are made to them, then the possibility of value change over time is partially dependent on the litigation strategies of appellants and their supporters in the interest group landscape. With increasing intervener activity taking place over the past four decades, the Canadian Supreme Court justices were subject to various postmaterialist justifications and value positions embedded in legal briefs. Thus, value change within the Supreme Court depends on two key elements: (1) social forces that advocate for value change and (2) individual justices who are predisposed to adopt the value change as a principled way of settling a legal dispute (see Alarie and Green [2010] for a similar argument). This essentially characterizes long-term value change within a court as dependent on social and attitudinal factors. As societal attitudes evolve, so will the individual attitudes of justices over time, and our quantitative and qualitative study of environmental, free speech, and equality cases clearly indicates that a value transformation of this type has indeed taken place. As the Canadian Supreme Court and other courts around the world move to centre stage in some of the most critical political conflicts of modern society, the mobilization of interest groups has come to play a key role in the deliberation process of the justices and in the decisions that reflect value change within the court.

A third overarching theme is that our findings documenting the prevalence of a postmaterialist value shift among Canadian judicial elites in key areas of law have important implications for other actors in the Canadian political system. Evidence of a postmaterialist shift within the Supreme Court in critical areas of law should (and arguably does) draw the attention of the prime minister and Parliament because this movement necessarily influences the Charter dialogue that emerges between the courts and political actors in the Canadian setting. As Manfredi and Kelly (1999) and others (see Manfredi 2001; Roach 2001; Hiebert 2002; Kelly 2005; Hogg, Bushell Thornton, and Wright 2007; Hogg 2011) have indicated, court rulings have a profound impact on the way that Parliament subsequently constructs new legislation in an effort to meet judicial mandates. Consequently, the values and language that justices articulate in their written opinions play an important role in shaping the political direction that policymakers take on key issues. To the extent that the Charter dialogue implicitly reflects a discussion about postmaterialist principles and values, the court's postmaterialist leanings necessarily shape the discussion that follows in the larger Canadian body politic.

Evidence of this type of postmaterialist dialogue can be clearly seen in the reference of constitutional questions to the Supreme Court – such as the *Reference re Same-Sex Marriage* case of 2004 (see also the lack of a dialogue response in *Vriend*). The politics of that reference might be characterized as a documentation of the power of changing postmaterialist values within society as intergenerational replacement resulted in Canadians growing increasingly comfortable with the rights of gays to equal treatment in society. Parliament's debate of the gay marriage law is a reflection of broader societal change and also a response to earlier Supreme Court rulings that had mapped out the possibilities of a gay rights legal agenda. As a result, the Charter dialogue over gay rights is one that fits the elements of a socio-attitudinal model of judicial behaviour. The dialogue on gay rights flows from multiple sources: an evolving landscape of liberalizing public opinion on gay rights, justices who are part of the intergenerational change in opinions, and a legislative body equally willing to discuss the legal contours of how these changing values would shape the practice and solemnization of gay marriage.

A fourth overarching theme from the book is that the operation of ideology within the Supreme Court of Canada matters in some critical areas of law, such as discrimination, but less so in others, such as environmental cases and free expression. In these two latter areas of law, other factors, such as case facts, interveners, regional differences, and, in the case of environmental cases, gender differences, play a critical role in influencing judicial voting patterns. These findings validate our prior research indicating that, in some areas of law, ideology plays an important role in the Canadian Supreme Court, while in other areas it does not; this suggests that, unlike the US Supreme Court context, the Canadian justices' attitudinal behaviour is more subtle, nuanced, and varied. This continues to be an important finding given the prevalence of attitudinal behaviour documented within the US Supreme Court and the belief among many US scholars that attitudinal behaviour is the major driver of judicial decision making of high courts (see Segal and Spaeth 1993, 2002).

We note that some Canadian critics have claimed that judges and scholars bristle at our attitudinal findings because they imply that judges are influenced by their ideology and are "pre-programmed" to decide cases in favour of particular types of litigants in particular types of cases (see Macfarlane 2013; McCormick 2015, 242). Moreover, one author has characterized attitudinal theory as portraying justices as visceral, unprofessional, unreflective, unprincipled, and lacking nuance in their judicial decisions (McCormick 2015, 242). This characterization fails to recognize that statistical data defy the claims of the justices themselves, to some extent, and document the importance of attitudinal behaviour, albeit more nuanced and subtle, in the decision-making process of the modern Canadian Supreme Court. It is an overreaction to reject the power of attitudinal forces that are at play in Canada, and it is an oversimplification to imply that attitudinal findings that occur in some areas of law but not others do not provide an important insight into the complexity of Canadian judicial behaviour.

Our work has consistently documented the complex array of forces that shape the justices' decisions, including their interest in writing opinions that have a strong legal grounding, forge consensus with their colleagues, pay attention to facts, and reflect their own ideological vision of the law (Ostberg and Wetstein 2007, 226–7; Songer et al. 2012, 6). Moreover, we have consistently documented that the impact of ideology is not as crystal clear or as systematic as in the US, but rather "weaves a more complex tapestry" that flows from the "different institutional structures and norms that operate in the high court" of Canada (Ostberg and Wetstein 2007, 226). In fact, ideology in the Canadian context, unlike that in the US, is prevalent in some areas of law and not others. It is notable that in an area where US scholars would expect ideology to be most prevalent in a democracy – namely, free expression – it has no impact on Canadian justices. This is an intriguing finding, worthy of further scrutiny. Yet ultimately, it is clear that attitudinal behaviour does play an important role in the Canadian context, although it is tempered by the distinctive cultural norms that guide the justices to a higher degree of unanimity and consensus within a collegial court, a propensity that is especially pronounced during the McLachlin years.

A fifth overarching theme of the book emanates from the postmaterialist approach that the Canadian justices have taken towards free expression cases and, to some extent, the environmental cases; this is illustrative of a long-running, cultural divide between the United States and Canada that has been recognized by scholars for decades (see Innis 1956; Hartz 1964; Porter 1965; Kornberg 1988; Lipset 1990). Our reading of the landmark political speech and First Nation fishing cases documents a court that is far more attentive to promoting postmaterialist equality concerns than promoting unfettered libertarian notions of free speech or protecting the environment against individual claims. US scholars would be surprised to find that ideology does not play a critical role in the quantitative analysis of free expression disputes, yet there is a degree of ideological consistency evident across the pro-equality rulings of the discrimination, political speech, and First Nation cases. The findings across these disparate areas of law provide consistent exemplars of a court that is far more interested in promoting postmaterialist values of equality over freedom and is indicative of a culture that has a heightened sensitivity for the creation of a polity that promotes the common good for all. This stands in stark contrast to the justices on the US Supreme Court and US culture generally, where the Lockean principles of liberty of individuals and limited government hold more sway (Lipset 1990, 8; Ostberg 1995, 11). The best example of the contrasting approaches of the two courts towards equality and liberty is illustrated in the area of campaign finance laws. Canada's court majority strongly endorsed campaign finance restrictions in *Harper* to enable all voices to be heard in the political realm, while the US court majority in *Citizens United* heralded the free speech rights of all at the expense of equality.[1] These disparate treatments of some free speech and environmental claims reflect an embedded cultural divide that remains salient in the high court rulings of these two cultures.

A sixth theme emerging from this book is the prominence of female justices leading the postmaterialist charge in the discrimination area and, to some extent, in the First Nation fishing rights cases. Their leadership points to the importance of elevating female justices to high courts because they bring a different voice to the value discussions that take place. Put simply, their background experiences, more often than not, make them more sensitive and sympathetic than their male colleagues to the pro-equality arguments brought forth by those who have faced discrimination or have experienced marginalized treatment within society. From the perspective of postmaterialist theory, female justices may have a greater tendency across cultures to elevate equality principles above freedom and liberty interests than their male counterparts. Given that women constitute over half the population in Canada and elsewhere, it is important that their voices be heard and reflected in the rulings of all high courts.

1 See Manfredi and Rush (2007) for a counterargument suggesting that there has been some convergence in thinking in campaign finance cases among some members of the two courts, most notably Chief Justice McLachlin and Justice Stephen Breyer.

One important question that emerges from our study is whether the postmaterialist transformation reflects majoritarian or anti-majoritarian principles. In other words, is this postmaterialist shift by the Canadian justices democratic in nature? On the one hand, the postmaterialist transformation may provide comfort to those who believe that the court should reflect the values of litigants and parties who have been shut out of mainstream politics and the legislative process. Seen in this light, the court's rulings that favour postmaterialist litigants flow from the mobilization of groups in Canadian society and recognize that many of the value positions taken by these groups reflect popular will. As a result, our findings that show a movement by the court in important postmaterialistic directions indicate that the justices are in step with important value changes taking place in the larger political landscape. This implies that the court's movement is indeed reflective of a majoritarian, democratic institution that responds to popular will.

On the other hand, such a finding is not without its critics. Some might argue that Supreme Court rulings that respond to mobilization efforts are anti-democratic and anti-majoritarian (see Morton and Knopff 2000). Advocates of this view would argue that since those litigants and parties have not won recognition for their policy stances in the halls of Parliament and provincial legislatures, they should not try to mitigate their losses in the judicial arena because doing so runs contrary to democratic principles. To the extent that this process has garnered fruitful results for some postmaterialist litigants, critics might argue that such efforts have essentially elevated the court to a policy-making position it was not meant to occupy; this is an argument that has been advanced in prior research (see Manfredi 1993, 2001; Morton and Knopff 2000). Regardless of which side of this normative debate you are on, there is no doubting that the Canadian court has moved in a postmaterialist direction in recent decades in key areas of law and that this movement has had a profound impact on Canadian society as a whole. Thus, court watchers, journalists, academics, and politicians alike should take heed and devote considerable attention to this value transformation in the years to come.

While the Supreme Court of Canada's movement in a postmaterialist direction invites the criticism that its decisions are anti-democratic, readers should recognize that the increasingly political profile of the court and its decisions is part of a wider pattern of the "judicialization of politics" across the globe (Tate and Vallinder 1995). The court's active taking of sides in materialist-postmaterialist disputes no doubt places it in the political fray. Moreover, these controversial policy decisions will necessarily trigger overt political tensions with Parliament, academics, and prominent media critics. In these instances, the court might invite Charter dialogue of a different kind, one that results in overt disagreement over fundamental principles of law, such as, how much equality should exist in a free and democratic society? The court's decisions on campaign finance laws in the 1990s and early 2000s are emblematic of the ways in which political issues become "judicialized" along postmaterialist value positions. Boiled down to their distinctive value conflicts, the *Libman* and *Harper* cases turn on the question of endorsing freedom of expression (through the vehicle of unrestricted spending during political campaigns) versus the position of endorsing more equitable participation in the democratic process. For some commentators, these are political questions best left to the rough-and-tumble of the political arena and the elected branches of government; they are not in the traditional purview of the judicial branch. Even so, the key actors involved in the disputes think differently, and they have no qualms about turning to the courts to resolve such disputes. In the end, the judicialization of political questions has garnered the participation of parties from all sides: citizens, corporations, interest groups, minorities, and even politicians themselves.

Another important question that arises from our study is whether the postmaterialist transformation in key areas of law, along with the increased judicialization of politics in Canada, will have an impact on the process of appointing Supreme Court justices in the Canadian setting. As the court has moved to centre stage in some of the critical disputes of the day, will the prime minister, who has virtually complete control over the selection process (with some important regional, linguistic, and statutory restrictions), start paying more attention to the values and background characteristics of those elevated to the high court? Recent appointment processes provide some preliminary answers to this question. As Hausegger, Hennigar, and Riddell (2009; see also Ziegel 2001; Alarie and Green 2008, 2009b) have pointed out, critics of the court's politicization have called for greater transparency and public accountability during the process of selecting new Supreme Court justices. The need for transparency is rooted in the fear that partisan motivations might lead prime ministers to appoint justices with similar ideological preferences. Alarie and Green suggest that the fear may be misguided since political parties in Canada are not that far apart on the ideological spectrum and prime ministers are not infallible when it comes to assessing the potential leanings of Supreme Court nominees (Alarie and Green 2009b, 44–5).

Since the adoption of the Charter, there has been movement towards transparent committee oversight, and in 2006, former prime minister Stephen Harper established a televised public hearing process, which required that, as part of earning the job, Supreme Court appointees meet with an ad hoc committee of members of Parliament selected from each of the parties (MacLeod 2014). Although some, such as Chief Justice McLachlin, were concerned that an American style of political rancour might emerge in this setting, in true Canadian style Justice Marshall Rothstein, who was the first to undergo this scrutiny, experienced a relatively benign, brief three-hour exchange in which a variety of questions were off limits (MacLeod 2014; see also Hausegger, Hennigar, and Riddell 2009, 141–3, 169–70). Even with this added public process, the prime minister still retained final selection power. However, this new public oversight process was short lived because it was not repeated during the subsequent appointment of Thomas Cromwell in 2008, with Stephen Harper expressing concerns about ensuring a "full staff" on the bench and an impending political election (Tibbetts 2008).

While the two appointees in 2011 went through the supposedly transparent hearing process, the process later suffered a political body blow with the failed appointment of Marc Nadon to the Supreme Court in the fall of 2013 and the "caretaker" appointment of Russell Brown by former prime minister Harper in 2015 (Cheadle 2013; Fine 2013; Fisher and Fekete 2014; MacLeod 2014; Plaxton 2016). Stephen Harper's selection of Marc Nadon made it through the obligatory ad hoc parliamentary committee review, only to be derailed by a claim that the Federal Court nominee was not qualified to serve as a Quebec appointee to the high court because he had not been a member of the Quebec Bar for 10 years and had not served on the Quebec courts. The appointment suffered a fatal blow when the Supreme Court rejected his nomination through the vehicle of a constitutional reference case (*Reference re Supreme Court Act, ss. 5 and 6*, [2014] 1 S.C.R. 433). The fact that Marc Nadon made it through the superficial questioning of the ad hoc committee within the so-called transparent, open nomination process, without hiccup begs the question of how transparent this process could actually be, and it reflects a weakness in the Canadian approach given that the ad hoc committee has no real power to reject a prime minister's nomination. The appointment of justices has once again become shrouded in mystery, although one could convincingly argue that the ad hoc committee, once established, was only for show, with the appointment of Canadian justices still subject to the whims and reasoning of one powerful politician in a democratic system. Stephen Harper's appointment of Russell Brown in 2015 validates this continuing political power, and his decision to replace Justice Rothstein one week before Parliament was dissolved was criticized by some as an overt political act that could have been avoided (see Plaxton 2016).

While many factors can impact an appointment decision, such as a desire to ensure legal expertise, collegiality, linguistic and regional balance, and gender concerns, and they have dominated many modern appointments, factors such as the political leanings and attitudinal predispositions of a nominee could take on more prominence going forward. The attempt by former prime minister Harper to put a legally unqualified nominee on the Supreme Court and the questionable elevation of a relative rookie with political ties from the Ontario Court of Appeal, while numerous more seasoned and well-qualified justices were serving on the same bench, reflects the fact that the potential political leanings of a nominee are still very relevant to modern prime ministers (*Globe and Mail* 2013). Subsequent criticism of the political nature of the Brown appointment further heightens this concern. Seen in this light, our research suggests that court watchers should pay more attention to the background and formative political years of new nominees to gain an understanding of the attitudes and values they will bring to the cases they hear as a justice on the bench. Such a conclusion makes sense when Canadian Supreme Court appointments remain solely in the hands of the prime minister.

Having recognized that a postmaterialist shift is evident in key areas of law, it is not a foregone conclusion that such a shift is inevitable in all areas of law or even permanent in the key areas of law where they have been documented. Indeed, Inglehart's intergenerational value change thesis recognizes that if the economic conditions and personal well-being of members of society deteriorate, concern for postmaterialist priorities may well give way to a resurgence of the materialistic concerns of basic survival and security needs (Inglehart and Welzel 2005, 46). This implies that societies that face a long-term economic downturn or the threat of war will likely see a resurgence in materialist value priorities, which will emphasize materialist concerns such as putting food on the table, the availability of jobs, concern over wages and prices, and national defence rather than emphasizing quality-of-life issues such as environmental protection and free speech and equality concerns. The terrorist attacks of the early 2000s in the United States, Spain, and the United Kingdom, and even more recently in Canada, France, Belgium, and Turkey, coupled with a significant economic recession in the late 2000s suggest that a generation of Canadians (and others) may come of age politically during a very different period than their generational predecessors. Thus, it is likely that conflicts between materialist and postmaterialist values will remain at the forefront of the political and legal agendas for the foreseeable future. and only time will tell whether the movement in the postmaterialist direction documented here will continue into the future.

Having said this, we believe that the Canadian court will continue to address timely, high-profile rights claims and that even with the Charter maturation, the court will remain at centre stage in the advancement of a postmaterialist political mindset in Canada. Recent decisions in the area of prostitution rights, union rights, the right to die, and First Nation land claims reflect a Supreme Court that is attentive to the ongoing push for postmaterialist notions of liberty and equality, and they suggest that claims that the Charter revolution has run its course are premature.[2] In the end, our application of Inglehart's theory in the 1973–2010 time frame sets a path for other scholars to follow, both inside and outside the Canadian setting, to see the degree to which a postmaterialist transformation is taking place in other high courts around the world.

2 Several prominent rulings in recent years have reflected a continuing postmaterialist trend. In *Canada (Attorney General) v. Bedford*, [2013] 3 S.C.R. 1101, the court overturned "bawdy house" provisions of the Criminal Code that infringed on the s. 7 rights of prostitutes to freely engage in their trade safely and securely. In *Carter v. Canada (Attorney General)*, [2015] 1 S.C.R. 331, the court struck down a law prohibiting physician-assisted suicide, forcing Parliament and the provinces to craft new laws guaranteeing this freedom. In several recent labour union decisions, the court upheld the rights of unions to organize and to strike (*Mounted Police Association of Ontario v. Canada*, [2015] 1 S.C.R. 3; *Meredith v. Canada*, [2015] 1 S.C.R. 125; and *Saskatchewan Federation of Labour v. Saskatchewan*, [2015] 1 S.C.R. 225). Finally, in *Tsilhqot'in Nation v. British Columbia*, [2014] 2 S.C.R. 256, the court extended land title rights to a British Columbia First Nation – a ruling that had the effect of revolutionizing the ability of First Nations to limit economic development on the part of governments and corporations.

List of Cases Cited

114957 Canada Ltée. v. Hudson, [2001] 2 S.C.R. 241
Abrams v. United States, 250 U.S. 616 (1919)
Andrews v. Law Society of British Columbia, [1989] 1 S.C.R. 143
Attorney General of Canada v. Lavell, [1974] S.C.R. 1349
Attorney General (Canada) and Dupond v. Montreal, [1978] 2 S.C.R. 770
Attorney General (Que.) v. Kellogg's Co. of Canada et al., [1978] 2 S.C.R. 211
Auton v. British Columbia, [2004] 3 S.C.R. 657
Baier v. Alberta, [2007] 2 S.C.R. 673
Beckman v. Little Salmon/Carmacks First Nation, [2010] 3 S.C.R. 103
Bedard v. Dawson, [1923] S.C.R. 681
Bliss v. Attorney General of Canada, [1979] 1 S.C.R. 183
Boucher v. The King, [1951] S.C.R. 265
British Columbia (Public Service Employee Relations Commission) v. BCGSEU, [1999] 3 S.C.R. 3
Brooks v. Canada Safeway Ltd., [1989] 1 S.C.R. 1219
Brown v. Board of Education, 347 U.S. 483 (1954)
Brown v. Board of Education II, 349 U.S. 294 (1955)
Canada (Attorney General) v. Bedford, [2013] 3 S.C.R. 1101
Canada v. Hislop, [2007] 1 S.C.R. 429
Canada v. JTI-MacDonald Corp., [2007] 2 S.C.R. 610
Canada (Human Rights Commission) v. Canadian Airlines International Ltd., [2006] 1 S.C.R. 3
Carter v. Canada (Attorney General), [2015] 1 S.C.R. 331
Committee for the Commonwealth of Canada v. Canada, [1991] 1 S.C.R. 139
Daniels v. White and The Queen, [1968] S.C.R. 517
Devine v. Quebec, [1988] 2 S.C.R. 790
Dunmore v. Ontario (Attorney General), [2001] 3 S.C.R. 1016

Egan v. Canada, [1995] 2 S.C.R. 513
Elk v. The Queen, [1980] 2 S.C.R. 166
Ford v. Quebec, [1988] 2 S.C.R. 748
Fowler v. The Queen, [1980] 2 S.C.R. 213
Fraser v. Public Service Staff Relations Board, [1985] 2 S.C.R. 455
Friends of Oldman River Society v. Canada (Minister of Transport), [1992] 1 S.C.R. 3
Gay Alliance Toward Equality v. Vancouver Sun, [1979] 2 S.C.R. 435
Gould v. Yukon Order of Pioneers, [1996] 1 S.C.R. 571
Haida Nation v. British Columbia (Minister of Forests), [2004] 3 S.C.R. 511
Harper v. Canada (Attorney General), [2004] 1 S.C.R. 827
Imperial Oil Ltd. v. Quebec (Minister of the Environment), [2003] 2 S.C.R. 624
Interprovincial Cooperatives Ltd. v. The Queen, [1976] 1 S.C.R. 477
Irwin Toy v. Quebec, [1989] 1 S.C.R. 927
Jack et al. v. The Queen, [1980] 1 S.C.R. 294
Janzen v. Platy Enterprises Ltd., [1989] 1 S.C.R. 1252
Law v. Canada (Minister of Employment and Immigration), [1999] 1 S.C.R. 497
Libman v. Quebec (Attorney General), [1997] 3 S.C.R. 569
M. v. H., [1999] 2 S.C.R. 3
Meredith v. Canada, [2015] 1 S.C.R. 125
Mikisew Cree First Nation v. Canada (Minister of Canadian Heritage), [2005] 3 S.C.R. 388
Miron v. Trudel, [1995] 2 S.C.R. 418
Montreal (City) v. 2952-1366 Quebec Inc., [2005] 3 S.C.R. 141
Mounted Police Association of Ontario v. Canada, [2015] 1 S.C.R. 3
Northwest Falling Contractors Ltd. v. The Queen, [1980] 2 S.C.R. 292
Ontario v. Canadian Pacific Ltd., [1995] 2 S.C.R. 1031
OPSEU v. Ontario (Attorney General), [1987] 2 S.C.R. 2
Osborne v. Canada, [1991] 2 S.C.R. 69
Parry Sound (District) Social Services Administration Board v. O.P.S.E.U. Local 324, [2003] 2 S.C.R. 157
Quebec (Attorney General) v. Canada (National Energy Board), [1994] 1 S.C.R. 159
R. v. Big M Drug Mart, [1985] 1 S.C.R. 295
R. v. Butler, [1992] 1 S.C.R. 452
R. v. Crown Zellerbach Canada Ltd., [1988] 1 S.C.R. 401
R. v. Gladstone, [1996] 2 S.C.R. 723
R. v. Hydro-Québec, [1997] 3 S.C.R. 213
R. v. Kapp, [2008] 2 S.C.R. 483
R. v. Keegstra, [1990] 3 S.C.R. 697
R. v. Marshall, [1999] 3 S.C.R. 456 (*Marshall I*)
R. v. Marshall, [1999] 3 S.C.R. 533 (*Marshall II*)

R. v. Marshall, [2005] 2 S.C.R. 221 (*Marshall III*)
R. v. Nova Scotia Pharmaceutical Society, [1992] 2 S.C.R. 606
R. v. N.T.C. Smokehouse Ltd., [1996] 2 S.C.R. 672
R. v. Oakes, [1986] 1 S.C.R. 103
R. v. Sparrow, [1990] 1 S.C.R. 1075
R. v. Turpin, [1989] 1 S.C.R. 1296
Reference re Alberta Statutes, [1938] S.C.R. 100
Reference re Newfoundland's Continental Shelf, [1984] 1 S.C.R. 86
Reference re Same-Sex Marriage, [2004] 3 S.C.R. 698
Reference re Supreme Court Act, ss. 5 and 6, [2014] 1 S.C.R. 433
Rio Hotel Ltd. v. New Brunswick (Liquor Licensing Board), [1987] 2 S.C.R. 59
Rio Tinto Alcan Inc. v. Carrier Sekani Tribal Council, [2010] 2 S.C.R. 650
RJR-MacDonald Inc. v. Canada, [1995] 3 S.C.R. 199
Rocket v. Royal College of Dental Surgeons of Ontario, [1990] 2 S.C.R. 232
RWDSU v. Dolphin Delivery, [1986] 2 S.C.R. 573
Saskatchewan Federation of Labour v. Saskatchewan, [2015] 1 S.C.R. 225
Slaight Communications Inc. v. Davidson, [1989] 1 S.C.R. 1038
Switzman v. Elbling, [1957] S.C.R. 285
The Queen v. Drybones, [1970] S.C.R. 282
Tsilhqot'in Nation v. British Columbia, [2014] 2 S.C.R. 256
Van Der Peet v. The Queen, [1996] 2 S.C.R. 507
Vriend v. Alberta (Attorney General), [1998] 1 S.C.R. 493
Westendorp v. R., [1983] 1 S.C.R. 43

Appendix of Cases

Cases Analysed in the Environmental Quantitative Chapter (*N* = 74)

114957 Canada Ltée. v. Hudson, [2001] 2 S.C.R. 241
Beckman v. Little Salmon/Carmacks First Nation, [2010] 3 S.C.R. 103
Berendsen v. Ontario, [2001] 2 S.C.R. 849
British Columbia v. Canadian Forest Products Ltd., [2004] 2 S.C.R. 74
British Columbia (Minister of Forests) v. Okanagan Indian Band, [2003] 3 S.C.R. 371
CanadianOxy Chemicals Ltd. v. Canada (Attorney General), [1999] 1 S.C.R. 743
Comeau's Sea Foods Ltd. v. Canada, [1997] 1 S.C.R. 12
Dick v. The Queen, [1985] 2 S.C.R. 309
Elk v. The Queen, [1980] 2 S.C.R. 166
Enterprise Sibeca Inc. v. Frelighsburg (Municipality), [2004] 3 S.C.R. 304
Fowler v. The Queen, [1980] 2 S.C.R. 213
Frank v. The Queen, [1978] 1 S.C.R. 95
Friends of the Oldman River Society v. Canada (Minister of Transport), [1992] 1 S.C.R. 3
Gauthier v. Quebec (CPTA), [1989] 1 S.C.R. 859
Haida Nation v. British Columbia (Minister of Forests), [2004] 3 S.C.R. 511
Hollick v. Toronto (City), [2001] 3 S.C.R. 158
Imperial Oil Ltd. v. Quebec (Minister of Environment), [2003] 2 S.C.R. 625
Interprovincial Co-ops. v. The Queen, [1976] 1 S.C.R. 477
Jack and Charlie v. The Queen, [1985] 2 S.C.R. 332
Jack et al. v. The Queen, [1980] 1 S.C.R. 294
Kitkatla Band v. British Columbia (Minister of Small Business, Tourism and Culture), [2002] 2 S.C.R. 147
Kruger et al. v. The Queen, [1978] 1 S.C.R. 104

Lebel v. Winzen Land Corp., [1989] 1 S.C.R. 918
LeBlanc v. Curbera, [1983] 2 S.C.R. 28
Leiriao v. Val-Belair (Town), [1991] 3 S.C.R. 349
Manitoba Fisheries Ltd. v. The Queen, [1979] 1 S.C.R. 101
Mikisew Cree First Nation v. Canada, [2005] 3 S.C.R. 388
MiningWatch Canada v. Canada (Fisheries and Oceans), [2010] 1 S.C.R. 6
Moosehunter v. The Queen, [1981] 1 S.C.R. 282
Myran v. The Queen, [1976] 2 S.C.R. 137
Nanaimo (City) v. Rascal Trucking Ltd., [2000] 1 S.C.R. 342
Northwest Falling Contractors Ltd. v. The Queen, [1980] 2 S.C.R. 292
Oakwood Development v. St. Francoise Xavier, [1985] 2 S.C.R. 164
Ontario v. Canadian Pacific Ltd., [1995] 2 S.C.R. 1031
Paul v. British Columbia (Forest Appeals Commission), [2003] 2 S.C.R. 585
Peralta v. Ontario, [1988] 2 S.C.R. 1045
Quebec (Attorney General) v. Canada (National Energy Board), [1994] 1 S.C.R. 159
Quebec (Attorney General) v. Moses, [2010] 1 S.C.R. 557
The Queen v. Mousseau, [1980] 2 S.C.R. 89
The Queen v. Sault Ste. Marie, [1978] 2 S.C.R. 1299
The Queen v. Sutherland et al., [1980] 2 S.C.R. 451
R. v. Adams, [1996] 3 S.C.R. 101
R. v. Badger, [1996] 1 S.C.R. 771
R. v. Blais, [2003] 2 S.C.R. 236
R. v. Consolidated Maybrun Mines, Ltd., [1998] 1 S.C.R. 706
R. v. Côté, [1996] 3 S.C.R. 139
R. v. Crown Zellerbach Canada Ltd., [1988] 1 S.C.R. 401
R. v. Fitzpatrick, [1995] 4 S.C.R. 154
R. v. Gladstone, [1996] 2 S.C.R. 723
R. v. Horse, [1988] 1 S.C.R. 187
R. v. Horseman, [1990] 1 S.C.R. 901
R. v. Howard, [1994] 2 S.C.R. 299
R. v. Hydro-Québec, [1997] 3 S.C.R. 213
R. v. Kapp, [2008] 2 S.C.R. 483
R. v. Lewis, [1996] 1 S.C.R. 921
R. v. Marshall, [1999] 3 S.C.R. 456 (*Marshall I*)
R. v. Marshall; R. v. Bernard, [2005] 2 S.C.R. 220 (*Marshall III*)
R. v. Morris, [2006] 2 S.C.R. 915
R. v. Nikal, [1996] 1 S.C.R. 1013
R. v. N.T.C. Smokehouse Ltd., [1996] 2 S.C.R. 672
R. v. Powley, [2003] 2 S.C.R. 207
R. v. Sappier, [2006] 2 S.C.R. 686

R. v. Sioui, [1990] 1 S.C.R. 1025
R. v. Sparrow, [1990] 1 S.C.R. 1075
R. v. Sundown, [1999] 1 S.C.R. 393
R. v. Van der Peet, [1996] 2 S.C.R. 507
Reference re Newfoundland Continental Shelf, [1984] 1 S.C.R. 86
Rio Tinto Alcan Inc. v. Carrier Sekani Tribal Council, [2010] 2 S.C.R. 650
Sierra Club v. Canada (Minister of Finance), [2002] 2 S.C.R. 522
Simon v. The Queen, [1985] 2 S.C.R. 387
Taku River Tlingit First Nation v. British Columbia (Project Assessment Director), [2004] 3 S.C.R. 550
Veilleux v. Quebec (CPTA), [1989] 1 S.C.R. 839
Venne v. Quebec (CPTA), [1989] 1 S.C.R. 880
Ward v. Canada (Attorney General), [2002] 1 S.C.R. 569

Cases Analysed in the Free Expression Quantitative Chapter ($N = 85$)

Ahani v. Canada (Minister of Citizenship and Immigration), [2002] 1 S.C.R. 72
Allsco Building Products Ltd. v. UFCW Local 1288P, [1999] 2 S.C.R. 1136
Attorney General (Canada) v. Law Society of B.C., [1982] 2 S.C.R. 307
Attorney General (Canada) and Dupond v. Montreal, [1978] 2 S.C.R. 770
Attorney General (Que.) v. Kellogg's Co. of Canada et al., [1978] 2 S.C.R. 211
Baier v. Alberta, [2007] 2 S.C.R. 673
BCGEU v. British Columbia (Attorney General), [1988] 2 S.C.R. 214
Botiuk v. Toronto Free Press, [1995] 3 S.C.R. 3
Canada v. JTI-MacDonald Corp., [2007] 2 S.C.R. 610
Canada (Human Rights Commission) v. Canadian Liberty Net, [1998] 1 S.C.R. 626
Canada (Human Rights Commission) v. Taylor, [1990] 3 S.C.R. 892
Canadian Newspapers Company v. Canada (Attorney General), [1988] 2 S.C.R. 122
Capital Cities Inc. v. Canadian Radio and TV Commission, [1978] 2 S.C.R. 141
CBC v. Lessard, [1991] 3 S.C.R. 421
CBC v. New Brunswick (Attorney General), [1991] 3 S.C.R. 459
CBC v. New Brunswick (Attorney General), [1996] 3 S.C.R. 480
CBC et al. v. The Queen, [1983] 1 S.C.R. 339
Cherneskey v. Armadale Publishing, [1979] 1 S.C.R. 1067
City of Prince George v. Payne, [1978] 1 S.C.R. 458
Committee for the Commonwealth of Canada v. Canada, [1991] 1 S.C.R. 139
CRTC v. CTV Network et al., [1982] 1 S.C.R. 530
Dagenais v. CBC, [1994] 3 S.C.R. 835
Davies and Davies Ltd. v. Kott, [1979] 2 S.C.R. 686
Dechow v. The Queen, [1978] 1 S.C.R. 951

Deslisle v. Canada (Attorney General), [1999] 2 S.C.R. 989
Dunmore v. Ontario (Attorney General), [2001] 3 S.C.R. 1016
Edmonton Journal v. Alberta (Attorney General), [1989] 2 S.C.R. 1326
Ford v. Quebec (Attorney General), [1988] 2 S.C.R. 712
Germain v. The Queen, [1985] 2 S.C.R. 241
G.V.T.A. v. Canadian Federation of Students – British Columbia Component, [2009] 2 S.C.R. 295
Harper v. Canada (Attorney General), [2004] 1 S.C.R. 827
Hawkshaw v. The Queen, [1986] 1 S.C.R. 668
Health Services and Support – Facilities Subsector Bargaining Association v. British Columbia, [2007] 2 S.C.R. 391
Hill v. Church of Scientology, [1995] 2 S.C.R. 1130
Irwin Toy v. Quebec, [1989] 1 S.C.R. 927
Johnson v. The Queen, [1975] 2 S.C.R. 160
Lavigne v. Ontario Public Service Employees Union, [1991] 2 S.C.R. 211
Libman v. Quebec (Attorney General), [1997] 3 S.C.R. 569
Little Sisters Book and Art Emporium v. Canada (Minister of Justice), [2000] 2 S.C.R. 1120
McLoughlin v. Kutasy, [1979] 2 S.C.R. 311
Montreal v. 2952-1366 Quebec Inc., [2005] 3 S.C.R. 141
Moysa v. Alberta (Labour Relations Board), [1989 1 S.C.R. 1572
Native Women's Association of Canada v. Canada, [1994] 3 S.C.R. 627
Newfoundland (Attorney General) v. N.A.P.E., [1988] 2 S.C.R. 204
Nova Scotia Board of Censors v. M., [1978] 2 S.C.R. 662
OPSEU v. Ontario (Attorney General), [1987] 2 S.C.R. 2
Osborne v. Canada (Treasury Board), [1991] 2 S.C.R. 69
P. (D.) v. S. (C.), [1993] 4 S.C.R. 141
PIPSC v. Northwest Territories (Commissioner), [1990] 2 S.C.R. 367
Provincial News Company v. The Queen, [1976] 1 S.C.R. 89
Public Service Alliance of Canada v. Canada, [1987] 1 S.C.R. 424
The Queen v. Skinner, [1990] 1 S.C.R. 1235
The Queen v. Stagnitta, [1990] 1 S.C.R. 1226
The Queen v. Video World Ltd., [1987] 1 S.C.R. 1255
R. v. Advance Cutting and Coring Ltd., [2001] 3 S.C.R. 209
R. v. Andrews, [1990] 3 S.C.R. 870
R. v. Bryan, [2007] 1 S.C.R. 527
R. v. Butler, [1992] 1 S.C.R. 452
R. v. Guignard, [2002] 1 S.C.R. 472
R. v. Jorgensen, [1995] 4 S.C.R. 55
R. v. Keegstra, [1990] 3 S.C.R. 697

R. v. Krymowski, [2005] 1 S.C.R. 101
R. v. Lucas, [1998] 1 S.C.R. 439
R. v. Mara, [1997] 2 S.C.R. 630
R. v. Sharpe, [2001] 1 S.C.R. 45
R. v. S. (T.), [1994] 3 S.C.R. 952
R. v. Zundel, [1992] 2 S.C.R. 731
Ramsden v. Peterborough, [1993] 2 S.C.R. 1084
Reference re Public Service Employee Relations Act (Alta.), [1987] 1 S.C.R. 313
Reference re ss. 193 and 195.1(1)(c) of the Criminal Code (Man.), [1990] 1 S.C.R. 1123
RJR-MacDonald Inc. v. Canada, [1995] 3 S.C.R. 199
Rocket v. Royal College of Dental Surgeons of Ontario, [1990] 2 S.C.R. 232
Ross v. New Brunswick School District, [1996] 1 S.C.R. 825
Ruby v. Canada, [2002] 4 S.C.R. 3
RWDSU Local 558 v. Pepsi-Cola Canada Beverages (West) Ltd., [2002] 1 S.C.R. 156
RWDSU Local 580 v. Dolphin Delivery Ltd., [1986] 2 S.C.R. 573
RWDSU v. Saskatchewan, [1987] 1 S.C.R. 460
Saint-Romuald (City) v. Olivier, [2001] 2 S.C.R. 898
Siemens v. Manitoba (Attorney General), [2003] 1 S.C.R. 6
Slaight Communications Inc. v. Davidson, [1989] 1 S.C.R. 1038
Suresh v. Canada (Minister of Citizenship and Immigration), [2002] 1 S.C.R. 3
Thomson Newspapers Co. v. Canada (Attorney General), [1998] 1 S.C.R. 877
Towne Cinema Theatres Ltd. v. The Queen, [1985] 1 S.C.R. 494
UFCW Local 1518 v. K-Mart Canada Ltd., [1999] 2 S.C.R. 1083
Vickery v. Nova Scotia Supreme Court, [1991] 1 S.C.R. 671
Young v. Young, [1993] 4 S.C.R. 3

Cases Analysed in the Discrimination Quantitative Chapter (*N* = *106*)

A. C. v. Manitoba (Director of Child and Family Services), [2009] 2 S.C.R. 181
Adler v. Ontario, [1996] 3 S.C.R. 609
Alberta v. Hutterian Brethren of Wilson Colony, [2009] 2 S.C.R. 567
Andrews v. Law Society of British Columbia, [1989] 1 S.C.R. 143
Athabasca Tribal Council v. Amoco Canada Petroleum Co. Ltd. et al., [1981] 1 S.C.R. 699
Attorney General of Canada v. Lavell, [1974] S.C.R. 1349
Auton v. British Columbia (Attorney General), [2004] 3 S.C.R. 657
B. v. Ontario (Human Rights Commission), [2002] 3 S.C.R. 403
Baier v. Alberta, [2007] 2 S.C.R. 673
Battlefords and District Co-operative Ltd. v. Gibbs, [1996] 3 S.C.R. 566
Béliveau St-Jacques v. Fédération des employées et employés de services publics inc., [1996] 2 S.C.R. 345

Benner v. Canada (Secretary of State), [1997] 1 S.C.R. 358
Bhinder v. Canadian National Railway Co., [1985] 2 S.C.R. 561
Bliss v. Attorney General of Canada, [1979] 1 S.C.R. 183
British Columbia (Public Service Employee Relations Commission) v. BCGSEU, [1999] 3 S.C.R. 3
British Columbia (Superintendent of Motor Vehicles) v. British Columbia (Council of Human Rights), [1999] 3 S.C.R. 868
Brooks v. Canada Safeway Ltd., [1989] 1 S.C.R. 1219
Brossard v. Quebec (Human Rights Commission), [1988] 2 S.C.R. 279
Caldwell et al. v. Stuart et al., [1984] 2 S.C.R. 603
Canada v. Hislop, [2007] 1 S.C.R. 429
Canada (Attorney General) v. Mossop, [1993] 1 S.C.R. 554
Canada (House of Commons) v. Vaid, [2005] 1 S.C.R. 667
Canada (Human Rights Commission) v. Canadian Airlines International Ltd., [2006] 1 S.C.R. 3
Canadian Foundation for Children, Youth and the Law v. Canada (Attorney General), [2004] 1 S.C.R. 76
Central Okanagan School District No. 23 v. Renaud, [1992] 2 S.C.R. 970
CN Railway v. Canadian Human Rights Commission, [1987] 1 S.C.R. 1114
Commission Scolaire Régionale de Chambly v. Bergevin, [1994] 2 S.C.R. 525
Cooper v. Canada (Human Rights Commission), [1996] 3 S.C.R. 854
Corbierre v. Canada (Minister of Indian and Northern Affairs), [1999] 2 S.C.R. 203
Council of Canadians with Disabilities v. VIA Rail Canada Inc., [2007] 1 S.C.R. 650
Deslisle v. Canada (Attorney General), [1999] 2 S.C.R. 989
Dick et al. v. Deputy Attorney General of Canada, [1980] 2 S.C.R. 243
Dickason v. University of Alberta, [1992] 2 S.C.R. 1103
Douglas/Kwantlen Faculty Association v. Douglas College, [1990] 3 S.C.R. 570
Eaton v. Brant County Board of Education, [1997] 1 S.C.R. 241
Egan v. Canada, [1995] 2 S.C.R. 513
Eldridge v. British Columbia (Attorney General), [1997] 3 S.C.R. 624
Employment and Immigration Commission v. Dallialian, [1980] 2 S.C.R. 582
Eve by Her Guardian v. Mrs. E., [1986] 2 S.C.R. 388
Gay Alliance Toward Equality v. Vancouver Sun, [1979] 2 S.C.R. 435
Gosselin v. Québec (Attorney General), [2002] 4 S.C.R. 429
Gould v. Yukon Order of Pioneers, [1996] 1 S.C.R. 571
Granovsky v. Canada (Minister of Employment and Immigration), [2000] 1 S.C.R. 703
Harrison v. University of British Columbia, [1990] 3 S.C.R. 451
Health Services and Support – Facilities Subsector Bargaining Association v. British Columbia, [2007] 2 S.C.R. 391
Hodge v. Canada, [2004] 3 S.C.R. 357

Insurance Corp. of British Columbia v. Heerspink, [1982] 2 S.C.R. 145
Janzen v. Platy Enterprises Ltd., [1989] 1 S.C.R. 1252
Large v. City of Stratford, [1995] 3 S.C.R. 733
Lavoie v. Canada, [2002] 1 S.C.R. 769
Law v. Canada (Minister of Employment and Immigration), [1999] 1 S.C.R. 497
Little Sisters Book and Art Emporium v. Canada (Commissioner of Customs and Revenue), [2007] 1 S.C.R. 38
Little Sisters Book and Art Emporium v. Canada (Minister of Justice) (Little Sisters II), [2000] 2 S.C.R. 1120
Lovelace v. Ontario, [2000] 1 S.C.R. 950
M. v. H., [1999] 2 S.C.R. 3
McGill University Health Centre (Montreal General Hospital) v. Syndicat des employés de l'Hôpital général de Montréal, [2007] 1 S.C.R. 161
McKinley v. British Columbia Telephone, [2001] 2 S.C.R. 161
McKinney v. University of Guelph, [1990] 3 S.C.R. 229
Miron v. Trudel, [1995] 2 S.C.R. 418
Montreal v. Arcade Amusements, [1985] 1 S.C.R. 368
Montréal (City) v. Quebec (CDPDJ), [2008] 2 S.C.R. 698
Multani v. Commission scolaire Marguerite-Bourgeoys, [2006] 1 S.C.R. 256
Native Women's Association of Canada v. Canada, [1994] 3 S.C.R. 627
Newfoundland Association of Public Employees v. Newfoundland (Green Bay Health Care Centre), [1996] 2 S.C.R. 3
Newfoundland (Treasury Board) v. NAPE, [2004] 3 S.C.R. 381
Nova Scotia (Attorney General) v. Walsh, [2002] 4 S.C.R. 325
Nova Scotia (Workers' Compensation Board) v. Martin; Nova Scotia (Workers' Compensation Board) v. Laseur, [2003] 2 S.C.R. 504
Ontario Human Rights Commission v. Etobicoke, [1982] 1 S.C.R. 202
Ontario Human Rights Commission v. Simpsons-Sears, [1985] 2 S.C.R. 536
Orlowski v. British Columbia (Forensic Psychiatric Institute), [1999] 2 S.C.R. 733
Parry Sound (District) Social Services Administration Board v. O.P.S.E.U., Local 324, [2003] 2 S.C.R. 157
Quebec (Attorney General) v. Quebec (Human Rights Commission), [2004] 2 S.C.R. 223
Quebec (CDPDJ) v. Maksteel Québec Inc., [2003] 3 S.C.R. 228
Quebec (CDPDJ) v. Montréal, [2000] 1 S.C.R. 665
Quebec (Human Rights Commission) v. Montreal, [2004] 1 S.C.R. 789
Quebec (Human Rights Commission) v. Quebec (Attorney General), [2004] 2 S.C.R. 185
The Queen v. Burnshine, [1975] 1 S.C.R. 693
The Queen v. Cornell, [1988] 1 S.C.R. 461

R. v. Kapp, [2008] 2 S.C.R. 483
R. v. LePage, [1999] 2 S.C.R. 744
R. v. S. (G.), [1990] 2 S.C.R. 294
R. v. S. (S.), [1990] 2 S.C.R. 254
R. v. Williams, [1998] 1 S.C.R. 1128
Radulesco v. Canadian Human Rights Commission, [1984] 2 S.C.R. 407
Reference re Same-Sex Marriage, [2004] 3 S.C.R. 698
Robichaud v. Canada (Treasury Department), [1987] 2 S.C.R. 84
Rodriguez v. British Columbia (Attorney General), [1993] 3 S.C.R. 519
Ross v. New Brunswick School District, [1996] 1 S.C.R. 825
Saskatchewan (Human Rights Commission) v. Moose Jaw, [1989] 2 S.C.R. 1317
Saskatchewan (Human Rights Commission) v. Saskatoon, [1989] 2 S.C.R. 1297
Sauvé v. Canada (Chief Electoral Officer), [2002] 3 S.C.R. 519
Schacter v. Canada, [1992] 2 S.C.R. 679
Seneca College v. Bhadauria, [1981] 2 S.C.R. 181
Stoffman v. Vancouver General Hospital, [1990] 3 S.C.R. 483
Symes v. Canada, [1993] 4 S.C.R. 695
Syndicat des Employés de Production du Québec et de l'Acadie v. Canada (Human Rights Commission), [1989] 2 S.C.R. 879
Syndicat Northcrest v. Anselem, [2004] 2 S.C.R. 551
Tetreault-Gadoury v. Canada (Employment and Immigration Commission), [1991] 2 S.C.R. 22
Thibaudeau v. Canada, [1995] 2 S.C.R. 627
Trociuk v. British Columbia (Attorney General), [2003] 1 S.C.R. 835
University of British Columbia v. Berg, [1993] 2 S.C.R. 353
Vancouver Society of Immigrants and Visible Minority Women v. Minister of National Revenue, [1999] 1 S.C.R. 10
Vriend v. Alberta (Attorney General), [1998] 1 S.C.R. 493
Winko v. British Columbia (Forensic Psychiatric Institute), [1999] 2 S.C.R. 625
Winnipeg School Division No. 1 v. Craton, [1985] 2 S.C.R. 150
Zurich Insurance Co. v. Ontario, [1991] 2 S.C.R. 321

References

Alarie, Benjamin, and Andrew Green. 2008. "Should They All Just Get Along? Judicial Ideology, Collegiality, and Appointments to the Supreme Court of Canada." *University of New Brunswick Law Journal* 58 (1): 73–91.

– 2009a. "Charter Decisions in the McLachlin Era: Consensus and Ideology at the Supreme Court of Canada." *Supreme Court Review* 47 (2d): 475–511.

– 2009b. "Policy Preference Change and Appointments to the Supreme Court of Canada." *Osgoode Hall Law Journal* 47 (1): 1–46.

– 2010. "Interventions at the Supreme Court of Canada: Accuracy, Affiliation, and Acceptance." *Osgoode Hall Law Journal* 48 (3): 381–410.

Aldrich, John H., and Forrest D. Nelson. 1984. *Linear Probability, Logit, and Probit Models*. Beverly Hills, CA: Sage. http://dx.doi.org/10.4135/9781412984744.

Armer, J. Michael, and John Katsillis. 2000. "Modernization Theory." *Encyclopedia of Sociology*. 2nd ed. Edited by Edgar F. Borgatta and Rhonda J.V. Montgomery. http://www.edu.learnsoc.org.

Asch, Michael, and Patrick Macklem. 1991. "Aboriginal Rights and Canadian Sovereignty: An Essay on *R. v. Sparrow*." *Alberta Law Review* 29 (2): 498–517.

Baar, Carl. 1976. "Judicial Behaviour and Comparative Rights Policy." In *Comparative Human Rights*, edited by Richard P. Claude, 353–81. Baltimore: Johns Hopkins University Press.

Babooram, Avani. 2008. "Canadian Participation in an Environmentally Active Lifestyle." *Envirostats* 2 (4): 7–11.

Baum, Lawrence. 1997. *The Puzzle of Judicial Behavior*. Ann Arbor: University of Michigan Press.

– 1998. *The Supreme Court*. 6th ed. Washington, DC: CQ Press.

– 2006. *Judges and Their Audiences: A Perspective on Judicial Behavior*. Princeton, NJ: Princeton University Press.

Berger, Thomas J. 1981. *Fragile Freedoms: Human Rights and Dissent in Canada*. Toronto: Clarke, Irwin.

– 2005. "My Idea of Canada." Speech to members of Citizens for Public Justice, June 2. Accessed May 7, 2015. http://www.cpj.ca/content/thomas-berger-my-idea-canada.

Black, Hugo L. 1968. *A Constitutional Faith*. New York: Random House.

Blais, André, Elisabeth Gidengil, Richard Nadeau, and Neil Nevitte. 2004. *Canadian Election Survey, 2000*. ICPSR03969-v1. Ann Arbor, MI: Inter-university Consortium for Political and Social Research. http://doi.org/10.3886/ICPSR03969.v1.

Boland, James. 2013. "Is Free Speech Compatible with Human Dignity, Equality, and Democratic Government: America, a Free Speech Island in a Sea of Censorship?" *Drexel Law Review* 6 (1): 1–46.

Boltken, Ferdinand, and Wolfgang Jagodzinski. 1985. "In an Environment of Insecurity: Postmaterialism in the European Community, 1970 to 1980." *Comparative Political Studies* 17 (4): 453–84. http://dx.doi.org/10.1177/0010414085017004003.

Borrows, John. 2015. "The Durability of *Terra Nullius: Tsilhqot'in Nation v British Columbia*." *UBC Law Review* 48 (3): 701–42.

Boyd, David R. 2003. *Unnatural Law: Rethinking Canadian Environmental Law and Policy*. Vancouver: UBC Press.

– 2012a. *The Environmental Rights Revolution: A Global Study of Constitutions, Human Rights and the Environment*. Vancouver: UBC Press.

– 2012b. *The Right to a Healthy Environment: Revitalizing Canada's Constitution*. Vancouver: UBC Press.

Brodie, Ian. 2002. *Friends of the Court: The Privileging of Interest Group Litigants in Canada*. Albany: State University of New York Press.

Brodie, Ian, and Neil Nevitte. 1993. "Evaluating the Citizens' Constitution Theory." *Canadian Journal of Political Science* 26 (2): 234–59.

Cairns, Alan. 1991. *Disruptions: Constitutional Struggles, from the Charter to Meech Lake*. Toronto: McClelland and Stewart.

Cameron, Jamie. 1997. "The Past, Present, and Future of Expressive Freedom under the Charter." *Osgoode Hall Law Journal* 35 (1): 1–74.

Cheadle, Bruce. 2013. "Supreme Court Quarantines Contested Nominee Nadon." *Calgary Herald*, November 4, B2.

Clarke, Harold D., Allan Kornberg, Chris McIntyre, Petra Bauer-Kaase, and Max Kaase. 1999. "The Effect of Economic Priorities on the Measurement of Value Change: New Experimental Evidence." *American Political Science Review* 93 (3): 637–47. http://dx.doi.org/10.2307/2585579.

Collins, Lynda M., and Meghan Murtha. 2010. "Indigenous Environmental Rights in Canada: The Right to Conservation Implicit in Treaty and Aboriginal Rights to Hunt, Fish, and Trap." *Alberta Law Review* 47 (4): 959–91.

Dahl, Robert. 1971. *Polyarchy: Participation and Opposition*. New Haven, CT: Yale University Press.

Danelski, David. 1989. "The Influence of the Chief Justice in the Decisional Process of the Supreme Court." In *American Court Systems*, edited by Sheldon Goldman and Austin Sarat, 486–99. New York: Longman.

Davis, Darren W., and Christian Davenport. 1999. "Assessing the Validity of the Postmaterialism Index." *American Political Science Review* 93 (3): 649–64. http://dx.doi.org/10.2307/2585580.

Dawood, Yasmin. 2006. "Democracy, Power, and the Supreme Court: Campaign Finance Reform in Comparative Context." *International Journal of Constitutional Law* 4 (2): 269–93. http://dx.doi.org/10.1093/icon/mol005.

Ducat, Craig R. 1978. *Modes of Constitutional Interpretation*. St. Paul, MN: West Publishing.

– 2004. *Constitutional Interpretation*. 8th ed. Boston: Wadsworth.

– 2013. *Constitutional Interpretation*. 10th ed. Boston: Cengage Learning.

Emerson, Thomas. 1963. "Toward a General Theory of the First Amendment." *Yale Law Journal* 72 (5): 877–956. http://dx.doi.org/10.2307/794655.

– 1970. *The System of Freedom of Expression*. New York: Random House.

English, Cynthia, and Lee Becker. 2013. Majorities in Most Countries Perceive Their Media as Free. Washington, DC: Gallup Poll. Accessed June 19, 2015. http://www.gallup.com/poll/162179/majorities-countries-perceive-media-free.aspx.

Environment Canada. 2012. Canada's Protected Areas. Ottawa: Environment Canada. Accessed March 1, 2013. http://ec.gc.ca/indicateurs-indicators.

Epp, Charles R. 1996. "Do Bills of Rights Matter? The Canadian Charter of Rights and Freedoms." *American Political Science Review* 90 (4): 765–79. http://dx.doi.org/10.2307/2945841.

– 1998. *The Rights Revolution: Lawyers, Activists, and Supreme Courts in Comparative Perspective*. Chicago: University of Chicago Press.

Epstein, Lee, and Jack Knight. 1998. *The Choices Justices Make*. Washington, DC: CQ Press.

Fine, Sean. 2013. "Nadon Barred from Supreme Court Office Amid Legal Challenge." *Globe and Mail*, November 4, A5.

Fisher, Matthew, and Jason Fekete. 2014. "Harper Won't Fight Court's Nadon Ruling: PM Will Respect 'Spirit of Decision' by Supreme Court." *Edmonton Journal*, March 26, C16.

Flemming, Roy B., and Glen S. Krutz. 2002. "Selecting Appeals for Judicial Review in Canada: A Replication and Multivariate Test of American Hypotheses." *Journal of Politics* 64 (1): 232–48. http://dx.doi.org/10.1111/1468-2508.00126.

Frank, Jerome. 1930. *Law and the Modern Mind*. New York: Coward-McCann.

Froc, Kerri. 2010. "Multidimensionality and the Matrix: Identifying Charter Violations in Cases of Complex Subordination." *Canadian Journal of Law and Society* 25 (1): 21–49. http://dx.doi.org/10.1017/S0829320100010206.

Fyfe, R. James. 2007. "Dignity as Theory: Competing Conceptions of Human Dignity at the Supreme Court of Canada." *Saskatchewan Law Review* 70: 1–26.

Galanter, Marc. 1974. "Why the 'Haves' Come Out Ahead: Speculation on the Limits of Legal Change." *Law & Society Review* 9 (1): 95–160. http://dx.doi.org/10.2307/3053023.

– 2003. "Why the 'Haves' Come Out Ahead: Speculation on the Limits of Legal Change." In *In Litigation Do the "Haves" Still Come Out Ahead?*, edited by Herbert Kritzer and Susan Silbey, 13–81. Palo Alto, CA: Stanford University Press.

Gilligan, Carol. 1982. *In a Different Voice: Psychological Theory and Women's Development*. Cambridge, MA: Harvard University Press.

– 1987. "Moral Orientation and Moral Development." In *Women and Moral Theory*, edited by Eva F. Kittay and Dianna T. Myers, 19–33. New York: Rowman & Littlefield.

Globe and Mail. 2013. "Weak Process for Weighty Choices," editorial, April 4, A16.

Greene, Ian. 2006. *The Courts*. Vancouver: UBC Press.

Greene, Ian, Carl Baar, Peter McCormick, George Szablowski, and Martin Thomas. 1998. *Final Appeal: Decision-Making in Canada's Courts of Appeal*. Toronto: James Lorimer.

Greenstein, Fred I. 1965. *Children and Politics*. New Haven, CT: Yale University Press.

Griffin, Larry J. 2004. "'Generations and Collective Memory' Revisited: Race, Region, and Memory of Civil Rights." *American Sociological Review* 69 (4): 544–57. http://dx.doi.org/10.1177/000312240406900404.

Haggan, Nigel, and Pamela Brown. 2002. "Aboriginal Fisheries Issues: The West Coast of Canada." In *Production Systems in Fishery Management*, edited by Daniel Pauly and Maria Palomares, 17–22. Vancouver: Fisheries Centre, University of British Columbia.

Harris, Douglas C. 2010. "Historian and Courts: *R. v. Marshall* and Mi'kmaq Treaties on Trial." *Canadian Journal of Law and Society* 18 (2): 123–31.

Hartz, Louis. 1964. *The Founding of New Societies*. New York: Harcourt Brace.
Hausegger, Lori, Matthew Hennigar, and Troy Riddell. 2009. *Canadian Courts: Law, Politics and Process*. Oxford: Oxford University Press.
Hein, Gregory. 2001. "Interest Group Litigation and Canadian Democracy." In *Judicial Power and Canadian Democracy*, edited by Paul Howe and Peter H. Russell, 214–54. Montreal: McGill-Queen's University Press.
Hendry, Jim. 2002. "The Idea of Equality in Section 15 and Its Development." *Windsor Yearbook of Access to Justice* 21: 153–84.
Hiebert, Janet. 1996. *Limiting Rights: The Dilemma of Judicial Review*. Montreal and Kingston: McGill-Queen's University Press.
– 2002. *Charter Conflicts: What Is Parliament's Role?* Montreal and Kingston: McGill-Queen's University Press.
Hirschl, Ran. 2004. *Towards Juristocracy: The Origins and Consequences of the New Constitutionalism*. Cambridge: Cambridge University Press.
Hogg, Peter W. 1997. *Constitutional Law of Canada*. 4th ed. Toronto: Carswell.
– 2011. *Constitutional Law of Canada*. 2011 Student Edition. Toronto: Carswell.
Hogg, Peter W., Allison A. Bushell Thornton, and Wade K. Wright. 2007. "Charter Dialogue Revisited: Or 'Much Ado about Metaphors.'" *Osgoode Hall Law Journal* 45 (1): 1–65.
Holmes, Oliver Wendell, Jr. 1881. *The Common Law*. Boston: Little Brown.
– 1897. "The Path of the Law." *Harvard Law Review* 10 (8): 457–78. http://dx.doi.org/10.2307/1322028.
Hsieh, Hsiu-Fang, and Sarah E. Shannon. 2005. "Three Approaches to Qualitative Content Analysis." *Qualitative Health Research* 15 (9): 1277–88. http://dx.doi.org/10.1177/1049732305276687.
Inglehart, Ronald. 1971. "The Silent Revolution in Europe: Intergenerational Change in Post-industrial Societies." *American Political Science Review* 65 (4): 991–1017. http://dx.doi.org/10.2307/1953494.
– 1977. *The Silent Revolution: Changing Values and Political Styles*. Princeton, NJ: Princeton University Press.
– 1990. *Culture Shift in Advanced Industrial Society*. Princeton, NJ: Princeton University Press.
– 1995. "Public Support for Environmental Protection: Objective Problems and Subjective Values in 43 Societies." *PS: Political Science & Politics* 28 (1): 57–72. http://dx.doi.org/10.1017/S1049096500056080.
– 1997. *Modernization and Postmodernization: Cultural, Economic, and Political Change in 43 Societies*. Princeton, NJ: Princeton University Press.
Inglehart, Ronald, and Paul R. Abramson. 1994. "Economic Security and Value Change." *American Political Science Review* 88 (2): 336–54. http://dx.doi.org/10.2307/2944708.

– 1999. "Measuring Postmaterialism." *American Political Science Review* 93 (3): 665–77. http://dx.doi.org/10.2307/2585581.

Inglehart, Ronald, Roberto Foa, Christopher Peterson, and Christian Welzel. 2008. "Development, Freedom, and Rising Happiness: A Global Perspective (1981–2007)." *Perspectives on Psychological Science* 3 (4): 264–85. http://dx.doi.org/10.1111/j.1745-6924.2008.00078.x.

Inglehart, Ronald, Neil Nevitte, and Miguel Basanez. 1996. *The North American Trajectory: Cultural, Economic, and Political Ties among the United States, Canada, and Mexico*. New York: Aldine de Gruyter.

Inglehart, Ronald, and Christian Welzel. 2005. *Modernization, Cultural Change, and Democracy: The Human Development Sequence*. Cambridge: Cambridge University Press. http://dx.doi.org/10.1017/CBO9780511790881.

Innis, Harold A. 1956. *Essays in Canadian Economic History*. Toronto: University of Toronto Press.

Jackman, Robert W., and Ross A. Miller. 2005. *Before Norms: Institutions and Civic Culture*. Ann Arbor, MI: University of Michigan Press.

Jackson, Robert J., Doreen Jackson, and Nicolas Baxter-Moore. 1986. *Politics in Canada: Culture, Institutions, Behaviour, and Public Policy*. Scarborough, ON: Prentice-Hall Canada.

James, Matt. 2006. *Misrecognized Materialists: Social Movements in Canadian Constitutional Politics*. Vancouver: UBC Press.

Janda, Kenneth, Jeffrey Berry, and Jerry Goldman. 2004. *The Challenge of Democracy*. 8th ed. Boston: Houghton-Mifflin.

Jennings, M. Kent, and Richard G. Niemi. 1974. *The Political Character of Adolescents*. Princeton, NJ: Princeton University Press.

Johnston, Richard, André Blais, Henry Brady, Elisabeth Gidengil, and Neil Nevitte. 1995. Canadian Election Study, 1993: Incorporating the 1992 Referendum Survey on the Charlottetown Accord. ICPSR06571-v1. Ann Arbor, MI: Inter-university Consortium for Political and Social Research. Accessed June 19, 2015. http://doi.org/10.3886/ICPSR06571.v1.

Johnston, Richard, et al. 1988. Canada Election Study. ICPSR09386-v1. Ann Arbor, MI: Inter-university Consortium for Political and Social Research. Accessed June 19, 2015. http://doi.org/10.3886/ICPSR09386.v1.

Kelly, James B. 2005. *Governing with the Charter: Legislative and Judicial Activism and Framers' Intent*. Vancouver: UBC Press.

Knopff, Rainer, and F.L. Morton. 1992. *Charter Politics*. Scarborough: ON: Nelson Canada.

Kornberg, Allan. 1988. *Politics and Culture in Canada*. Ann Arbor, MI: Center for Political Studies.

Koshan, Jennifer, and Jonette Watson Hamilton. 2013. "The Continual Reinvention of Section 15 of the Charter." *University of New Brunswick Law Journal* 64: 19–53.

Kritzer, Herbert. 2003. "The Government Gorilla: Why Does the Government Come Out Ahead in Appellate Courts?" In *In Litigation Do the "Haves" Still Come Out Ahead?*, edited by Herbert Kritzer and Susan Silbey, 342–70. Palo Alto, CA: Stanford University Press.

Kymlicka, Will. 1994. "Individual and Community Rights." In *Group Rights*, edited by Judith Baker, 17–33. Toronto: University of Toronto Press.

– 1995. *Multicultural Citizenship: A Liberal Theory of Minority Rights*. Oxford: Oxford University Press.

Langer, Rosanna. 2005. "Five Years of Canadian Feminist Advocacy: Is It Still Possible to Make a Difference?" *Windsor Yearbook of Access to Justice* 23 (1): 115–44.

Lasswell, Harold, and Nathan Leites. 1965. *Language of Politics*. Cambridge, MA: MIT Press.

Lehman, Mark Warren. 2006. "Affect Change: The Increased Influence of Attitudinal Factors on Canadians' Support for Legal Same-Sex Marriage." Master's thesis, Department of Political Science, University of Toronto.

L'Heureux-Dubé, the Honourable Claire. 2000. "The Search for Equality: A Human Rights Issue." *Queen's Law Journal* 25: 401–15.

Lipset, Seymour M. 1990. *Continental Divide: The Values and Institutions of the United States and Canada*. New York: Routledge.

Lipset, Seymour M., Martin Trow, and James Coleman. 1956. *Union Democracy*. Glencoe, IL: Free Press.

Locke, John. 1689. *Two Treatises of Government*. Reprint, London: Everyman, 1993.

Lu, Vanessa. 2013. "Canada Post, Union End 30-Year Pay Equity Fight." *Toronto Star*, June 27, 2013. Accessed August 2, 2014. https://www.thestar.com.

Lyons, Nona Plessner. 1988. "Two Perspectives: On Self, Relationships, and Morality." In *Mapping the Moral Domain*, edited by Carol Gilligan and Hanis Ward, 221–45. Cambridge, MA: Harvard University Press.

Macfarlane, Emmett. 2013. *Governing from the Bench: The Supreme Court and the Judicial Role*. Vancouver: UBC Press.

MacKay, A. Wayne. 1983. "Judicial Process in the Supreme Court of Canada: The Patriation Reference and Its Implications for the Charter of Rights." *Osgoode Hall Law Journal* 21 (1): 55–81.

– 2013. "The Marriage of Human Rights Codes and Section 15 of the Charter in Pursuit of Equality: A Case for Greater Separation in Both Theory and Practice." *University of New Brunswick Law Journal* 60: 54–102.

MacKinnon, Catherine. 1993. *Only Words*. Cambridge, MA: Harvard University Press.
Macklem, Patrick. 1995. "Normative Dimensions of an Aboriginal Right of Self-Government." *Queen's Law Journal* 21: 173–220.
MacLeod, Ian. 2014. "Passing Judgment: Supreme Court Appointees Return to Secret Process." *Windsor Star*, November 22, C8.
Madison, James. 1788. The Federalist Papers. The Federalist Papers Project. Accessed December 30, 2016. http://thefederalistpapers.org.
Maltzman, Forrest, James F. Spriggs II, and Paul Wahlbeck. 2000. *Crafting Law on the Supreme Court: The Collegial Game*. Cambridge: Cambridge University Press.
Mandel, Michael. 1994. *The Charter of Rights and the Legalization of Politics in Canada*. Toronto: Thompson Educational.
Manfredi, Christopher P. 1993. *Judicial Power and the Charter: Canada and the Paradox of Liberal Constitutionalism*. Norman: University of Oklahoma Press.
– 2001. *Judicial Power and the Charter: Canada and the Paradox of Liberal Constitutionalism*. 2nd ed. Oxford: Oxford University Press.
– 2004. *Feminist Activism in the Supreme Court of Canada*. Vancouver: UBC Press.
Manfredi, Christopher P., and James B. Kelly. 1999. "Six Degrees of Dialogue: A Response to Hogg and Bushell." *Osgoode Hall Law Journal* 37 (3): 513–27.
Manfredi, Christopher P., and Mark Rush. 2007. "Electoral Jurisprudence in the Canadian and U.S. Supreme Courts: Evolution and Convergence." *McGill Law Journal* 52 (3): 457–93.
– 2008. *Judging Democracy*. Peterborough, ON: Broadview Press.
Manheim, Jarol B., and Richard C. Rich. 1991. *Empirical Political Analysis*. 3rd ed. White Plains, NY: Longman.
Matthews, J. Scott. 2005. "The Political Foundations of Support for Same-Sex Marriage in Canada." *Canadian Journal of Political Science* 38 (4): 841–66. http://dx.doi.org/10.1017/S0008423905040485.
McCormick, Peter. 1993. "Party Capability Theory and Appellate Success in the Supreme Court of Canada, 1949–1992." *Canadian Journal of Political Science* 26 (3): 523–40. http://dx.doi.org/10.1017/S0008423900003437.
– 1994. *Canada's Courts*. Toronto: James Lorimer.
– 2000. *Supreme at Last: The Evolution of the Supreme Court of Canada*. Toronto: James Lorimer.
– 2015. *The End of the Charter Revolution: Looking Back from the New Normal*. Toronto: University of Toronto Press.
Meiklejohn, Alexander. 1960. *Political Freedom*. New York: Harper.
Merelman, Richard M. 1971. *Political Socialization and Educational Climates*. New York: Holt, Rinehart and Winston.

Mill, John Stuart. 1859. *On Liberty*. Reprint, London: Dover, 2002.
Montesquieu, Baron Charles Louis de Secondat. 1748. *The Spirit of the Laws*. Reprint, Cambridge: Cambridge University Press, 1989.
Moon, Richard. 1995. "Comment on *RJR-MacDonald v. Canada*." *Constitutional Forum* 7: 1–8.
Morton, F.L. 1995. "The Effect of the Charter of Rights on Canadian Federalism." *Publius: The Journal of Federalism* 25 (3): 173–88.
Morton, F.L., and Rainer Knopff. 2000. *The Charter Revolution and the Court Party*. Peterborough, ON: Broadview Press.
Morton, F.L., Peter H. Russell, and Michael Withey. 1991. "Judging the Judges: The Supreme Court's First One Hundred Charter Decisions." In *Politics: Canada*, 7th ed., edited by Paul W. Fox and Graham White, 59–79. Toronto: McGraw-Hill Ryerson.
Murphy, Walter. 1964. *Elements of Judicial Strategy*. Chicago: University of Chicago Press.
Nevitte, Neil. 1991. "The Dynamics of Canadian Political Culture(s)." In *Introductory Readings in Canadian Government and Politics*, 2nd ed., edited by Robert M. Krause and R.H. Wagenberg, 1–23. Toronto: Copp Clark.
Nichols, Joshua. 2015. Introduction to Special Issue on *Tsilhqot'in Nation v British Columbia*. *UBC Law Review* 48 (3): 693–6.
Niemi, Richard G., and Mary A. Hepburn. 1995. "The Rebirth of Political Socialization." *Perspectives on Politics* 24 (1): 7–16. http://dx.doi.org/10.1080/10457097.1995.9941860.
Nowak, John E., and Ronald D. Rotunda. 1995. *Constitutional Law*. 5th ed. St. Paul, MN: West Publishing.
Ostberg, C.L. 1995. "A Comparison of U.S. and Canadian Supreme Court Decisions after the Addition of the *Charter of Rights and Freedoms* to the Canadian Constitution." PhD diss., Department of Political Science, Northern Illinois University.
– 1998. "The Canadian Supreme Court and Free Expression Cases under the Charter of Rights and Freedoms." *American Review of Canadian Studies* 28 (4): 489–516. http://dx.doi.org/10.1080/02722019809481615.
Ostberg, C.L., and Matthew E. Wetstein. 1998. "Dimensions of Attitudes Underlying Search and Seizure Decisions of the Supreme Court of Canada." *Canadian Journal of Political Science* 31 (04): 767–87. http://dx.doi.org/10.1017/S000842390000963X.
– 2007. *Attitudinal Decision Making in the Supreme Court of Canada*. Vancouver: UBC Press.
Ostberg, C.L., Matthew E. Wetstein, and Craig R. Ducat. 2002. "Attitudinal Dimensions of Supreme Court Decision Making in Canada: The Lamer

Court, 1991–95." *Political Research Quarterly* 55 (1): 235–56. http://dx.doi.org/10.1177/106591290205500110.

– 2004. "Leaders, Followers, and Outsiders: Task and Social Leadership on the Supreme Court of Canada in the Early Nineties." *Polity* 36: 505–28.

Parrish, Michael D. 1995. "On Smokes and Oakes: A Comment on *RJR-MacDonald Inc. v. Canada (A.G.)*." *Manitoba Law Journal* 24: 665–96.

Peck, Sidney R. 1987. "An Analytical Framework for the Application of the Canadian Charter of Rights and Freedoms." *Osgoode Hall Law Journal* 25 (1): 1–85.

Plaxton, Michael. 2016. "The Caretaker Convention and Supreme Court Appointments." *Supreme Court Law Review* 72 (2d): 449–77.

Pomeranz, Jennifer. 2010. "Television Food Marketing to Children Revisited: The Federal Trade Commission Has the Constitutional and Statutory Authority to Regulate." *Journal of Law, Medicine & Ethics* 38 (1): 98–116. http://dx.doi.org/10.1111/j.1748-720X.2010.00470.x.

Porter, John. 1965. *The Vertical Mosaic: An Analysis of Social Class and Power in Canada*. Toronto: University of Toronto Press.

Prasad, B. Devi. 2008. "Content Analysis: A Method in Social Science Research." In *Research Methods for Social Work*, edited by D.K. Lal Das and V. Bashkaram, 173–93 (Chapter 10). New Delhi: Rawat.

Prescott-Allen, Robert. 2001. *The Well-Being of Nations: A Country-by-Country Index of Quality of Life and the Environment*. Washington, DC: Island Press.

Pritchett, C. Hermann. 1941. "Divisions of Opinion among Justices of the U.S. Supreme Court, 1939–41." *American Political Science Review* 35 (5): 890–8. http://dx.doi.org/10.2307/1948251.

– 1948. *The Roosevelt Court*. New York: Macmillan.

Roach, Kent. 2001. *The Supreme Court on Trial: Judicial Activism or Democratic Dialogue*. Toronto: Irwin Law.

Rohde, David W., and Harold J. Spaeth. 1976. *Supreme Court Decision Making*. San Francisco: Freeman.

Rosenberg, Gerald N. 1991. *The Hollow Hope: Can Courts Bring About Social Change?* Chicago: University of Chicago Press.

Rostow, W.W. 1971. *The Stages of Economic Growth*. 2nd ed. Cambridge: Cambridge University Press.

Rousseau, Jean-Jacques. 1762. *The Social Contract*. Reprint, London: Penguin Classics, 1968.

Roxborough, Ian. 1988. "Modernization Theory Revisited: A Review Article." *Comparative Studies in Society and History* 30 (4): 753–61. http://dx.doi.org/10.1017/S0010417500015528.

Russell, Peter H. 1987. *The Judiciary in Canada*. Toronto: McGraw-Hill Ryerson.

Ryder, Bruce, Cidalia C. Faria, and Emily Lawrence. 2004. "What's *Law* Good for? An Empirical Overview of Charter Equality Rights Decisions." *Supreme Court Law Review* 24 (2d): 103–36.
Schubert, Glendon. 1965. *The Judicial Mind: Attitudes and Ideologies of Supreme Court Justices, 1946–1963*. Evanston, IL: Northwestern University Press.
– 1974. *The Judicial Mind Revisited*. New York: Oxford University Press.
Segal, Jeffrey A. 1984. "Predicting Supreme Court Cases Probabilistically: The Search and Seizure Cases, 1962–1981." *American Political Science Review* 78 (4): 891–900. http://dx.doi.org/10.2307/1955796.
– 1986. "Supreme Court Justices as Human Decision Makers: An Individual-Level Analysis of the Search and Seizure Cases." *Journal of Politics* 48 (4): 938–55. http://dx.doi.org/10.2307/2131006.
Segal, Jeffrey A., and Albert D. Cover. 1989. "Ideological Values and Votes of U.S. Supreme Court Justices." *American Political Science Review* 83 (2): 557–65. http://dx.doi.org/10.2307/1962405.
Segal, Jeffrey A., and Harold J. Spaeth. 1993. *The Supreme Court and the Attitudinal Model*. New York: Cambridge University Press.
– 2002. *The Supreme Court and the Attitudinal Model Revisited*. New York: Cambridge University Press.
Segal, Jeffrey A., Harold J. Spaeth, and Sara C. Benesh. 2005. *The Supreme Court in the American Legal System*. Cambridge: Cambridge University Press. http://dx.doi.org/10.1017/CBO9780511614705.
Sharpless, Andy, and Josh Laughren. 2016. "CEO Note: Fighting for Transparency in Canada." Blog entry, March 30. *Oceana Canada*. https://www.oceana.ca/en/blog.
Smith, Miriam. 2002. "Ghosts of the Judicial Committee of the Privy Council: Group Politics and Charter Litigation in Canadian Political Science." *Canadian Journal of Political Science* 35 (1): 3–30. http://dx.doi.org/10.1017/S000842390277813X.
Sniderman, Paul M., Joseph F. Fletcher, Peter H. Russell, and Philip E. Tetlock. 1996. *The Clash of Rights: Liberty, Equality, and Legitimacy in Pluralist Democracy*. New Haven, CT: Yale University Press.
Songer, Donald R. 2008. *The Transformation of the Supreme Court of Canada: An Empirical Examination*. Toronto: University of Toronto Press.
Songer, Donald R., and Susan W. Johnson. 2007. "Judicial Decision Making in the Supreme Court of Canada: Updating the Personal Attribute Model." *Canadian Journal of Political Science* 40 (4): 911–34. http://dx.doi.org/10.1017/S0008423907071156.
Songer, Donald R., Susan W. Johnson, C.L. Ostberg, and Matthew E. Wetstein. 2012. *Law, Ideology, and Collegiality: Judicial Behaviour in the Supreme Court of Canada*. Montreal: McGill-Queen's University Press.

Spaeth, Harold J. 1963. "An Analysis of Judicial Attitudes in the Labour Relations Decisions of the Warren Court." *Journal of Politics* 25 (2): 290–311. http://dx.doi.org/10.2307/2127466.

Tate, C. Neal, and Roger Handberg. 1991. "Time Binding and Theory Building in Personal Attribute Models of Supreme Court Voting Behavior." *American Journal of Political Science* 35 (2): 460–80. http://dx.doi.org/10.2307/2111371.

Tate, C. Neal, and Panu Sittiwong. 1989. "Decision Making in the Canadian Supreme Court: Extending the Personal Attributes Model across Nations." *Journal of Politics* 51 (4): 900–16. http://dx.doi.org/10.2307/2131540.

Tate, C. Neal, and Torbjorn Vallinder, eds. 1995. *The Global Expansion of Judicial Power*. New York: New York University Press.

Thomassen, Jacques A., and Jan van Deth. 1989. "How New Is Dutch Politics?" *West European Politics* 12 (1): 61–78. http://dx.doi.org/10.1080/01402388908424723.

Thomson, Aly. 2013. "Canada Overfishing: Cod Stock, Other Species May Never Bounce Back." *Canadian Press*, April 18.

Tibbetts, Janice. 2008. "Nova Scotia Judge Named to Top Court: Harper Picks 'Triathlete of Jurists.'" *Calgary Herald*, September 6, A2.

Ulmer, S. Sidney. 1973. "Social Background as an Indicator to the Votes of Supreme Court Justices in Criminal Cases, 1947–1956 Terms." *American Journal of Political Science* 17 (3): 622–30. http://dx.doi.org/10.2307/2110748.

– 1986. "Are Social Background Models Time-Bound?" *American Political Science Review* 80 (3): 957–67. http://dx.doi.org/10.2307/1960547.

van Deth, Jan. 1983. "The Persistence of Materialist and Post-materialist Value Orientations." *European Journal of Political Research* 11: 63–79.

Wenner, Lettie. 1982. *The Environmental Decade in Court*. Bloomington: Indiana University Press.

West, Robin. 1991. "Jurisprudence and Gender." In *Feminist Legal Theory*, edited by Katherine T. Bartlett and Rosanne Kennedy, 201–34. Boulder, CO: Westview Press.

Wetstein, Matthew E., and C.L. Ostberg. 1999. "Search and Seizure Cases in the Supreme Court of Canada: Extending an American Model of Judicial Decision Making across Countries." *Social Science Quarterly* 80 (4): 757–74.

Wetstein, Matthew E., C.L. Ostberg, Donald Songer, and Susan W. Johnson. 2009. "Ideological Consistency and Attitudinal Conflict: A Comparative Analysis of the U.S. and Canadian Supreme Courts." *Comparative Political Studies* 42 (6): 763–92. http://dx.doi.org/10.1177/0010414008329897.

Woodrum, Eric. 1984. "Mainstreaming Content Analysis in Social Science: Methodological Advantages – Obstacles and Solutions." *Social Science Research* 13 (1): 1–19. http://dx.doi.org/10.1016/0049-089X(84)90001-2.

World Values Survey. 2000. World Values Survey Wave 4, 2000–2004 (v.20140429). World Values Survey Association. Aggregate File Producer: Asep/JDS, Madrid, Spain. Accessed June 19, 2015. http://www.worldvaluessurvey.org/WVSDocumentationWV4.jsp.

– 2005. World Values Survey Wave 5, 2005–2008 (v.20140429). World Values Survey Association. Accessed June 19, 2015. http://www.worldvaluessurvey.org/WVSDocumentationWV5.jsp.

– 2011. World Values Survey: 1981–2008 Integrated Data File. Accessed March 1, 2013. http://www.worldvaluessurvey.org/index_surveys.

Ziegel, Jacob. 2001. "Merit Selection and Democratization of Appointments to the Supreme Court of Canada." In *Judicial Power and Canadian Democracy*, edited by Paul Howe and Peter H. Russell, 131–64. Montreal: McGill-Queen's University Press.

Index

www.ingramcontent.com/pod-product-compliance
Lightning Source LLC
LaVergne TN
LVHW090149080826
844660LV00013B/730/J

* 9 7 8 1 4 8 7 5 0 1 3 9 6 *